Reinhard Gagel, Matthias Schwabe (Hg./eds.)
Improvisation erforschen – improvisierend forschen /
Researching Improvisation – Researching by Improvisation

Musik und Klangkultur/Music and Sound Culture

Reinhard Gagel, Matthias Schwabe (Hg./eds.)

Improvisation erforschen – improvisierend forschen

Beiträge zur Exploration musikalischer Improvisation

Researching Improvisation – Researching by Improvisation

Essays About the Exploration of Musical Improvisation

[transcript]

Bibliografische Information der Deutschen Nationalbibliothek
Die Deutsche Nationalbibliothek verzeichnet diese Publikation in der Deutschen Nationalbibliografie; detaillierte bibliografische Daten sind im Internet über http://dnb.d-nb.de abrufbar.

Umschlaggestaltung: Kordula Röckenhaus, Bielefeld
Umschlagabbildung: Fridhelm Klein, Berlin/München 2014
Zeichnungen: Fridhelm Klein, http://www.fridhelmklein.com
Projektleitung: Iris Broderius, http://www.impressum-berlin.de
Lektorat (Deutsch): Iris Broderius, http://www.impressum-berlin.de
Lektorat (Englisch): Louise & Phil Loxton, http://www.loxton-english.de
Korrektur (Deutsch): Barbara Bachinger
Korrektur (Englisch): Solveig Raschpichler
Satz: Tanja Jentsch, http://www.7silben.de
Printed in Germany
Print-ISBN 978-3-8376-3188-3
PDF-ISBN 978-3-8394-3188-7

Gedruckt auf alterungsbeständigem Papier mit chlorfrei gebleichtem Zellstoff.
Besuchen Sie uns im Internet: *http://www.transcript-verlag.de*
Bitte fordern Sie unser Gesamtverzeichnis und andere Broschüren an unter: *info@transcript-verlag.de*

Inhalt

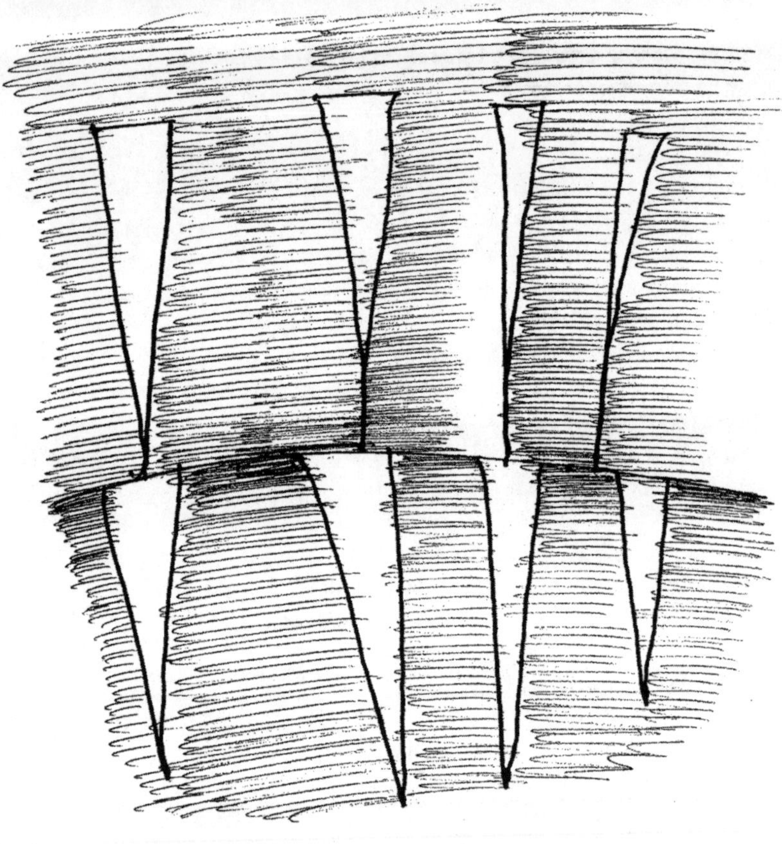

Improvisation erforschen – improvisierend forschen | Researching Improvisation – Researching by Improvisation

Einleitung | Introduction

Reinhard Gagel

Warum Forschung in der Improvisation?

Musikalische Improvisation ist eine hoch differenzierte Kunstrichtung mit eigener Geschichte und Reflexion. Ihr Wirkungsgrad in unserer Kultur ist klein, aber doch groß genug, um hervorragende Protagonisten, Spielstätten und Festivals hervorzubringen, zu denen die Zuhörer strömen. Improvisierende Musiker sind daran interessiert, die Verfahren ihrer Kunst zu verfeinern, Grundlagen zu erkennen und Methoden zur Probenarbeit und Vermittlung zu entwickeln. Wenn wir in diesem Buch den Begriff der Forschung ins Spiel bringen, meinen wir einerseits dieses vertiefende Erforschen und Nachforschen, andererseits aber auch das wissenschaftliche Forschen. Wir sind der Meinung, dass es an der Zeit ist, auch Methoden der Wissenschaft in das Nachdenken über Improvisation einzubeziehen. Sie erschließen eine zusätzliche Dimension, die es uns auf noch differenziertere Weise ermöglicht zu hinterfragen, was vielleicht bloße Meinung ist, in Daten zu verwandeln, was an Mythen herumschwirrt und so zu vertiefen, was an Begriffen bereits existiert. Die Sozialwissenschaft interessiert sich zunehmend für die Forschung der Improvisation, weil diese das Handeln in unserer komplexen Gesellschaft prägt. Auch in der Musik kann Forschen die Improvisation vertiefen und aus ihrem kulturellen Schattendasein herausholen. Ihre Bedeutung für Musikproduktion und Musikpädagogik und das in ihr schlummernde gesamtgesellschaftliche kulturelle Potential ist nur so in vollem Maße zu erfassen.

Der britische Perkussionist und Theoretiker **Edwin Prévost** – ein Musiker der ersten Stunde freier Improvisation – vertritt streitbar, dass Improvisation der ästhetische, aber auch politische Gegenentwurf zum Establishment und Forschen eine menschliche kreative Konstante ist. Wer Unbekanntes und Neues entdecken will, geht den Weg der Erforschung. Der Gedanke der Exploration steht deshalb im Mittelpunkt des improvisatorischen Denkens. In seinem Beitrag hier im Buch entfaltet er den Gedanken, Improvisation sei die verschüttete Quelle der Musik und ihre Wiederaufdeckung eigne sich als Modell eines alternativen, partizipativen Kulturverständnisses. Dieses Begründungsszenario weist der Improvisation einen ihr gemäßen Platz zu: Sie ist ein Gewinn für das Kultur- und Musikleben.

Soll also Improvisation substantiell hinterfragt und begründet werden, muss man sie erforschen. Dies stelle ich als Grundthese in den Raum. Ein Indiz dafür, dass auch andere das so sehen, ist die zunehmende Anzahl von wissenschaftlichen Projekten, die sich der Improvisation widmen. Diese sind vor allem im angelsächsischen Raum auf universitärem Level zu finden und dort haben auch Künstler[1] ihren Platz: Kunst und Wissenschaft kommen zusam-

1 | Wir verwenden in Anlehnung an Gepflogenheiten des Verlages im gesamten Buch die männliche oder – wenn möglich – die genderneutrale Schreibweise.

Why research improvisation?

Musical improvisation is a highly diverse art form with its own distinct history and reflections. Its impact on our culture is relatively small, yet it is still large enough to have produced exceptional protagonists, performance venues and festivals to which many people flock in order to appreciate it. Improvisational musicians are focused on refining their art, uncovering principles and developing methods for their rehearsal work and in order to better convey their craft. When we talk about "research" in this book, we mean going deeper in terms of exploration and investigation, however, at the same time, we are also referring to scientific research. We believe that the time has come to include and utilize scientific methods when we reflect on improvisation. These methods open up an additional dimension that enables us to scrutinize more diversely what could, after all, just be an opinion. It also enables us to transform the myths that are flying around into data and, by doing so, go into even more depth regarding the terms that already exist. Social sciences are becoming increasingly interested in researching improvisation because it influences our behavior in today's complex society. The same is true of music, where research can add more depth to improvisation, bringing it out of its shadowy existence. Only by carrying out such research can we fully grasp the significance of improvisation for the production of music and musical pedagogy and, at the same time, for the dormant cultural potential of society as a whole.

The British percussionist and theorist **Edwin Prévost** – a pioneer of free improvisation – tenaciously expounds the view that improvisation is an aesthetic and a political alternative to the establishment and that research is a creative constant in human beings. Whoever wishes to discover the unknown, or find new things, treads the path of exploration. The idea of exploration is therefore central to improvisational thought. In his contribution to this book, Prévost develops the idea that improvisation is the submerged source of music and its re-emergence the perfect model for an alternative participatory understanding of culture. This argumentation gives improvisation an appropriate standing: it is an asset to cultural and musical life.

If improvisation is to be scrutinized and justified sufficiently, one must explore it. I would now like to put this theory forward for discussion. The increasing number of scientific projects dedicated to the topic of improvisation is proof that others share this opinion. These projects are mainly conducted in universities in the Anglo-Saxon world, and it is on this level that artists can also be found: art and science come together.[1] In Germany there are theses and research projects

1 | The American trombonist, improviser, composer and musicologist George Lewis is a living example of this. He is co-editor of the "Oxford Handbook of Critical Improvisation Studies". An interdisciplinary project *Improvisation, Community and Social Practice*

men.[2] In Deutschland gibt es verstreute Dissertations- und Forschungsprojekte, von denen wir in diesem Band einige vorstellen. Eine breitere – auch interdisziplinäre – Forschungslandschaft wäre hier durchaus wünschenswert. Das Gleiche gilt für den Austausch unter Musikern und Denkern. Beispielhaft sei hier die *Internationale Tagung für Improvisation* in Luzern erwähnt. Walter Fähndrich, Christoph Baumann und Peter K Frey haben mit dieser Veranstaltung, die sie von 1992 bis 2005 alle drei Jahre ausrichteten, Pionierarbeit geleistet. Dort trafen sich Künstler, Wissenschaftler, Feuilletonisten und Literaten. In ihren Beiträgen thematisierten sie Improvisation aus vielfältiger Perspektive.[3] Kontinuierlich trifft sich in Berlin eine Gruppe von Forschenden der Improvisation. Die Mitglieder der *Berlin Improvisation Research Group (BIRG)*[4] sind allesamt meist selbst improvisierende Musiker und darüber hinaus Forschende, die über internationale Kontakte verfügen und auch Forscher anderer Länder einladen. Einige Mitglieder dieser Gruppe waren auch Vortragende im nachfolgend beschriebenen Symposium.

Das Symposium »Improvisation erforschen – improvisierend forschen«

Zu der hier nur angedeuteten Vielzahl von Konferenzen, Tagungen und Forschungsgruppen befindet sich das Symposium »Improvisation erforschen – improvisierend forschen«, dessen Vorträge in diesem Band veröffentlicht sind, in enger Nachbarschaft. Und es ist doch auf eine ganz besondere Weise durchgeführt worden. Zum 10jährigen Jubiläum veranstaltete das Veranstaltungszentrum für improvisierte Musik *exploratorium berlin* im Mai 2014 ein Festival mit dem Titel *Exploring Improvisation*. Wie der Name »exploratorium« schon sagt, ist dort Forschen und Explorieren ein zentrales Anliegen (siehe den Beitrag von Matthias Schwabe) und existiert seit 2012 auch als eigene Abteilung.

2 | Der amerikanische Posaunist, Improvisator, Komponist und Musikwissenschaftler George Lewis ist dafür ein lebendes Beispiel. Er ist Mitherausgeber des »Oxford Handbook of Critical Improvisation Studies«. Mit dem Project ICASP (*Improvisation, Community and Social Practice*) existiert in Kanada seit Jahren ein interdisziplinäres Projekt, das Improvisation als künstlerische Praxis und als Modell für anderweitige gesellschaftliche Felder erforscht.

3 | Als weitere Projekte und Tagungen sind zu erwähnen: In Basel veranstalteten Nikolas Rihs und Hansjürgen Wäldele von 2003 bis 2010 eine jährliche Konzert- und Diskussionreihe »Aspekte der freien Improvisation«. Die *International Society of Improvisation* (ISIM) lädt jährlich zu einer Konferenz, die Universität Oxford richtet alle zwei Jahre eine Konferenz aus. Die Prager Agosto-Stiftung hat in 2014 mit »vs. Interpretation« eine Serie von jährlichen Tagungen begonnen.

4 | *URL: https://berlinimprovisationresearchgroup.wordpress.com/*

scattered around; a selection of which we will cover in this book. A wider – also interdisciplinary – research landscape would definitely be desirable here. The same is true of the dialog between musicians and thinkers. The *International Conference on Improvisation* in Lucerne is mentioned here as an example. Walter Fähndrich, Christoph Baumann and Peter K. Frey achieved pioneering work with this event, which they organized every three years from 1992 to 2005. Artists, scientists, art critics and writers came together at this conference and discussed the topic of improvisation from many different perspectives.[2] An improvisation research group meets regularly in Berlin. The members of the *Berlin Improvisation Research Group (BIRG)*[3] are mostly all improvising musicians and, in addition, researchers who have international contacts and invite other researchers from abroad to participate in their meetings and events. A few members of this group were also keynote speakers at the symposium which is described below.

The symposium "Researching Improvisation – Researching by Improvisation"

The symposium "Researching Improvisation – Researching by Improvisation", whose lectures are published in this book, is closely related to the vast number of congresses, conferences and research groups which address this topic. The symposium has been organized and conducted in a unique way. In May 2014, the Berlin *exploratorium*, which is a venue for improvised music events, put on a festival to mark its 10th anniversary; the title of the festival was *Exploring Improvisation*. As the name *"exploratorium"* suggests, research and exploration are a central theme at this institution (see the article by Matthias Schwabe) and have had their own dedicated department since 2012. It was no surprise, therefore, to find the topic of research on the festival program. The symposium formed part of the festival program and consisted of concerts, workshops and panel discussions. There were keynote speeches and discussions every morning. In the afternoon, there were round-table discussions called seminars, which took the form of debates between the keynote speakers and the festival attendees. As

(ICASP) has been running in Canada for many years. This project explores improvisation as an artistic practice and as a model for other areas in society.

2 | Additional projects and congresses: the annual concert and discussion series "Aspects of Free Improvisation" was organized and put on by Nikolas Rihs und Hansjürgen Wäldele in Basel from 2003 to 2010. The *International Society of Improvisation* (ISIM) holds an annual conference. Oxford University holds one every two years. The Agosto Foundation in Prague began a series of annual conferences in 2014 titled "vs. Interpretation".

3 | *URL: https://berlinimprovisationresearchgroup.wordpress.com/*

Es war also nur konsequent, dass das Thema Forschen selbst auf der Tagesordnung stand. Das Symposium fand im Rahmen des Festival-Programms mit Konzerten, Workshops und Offenen Bühnen statt. Jeweils vormittags gab es Vorträge und Diskussionen, nachmittags fand eine Gesprächsrunde – Seminar genannt – der Vortragenden und Gäste statt. Als Initiator und Leiter des Symposiums war mir wichtig, dass es mit den übrigen Festival-Veranstaltungen verbunden war. Konzerte, Workshops, Vorträge, Diskussionen und Offene Bühnen sollten sich mischen. Programmatische Schnittstelle von Symposium und Festival war die sogenannte SOUP, eine Improvisation mit Musik und Texten aller beteiligten Wissenschaftler und Musiker. Gegenstand des Symposiums war die sogenannte Freie Improvisation im Sinne eines stilistisch offenen musikalischen Verfahrens. Forschen war Thema unter zwei Aspekten: einerseits wurden Forschungsprojekte und theoretische Ansätze präsentiert (*Improvisation erforschen*), zum anderen diskutierten wir, ob und in welcher Form es eine improvisierende und künstlerische Art des Forschens gibt oder geben könnte (*improvisierend forschen*). Eingeladen waren zehn Forscher aus unterschiedlichen Ländern und Fachbereichen. Alle stehen für aktuelle künstlerisch-wissenschaftliche Forschungs- und Reflexionsansätze zur Improvisation. Ihre Beiträge, die während des Symposiums als Kurzvorträge präsentiert wurden, haben sie für die vorliegende Publikation überarbeitet.

Improvisation erforschen

Den Anfang machen Beiträge aus dem Kontext zweier europäischer Ausbildungsgänge, die Improvisation erforschen. Das von **Urban Mäder** vorgestellte Forschungsprojekt an der Hochschule für Musik Luzern wurde aus der Einsicht der Lehrenden begonnen, sich auszutauschen – ein wichtiger Aspekt, denn Improvisatoren haben ihren individuellen künstlerischen Zugang und ihre eigene Strategie, die aber zu wenig untereinander kommuniziert wird. Des Weiteren – und hier wird es Forschung – war ihr Ziel, gemeinsame Begriffe zu entwickeln, diese zu reflektieren, zu befragen und zusammengefasst zu veröffentlichen. Herausgekommen ist ein Kompendium, das viele Aspekte der Improvisation sammelt und vor allem in Bezug auf das Unterrichten und seine Didaktik hin breit ausformuliert.

Ein Forschungsprojekt an der Universität Potsdam widmet sich explizit der vertiefenden Analyse improvisatorischer Prozesse: **Marc Godau** und **Matthias Haenisch** sammeln Daten zu dem Thema, wie Improvisierende das Improvisieren eigentlich lernen. Es geht also um Aneignung von Wissen: Erlernen wir Improvisieren überhaupt? Haben wir es möglicherweise als implizites Wissen, das heißt Erfahrungswissen, das selbständig und en passant erworben wird, verfügbar? Welche Rolle spielt dann das angeleitete Lernen? Und können Improvisierende überhaupt Aussagen über ihr Lernen machen?

the instigator and head of the symposium, it was important to me that these were linked to, and in keeping with, the other events at the festival. Therefore, the events – concerts, workshops, talks, debates and open panel discussions – needed to blend in with the other activities. The so-called SOUP, which was an improvisation using music and texts from all the participating scientists and musicians, was the interface between the symposium and the festival itself. The subject of the symposium was so-called *free improvisation*, in the sense of a stylistically-open musical process. Research was the topic, in particular two aspects pertaining to it: one aspect was about research projects and theoretical approaches (*Researching Improvisation*), the other aspect saw us discuss whether, and in what form, improvising and artistic research exists or could exist (*Researching by Improvisation*). Ten researchers from different count:ries and with different areas of expertise were invited. All of them represent and support current artistic-scientific research and reflection approaches to improvisation. They presented contributions during the symposium in the form of short lectures. They have subsequently revised these for this publication.

Researching Improvisation

The beginning of the book consists of contributions taken from the work of two European training programs that explore improvisation. The research project at the *Lucerne University of Applied Sciences and Arts,* which is presented here by **Urban Mäder**, was initiated by lecturers with the aim of allowing them to exchange experiences and ideas – an important aspect because improvisers have their own individual approach and strategy towards art, however, they do not often communicate sufficiently with one another. Furthermore – and this is where the work becomes research – it was their goal to develop common terms and terminology, to reflect on these, to question them and to publish them. The result was a compendium containing many aspects of improvisation and, above all, elaborating on its teaching and didactics in great detail.

A research program at the University of Potsdam is dedicated exclusively to the in-depth analysis of improvisational processes: **Marc Godau** and **Matthias Haenisch** collect data on the topic of how improvisers actually learn to improvise. It is therefore about the acquisition of knowledge: do we even learn how to improvise? Do we have implicit knowledge, in other words practical knowledge, that we accumulate by ourselves and pick up as we go along? If this is so, then what role does guided learning play? Are improvisers even able to make statements about their learning? Interviews, which were based on video footage of lessons and/or rehearsals, were evaluated. This project makes it very clear how precisely one must reflect on the methodological setting in order to be able to explore improvisation. The methodological approach is outlined in great detail. The data is obtained from the live practice of teaching, not from a laboratory.

Ausgewertet werden Interviews, die anhand der Videos des Unterrichts beziehungsweise der Proben durchgeführt wurden. Gerade hier in diesem Projekt wird deutlich, wie genau man das methodische Setting reflektieren muss, um Improvisation zu erforschen. Der methodische Zugang ist präzise ausgewiesen. Die Daten lassen sich aus einer lebendigen Praxis des Unterrichtens, nicht aus einem Labor gewinnen. Die verwendete Methode der *grounded theory* kann auf den Gegenstand Improvisation angewendet werden, ja ist eigentlich selbst Improvisation. Die Arbeit der Potsdamer Forscher ist ein Beispiel dafür, Lernen und Lehren von Improvisation differenziert zu betrachten, Daten dem Gegenstand entsprechend zu erheben und sorgfältig auszuwerten. Sie macht auch deutlich, wie aufwändig und komplex es ist, gesicherte Aussagen über Improvisation zu machen. Solch ein Ansatz ist beispielhaft und weist einen Weg für die kommende Forschung. Folgeprojekte mit ähnlicher Sorgfalt könnten langfristig das Fremdeln der Wissenschaft mit improvisatorischer Theoriebildung und Praxis aufbrechen. Sie könnten damit einen Prozess anstoßen, den die Neue Musik seit langem durchlaufen hat: eine ständige wissenschaftliche Begleitung und Publikations-, Lehr- und Forschungstätigkeit zu etablieren. Ein Lehrstuhl, in dem sich die Inhaberin einem Komponisten widmet? Das ist ganz normal. Ein Lehrstuhl für Freie Improvisation, der sich einem Improvisator, einem Ensemble widmet? Sowohl der Lehrstuhl als auch die thematische Konzentration wären für die Improvisation durchaus wünschenswert.

Blicken wir also in die hier vorgestellten Einzelstudien. *Present-Time Composition*, das Konzept von **Alan Bern**, will künstlerisches Improvisieren durch die Anwendung neurologischer Forschungserkenntnisse effektiver und origineller befördern. Sein hier abgedruckter Beitrag stellt in aller Kürze Grundlagen und Grundsätze des methodischen Vorgehens vor. Die Basis seiner Denk- und Konzeptüberlegungen bilden die Forschungen des Neurowissenschaftlers Daniel Kahneman. Dieser untersucht – bewusste und unbewusste – Denkstrategien, mit denen die Menschen Entscheidungen treffen und handeln. Bern folgt Kahneman, indem er dessen Ansatz des »schnellen Denkens«, das auf dem Entfalten nichtlinearer Denk- und Aktionsprozesse beruht, auf das Improvisieren überträgt. Methoden, die dieses Denken und Handeln in Gang setzen, sind für den schöpferischen – und hochkomplexen – Moment der Improvisation nützlich. Langsame Entscheidungsvorgänge in Einzelschritten, Kennzeichen einer kontrollierten – und oft das Improvisieren hemmenden – Handlungsweise können ersetzt werden. Impulse, die man nicht aufgrund von Nachdenken abwägen kann, können so in der Spielsituation ausgelöst werden. Berns Ansatz ist universell, da er nicht stilistisch argumentiert, nicht mit Kriterien von Klangproduktion oder Soundstudies, sondern das tief im Menschen verwurzelte – und oft nicht frei verfügbare – kreative Potential ansteuert.

The method used – that of *grounded theory* – can be applied to the theory of improvisation because it is, in fact, itself a form of improvisation. The work of the Potsdam researchers is an example of how to observe the learning and teaching of improvisation in different ways and, what is more, how to collect corresponding data about this subject and evaluate it appropriately. This work also makes clear to us how complicated and complex it is to make verifiable statements about improvisation. This is a perfect example of research and shows the way for future endeavors. Subsequent projects, if carried out with a similar level of precision, could, in the long-term, end the estrangement between science and the development of improvisational theory and practice. They could give impetus to a process which contemporary music already passed through some time ago: namely, establishing constant scientific monitoring together with publishing, teaching and research activities. A professorship in which the incumbent dedicates themselves to a composer is totally normal in contemporary music, whereas a professorship for free improvisation which dedicates itself to an improviser or an ensemble is not. Having such a professorship and a thematic focus would therefore be most welcome for improvisation.

Let us now have a look at the individual studies presented in this book. **Alan Bern's** concept of *Present-Time Composition* aims to make artistic improvisation more effective and original through the application of neurological research findings. In his article, he presents a brief overview of the principles of the methodological approach. His thoughts and reflections are based on the research of the neuroscientist Daniel Kahneman. Kahneman investigates thought strategies – both conscious and unconscious – that human beings use to make decisions and take actions. Bern expands on the work of Kahneman by applying his approach of "rapid thought", which is based on the unfolding of non-linear thought and action processes, to improvisation. Methods which instigate this kind of thinking and acting are useful to the creative – and highly complex – moment of improvisation. Slow decision processes, made up of single steps, are indicators of a controlled, and in terms of improvisation, often limiting way of acting and can be replaced. Impulses that cannot be accessed by thinking about them, can, in this way, be triggered during the playing performance. Bern's approach is universal because he does not argue in terms of style nor in terms of criteria of sound production or sound studies, but rather he focuses on the creative potential which is deeply rooted in human beings and not often freely accessible.

Mirio Cosottini's *non-linear music* approach is very similar and reflects his own artistic work but also produces results that go beyond this work. Cosottini has also developed his own teaching method, which he calls *Complete Restitution Exercise*. However, Cosottini argues from the perspective of sound and listening. According to him, non-linearity is not a neuro-physiological quality but rather a principle of sound creation. The composition of sounds ta-

Ganz ähnlich ist **Mirio Cosottinis** *nonlinear music* ein Denkansatz, der seine eigene künstlerische Arbeit reflektiert, aber zu darüber hinaus weisenden Ergebnissen kommt. Auch Cosottini entwickelt eine eigene Lehrmethode, die er *Complete Restitution Exercise* nennt. Cosottini argumentiert allerdings vom Klang und vom Hören aus. Nonlinearität ist bei ihm keine neurophysiologische Qualität, sondern ein klangliches Gestaltungsprinzip. Das Zusammenstellen von Klängen geschieht, indem man ihre Verbindungen sucht. Cosottini nennt sie *Invarianzen*, gleichbleibende Eigenschaften eines Klanges oder einer Struktur. Damit werden der Klang und seine Eigenschaft zum Zentrum des Handelns, nicht seine einzelnen zusammengesetzten Elemente (zum Beispiel Harmoniefolgen, stilistische Muster). Musiker (und Hörer) hören das als Kumulation, als Anhäufung (kumulatives Hören) im Gegensatz zur Abfolge einzelner Bausteine (analytisches Hören). Als Lehrmethode schlägt Cosottini einen methodischen Dreischritt vor: das Identifizieren von Invarianzen (in einem Stück, einer Improvisation), das Umsetzen in musikalische Grafiken (statt in Worte und Noten) und das Ausführen als (erneute) Improvisation. Cosottini zeigt damit einen Aspekt künstlerischer Analyse der dem Improvisieren zugrundeliegenden Kompositionsprozesse auf, die nicht nur für non-idiomatische Improvisationen gelten, sondern auch in stilistischen Improvisationen wirken.

Auch **Rogério Costa** reflektiert die eigene Spielpraxis als Saxophonist – er untersucht die Handhabung einer Live-Schnittstelle zu Soundmodulen während eines Spielvorgangs. Es geht dabei um musikalische Spieltechnik; diskutiert wird, wie der Spieler seinen Körper auf den Umgang mit dem Modul und den zu erreichenden Klang »einstellt«. Costa geht von der Vorstellung aus, dass, anstatt den Klang aufzubauen, der Spieler in den Klang eintaucht. Er postuliert ein enges energetisches Verhältnis zwischen Spieler und Klangmaterial: Der Klang wird erschaffen und erschafft umgekehrt auch seine Wege im Musiker. Improvisieren mit den Eigenschaften des Klanges ist also quasi ein direktes ineinander Übergehen zwischen Instrument und Spieler und das lässt sich nicht nur auf das Saxophon, sondern auch auf eine elektronische Schnittstelle übertragen. Costas Text ist ein Beispiel für die Erweiterung der eigenen Spielfähigkeit durch die konsequente Nutzung wissenschaftsbasierter Reflektion: Musikwissenschaftler der aktuellen Musik (Makis Solomos) ebenso wie Philosophen (Jacques Deleuze) und Komponisten (Helmut Lachenmann) stehen Pate. Er kommt damit zu Aussagen, die sehr relevant für die Analyse, das Spielen und das Lehren von Improvisation sind. Costa argumentiert als Wissenschaftler und wendet die daraus gewonnenen Erkenntnisse für sein Improvisieren an.

Corinna Eikmeier erforscht den musikalisch handelnden Körper in der Improvisation. Sie konstatiert einen Unterschied zwischen interpretatorischen und improvisatorischen Spielbewegungen. Ihre Forschungsarbeit nutzt Me-

kes place as one searches for their connections to each other. Cosottini calls these *invariances*; unchanging properties of sound or structure. These invariances make sound and its properties the focal point of the performance, rather than the individual elements (for example, harmonic sequences or stylistic patterns). Musicians (and listeners) hear the performance as an accumulation, as an assembled collection (cumulative listening), as opposed to a sequence of individual modules (analytical listening). As a teaching method, Cosottini suggests a three-step approach: identify invariances (in a piece, in an improvisation), transfer them into musical graphics (instead of words and notes) and perform them as a (revised) improvisation. As such, Cosottini illustrates an aspect of artistic analysis of the composition processes fundamental to improvising. These do not just apply to non-idiomatic improvisation; they also have an impact on stylistic improvisation.

Rogério Costa also reflects on his own playing experience as a saxophonist; he investigates how, during a performance, one can work with live interfaces to sound modules. With regard to musical playing technique, he discusses how the musician can "attune" their body to handle the module and achieve the sound they are aiming for. Costa assumes that instead of constructing the sound the musician immerses themselves in it. He presumes a close-knit relationship between the musician and the sound material. The musician creates the sound and, at the same time, the sound creates its own paths within the musician. Improvising using the properties of sound is therefore a virtual merging of instrument and musician. This does not only apply to the saxophone, it is also valid for the electronic interface. Costa's text is an example of how one can expand one's own performance ability through the consistent use of scientifically-based reflection. Musicologists of contemporary music (Makis Solomos), philosophers (Jacques Deleuze) and composers (Helmut Lachenmann) are models for this concept. Costa comes to conclusions which are highly significant for the analysis, teaching and performance of improvisation. Whilst arguing and reasoning from a scientific point of view, Costa uses the resulting insights for his own improvisational work.

Corinna Eikmeier explores how the body behaves in a musical sense during improvisation. She establishes a difference between interpretational and improvisational playing movements. Her research work utilizes methods of qualitative heuristics. She evaluates the improvisations of test participants from different age groups. She participates in these improvisations as a musician. She takes her own experiences as a Feldenkrais teacher as a starting point. She makes extensive analogies between optimum movements described by Feldenkrais and the quality of movements in improvisation. In fact, this catalog reads like a description of improvisational procedures and qualities. Eikmeier develops performance exercises for each participant; these exercises focus on the individual aspects of improvisational movement quality. For example, she

thoden der qualitativen Heuristik. Sie wertet die Improvisationen von Probanden unterschiedlichen Alters aus. In diese war sie immer unmittelbar als Mitspielende einbezogen. Als Ausgangspunkt nimmt sie ihre Erfahrungen als Feldenkrais-Lehrerin: Sie listet umfangreiche Analogien von Feldenkrais´ Bewegungstugenden zu improvisatorischer Bewegungsqualität auf. Dieser Katalog liest sich in der Tat wie eine Beschreibung von improvisatorischen Handlungsweisen und Qualitäten. Eikmeier entwickelt für die jeweiligen Probanden Spielübungen, die den Fokus auf einzelne Aspekte improvisatorischer Bewegungsqualität legen. Zum Beispiel lässt sie Versuchsspieler improvisieren, indem diese sich von der Fokussierung auf die Bewegungen eines Körperteils leiten lassen. Sie hat diese Sitzungen aufgenommen und durch Interviews ausgewertet. Es lassen sich Tendenzen beobachten, dass durch Fokussierung körperlicher Aspekte die Improvisationsfähigkeit zunimmt. Damit schafft ihr systematisches Forschungsvorgehen Daten und Erkenntnisse, die Erfahrungen über die Relevanz des Körperbewusstseins in der Improvisation untermauern.

Forschung über Improvisation kann auch Sprache selbst zum Thema machen. Über Improvisation zu sprechen ist etwas anderes, als sie zu praktizieren. Über sie zu schreiben, schafft noch zusätzliche Distanz. In Diskussionen während des Symposiums wurde sogar von einem Abgrund zwischen Sprache und Musik gesprochen. **Lara Frisch** thematisiert in ihrem Beitrag das Sprechen der Improvisatoren über ihre Probenarbeit. Ob uns das Klischee von Improvisation als musikalischem Gespräch aber weiterhilft? Ist musikalische Kommunikation auch von der von Luhmann konstatierten Unwahrscheinlichkeit des Verstehens geprägt? Und hat das Sprechen vorher und nachher Auswirkungen auf das musikalische Geschehen? Eine verbale Konfliktsituation kann im äußersten Fall dazu führen, dass die Musiker sich sogar auf der Bühne prügeln. Miles Davis soll durch verbale Beleidigungen während des Spielens seine Musiker herausgefordert haben, noch intensiver zu spielen. Die Musiker, die Frisch untersucht hat, bevorzugten friedlichere Lösungen, um weiter zu arbeiten. Sie fanden Worte für ihre musikalischen Strategien in Form von Metaphern: zum Beispiel ist eine »Welle« übertragbar in Musik wie in Sprache. Dieser Befund hat Anschlussmöglichkeiten. In die bildliche Ebene zu wechseln bedeutet, für das eigene Tun Verständigung zu suchen und die verbale Anwendung dem Medium Kunst anzupassen.

Die Erforschung und Benennung der Performativität als Aspekt der Improvisation, wie ihn **Mathias Maschat** darstellt, halte ich für einen wichtigen Paradigmenwechsel der letzten Jahre in Bezug auf Improvisation als Kunstform. Das, was sie phänomenal am deutlichsten kennzeichnet, kann nun erfasst werden. Das Erscheinen selbst – als musikalische Praxis, ob für sich oder vor Publikum – ist ihr wichtigstes Merkmal. Improvisieren manifestiert sich erst dort und nur dort. Musikalische Erörterungen, Stilübungen, Material- und

encourages the participants to focus on the movements of a particular part of their body whilst improvising. She recorded these sessions and evaluated them by means of subsequent interviews. She observed that the improvisational ability of the participants tended to increase when they focused on aspects of bodily movement. Her systematic approach to research provided her with data and insights that support the significance of being aware of the body during improvisation.

Researching improvisation can also be a language issue. Speaking about improvisation is quite another thing compared to actually practicing it. Writing about it creates even more distance. Discussions which took place during the symposium even spoke about the gulf between language and music. In her article, **Lara Frisch** deals with the topic of improvisers talking about their rehearsal work. Does the question of improvisation as a musical conversation even help us? Is musical communication also influenced by what Luhmann terms "the improbability of understanding"? Moreover, does speaking before and after the musical event have an impact on it? A verbal conflict situation can, in an extreme case, even lead to the musicians coming to blows on stage. Miles Davis is said to have encouraged his musicians to play even more intensively by verbally insulting them during performances. The musicians whom Frisch investigated preferred more peaceful solutions in order to be able to proceed with their work. They found words for their musical strategies in the form of metaphors: for example, "a wave" is capable of being communicated both in music and in language. This finding opens up more possibilities. Changing to a metaphorical level means searching for an understanding of one's own actions, whilst adapting the verbal application to the medium of art.

In his article, **Mathias Maschat** discusses exploring and labelling the performative as an important aspect of improvisation. In my opinion, this aspect represents a significant paradigm shift, one that has taken place in the last few years, with regard to improvisation as an art form. This aspect, one that has always been very apparent, can now be captured and recorded. Its coming into being as a musical practice, whether by itself or in front of an audience, is its most important feature. First and foremost, improvisation manifests itself only in the here and now. Musical analyzes, stylistic exercises, material and structure analyzes are all irrelevant to this feature. Improvisation is an event, and within this event there is something that written work does not possess, although it can sometimes achieve it (for example, in its interpretation on stage). Nevertheless, music and musicological thinking are influenced by the aesthetics of the work. In terms of improvisation, the aesthetics differ. One cannot assume that aspects which do not appear to belong to improvisation are not, in fact, improvisation, rather one must discuss and evaluate as one goes along: all characteristics which distinguish a performance are important for improvisation. All music, even composed, can be analyzed and even composed with the help of

Strukturanalysen gehen im Grunde an diesem Charakteristikum vorbei. Improvisation ist Ereignis, und in diesem ist sie etwas, was das schriftliche Werk manchmal erreicht (in der Interpretation auf der Bühne), aber sonst von sich aus nicht hat. Dennoch ist das musikalische und musikwissenschaftliche Denken von der Werkästhetik geprägt. Eine Improvisationsästhetik, die sich davon unterscheidet, darf nun nicht davon ausgehen, was alles die Improvisation nicht ist, sondern kann nur nach vorne argumentieren: Alle Merkmale, die eine Performance auszeichnen, sind wesentlich für die Improvisation. Mit ihrer Hilfe lässt sich Musik analysieren, durchaus auch komponierte, aber vor allem improvisierte Musik. Einige von Maschat gegenübergestellte Begriffe verdeutlichen auch den cultural turn, den die Improvisation darstellt: Präsenz statt Repräsentation, Aura statt Reproduktion, Emergenz statt Konstruktion und körperlicher Eigensinn statt Disziplinierung. Mit dem letzteren befassen sich auch Corinna Eikmeiers Forschungen zum improvisierenden Körper. Der Blickwinkel der Performativität verändert das Bild: Statt Improvisation defizitär zu definieren, werden die originären Merkmale in den Vordergrund gerückt. Vielleicht nennen wir unsere *improvisierte Musik* besser *improvisierende Musik?*

Improvisierend forschen

Improvisierend forschen war der zweite Aspekt des Symposiums. Mit improvisierend ist die Charakteristik eines Vorgehens gemeint, das möglicherweise im Gegensatz zu wissenschaftlichem Vorgehen stehen könnte, aber dennoch zu Erkenntnis aus Forschung führt. Wird in der Wissenschaft improvisiert? Ist künstlerisches Improvisieren als wissenschaftliche Forschung anzusehen? Wie kann das relevant sein für die Erforschung von Improvisation? Was ist eigentlich Improvisieren als Forschung? Wie sieht das Setting performativen Forschens aus, wie ist ein Ort beschaffen, in dem das stattfindet? Es tauchen Bezüge zu einem sehr aktuellen – und kontrovers betrachteten – Forschungsbereich, nämlich der künstlerischen Forschung auf. Wäre Improvisieren nicht dafür die Idealbesetzung? Könnte man nicht künstlerische Präsenz und Dynamik als Katalysator für Forschungsprozesse verwenden? Das Thema Improvisieren durch das künstlerische Improvisieren darüber erforschen?

Der schon erwähnte Altmeister improvisatorischer Kunst, **Edwin Prévost**, spannt den weitesten Bogen. Er besteht konsequenterweise auf der geräuschhaften Klanglichkeit freier Improvisation und nimmt, was er seit über sechs Jahrzehnten klanglich entwickelt, auch theoretisch als unbedingten Bezugspunkt. Er verortet das non-idiomatische Improvisieren anthropologisch. *Exploratoria* sind für ihn verlorengegangene kreative Wurzeln des Menschen. Er skizziert den menschlichen Entwicklungsgang als *erste, zweite* und *dritte Natur* des Menschen. Nur der Klang – nicht eine Phrase, ein Motiv – schlägt eine Brücke zu den menschlichen Urlauten, zur *ersten Natur.* Das Heulen des Urmenschen

these characteristics, but in the case of improvised music this is especially so. Some of the terms diametrically opposed by Maschat also illustrate the cultural turn embodied by improvisation: presence instead of representation, aura versus reproduction, emergence instead of construction and self-determination instead of discipline. Corinna Eikmeier's research on the role of the body in improvisation also concerns itself with the matter of self-determination versus discipline. The perspective of performativity changes one's impression of it: instead of defining what is missing or lacking, one focuses on the original features which come to the fore. Perhaps it would be better instead to refer to *improvised music* as *improvising music.*

Researching by Improvisation

Researching by Improvisation was the second aspect of the symposium. By improvising, I mean the characteristics of a research process that could potentially be the opposite of a scientific procedure, but one which could still lead to insight. Is improvisation conducted in the world of science? Can artistic improvisation be viewed as scientific research? How can this be relevant for exploring improvisation? What *is* improvised research? What does a setting for performative research look like? How can we create a venue in which it can take place? References emerge that relate to a highly topical area of research – one that is often viewed as controversial – namely that of artistic research. Could improvised research in fact be the perfect example? Could one not utilize artistic presence and dynamic as a catalyst for research processes? Could we explore the topic of improvising using artistic improvisation itself?

The aforementioned grandmaster of improvisational art, **Edwin Prévost**, bridges the widest gaps. He consistently demands the noisy sonority of free improvisation and uses what he has developed in sound over the past six decades, both practically and theoretically, as his essential reference point. He positions non-idiomatic improvisation anthropologically. For him, *Exploratoria* are the lost creative roots of mankind. He defines the course of human development as man's *first, second* and *third nature.* Only sound, not a motif or a phrase, spans the bridge to the ancient sounds of man, namely the *first nature.* Thomas Mann had already perceived the howling of cavemen with secret desire as an escape from civilization and convention, which had become the *second nature* of man. Today we have added to this the aesthetics of commercial goods and technology, which manipulate us with their branding and packaging, and without which we are hardly able to perceive music anymore. Music is standardized. The division of labor in culture means that we no longer carry out research ourselves, but instead employ others to do it for us. Exploratory processes in music, with all their potential richness, are normally closed off to us. We listen in a culturally-accepted way. Only when people begin to reflect on this and act differently will they find their

hatte schon Thomas Mann mit heimlicher Lust als Ausweg aus der Zivilisiertheit und Konvention angesehen, die zur *zweiten Natur* des Menschen geworden sind. Heute kommen die Warenästhetik und die Technologien hinzu, die mit ihren Marken und Verpackungen manipulieren und ohne die wir Musik kaum mehr wahrnehmen können. Musik wird standardisiert. Die Arbeitsteilung der Kultur hat dazu geführt, dass wir nicht mehr selbst forschen, sondern andere beauftragen. Erkundungsprozesse in der Musik sind uns in ihrer möglichen Reichhaltigkeit normalerweise verschlossen. Wir hören in einer kulturell akzeptierten Weise. Erst wenn die Menschen dies reflektieren und beginnen neu zu handeln, finden sie zu ihrer *dritten Natur*. Kunst wäre eine gegen den Strom – den main stream – anschwimmende Bewegung: mit Investigation und Kooperation als wesentlichen Eigenschaften. So gesehen richtet sich Prévost auch gegen den allein sich behauptenden Künstler als Held. Haben nicht alle Menschen eine *dritte Natur* und damit genügend »kognitive Fluidität«, kreativ zu werden in der Art und Weise, dass sie suchen, was zu ihnen passt, anstatt sich mit dem zu beschäftigen, was gewünscht, gemocht, verkauft wird?

Improvisierend forschen zielte auch auf die Frage, wie man Improvisation als Kunstform mit dem Forschen näher in Verbindung bringt. Prévost legt nahe, das Improvisieren insgesamt als Forschen zu bezeichnen. Passt dazu der Begriff der künstlerischen Forschung, der momentan Furore macht, als dritter Erkenntnisweg zwischen Kunst und Wissenschaft? Zu diesem Thema hatte ich den Künstler **Fridhelm Klein** eingeladen, der seine Zeichenkunst explizit als Forschung versteht. Zeichnen als Erkenntnismethode ist sein Credo. Er hielt während des Symposiums seine Eindrücke zeichnerisch fest. Charakteristisch in seinen Skizzen ist das Miteinander von Bild und Text, indem er Erkenntnisse pointiert und auf den Punkt bringt. Dabei entstand ein Konvolut von Zeichnungen, ein Teil ist in diesem Band veröffentlicht.

Nina Polaschegg beschäftigt sich in ihrem Impuls-Beitrag mit dem Begriff »künstlerische Forschung«. Passt dieser für die Aktivitäten und Reflexionen improvisierender Musiker? Sollen künstlerische Methoden Forschung sein, die sich auch im Wissenschaftssystem platzieren lassen, dann müssen sie nachvollziehbar und vergleichbar sein. So jedenfalls sieht es der österreichische Forschungsverband FWF, der ein Förder-Programm für künstlerisches Forschen entwickelt hat. Ergebnisse des künstlerischen Forschens können, müssen aber nicht zu einem Kunstwerk führen. Sie können auch im Schreiben über etwas bestehen. Sprechen zum Beispiel die in diesem Band veröffentlichten Autoren, weil sie auch oder gerade Musiker sind, als Künstler? Oder sind sie nicht doch wieder Wissenschaftler, wenn sie sich der Sprache bedienen, über ihren Gegenstand schreiben, Methoden und Verfahren anwenden, mithin vom Künstler zum Beobachter werden? Polascheggs Beitrag stellt vor allem Fragen, die deutlich machen, wie schwierig es ist, künstlerische Forschung zu definieren. Sie entwickelt als Alternative den Begriff einer angewandten Forschung.

third nature. Art, with investigation and cooperation as its main characteristics, is a movement that swims against the current, in other words against the mainstream. Prévost also opposes the artist who believes they can succeed alone and, in effect, be perceived as a hero. Is it not true, in fact, that all people possess a *third nature,* and with it sufficient "cognitive flexibility" to become creative in the way that they are searching for? Are they, in fact, looking for what fits them, instead of focusing on what they want, like, or are being offered?

Researching by Improvisation aims to answer the question "How can you bring improvisation as an art form closer to research?" Prévost urges us to perceive all improvisation as research. Can we therefore say that "artistic research", which is currently a very hot topic, is a suitable way to describe this third approach, one which lies between art and science? In order to address this topic, I have invited the artist **Fridhelm Klein**, who perceives the art of drawing as research. His motto is: drawing as a method of knowledge acquisition. During the symposium, he kept a record of his impressions in the form of drawings. The co-existence of picture and text, through which he emphasizes and summarizes his knowledge, is characteristic of his sketches. As a result of his undertakings, a collection of drawings was produced, several of which can be found in this publication.

In her impulse article, **Nina Polaschegg** also addresses the term "artistic research". Does this fit to the activities and reflections of improvisational musicians? Should artistic methods which are understandable and comparable and, as such, capable of being researched be given a place within a scientific system? The Austrian Science Fund (the FWF) believes they should, as it has developed and funded a program for artistic research. The findings or results from artistic research can, but do not have to, lead to art itself. They can also take the form of something written. Do, for example, the authors published in this book, who are also musicians, speak as artists? Or are they rather scientists when they use language to describe their subject, methods and procedures, thus shifting their position from that of being an artist to that of being an observer? Above all, Polaschegg asks those questions which demonstrate how difficult it is to define artistic research. She develops the term "applied research" as an alternative in which musicians explore differentiating sound (sound research), compose texts regarding the principles of their work (principle research) and create artistic works which are founded on research. Based on sound research, music – from a historical perspective of improvisation – led to the rejection of traditional styles, new playing techniques and the invention of new instruments. This is new art, and it is also research leading to art. It would be a contribution towards Prévost's concept of the *third nature* of man. Such explorations also give art a societal function.

The artistic-scientific project that I advocate in my article is a potential model for researching knowledge in which art can act as a catalyst. It brings together several of the features already mentioned here in one entity. It is not

Musiker finden zu differenzierten Klängen (Klangforschung), zu Texten über die Grundlagen ihrer Arbeit (Grundlagenforschung) und zu Kunstwerken, die auf den Forschungen beruhen. Auf der Basis von Klangforschung fand die Musik – improvisationsgeschichtlich gesehen – in Ablehnung traditioneller Stilistiken zu neuen Spieltechniken und zur Erfindung neuer Instrumente. Das ist neue Kunst, das ist auch Forschung hin zur Kunst. Es wäre ein Beitrag hin zu Prévosts Vorstellung von der *dritten Natur* des Menschen. Solche Exploratoria geben der Kunst auch eine gesellschaftliche Funktion.

Das künstlerisch-wissenschaftliche Projekt, für das ich in meinem Beitrag plädiere, ist ein mögliches Modell forschenden Erkennens, in dem Kunst Katalysator sein kann. Es führt einige hier bereits aufgezählte Merkmale in einer Anwendung zusammen. Es geht nicht um neue Musik im Konzert. Ich entwickele Formate, in denen das gemeinsame Musikmachen, Nachdenken, Lesen, Hören und Diskutieren in der Performanz einer ritualisierten Form stattfinden können. Diese Formate beteiligen Künstler und Nichtkünstler, Laien und Wissenschaftler als Denkende und Improvisierende auf einer Bühne. Nachdenken, Sprechen, Diskutieren, Erproben, und Performen fallen zusammen. Die Dynamiken, die Improvisierende in der Performance entfalten (zum Beispiel durch ihre Präsenz und Aura), können mit dem kühlen Forschen, mit Theorie und Forschungsergebnissen verbunden werden.

Der Gewinn eines solchen Vorgehens für die Improvisation ist die Nähe und Unmittelbarkeit von Theorie und Praxis. Hier könnte gelingen, was bereits angedeutet wurde: angewandte Forschung der Musiker in unmittelbarer Verschränkung mit Theorie als künstlerisches Format.

Die bereits erwähnte SOUP ist dafür ein Beispiel. Sie war eine gemeinsame Adhoc-Performance aller Beteiligten an prominenter Stelle jedes Symposiumtages. Musikalisches und Sprachliches, Instrumente und Stimmen, strukturiert durch musikalische Spielregeln, vermischten sich in einer gemeinsamen Improvisation. Sie verlief als ein einstündiges Ritual in konzentrierter Atmosphäre, voller Achtsamkeit aufeinander und auf die musikalische und performative Qualität. Instrumentenensembles spielten zusammen, Texte wurden gelesen, andere gesungen. Diese Performance war ein Experiment. Es fragte: Finden Wissenschaft und Kunst auf diese Weise zusammen? Zusammenfinden meint: ineinander verschränkt zusammen spielen und nachdenken, um etwas zusammen zu finden. Diese Immersionen waren konzeptuell und konzentriert in der SOUP, aber sie waren im gesamten Verlauf des Symposiums ebenso präsent: der Wissenschaftler, der auf der Bühne mitspielt, der Musiker, der im Seminar mitredet, der Zuhörer, der aktiv wird in der Offenen Bühne und im Seminar, das Gespräch am Rande zwischen den Konzerten und Vorträgen.

Eine etwas andere Form des Ineinander-Verschränkens bieten die »Intermezzi« in diesem Buch. Es sind kurze Einwürfe und Originaltöne, »Gedan-

just a matter of a concert with new music. I develop formats in which collective music-making, reflection, reading, listening and discussing can take place during the performance according to a ritualized structure. These formats bring together artists and non-artists, laymen and scientists, as thinkers and improvisers on a stage. Reflecting, speaking, discussing, experimenting and performing all come together. The dynamic improvisers develop during the performance (for example, via their presence and aura) can be merged with cold, hard research, with theory and findings.

The benefit of such a process for improvisation is the closeness and the immediacy of theory and practice. Here, what has already been hinted at could be successfully achieved: applied research by musicians is immediately interwoven with theory, thus creating an artistic format.

The aforementioned SOUP is an example of this. It was a collective ad hoc performance of all participants and had a prominent position on each day of the symposium. The musical and the linguistic, instruments and voices, all of which were structured by musical rules of playing, merged together to form a collective improvisation. It ran as a one-hour ritual in an intense atmosphere full of mutual attentiveness and the performative quality of the music. Instrumental ensembles played together, texts were read and sung. This performance was an experiment. It posed the question: can science and art find a way together using such an approach? Finding a way together means: interweaving play with one another and reflecting, in order to discover something together. In SOUP this immersion was conceptual and concentrated, however, it was also evident throughout the entire course of the symposium: the scientist who performed on stage, the musician who spoke during the seminar, the listener who was active on the open stage and in the seminar, the discussion which took place on the fringe – between concerts and lectures.

The "intermezzi" in this book offer a different kind of interweaving. These are brief interjections and original recordings – "snippets of thought" – which we have scattered between the more detailed articles. They arose out of one of the aforementioned afternoon seminars as well as from the podium discussion with Barre Phillips and Edwin Prévost, which opened the whole festival. They encompass the topics of this book but are not meant to be seen as an introduction or as an interface between the articles. Rather, their purpose is to present additional thought input in a miniaturized way.

The Berlin *exploratorium* and exploration

The symposium took place in a location: the Berlin *exploratorium*, whose name alone serves to embody exploration, something which Prévost highlights in the title of his article. The entire festival and symposium – and indeed this book – was made possible thanks to the Lilli Friedemann Foundation. In his article,

ken-Schnipsel«, die wir zwischen die ausführlichen Beiträge gestreut haben. Sie entstammen einem der erwähnten Nachmittags-Seminare sowie einem Podiumsgespräch mit Barre Phillips und Edwin Prévost, mit dem das Festival eröffnet wurde. Sie kreisen um die Themen dieses Buches, sind aber weder als Einleitung zu noch Verbindung zwischen den Artikeln gedacht, sondern vielmehr als zusätzlicher gedanklicher Input im Miniatur-Format.

exploratorium berlin und Exploration

Das Symposium fand statt an einem Ort, der schon im Namen (und darauf verweist Prévosts Beitragsüberschrift) das Explorieren zum Hauptthema macht: dem *exploratorium berlin*. Das gesamte Festival und Symposium – und dieses Buch – hat die Lilli Friedemann Stiftung als Trägerin ermöglicht. **Matthias Schwabe** als Gründer und Leiter gibt in seinem Beitrag einen Einblick in das alltägliche Explorieren an diesem Ort, der offen ist für Profimusiker, für musikalische Semiprofis und Amateure, für Wissenschaftler und für Kunstschaffende anderer Sparten. Dabei ist der Vorgang des Explorierens und Experimentierens Ausgangspunkt und praktische Ausformung in einem. Erkunden und Erproben, Reflektieren und Erkennen, Konzepte und Regeln finden stehen in einem sich gegenseitig befruchtenden Verhältnis, sei es in den pädagogischen, den künstlerischen oder den theoretischen Ausformungen.

Musikalische Improvisation wird in absehbarer Zeit in Deutschland wahrscheinlich eher marginal bleiben. Dort wird Improvisation eher als Spezialgebiet angesehen. Wir sind aber überzeugt, dass Improvisieren ein sehr breites und generelles Thema der Gesellschaft, der Kunst, der Musik und der Musikpädagogik ist. Das *exploratorium berlin* hat glücklicherweise die Möglichkeit, sich diesem Thema speziell zu widmen und Fragen, Konzepte, und Themen weiter zu entwickeln, zu erproben und öffentlich zu machen. Zwar ist es zu klein und dünn besetzt, um in großem Stil forschend, lehrend und performend zu wirken. Doch wir verstehen es als Ort, der exemplarisch wissenschaftliche, künstlerische und pädagogische Impulse setzen soll. Kunst, Pädagogik und Wissenschaft befinden sich in Theorie und Praxis auf Augenhöhe.

Aus den hier versammelten Beiträgen ergibt sich ein erhebliches Potential für die Improvisation. Sie sind in gewisser Weise zufällig. Sie versammeln Forschende, die genau an diesem Thema arbeiteten, als wir sie einluden. Sie bringen zusammen, wen ich zu diesem Zeitpunkt im Blickfeld hatte, und lassen andere außen vor. Das Buch hat und das Symposium hatte nicht den Anspruch, umfassend sein zu wollen. Aber es ist – auch für mich – erstaunlich, wie in der Zusammensetzung, in den Argumentationen, in den dargestellten großen thematischen Bögen dann Erkenntnisse zusammenfanden und in vielfältiger Weise emergierten.

Matthias Schwabe, the head and founder of this institute, gives an insight into everyday exploration at this location, which is open to professional musicians, semi-professional musicians and amateurs, scientists, and artists from other fields. As such, the process of experimenting and exploring refers to both the starting point and its subsequent practical formation. The aspects of discovering and experimenting, reflecting and realizing, identifying concepts and rules, all have a mutually-beneficial relationship, whether that be in terms of pedagogical, artistic or theoretical form.

Musical improvisation in Germany will, in the foreseeable future, continue to be marginalized. There, improvisation is seen more as a special field. We are convinced, however, that improvisation is a very diverse and general theme in terms of society, art, music and musical instruction. The Berlin *exploratorium* is fortunate to be able to dedicate itself entirely to this theme and to develop further questions, concepts and themes, to investigate them and publish the results. However, it is too small and too sparsely staffed to be able to research, teach and perform effectively on a larger scale. Nevertheless, we see it as a location that should inspire scientific, artistic and pedagogical impulses. Art, pedagogy and science find themselves on an equal footing in terms of theory and practice.

There is an enormous potential for improvisation contained in the articles present in this book. To a certain extent, this is a coincidence. The articles were written by researchers who were engaged in work on this theme at the very moment in which we asked them to contribute. The articles bring together the people who were on my radar at this time. There are, of course, others. Neither this book nor the symposium claim to be exhaustive. Nevertheless, in my opinion, it is astonishing how, in the constellation, the argumentation and the far-reaching thematic scope of this work, common insights were discovered and then emerged in a variety of different ways.

Translation into English: Louise & Phil Loxton, GB-Wales

Urban Mäder – Uni Luzern
'Freie Improvisation als Herausforderung'
Free Improvisation as Challenge

• Wir forschen über das Vermitteln • Forschungsarbeit als Standortbestimmung.

Lernziele u.a.
- reflektierend sprechen
- Höranalyse (wir sprechen nach dem Spiel)
- Improvisationsarbeit hat direkten Einfluss auf Klassik u. Jazz …
- Objektivierbarkeit der Improvisation
- musikalische Qualität

Freie Improvisation als Herausforderung | The Challenge of Free Improvisation

Vermittlung und Forschung an der Hochschule Luzern – Musik | Teaching and Research at the Lucerne University of Applied Sciences and Arts – School of Music

---

Urban Mäder

Freie Improvisation, welch wunderbares wörtliches Versprechen! Im Grunde gibt es doch nichts Anderes, in der Musik, im Alltag, wann und wo auch immer. Und doch wird es dann komplizierter oder komplexer zumindest, wenn es um Forschen und Vermitteln geht; wenn sich alle ihre Gedanken machen, wieviel Freiheit beim Improvisieren tatsächlich möglich sei und ob man denn dieses Frei-Sein oder Freie Tun überhaupt vermitteln könne ...

1. London Improvisers Orchestra

Sonntag, 6. April 2014, 20.30 Uhr. Das *London Improvisers Orchestra* spielt in der St Mary's Church in London. Ich erreiche im abendlichen Halbdunkel die am Rand des Clissold Parks gelegene hübsche alte Kirche. Gute 15 Minuten vor Konzertbeginn bin ich einer der ersten zahlenden Besucher, Eintritt 6 Pfund. Ein paar Stühle vorne im Chor lassen den bevorstehenden Konzertabend erahnen. Einige weitere Personen, verteilt in kleine Gruppen, heben sich mit ihrer ungezwungenen englischen Art der Konversation unmerklich von der Stille ab. Nach und nach betreten Musikerinnen und Musiker den Spielbereich, packen ihre Instrumente aus und spielen sich unaufdringlich in die transparente Akustik des Raumes ein.

Die Liste der beim *London Improvisers Orchestra* aktiv Mitbeteiligten beträgt ungefähr 150 Musiker. Ein engerer Pool spielt oft. Zwölf haben sich an diesem Abend im Konzert eingefunden. Bis zum Konzertbeginn hat sich eine Zuhörerschaft von ungefähr 20 Menschen versammelt. Nach den leisen Begrüßungsworten der Saxophonistin und Bassklarinettistin Caroline Kraabel, die so vor allem den Beginn des Konzerts markieren will, erhebt sich ein ebenso feines und unaufdringliches Klanggewebe aus der gespannten Stille. Das Konzert besteht aus einer Mischung von Freien Improvisationen und Stücken, die durch das sogenannte Conducting einiger Musiker aus den eigenen Reihen konzeptionelle Form erhalten. Ich erlebe einen Konzertabend, der in erster Linie durch Uneigennützigkeit, Bescheidenheit und Gelassenheit in der Haltung ausnahmslos aller Mitwirkenden geprägt ist. Gleichzeitig strahlt das Ensemble eine derart hohe Konzentration und Intensität aus, wie ich das selten in einem Konzert mit improvisierter Musik erlebt habe. Auf dem Nachhauseweg denke ich äußerst angeregt über das Konzert nach und stelle mir unter anderem die Frage: Wie wohl das *London Improvisers Orchestra* gespielt hätte, hätten diese Musiker in ihren Anfängen oder in ihrer Studienzeit Workshops in Freier Improvisation besucht?

Wenn Musik geschieht, herrscht Unberechenbarkeit. Dann weckt, überrascht, provoziert, bezaubert, überwältigt sie. Das Konzert mit dem *London Improvisers Orchestra*, kurz *LIO* genannt, macht alle diese Aspekte besonders deutlich. Wenn Musik geschieht, geht es um »die unmittelbare Lust, den Ernst

We might conceive of free improvisation as part of an overarching *Weltanschauung*, a way of looking at the world that, with its ostensible emphasis on spontaneity, covers more or less everything – music, everyday life, whenever and wherever. However, the situation becomes a little more complicated, or at least more complex, when applied to research and teaching; if we think about how much freedom is genuinely possible in improvisation and if it is even possible to teach this kind of "freedom".

1. London Improvisers Orchestra

Sunday, 6 April 2014 at 8.30 pm. *The London Improvisers Orchestra* (*LIO*) is playing at St Mary's Church in the borough of Hackney. I arrive at the attractive old building on the edge of Clissold Park in the twilight of early evening. Some 15 minutes before the concert starts, I am one of the first paying visitors, handing over my six pounds for entry. Scattered chairs in the chancel tell of the concert to come, and a few other people, dotted around the church in groups, inconspicuously punctuate the silence with their easy English style of conversation. Musicians gradually assemble, unpack their instruments and unobtrusively warm up in the airy acoustics of the space.

The *LIO* has around 150 active musicians on its books; however, its core of frequent performers is smaller than that. Twelve have gathered for this evening's concert, the audience numbers around twenty by the time it starts. Following hushed words of welcome from saxophonist and bass clarinettist Caroline Kraabel to indicate the start of the concert, a graceful and restrained mosaic of sound breaks through the solemn silence. The performances are a mixture of free improvisation and pieces given structure by "conductors" within the orchestra. I experience a concert marked by the altruism, modesty and composure of everyone involved. At the same time, the ensemble exudes a level of concentration and intensity I have rarely witnessed in a concert of improvised music. On my way home, my mind is full of thoughts and the question of how the *LIO* might have played if its musicians had attended free improvisation workshops when young or at university.

Music-making is full of unpredictability: it rouses, surprises, provokes, enchants and overwhelms. All of these facets are brought out in the concert given by the *LIO*. Music involves "the direct desire, the earnestness and risk of performing and listening, of trying new things, of simulating and of playful transformation," says Hartmut von Hentig in his essay on creativity (Beltz 2000). What fascinates us about music is the vitality of the moment, the magic of being in the present, the sound as a living thing felt physically and, with that, our awareness of being present. This is what music makes possible – improvised music with its intentional focus on the unpredictable even more so. Free

und das Wagnis des Spielens und Hörens, des Erprobens, des Simulierens und des spielerischen Verwandelns«, so Hartmut von Hentig in seinem Essay über Kreativität (Beltz 2000). Es ist das, was uns an Musik fasziniert, die Lebendigkeit des Augenblicks, die Magie der Präsenz, der körperlich lebendige Klang und gleichzeitig die Wahrnehmung der eigenen Anwesenheit. Das kann jede Musik möglich machen. Improvisierte Musik vermag es besonders, und sie betont mit Absicht das Unberechenbare. Freie Improvisation steigert dies zusätzlich. Ob Freie Improvisation im schulischen Kontext lehr- und lernbar ist, hat sich gezeigt, muss sich aber immer wieder neu weisen.

2. Freie Improvisation an der Hochschule Luzern

Improvisation ist seit 60 Jahren auf neue Weise Teil der Musikgeschichte geworden und wird mehr und mehr in den Curricula und Forschungsprogrammen von Hochschulen und Universitäten präsent. Das hat auch den ganz einfachen Grund, dass Exponenten der Improvisationsszene an den Instituten zu lehren begannen. So auch an den meisten Musikhochschulen der Schweiz. Die Hochschule Luzern – Musik bietet Improvisationskurse und hat im speziellen die »Freie Improvisation« seit 1989 im Lehrangebot. Die Ausschreibung im Studienführer lautet: »Den Schwerpunkt bildet in diesem Kurs das Spiel auf dem Hauptinstrument in kleinen Gruppen. Improvisierend und analysierend wird Fragestellungen nachgegangen: Wie entsteht Energie? Wie entsteht Form? Wie entsteht Qualität? Wie kann ich musikalisches Material entwickeln? Was kann Improvisation leisten, was nicht? Wichtiger Teil der Arbeit ist das Entwickeln und Erarbeiten eines individuellen Repertoires von Materialien und Spielmöglichkeiten in der Gruppe«.

Alle Bachelor-Studierenden machen diesen Gruppenkurs, Klassiker und Jazzer zusammen. Da kommen oft die unterschiedlichsten Instrumente respektive Instrumentalisten zusammen, was auf positive Weise dazu beitragen kann, alle möglichen Fragen wie Stil, Rolle, Funktion, Form, Dichte, Präsenz et cetera auf vielfältige Weise aufkommen zu lassen. Im Anschluss können weiterführende Workshops während des Bachelor- oder Masterstudiums besucht werden.

Seit dem Herbstsemester 2014 gibt es die Möglichkeit, neben der Hauptstudienrichtung Klassik oder Jazz einen zusätzlichen Schwerpunkt »Improvisation« zu wählen. Die Studierenden belegen ein zweites Hauptfach in Improvisation und partizipieren an möglichst vielen bereits bestehenden Angeboten in diesem Themenbereich. Diese Leute machen nach dem Bachelor höchstwahrscheinlich Masterstudien wie den seit 2012 existierenden Studiengang »Music and Art Performance« in Luzern oder den »Master Performance mit Schwerpunkt Improvisation« an der Musikhochschule Basel oder auch »Contemporary Arts Practice« an der Hochschule der Künste Bern.

improvisation ups the ante further, but whether it can be taught and learned in an educational environment is a matter of persistent doubt.

2. Free improvisation at the Lucerne University of Applied Sciences and Arts

Improvisation has been a part of music history for 60 years and increasingly features on the lecture lists and research programs of colleges and universities. This is simply down to a growing number of musicians in the improvisation scene now teaching at higher education institutions. This is also true of most music colleges in Switzerland. The Lucerne University of Applied Sciences and Arts runs courses in improvisation and, since 1989, one specifically in "free improvisation". The student guide describes it as follows: "This course focusses on playing your main instrument in small groups. Issues are discussed in an improvisatory and analytical context: where does the energy come from? How is the form created? How do we ensure quality? How can I develop musical material? What can improvisation do, and what can it not do? A key component of work involves developing and exploring an individual repertoire of materials and performance opportunities in the group." All BA students, whether they are studying classical or jazz, take this group course. It brings together a wide range of different instruments and instrumentalists, helping to raise wide-ranging questions relating to style, roles, function, form, density, presence and so on. On completion, BA and master's students can also go on to advanced workshops.

The winter term 2014 gave students a brand new option to take "improvisation" as a second core subject alongside their main field of study in classical music or jazz, allowing them to participate in a large number of existing courses in this field. After obtaining their BAs, most of them will likely continue on to a master's course such as "Music and Art Performance", which has been available at Lucerne since 2012, with a major in Performance and a minor in Improvisation at the Bern School of Music or "Contemporary Arts Practice" at Bern University of the Arts.

3. Teaching and research in Lucerne

The idea of a research project on "The Possibilities and Limits of Teaching Free Improvisation" (Freie Improvisation: Möglichkeiten und Grenzen der Vermittlung) originated in 2009. After many years of teaching experience, the lecturers in Lucerne expressed a desire to share views on the question of how their colleagues deal with the potentially explosive force of free improvisation as a

3. Vermittlung und Forschung in Luzern

2009 entstand die Idee, eine Forschungsarbeit zum Thema »Möglichkeiten und Grenzen in der Lehre der Freien Improvisation« zu machen. Nach vielen Jahren Unterrichtserfahrung hat sich im Luzerner Dozententeam der Wunsch nach Austausch aufgedrängt, nach der Frage, wie wohl die Kolleginnen und Kollegen mit der in gewisser Weise widersprüchlichen Sprengkraft von Freier Improvisation als Unterrichtsfach umgehen. Auch die Gespräche nach den Konzerten, jeweils am Ende des Semesters, waren immer sehr angeregt. Wiederholt stellten wir fest, dass wir die Gruppen aufgrund ihrer Spielart leicht den betreffenden Lehrpersonen zuordnen konnten, ein in der Bildung bekanntes Phänomen.

Das Dozententeam: Lauren Newton ist klassisch ausgebildete Sängerin und bestens bekannt als Vokalistin in der experimentellen Musik; Dieter Ammann, zeitgenössischer Komponist und Trompeter mit Erfahrung im Jazz und Funk; Urban Mäder, klassischer Komponist, arbeitet häufig mit Installationen und raumbezogenen Projekten; Thomas Mejer, ist Saxophonist und hat Erfahrung mit experimentellen Projekten; Marc Unternährer, klassisch ausgebildeter Tubist, spielt in unzähligen Formationen und Projekten Freier Musik; Christy Doran, Gitarrist, hat eine lange Erfahrung in zahlreichen Jazzformationen; Christoph Baumann, Jazzpianist, komponiert für Bands, Theater und Film; Gerry Hemingway, Schlagzeuger, spielt in vielen bekannten Formationen und hat Erfahrung mit interdisziplinären Arbeiten.

Eine wichtige Motivation, die Forschungsarbeit wirklich anzugehen, entstand dadurch, dass wir improvisierte Musikstücke, auch jene unserer Semesterabschlusskonzerte, trotz ihrer Unterschiedlichkeit in ihrer Qualität überraschend ähnlich beurteilten. Wir haben fünf Jahre lang Material zusammengetragen, Video-Studien und Teamteaching gemacht, haben die wichtigsten Methoden des Vermittelns hinterfragt und daraus ein Situationspapier geschaffen, das heute die Luzerner Arbeit dokumentiert.

Hier die Lernziele dieses Kurses:

- Die Studierenden haben ihre Wahrnehmungsfähigkeit gesteigert.
- Sie sind in der Lage, musikalische Prozesse zu steuern und zu gestalten.
- Ihre Fähigkeit, Verantwortung für das eigene musikalische Tun zu übernehmen, ist weiterentwickelt.
- Die Studierenden können Position beziehen gegenüber den gestalterischen Grundfragen (»was – wann – wieso«).
- Sie verfügen über ein Repertoire an Materialien und Spielstrategien.
- Sie erleben eine Erhöhung der Konzentration und Wachheit.
- Sie verstehen Offenheit als (Spiel-)Haltung und haben ihre Kommunikationsfähigkeit gesteigert.

subject of teaching. Post-concert discussions at the end of each term were also highly animated. We repeatedly found that we could identify the member of staff who taught each group on the basis of their performance style, a well-known phenomenon in the educational field.

The team of lecturers: Lauren Newton is a classically trained singer and best known as an experimental music vocalist; Dieter Ammann is a composer and trumpeter with experience in jazz and funk; Urban Mäder, a classical composer, frequently works with installations and on spatial projects; Thomas Mejer is a saxophonist with experience in experimental projects; Marc Unternährer, a classically trained tuba player, plays in numerous groups and free improvisation projects; Christy Doran, a guitar player, has longstanding experience in a wide range of jazz groups; Christoph Baumann, a jazz pianist, composes for bands, theater and film; Gerry Hemingway, a percussionist, plays in many well-known groups and has experience of interdisciplinary projects.

One primary motivation to genuinely tackle the research project was the fact that we all took a surprisingly similar view of improvised works, including those of disparate quality performed at our end-of-term concerts. We collected five years' worth of material, undertook video studies and team-based teaching, and scrutinized key teaching methods to arrive at a situation report that documents present work in Lucerne.

The objectives of the course:

- Increase students' perceptive faculties.
- Put students in a position to manage and shape musical processes.
- Develop their ability to take responsibility for their own music-making.
- Enable students to express an opinion on creative issues ("what–when–why").
- Ensure they have a repertoire of materials and performance strategies.
- Boost their concentration and alertness.
- Ensure they understand freedom as an approach (to performance) and are better communicators.
- Expand their aural analytical skills and knowledge of new and contemporary music.
- Give them experience of free improvisation, which in turn can directly affect their style of performance in jazz and classical chamber music.
- Ensure that students can identify and quantify quality and are aware of the conflict between personal preferences and "objectifiable" quality when assessing musical soundscapes.

Musical quality, mentioned above, is a notion we approached with the greatest respect. The evaluation of the tonal outcomes of free improvisation frequent-

- Die höranalytische Kompetenz sowie der Zugang zu neuer und zeitgenössischer Musik werden erweitert.
- Die Erfahrung mit Freier Improvisation hat direkte Auswirkung auf das Spielverhalten im Jazz und in der klassischen Kammermusik.
- Die Studierenden können Qualität erkennen und benennen und sind sich des Konfliktes zwischen persönlichen Präferenzen und »objektivierbarer« Qualität in der Beurteilung von musikalischen Klangresultaten bewusst.

»Musikalische Qualität« ist erwähnt, eine Begrifflichkeit, an die wir uns mit höchstem Respekt angenähert haben. Die Beurteilung von Klangergebnissen der Freien Improvisation bewegt sich immer im Spannungsverhältnis zwischen individueller und einer vielleicht kollektiven Beurteilung. Mit diesem Bewusstsein haben wir mutig versucht, ein paar Thesen auszuformulieren und haben die Kriterien Intensität, Authentizität und musikalische Gestalt als übergeordnete Titel gewählt.

a) Intensität

- Das klangliche Ergebnis ist Resultat eines wahrnehmbaren Gestaltungswillens.
- Der Ausdruck des Spiels lässt eine wache Kommunikation vermuten.
- Das Klangergebnis ist zugleich Ausdruck verschiedener Energielevels.

b) Authentizität/Originalität

- Klangforschung und Erfindung als Spielhaltung führen zu originellen musikalischen Ergebnissen.
- Die Originalität der Einfälle ist Ergebnis eines wachen Bezugs zur Gruppe und zum momentanen Klangereignis.

c) Musikalische Gestalt (Auswahl von Grundkriterien)

- Die Musik zeichnet sich durch eine verbindliche und spannungsvolle Gestalt aus.
- Die Musik ist Ausdruck von Risikobereitschaft.
- Die Aussagedichte einzelner Spieler stimmt im Verhältnis zum Kollektivgeschehen.
- Dichte und Transparenz werden bewusst gewählt.
- Der Formverlauf der Musik entwickelt sich konsequent aus dem gewählten Spielmaterial heraus.
- Der Verlauf des Stücks ist gut nachvollziehbar und lässt gleichzeitig genug Überraschungsraum zu.

ly involves shifting the dynamic relationship between the individual and the collective. Aware of this, we bravely ventured to develop a number of hypotheses, selecting the criteria of intensity, authenticity and musical form as priorities.

a) Intensity

- The musical outcome is the result of a perceptible creative impulse.
- The performance exudes a sense of lively communication.
- The musical outcome is also the expression of differing energy levels.

b) Authenticity/originality

- Sound research and inventive sonority as an approach to music-making results in original musical outcomes.
- The originality of ideas is the result of responsiveness to the group and the sound of the moment.

c) Musical form (selection of basic criteria)

- The music has an essential, compelling form.
- The music reveals a willingness to take risks.
- The expressive force of individual players is well-balanced against the collective performance.
- Full and transparent passages are deliberately contrasted.
- Formal development of the music is consistent with the chosen performance material.
- The progress of the piece can be easily followed while allowing sufficient opportunity for surprising elements.
- Stylistic or idiomatic references do not take over but remain an aspect of the free improvisation.
- The music is not only meaningful to the players but develops a universal communicative force.
- In addition to original and unique moments, the music builds on archetypes[1], but uses them creatively and flexibly.

4. The Promise of Free Improvisation, Research Phase I

Twenty-five years of experience have shown that the students at the Department of Music at Lucerne University of Applied Sciences and Arts view the

1 | For more on "archetypes", see p. 61.

- Stilistische oder idiomatische Bezugsmomente werden nicht zum Selbstläufer, sondern bleiben Gegenstand der Freien Gestaltung.
- Die Musik dreht nicht nur im persönlichen (oder gar privaten) Ausdruckskreis, sondern entwickelt eine allgemeingültige kommunikative Kraft.
- Die Klangergebnisse bauen nebst originellen und einmaligen Momenten auf Archetypen[1], gehen mit diesen allerdings kreativ und flexibel um.

4. Das Versprechen Freie Improvisation, Forschungsphase I

Die mittlerweile 25 Jahre Erfahrung haben gezeigt, dass die Studierenden unserer Hochschule den Fachtitel »Freie Improvisation« als ganz besonderes Versprechen sehen. Sowohl die mit Improvisation bewanderten wie auch die unerfahrenen Studierenden betrachten die didaktische Relevanz dieser radikalen Idee besonders kritisch. Sie prüfen die Ehrlichkeit des Fachversprechens, die Transparenz und Relativierbarkeit der Vermittlungsansätze.

Wir betrachten unsere Vermittlungsarbeit: Sie knüpft teilweise durchaus an die Primärerfahrungen der ersten frei Improvisierenden (ich denke an die Musiker des *LIO*) an, als eine Art neutrales Labor, in dem zunächst weder musikalisch noch sozial oder gesellschaftspolitisch eine Richtung auszumachen ist. Man beginnt mit einem radikalen NICHTS. Freiheit in Lehre und Forschung in aller Form. Gleichzeitig ist die Herausforderung immens, will man nicht einfach eine beliebige Ästhetik auswählen und es sich bequem machen. Die Herausforderung besteht darin, dass die Studierenden eine Produktionsform von Musik ausüben sollen, die sie meist nicht kennen. Die Studierenden müssen in die Rolle des Autors steigen, was sie ebenfalls nicht gewohnt sind. Und die Musik soll im Kollektiv und unvereinbart entstehen und dazu möglichst selbstbewusst und kritisch. Nicht unerheblich ist auch unsere Gewohnheit, am Ende des Semesters zu konzertieren und somit eigentlich schon früh zur Auseinandersetzung mit den künstlerisch-kommunikativen Aspekten eines ästhetischen Produktes anzuregen – eines Produktes, das man auf der Bühne mit einer gewissen Risikobereitschaft spontan entwirft.

Eine überzeugende Umsetzung des Versprechens »Freie Improvisation« als Bildungsfach steht und fällt mit der Qualität der Vermittlungskompetenz. Wir haben folgende pädagogische Qualitätskriterien formuliert.

1. Eine Kernqualität der Vermittlung geht von der didaktischen Idee aus, dass die Prozessarbeit mit einer Gruppe im weitesten Sinne auch die Form einer Freien Improvisation hat.

---

1 | Zum Begriff »Archetypen« s. Erläuterungen auf S. 60.

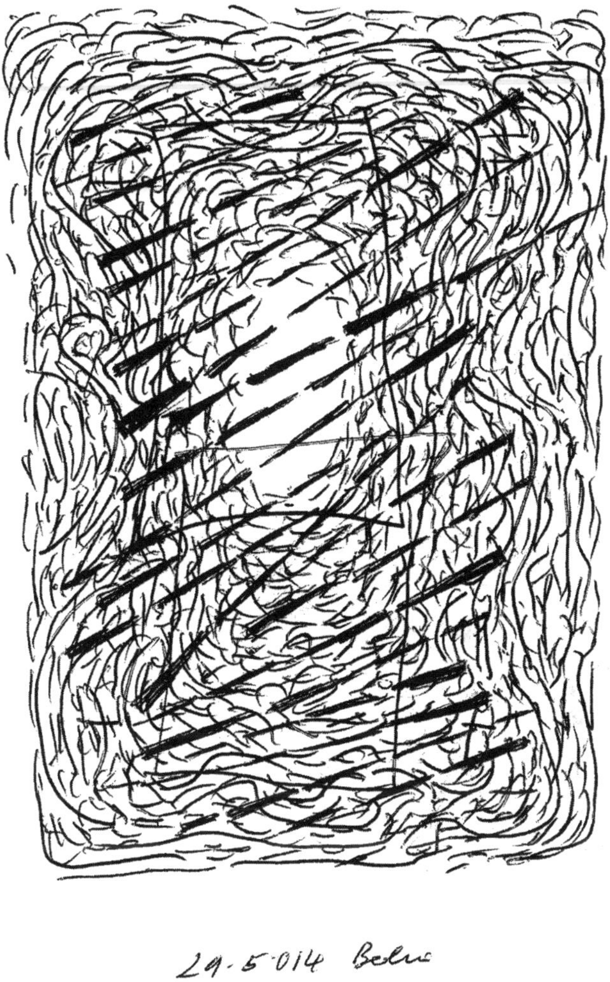
29-5-014

2. Die Philosophie der Freien Improvisation, die davon ausgeht, ohne vorausgehende Vereinbarungen Musik zu machen, führt zum Anspruch, dass bei der Vermittlung eine gute Balance zwischen dem Erreichen von qualitativ hochwertigen musikalischen Ergebnissen und der entwickelten Erfahrung jeglicher Aspekte der Gruppenimprovisation angestrebt wird.
3. Die Lehrperson setzt ihre musikalische und musikpädagogische Erfahrung ein, nutzt deren inspirierendes Potenzial und motiviert dadurch und im interaktiven Dialog mit den Studierenden diese zu interessiertem musikalischem Forschen.
4. Die Lehrperson ist fähig, die Wahrnehmung und das Bewusstsein für die Komplexität der Freien Improvisation und für die Entscheidungsverantwortung zu steigern.
5. Sie ist fähig, zur Reflexion über musikalische Ereignisse zu motivieren und erreicht dies auf eine situationsbezogene und flexible Weise.
6. Die Lehrperson ist fähig, die Ideen und Anregungen der Studierenden in konstruktiver und effizienter Weise in den Arbeitsprozess zu integrieren.
7. Die Lehrperson ist fähig, Methoden einzusetzen, um die musikalische Qualität zu steigern.

5. Das Luzerner Modell

Ein zentrales Kapitel im Forschungspapier »Freie Improvisation: Möglichkeiten und Grenzen der Vermittlung« (Phase I) sind die Themen, die dort in Kapitel 5.3 beschrieben werden. Es sind die Themen oder Momente, die sich in Gruppenimprovisationen typischerweise oft ereignen und die dann folglich auch Inhalt der Auseinandersetzung sind. Die Beschreibungen lassen einerseits die Komplexität der Vorgänge erahnen und sind andererseits Basisgedanken der Fortsetzung der Forschungsarbeit in Luzern.

Themen[2]

Das Kapitel beschreibt Themen oder Aspekte der Unterrichtssituation mit Freier Improvisation. Sie sind hier in drei übergeordnete Begriffsbereiche (Soziale Aspekte, Musikalische Aspekte, Reflexionsaspekte) unterteilt. Dazu ist zu bemer-

2 | Leicht gekürztes Kapitel 5.3 »Themen« aus der Forschungsarbeit »Freie Improvisation: Möglichkeiten und Grenzen der Vermittlung« von Mäder, Urban; Baumann, Christoph; Mejer, Thomas. Erhältlich unter *URL: IDS%20Luzern%20-%20Bibliothekskatalog%20:%20Library%20catalog.webarchive.*

course title "free improvisation" with very critical eyes. Whether or not they have experience of improvisation, they initially consider the teaching of this radical idea to be problematic. They question the principles of the topic as a subject and the transparency and impartiality of the teaching methods employed.

We analyze our teaching, a process that in part arises from our initial experience of free improvisation (the *LIO* musicians, for example), as a kind of neutral testing ground in which no clear social or societal biases are initially evident. We start with a radical NOTHING: freedom to teach and research spontaneously. At the same time, we face the considerable challenge of avoiding selecting a random aesthetic stance and making it easy for ourselves; the challenge for students is to practice a way of making music that most of them are unaware of. They must adopt the role of the author, another situation they are not used to. Furthermore, the music should be created collectively and without prior agreement, while at the same time being as assured and critical as possible. Our end-of-term concert routine that encourages critical engagement with the artistic and communicative aspects of an aesthetic outcome at an early stage is also an important factor – a musical creation spontaneously enacted on the stage in full knowledge of the potential risks.

Persuasive results in "free improvisation" critically depend on the quality of the teaching skills employed. We have developed the following quality criteria:

1. One core aspect of teaching is based on the idea that developing processes within a group is, in the broadest sense, also a type of free improvisation.
2. The philosophy of free improvisation that argues for making music with no prior consensus produces the need to achieve a teaching balance between ensuring high-quality musical results and developing experience in all aspects of group improvisation.
3. The tutor deploys their musical and teaching experience, uses their potential to inspire and thus encourages active musical research in dialog with the students.
4. The tutor is able to increase knowledge and awareness of the complexity of free improvisation and decision-making responsibility.
5. The tutor is able to encourage reflection on musical events and does so in a context-sensitive, flexible manner.
6. The tutor is able to integrate students' ideas and suggestions constructively and efficiently within the work process.
7. The tutor is able to employ methods that increase the quality of the music-making.

ken, dass gewisse Themen aus der Perspektive der Spielenden eine möglicherweise ganz andere Bedeutung und Gewichtung haben als aus der Perspektive der Rezeption (Zuhörer, begleitender Dozent).

Soziale Aspekte

Freies Improvisieren ist in erster Linie ein spontanes Agieren in einer Zweckgemeinschaft. Gerade deshalb haben hier soziale Aspekte, welche in der Kunst allgemein und der Kunstmusik im Besonderen häufig ausblendet werden, eine zentrale und in Bezug auf das (Klang-)Resultat immanente Bedeutung. Das erste Unterthema umfasst unsere körperliche Wahrnehmung und Präsenz im Raum und im zwischenmenschlichen Kontakt. Wir gehen davon aus, dass sich Wahrnehmungs- und Verhaltenskompetenzen durch die soziale Motivation bilden.

Hören als umfassendes Wahrnehmen (räumlich, fokussiert, analytisch)

Unsere auditive Wahrnehmung ist komplex. Wahrnehmung beinhaltet Herstellung von Beziehungen zur dinglichen und personalen Umwelt. Wahrnehmung schließt sinnliche (nebst der auditiven auch die visuelle, taktile und kinästhetische) Reizaufnahme, körperliche und gedankliche Verarbeitung, Erkennung und sprachliche oder motorische Reaktion mit ein. Wahrnehmung ist abhängig von der räumlichen Position, von der momentanen Beweglichkeit, von Wachheit, der emotionalen Befindlichkeit, den Erfahrungen und dem Denkvermögen der Person.

Das Hören beim gemeinsamen Musizieren hat verschiedene Dimensionen und kann verschieden geübt werden. Das eine ist die Fähigkeit, möglichst alle klanglichen Ereignisse gleichzeitig wahrzunehmen. Dieses Hören muss in ganz entspannter Form geschehen.

Dem gegenüber steht das fokussierte Hören. Das kann heißen, dass man sich auf eine Auswahl von Mitspielern respektive Instrumenten konzentriert. Es kann auch bedeuten, dass man sich primär auf die Artikulation der Töne oder Geräusche konzentriert. Solche und ähnliche Übungen fördern ein fokussiertes Hören. Ein fokussiertes Hören führt direkt zum analytischen Hören.

Analytisches Hören baut auf einer Höraufgabe auf. Hier konzentriert man sich zum Beispiel auf die Klangstruktur, die Besetzungsdichte, die Spielfunktion der einzelnen Mitspieler oder die Spannung des Formverlaufs et cetera. Dieses Fokussieren führt zum »Festhalten von Ereignissen«, was für die Steigerung der musikalischen Qualität förderlich ist. Das bewusste Hören und Erkennen ist eine der wichtigsten Voraussetzungen für das »Erinnerungsvermögen«. Was sich letztlich im Gedächtnis festsetzt, kann ganz unterschiedlich sein, wobei der eingenommene Hörfokus bestimmt maßgeblich Einfluss hat.

5. The Lucerne model

Chapter 5.3 of the research paper "Freie Improvisation: Möglichkeiten und Grenzen der Vermittlung" (phase I) crucially examines topics or moments that frequently occur in group improvisation and thus warrant detailed investigation. The descriptions given hint at the complexity of the processes involved whilst at the same time forming the fundamental basis for continuing research in Lucerne.

Topics[2]

The chapter examines topics and aspects of teaching free improvisation and is subdivided into three main areas (social, musical, reflective). It should be noted that certain topics may have very different meanings and importance for performers than they do for recipients (listeners, lecturers).

Social aspects

Free improvisation is primarily a spontaneous act within a functional community. Social aspects frequently ignored in art generally and in "art music" specifically here assume central and immanent meaning for the (musical) outcome. The first subtopic covers our physical perception and presence in space and interpersonal contact. We assume that perception and behavioral skills are a result of the social drivers.

Listening as sweeping perception (spatial, focused, analytical)

Our auditory perception is a complex system. Perception establishes connections with the physical and personal environment. It includes sensory perception (covering visual, tactile, and kinaesthetic in addition to auditory), physical and mental processing, detection, and linguistic or motor responses. Perception is dependent on the spatial position, mobility, alertness, emotional state, experience and the intellectual capacity of any one person.

In the act of joint music-making, listening assumes varying dimensions and can be practiced in diverse ways. One is the ability to hear as many tonal events as possible at the same time, a form of listening that must be undertaken in an easy and relaxed manner. At the other end of the spectrum is focused listening, which involves concentrating on a selection of players or instruments. It may also mean focusing attention on the articulation of notes or sounds.

---

2 | Abridged translation of chapter 5.3, "Themen", in Mäder, Urban; Baumann, Christoph; Mejer, Thomas: Freie Improvisation: Möglichkeiten und Grenzen der Vermittlung, available at *URL: IDS%20Luzern%20-%20Bibliothekskatalog%20:%20Library%20catalog webarchive.*

Körperliche Präsenz (Spannung, Impuls)

Musik ist lebendig, weil sie mit der körperlichen Präsenz des Spielenden kongruent ist. Das bewusste Wahrnehmen von Meldungen der Haut, der Muskeln, Sehnen, Gelenke; das Wahrnehmen der Temperatur, der Regulierung von Körperspannungen, der feinmotorischen und koordinatorischen Fertigkeiten sowie der Geschicklichkeit; das Wahrnehmen der Atembewegung und -spannung. Körperliche Präsenz soll in den Fokus rücken, soll Anlass und Aufschluss geben für das interaktive Spiel.

Vom Verhalten oder von Spielverhalten ist oft die Rede. Inwieweit die körperliche Präsenz oder eine Form von Wachheit dieses Spielverhaltens mitprägt, kann beobachtet werden. Der Grad der Wachheit kommt im Spiel zum Ausdruck und kann sich auf den Spannungsgrad der Mitspieler übertragen. Ein hoher Grad an Wachheit gilt in unserer Kultur als Qualitätskriterium. Vielleicht vermag ein hoher Grad an Wachheit das Bewusstsein für Freiheit zu steigern.

Die Orientierung im Verlauf einer Kollektivimprovisation stellt komplexe Ansprüche. Es bedarf der Bemühung, den aktuellen Stand der Musik bewusst zu hören, sich zu erinnern, was war, und eine Vorstellung zu haben, in welche Richtung sich die Musik bewegen könnte. Die Orientierungsfähigkeit verändert sich je nachdem, ob man spielt oder nicht spielt. Mit der Orientierung unmittelbar gekoppelt ist die Flexibilität des Verhaltens. Die Musik kann sich jederzeit in Richtungen bewegen, die gerade nicht den eigenen Vorstellungen entsprechen, sodass man sich jederzeit zu neuen musikalischen Vorläufen gesellt. Übergänge oder Neuanfänge fordern meist einen besonders hohen Grad an Wachheit oder Flexibilität.

Kommunikation (Interesse, Offenheit, Demokratie, Klarheit, Interaktion)

Der im Grunde neutrale Begriff *Kommunikation* wird hier durch verschiedene für das Zusammenleben und die Kreativität von Menschen prägende Teilaspekte ergänzt. Künstlerisches Tun geht von einem grundsätzlichen Interesse für Kommunikation aus. Dieses Interesse, zu dem unmittelbar die Offenheit gehört, hat beim Musikmachen eine besondere Bedeutung. Bei der Musik – ähnlich wie bei Theater und Tanz – entsteht das kommunikative Objekt im Kollektiv. Das qualitative Ergebnis ist immer Ausdruck des Potentials des kollektiven Kommunikationsvermögens. Freie Improvisation auszuüben verlangt selbstverständlich eine Offenheit und ein hohes Interesse am musikalischen Produktionsprozess, der als künstlerisches Produktionsprinzip in gewisser Weise radikal und höchst komplex ist. Zum Interesse hinzu kommt die Klarheit der Kommunikation respektive des Interaktionsverhaltens. Der Begriff *Demokratie* betont die Gleichberechtigung aller Beteiligten. Die basisdemokratische Grundhaltung ist ein sozialpolitischer Aspekt, dessen Diskussion seit dem Free Jazz und dem konzeptuellen Ansatz der Neuen Musik bedeutsam ist.

These and other exercises promote focused listening, which in turn leads directly to analytical listening.

Analytical listening develops from specific aural tasks. It involves, for example, concentration on the sound structure, instrumental texture, and the activity of individual players or the tightness of the formal design. This act of focusing serves to isolate particular events and is conducive to increasing musical quality. Conscious listening and understanding is one of the key requirements for boosting "powers of recollection". What ultimately remains in the memory may vary from person to person and is crucially dependent on the listening focus adopted.

Physical presence (energy, stimuli)

Music is "alive" because it is congruent with the player's physical presence. Conscious awareness of signs sent out by the skin, the muscles, the tendons and the joints; awareness of temperature, regulation of body tension, fine motor skills, coordination and agility; awareness of respiratory movement and tension. The physical presence should be placed in the foreground. It should be the reason and explanation for the interactive performance. Playing behavior is often discernable, and the extent to which physical presence or a form of alertness contributes to this behavior is an observable quantity. Levels of alertness are expressed in performance and may affect the other players' levels of energy. A high level is considered a sign of quality in our culture, and may help to enhance our experience of freedom.

Maintaining one's bearings in the course of a collective improvisation is a complex challenge, demanding effort to know what is happening in the music at any one moment, recollection of what preceded it and an idea of the direction it may take. This skill varies according to whether a player is actually performing or not and is directly related to flexibility of behavior. At any time, the music may branch out in an unexpected direction, requiring rapid adaptation to new material or structures. Transitions or new starts usually demand a particularly high level of alertness or flexibility.

Communication (interest, receptiveness, democracy, clarity, interaction)

The essentially neutral term *communication* is augmented by various defining characteristics relevant to the coexistence and creativity of humans. Artistic activity assumes a basic interest in communication, one that is directly associated with receptiveness, which has special significance in music-making. In music – as in theater and dance –, the communicative object is created in a collective environment. The qualitative result is always the expression of the potential that is inherent in the collective ability to communicate. Free improvisation naturally demands a level of receptiveness to and interest in the musical production process that, as an artistic practice, is in some ways radical and extremely complex. Interest is joined by clarity of communication or in-

Verantwortung (in Relation zur Freiheit, Unabhängigkeit, Position in der Gruppe)

»Freiheit, Gleichheit, Brüderlichkeit« waren die Schlagworte der Französischen Revolution. Es sind Grundwerte, die in den von uns gesetzten Unterbegriffen zum Thema Verantwortung ähnlich erscheinen. Obwohl die Bezeichnung »Freie Improvisation« besonders betont, dass das Spiel im Prinzip an keine Regeln gebunden ist, bleibt diese Freiheit immer eingeschränkt. Jeder Mitspieler nämlich bringt seine persönliche Erfahrungsperspektive, seinen ästhetischen und instrumentaltechnischen Hintergrund mit; seine Freiheit endet dort, wo sie die Freiheit der anderen einschränkt, das heißt, anderen die Möglichkeit genommen wird, gleichberechtigt zu kommunizieren.

Die Verantwortung ist eine soziale und zugleich inhaltliche Prämisse, die vom Bewusstsein ausgeht, dass zwischen dem Eigenen gegenüber Anderen und Anderem immer eine Diskrepanz besteht und dass die Überwindung dieser zwar eine Utopie ist, die Kunst aber mitunter danach strebt, Utopien erahnen zu lassen. Die Entscheidung, einer Sache (dem entstehenden Musikstück) zu dienen, relativiert das eigene Tun. Alle Entscheide stehen immer in Bezug zum gemeinsam anzustrebenden Klangresultat. Wie die Freiheit ist auch die Unabhängigkeit immer relativ. Es besteht die Abhängigkeit vom Verlauf des Stücks; die Abhängigkeit von der ästhetischen Beurteilung eines Jeden in jedem Moment des Spiels; die Abhängigkeit von der Beurteilung durch das Publikum; die Abhängigkeit davon, dass man in jedem Moment im Spiel eine bestimmte Position einnimmt und davon ausgehen will, dass die Gruppe diese Position wahrnimmt und respektiert.

Musikalische Aspekte (Material, Form)

In der Vermittlungsarbeit stehen die Klangereignisse im Zentrum. Die erinnerbaren musikalischen Prozesse und auch die im Nachhinein hörbaren Resultate sind Inhalt des Gesprächs, der Analyse. Sie sind Ausgangspunkt für immer neue Vorhaben, seien sie frei improvisiert oder seien es spezifische Übungen im Kontext des Arbeitsprozesses. Die Reflexion über die Klangereignisse ist komplex, einerseits aufgrund der Komplexität der Klangereignisse selber, andererseits aufgrund der ganz unterschiedlichen Reflexionsansätze der Mitwirkenden. Die Erfahrung zeigt, dass Reflexion einen wichtigen Beitrag zur Steigerung der Wahrnehmungsfähigkeit bedeutet und damit weitere Entwicklungsprozesse ermöglicht.

Instrumentale Möglichkeiten (Gewohnheit, Technik, Kenntnis)

Die Frage der »Freiheit« bei der Freien Improvisation wird fürs erste meist im Zusammenhang mit den instrumentalen Möglichkeiten thematisiert. Diese machen schnell und klar deutlich, dass Freiheit nicht mit Grenzenlosigkeit oder Unerschöpflichkeit (oder gar Beliebigkeit) verwechselt werden sollte. Da

teraction. The idea of "democracy" stresses the equal rights of all the parties involved. Basic democratic credentials represent a sociopolitical issue that has been the subject of significant discussion since the emergence of free jazz and the conceptual approach taken by new music.

Responsibility (in relation to freedom, independence, position in the group)

"Liberty, equality, fraternity" were the calls-to-arms of the French Revolution and are fundamental values that resemble the ideas that we have subsumed under the heading of *responsibility*. Although the concept of "free improvisation" emphazises the notion of performance not bound by any rules, this perceived freedom is delimited: every player contributes their own experience, their aesthetic values and instrumental proficiency; their freedom is curtailed at the point at which it limits the freedom of others, in other words, deprives them of the ability to communicate on an equal footing.

Responsibility is a social and substantive premise arising from the awareness of a discrepancy between the self and the other and the realization that, while resolving this dichotomy may be utopian, one of art's aspirations is to concretize the possibility of such utopias. The decision to serve a cause (the piece of music) relativizes the actions of the individual. Any decision always relates to the objective of producing the music which is desired by the group. Just like freedom, independence is also always relative: anything a player does is dependent on the course of the piece, the aesthetic judgment of others at any time during the performance, the opinion of the audience, and the desire to play a certain role at any moment during the performance, combined with the hope that the group will accept and respect this role.

Musical aspects (material, form)

Musical events are at the heart of our teaching; musical processes that can be recalled as well as the audible results that form the content of discussion and analysis. They are the point of departure for new projects, be they free improvisations or specific exercises in the context of the working process. Reflecting on musical events is a complex matter, due both to the complexity of the events themselves and the very different ways people approach them. Experience suggests that reflection and contemplation greatly assist the perceptive faculties and facilitate further personal and musical development.

Instrumental possibilities (habits, technique, knowledge)

In free improvisation, initially the question of "freedom" is usually explored in the context of instrumental possibilities, which in turn quickly reveal that freedom is not to be confused with boundlessness or inexhaustibility (or even randomness). There is the instrument, with the musical and technical material

ist das Instrument mit dem musikalischen und technischen Material, das unsere Hände je ausgeführt haben, und auch die Kenntnis, was das Instrument noch hervorbringen könnte. All dies ist mit uns als Person verbunden, ist unser Fundus, unser persönlicher Dialekt. Dieses Klangmaterial steht uns zur Verfügung und setzt uns zugleich Grenzen. Aus diesem Fundus zu schöpfen, auszuwählen und damit zu handeln, ist unsere Möglichkeit, unsere Freiheit, unsere Herausforderung.

Material (Tonhöhe, Tondauer, Artikulation, Klangfarbe, Dynamik)

Jeder Ton – oder allgemeiner: jedes *Material* – kann aufgrund der fünf Aspekte Tonhöhe, Tondauer, Artikulation, Klangfarbe, Dynamik definiert und entwickelt werden. Mit Material ist, wie gesagt, ein Ton, ein Geräusch, ein Motiv oder eine Spielgeste gemeint – vielleicht vergleichbar mit einem Laut, einem Wort oder einer Redewendung in der Sprache. Die Bewusstseinsbildung für die Komplexität der Gestalt dieses Kernmaterials ist ein wesentlicher Bestandteil der Arbeit. Kleinste Veränderungen von nur einem der fünf genannten Aspekte können die musikalische Wirkung stark verändern. Vielleicht ist der Beobachtungsfokus auf Details deswegen so wichtig, weil durch das Aufeinandertreffen von Materialien mehrerer Mitwirkenden erfahrungsgemäß ohnehin schnell eine große oder gar zu große Dichte entsteht. Die Einschränkung auf das rudimentäre Ausgangsmaterial ermöglicht genug interaktiven Spielraum, ermöglicht eventuell durch die Einfachheit eine unmittelbarere Klarheit in der Interaktion.

Homogenität – Heterogenität

Die beiden Begriffe als Gegensatzpaar sind oft sowohl Teil des musikalischen Ereignisses wie Gesprächsthema. Die Bedingung, dass sozusagen kollektiv und zeitgleich mit der Klangrealisation komponiert wird, ist im Vergleich zur üblichen Produktionsform Komposition außergewöhnlich. Mehrere Charaktere und Vorstellungen, welche von der Erfahrung mit komponierter Musik stammen, treffen hier aufeinander. Die Zeit für eine gemeinsame Absprache ist erstens nicht erwünscht und zweitens im Verlaufe des Klangprozesses gar nicht gegeben. Man kann insofern sagen, dass in jedem Fall ein heterogener Kreationsprozess stattfindet.

Diese Heterogenität muss allerdings nicht zwingend zur Folge haben, dass auch das musikalische Ergebnis heterogen ist. Mit heterogener Spielweise wäre gemeint, dass alle Spieler unterschiedliches musikalisches Material spielen und unterschiedliche Verlaufsvorstellungen haben. Das muss grundsätzlich nicht problematisch sein, doch empfinden die Mitwirkenden solche Situationen oft als »chaotisch«, als ein Geschehen, das zu dicht, zu unübersichtlich, zu undurchschaubar (besser »undurchhörbar«) wahrgenommen wird.

Demgegenüber steht eine homogene Spielweise, bei der die Spieler ähnliches oder gar gleiches Spielmaterial verwenden und dazu noch ähnliche Ver-

that our hands have performed, and the knowledge of what else it could do. All of it is closely wedded to our persona, our pool of resources, our personal dialect. This musical material is available to us, but, at the same time, it sets boundaries. Drawing on these resources, selecting them and using them is our choice, our freedom, our challenge.

Material (pitch, duration, articulation, timbre, dynamics)

All notes – or, more generally, *material* – can be defined and developed using the five characteristics of pitch, duration, articulation, timbre and dynamics. Material can indeed be notes as well as sounds, motifs or performance gestures – perhaps comparable with a linguistic sound, word or figure of speech. Raising awareness of the complexity involved in shaping this core material is a key aspect of our work. The smallest changes to just one of the five characteristics noted above can greatly impact the musical effect. It may be that focusing on details is so important because, as experience suggests, the convergence of materials performed by different players rapidly produces a thick or even overbearing texture. Limiting ourselves to the rudimentary starting material provides sufficient interactive room for maneuver; maintaining simplicity leads to greater clarity in interaction.

Homogeneity/heterogeneity

These two contrasting terms frequently form both part of a musical event and its discussion. Compared to the traditional method of composition, the condition of collective composition in the moment of its genesis is of crucial importance. Multiple personae and ideas, familiar with the experience of composed music, come together, and taking the time to reach a common understanding is neither desired nor possible in the course of the actual music-making. This ultimately produces a heterogeneous creative process.

It does not follow, however, that this heterogeneity must result in a heterogeneous musical outcome. Heterogeneous performance implies that each instrumentalist plays different musical material and has their own conception of the course the music will take. In itself, that need not be problematic, but in practice players often see such situations as "chaotic", as an event that is perceived as too dense, unclear and inscrutable.

This contrasts with homogeneous performance, in which the players use similar or identical material and also share a common idea of the musical trajectory. Unfavorable opinions may, however, also greet this phenomenon: too uniform, too monotonous or simply boring. Critical engagement with these two styles of performance – accepting that they are not absolute but rather nuanced – cannot involve a simple contrast between them; the objective must be to make constructive use of the opportunities each presents and raise awareness of their formal possibilities or conditions required to achieve maximum

laufsvorstellungen haben. Auch da kann es negative Rückmeldung geben: zu gleichförmig, zu monoton oder schlicht langweilig. Die Auseinandersetzung mit den beiden (in Abstufungen erscheinenden) Spielweisen kann nicht dahin gehen, dass man sich suchend von der einen in die andere bewegt. Es muss das Ziel sein, die Möglichkeiten und Chancen jeder Spielweise konstruktiv zu nutzen, sich der formalen Möglichkeiten oder gar Bedingungen der beiden Spielweisen bewusst zu werden, um sich möglichst frei und differenziert mit ihnen und in ihnen zu bewegen. Ein Kollektivspiel, das ähnlich oder imitierend ist, muss nicht eingleisig und flach werden. Feinste Nuancen und Schattierungen des Gesamtklanges können zu einem spannenden musikalischen Gehalt führen. Ebenso ist die spannende Qualität einer heterogenen Spielweise mit einem wachen und flexiblen Hinhören aufzunehmen und auszuschöpfen, ohne dies allzu rasch als beliebiges oder bezugsloses Durcheinander zu verurteilen.

Bewegung (Geste, Figur, Melodie, Charakter, Tempo, Dichte)

Musik ist Bewegung. Bewegung ist Musik. Diese wechselseitige Aussage basiert auf einem rudimentären Gestaltdenken. Rudimentär insofern, als man davon ausgeht, dass dem musikalisch-instrumentalen Spielfluss die pure Motion, die Regung, die Bewegung, die Bewegungsgeste zugrunde liegt, respektive, dass die Bewegung die Musik initiiert.

Diese Aussage erscheint lapidar und ist dennoch ein wichtiger Aspekt, was die Authentizität des instrumentalen Spiels betrifft. Authentizität ist dann spürbar, wenn die körperliche, mentale und klangliche Bewegung eins sind. Die Lebendigkeit dieser Bewegung zeichnet sich durch ihre im weitesten Sinne organische Nachvollziehbarkeit aus. Geste, Figur und Melodie sind Formbegriffe. Sie erscheinen uns in ihrer gestalterischen Ausrichtung, in ihrem Spannungsverlauf, verständlich durch die Anlehnung an unser körperliches und sprachliches Bewegungsrepertoire. Sie stehen im Verhältnis zu unserem Atem- und Blutkreislauf und lassen sich daher als kürzer oder länger bezeichnen. Sie zeichnen sich durch die unterschiedlichsten Charaktere aus und fügen sich in ein durch das Kollektiv getragenes, geführtes, erwidertes oder in Opposition befindliches Zusammenspiel ein. Tempo (nicht mit dem messbaren Metrum zu verwechseln) und Dichte sind dann übergeordnete Gestaltungsebenen, welche die musikalischen Bewegungsmaterialien im Formfluss fortführen.

Form (Wiederholung, Variation, Kontrast, Fortspinnen, ohne Zusammenhang, Gliederung)

Die Verwendung des Begriffs ist im Kontext der Freien Improvisation für sich zu untersuchen. *Form* als Bezeichnung der Architektur einer Musik im herkömmlichen Sinn steht in Verbindung zur Planung respektive Komposition. Das im Voraus nicht abgesprochene kollektive Schöpfungsverfahren lässt die formale Planung indes nicht zu. Es geht aber auch gar nicht darum, als im-

freedom and differentiation. Collective performance that is homogeneous and imitative need not be restrictive or shallow. Fine nuances and subtleties in the overall sound can produce exciting musical content. In turn, the stimulating quality of a heterogeneous performance must be accepted with alert and flexible listening, avoiding premature judgment of the whole as a random or disconnected jumble of sounds.

Movement (gestures, figures, melody, character, tempo, density)

Music is movement. Movement is music. This reciprocal statement is derived from the rudiments of Gestalt psychology – rudimentary that is, to the extent that we assume that pure motion, movement and gestures underlie the musical and instrumental performance, or that movement gives rise to the music.

This notion – despite its deceptive brevity – is a key aspect of authenticity in instrumental performance. Authenticity is tangible when physical, mental and musical movement are united. The vitality of this movement is evident, in the broadest sense, from its organic credibility. Gestures, figures and melody are formal terms; as artistic elements that wax and wane, they acquire meaning by playing on our repertoires of physical and linguistic movement. They are directly related to our breathing and circulation and can thus be described as shorter or longer. They evince a wide range of qualities and embed themselves within collective, directed, reciprocal or antagonistic ensemble playing. Tempo (not to be confused with meter) and density are higher-level creative strata that advance the musical movement material within the performance.

Form (repetition, variation, contrast, development, disjunction, structure)

In the context of free improvisation, the use of this term demands separate analysis. *Form*, the musical architecture in the conventional sense, is closely related to planning or composition. A collective creative process that is not discussed in advance cannot therefore allow for formal planning. Indeed, specific forms are anathema to free improvisation, which prefers to engage with its material and create a form that is effective in the here and now of collective improvisation. The form that results is then subjected to analysis when listened to after the performance. The question concerns the extent to which the improvisation process has adopted traditional formal principles in full, in part, or not at all. It may be a case of accepting that while formal architecture is conventional and thus – consciously or unconsciously – shapes our ideas, it is relegated to marginal status as a creative criterion for improvising in an ensemble. What is important when re-listening is to increase aural analytical powers of perception in the performance process itself, thus allowing formal aspects/principles to come to the fore when playing and creating clarity and transparency of the whole. We then work on raising awareness of formal principles such as repetition, variation, contrast, texture, thrust, development and rhythm in the

provisierende Gruppe eine bestimmte Form zu realisieren. Vielmehr zielt die Freie Improvisation darauf, in eine Gestaltung einzusteigen und eine Form entstehen zu lassen, die für die kollektive Improvisation hier und jetzt gilt.

Es geht zunächst um die analytische Beobachtung der entwickelten Form beim Nachhören nach dem Spiel. Es stellt sich die Frage, inwieweit sich herkömmliche Formprinzipien vollständig, fragmentarisch oder gar nicht im Improvisationsprozess ergeben haben. Vielleicht gilt es festzustellen, dass formale Architektur zwar gelebte Konvention ist und bewusst oder unbewusst Vorstellungen prägt, ihr doch als Gestaltungskriterium für die Improvisation im Ensemble sekundäre Bedeutung zukommen sollte. Entscheidend ist, dass beim Nachhören die höranalytische Wahrnehmungsfähigkeit im Spielprozess selber gefördert wird. Damit sollen formale Tendenzen während des Spielens erkennbar werden und Klarheit und Übersicht im Ganzen ermöglichen. So ist vorerst daran zu arbeiten, sich formaler Gestaltungsprinzipien wie Wiederholung, Variation und Kontrast sowie Textur, Richtung, Entwicklung im Dichtegrad, Rhythmisierung et cetera im überhörbaren Moment bewusst zu werden, dies immer in einer Balance zu allen möglichen interaktiven Vorgängen und Ansprüchen.

Stil (Idiomatisches – Nicht-Idiomatisches)

Stilistische Fragen sind zentral und komplex. Derek Baileys Aussage, dass in der Freien Improvisation das »Nicht-Idiomatische« mit der Bedingung des Kollektiv-Verfahrens gegeben ist, wird immer wieder diskutiert und in Frage gestellt: Das komplexe System der Freien Improvisation in der Gruppe stellt als Gegenposition zum komponierten Werk eine Form des Chaos dar. Die Frage ist nun aber, was denn ein Idiom ist und ob das Nicht-Idiomatische überhaupt möglich ist. Der Begriff *Idiom* wird im Zusammenhang mit Eigenschaften von Sprachen, Dialekten und Soziolekten verwendet. Die Verwendung von Idiom im musikalischen Zusammenhang ist insofern sinnvoll, als damit die Bindung an eine bestimmte soziale Gruppe (beispielsweise von Bebop-Musikern) herausgestrichen wird. »Nicht-idiomatisch« meint also, dass Gruppen mit unterschiedlicher musikalischer Sozialisation beziehungsweise musikstilistischen Hintergründen zusammenkommen, dabei aber ihre jeweiligen Idiome zugunsten der gemeinsam entstehenden Musik »aufheben«. Zwei Überlegungen sind für die Vermittlungspraxis von Freier Improvisation von Relevanz:

1. Das Spielmaterial und das Spielverhalten eines Mitwirkenden in einem Improvisationsensemble besitzt grundsätzlich idiomatisches Potenzial. Es gibt kaum (vokales oder instrumentales) Material, das nicht schon irgendwo gehört wurde und insofern einen Erinnerungs- und Bedeutungshintergrund hat. Der gestrichene Klang einer Violine erinnert sofort an eine Streicherwelt und ist als solcher mit Bedeutung behaftet, auch wenn er noch so karg und monoton gehalten ist. Und wird auf diesem Instru-

fleeting moment, while always striking a balance with potential interactive processes and intentions.

Style (idiomatic/non-idiomatic)

Questions of style are important and complex. Derek Bailey's claim that free improvisation has "no stylistic or idiomatic commitment" is frequently the subject of discussion: the complex system of free improvisation in a group represents a form of chaos in contrast to the composed work. The question, however, is what an idiom really is and if the non-idiomatic is at all possible. The term *idiom* is used in connection with qualities of language, dialects and sociolects. In music, idiom acquires meaning by celebrating links to specific social groups (bebop musicians, for example). The "non-idiomatic", then, implies the meeting of persons experienced in differing music and styles who nevertheless "break" with their idioms for the benefit of the music created together. In this context, two considerations are of relevance to teaching free improvisation:

1. The performance material and behavior of a player in an improvisation ensemble generally exhibits idiomatic potential. There is very little (vocal or instrumental) material that has not already been heard somewhere and thus has recollection and meaningful value. The bowed sound of a violin immediately conjures up the memory of stringed instruments and is imbued with meaning, no matter how sparse and monotonous it sounds. Moreover, playing a sequence of notes on this instrument creates another (melodic) level of meaning. The melody may have qualities typical of a style, or it may be so far developed that it is perceived as a quotation from a composition. One aspect of teaching is to maintain awareness of the individual players' level of idiomatic density in their performance material.
2. Free group improvisation is a meeting of several musicians with separate idioms. We might describe this situation as "poly-idiomatic" instead of "non-idiomatic". Aside from similarities in material and aesthetics that exist among idioms or develop during interaction, the stylistic orientation in the creative musical process is always an important issue. Working together for lengthy periods of time can cause platitudes to emerge, typical musical material, specific sound aesthetics or a characteristic density of events to become established. This may result in a group idiom or even style distinct from jazz or classical idioms. An established, self-critical stance must then retain the vivid adaptability of these platitudes and uncover complacency or stagnation. Groups may thus potentially be characterized by how they deal with established styles and clichés, how they work with and question them.

ment eine Tonfolge gespielt, entwickelt diese eine weitere (melodische) Bedeutungsebene. Diese Melodik kann stiltypische Merkmale aufweisen, sie kann aber so konkret sein, dass sie quasi als Zitat einer Komposition wahrgenommen wird. Bei der Vermittlungsarbeit geht es unter anderem darum, sich der idiomatischen Informationsdichte von Spielmaterial der einzelnen Mitwirkenden bewusst zu werden.

2. Die Freie Gruppenimprovisation ist die musikalische Begegnung mehrerer Musiker mit individuell unterschiedlichen Idiomen. Diese Situation könnte man statt »Nicht-Idiomatik« zunächst einmal als »Poly-Idiomatik« bezeichnen. Abgesehen von materiellen oder ästhetischen Gemeinsamkeiten, die zwischen Idiomen bestehen oder bei der Interaktion sich entwickeln, ist die stilistische Ausrichtung im musikalischen Findungsprozess immer ein besonderes Thema. Bei der gemeinsamen Arbeit über längere Zeit können sich bestimmte stilistische Gemeinplätze herausschälen, kann sich typisches musikalisches Material, eine bestimmte Klangästhetik oder eine charakteristische Ereignisdichte etablieren. So entwickelt sich ein von Jazz- und Klassik-Idiomen verschiedenes Gruppenidiom oder gar ein Gruppenstil. Eine entwickelte, selbstkritische Haltung muss sich dann zur Aufgabe machen, die lebendige Modulierbarkeit dieser Gemeinplätze beizubehalten und Genügsamkeit oder Stagnation aufzuspüren. Eine Gruppencharakteristik zeichnet sich möglicherweise dadurch aus, wie mit etablierten Stilbildungen und Klischees umgegangen wird, wie sie reflektiert und in Frage gestellt werden.

Reflexionsaspekte

Der dritte Bereich unserer Themen, betitelt mit «Reflexionsaspekte», behandelt die zentralen Methoden der Vermittlungsarbeit: das Nachdenken, Besprechen, Analysieren, Kritisieren und Beurteilen. Sie sind neben den sozialen und musikalischen Aspekten nicht selten selber Gegenstand der Gespräche, was sie auf eine Sekundärebene, die Reflexion über die Unterrichtssituation, führt. Die Reflexion ist ein grundsätzlicher Bestandteil zur Förderung der Wahrnehmung. Sie deckt auch Mängel oder Missverständnisse im Umgang mit dem verwendeten Material auf. Das Vokabular ist wiederum wichtig für das Erkennen von Gestaltungsaspekten innerhalb der musikalischen Prozesse (»man hört, was man weiß«).

Soziale und musikalische Aspekte

Die Beobachtung von musikalischen Vorgängen geht gerade in der Freien Improvisation oft einher mit der Beobachtung sozialer Vorgänge. Das ist bei dieser Form von kollektiver Kreation naheliegend. Interessant ist die Beobachtung, dass dieser Zusammenhang von Studierenden respektive Studierendengruppen ganz unterschiedlich wahrgenommen wird. Je nach Gruppenzusammen-

Berlin 29. 5. 2014
Konzert 1

setzung werden Beobachtungen sozialer Verhaltensweisen vor der Beschreibung musikalischer Aspekte thematisiert.

Andere Gruppen vermeiden bewusst oder unbewusst die Fragen, die soziale Aspekte betreffen. In diesem Falle ist es die Aufgabe des Dozierenden, der den Gruppenprozess begleitet, die sozialen Aspekte zu thematisieren. Denn im Gegensatz zur komponierten Musik, bei der die sozialen Beziehungen vom Komponisten geregelt werden, sind diese in der Freien Improvisation offen. Gleichsam sind sie für die Gestaltung des Klangprozesses entscheidend. Das Wissen um die unterschiedlich möglichen »sozialen Positionen« in einer improvisierenden Gruppe während eines musikalischen Prozesses erweitert die gestalterischen Möglichkeiten.

Zufälligkeit – Präzision

Dass Studierende, die sich primär mit musikalischer Literatur und deren Interpretation befassen, das Zusammenspiel in der nicht geplanten Freien Gruppenimprovisation als »zufällig« empfinden und beschreiben, ist sehr oft der Fall. Dies liegt an idiomatisch gebundenen Vorstellungen und Erwartungen, die in der Freien Improvisation jedoch einer offenen Haltung weichen müssen. Denn nur dann sind wir fähig, Zufälligkeit nicht als Beliebigkeit, sondern als unausweichliche Möglichkeit, als eine allen Bedingungen entsprechende, höchst präzise musikalische Gestalt zu betrachten. Hier sei ein Zitat aus dem Roman *Ohio* von Ruth Schweikert (2005) angefügt, in dem der Begriff »Zufall« unüblich verwendet wird: »Es gibt nichts Präziseres als den Zufall, wobei jetzt die Frage gilt, welche Aufmerksamkeit wir ihm schenken und welche Bedeutung wir ihm beimessen«.[3]

Hierarchie der Aufmerksamkeit (Parameter des musikalischen Materials)

Als musikalisches Material muss man im Prinzip alles bezeichnen, was klingt. Dazu gehören die kleinsten Lautäußerungen, Geräusche und Töne, bis zu den gemeinsamen Klang-, Strukturentwicklungen und Formen. Im Vergleich zu der Arbeit an einer Komposition, bei der man vor und zurück gehen und endlos streichen, ergänzen und korrigieren kann, ist bei der Improvisation nur immer das unmittelbar Gegenwärtige und Zukünftige verhandelbar. Dadurch rückt das Zusammentreffen der rudimentären Instrumentalklänge und Materialien vergleichsweise stärker in den Fokus.

Hinzu kommen die Aspekte der Klangbildung. Bei einem einzelnen Ton oder Geräusch geht es um Tonhöhe, Tondauer, Dynamik, Artikulation und Klangfarbe. Interessanterweise sind Tonhöhe und Tondauer anfänglich meist wichtiger. Die Arbeit in der Freien Gruppenimprovisation setzt klar zum Ziel,

3 | Zitiert nach Ruth Schweikert (2007): Ohio, Frankfurt/Main, Fischer Taschenbuch Verlag, S. 14 (Originalausgabe Ammann Verlag, Zürich 2005).

Reflection

The third main area of our investigations, entitled “reflections”, addresses key aspects of teaching: thinking, discussion, analysis, criticism, and judgment. Alongside social and musical aspects, they are, not uncommonly, themselves the subject of discussion, leading on to a deeper level, that of reflection on the teaching itself. Reflection is a fundamental way of developing the perceptive faculties. It uncovers shortcomings or misunderstandings when handling the material. The vocabulary used, in turn, is an important indicator of creative aspects within the musical processes (“we hear what we know”).

Social and musical aspects

In the collective creative process of free improvisation, observation of musical interaction is frequently accompanied by an observation of social interaction. It is interesting to note that students, whether singly or in groups, make the connection in very different ways. Depending on the composition of the group, observations of social behavior take precedence over musical aspects as the subject of discussion.

Other groups consciously or unconsciously avoid questions that concern social aspects. In this case, it is the task of the tutor accompanying the group process to bring these into play. In contrast to composed music, in which the social component is dictated by the composer, these aspects are set far more loosely in free improvisation. They are, as it were, decisive factors for the musical process: knowledge of the various different “social functions” in an improvising group during the musical process expands the creative possibilities that can be exploited.

The chance occurrence/precision

It is very often the case that students who deal mainly with the musical canon and its interpretation consider and describe the interplay in unplanned free group improvisation as “random”. This is generally due to ingrained ideas and expectations that, in free improvisation, need to give way to a more open-minded attitude. Only then can we see the chance occurrence not as randomness but as an inevitability, an extremely precise musical creation that meets all expectations.

Hierarchy of musical elements

In principle, anything that “sounds” must be considered musical material. This includes the quietest vocalizations, noises and notes, all the way through to developed sounds, structures and forms. In comparison to working on a composition in which we can move forward and back, cut, add and correct at will, in improvisation only the immediate present and future is negotiable. This brings the meeting of rudimentary instrumental sounds and materials more strongly into focus.

Dynamik, Artikulation und Klangfarbe stärker in den Vordergrund zu rücken. Die Erfahrung zeigt, dass durch diese Umstellung der Hierarchie das Potenzial der musikalischen Kommunikation breiter wird. Dynamik, Klangfarbe und Artikulation sind Aspekte des Materials, die die musikalische Kommunikation meist schneller möglich machen. Der Kontakt wird unmittelbarer.

Ästhetische Reife

Ästhetische Reife ist ein umfassendes Thema. Ästhetik heißt ursprünglich Wahrnehmung. Wahrnehmung ist allerdings eine höchst komplexe Sache, bei welcher verschiedene sinnliche und reflexive Vorgänge geschehen. Diese Vorgänge werden unterschiedlich erlebt, da sie an individuelle Erfahrungen gebunden sind. Der Erfahrungshintergrund und der persönliche Wahrnehmungsfilter prägen gemeinsam die ästhetische Position. Da die ästhetische Position respektive Reife von einigen Faktoren abhängt, wird die Auseinandersetzung in einer Arbeit mit Freier Gruppenimprovisation komplex. Da kann folgende These gelten: Je mehr Erfahrung in Improvisation vorhanden und je höher die ästhetische Reife aller Mitwirkenden ist, desto höher ist das gemeinsame Verständnis beim interaktiven musikalischen Gestaltungsprozess.

Individuelle Präferenzen

Dieses Stichwort lehnt sich unmittelbar an den Punkt »ästhetische Reife« an. Die individuelle Präferenz weist auf einen Aspekt hin, der immer wirksam ist. Es geht um die Dynamik eines Gruppenprozesses, der von den Charakteren der Mitwirkenden abhängig ist. Gerade dadurch, dass das musikalische Ereignis das Resultat der Summe der einzelnen, in ihren Voraussetzungen verschiedenen und momentanen Entscheidungen ist, bleibt eine natürliche Dynamik für die Arbeit stets bestimmend.

Archetypisches

Bei der Arbeit mit Studierenden einer Musikhochschule ist die Bezugnahme zu sogenannten »musikalischen Archetypen« äußerst wertvoll. Studierende sind oft überrascht, wie schnell sie beurteilen können, ob ihnen eine Improvisation gefallen hat oder warum sie diese als gelungen bezeichnen. Sie sind überrascht, dass – trotz unterschiedlicher Erfahrung und unterschiedlichen Musikpräferenzen – Stücke oft ähnlich beurteilt werden. Um diesen kollektiven Übereinstimmungen nahe zu kommen, ist die Analyse des Gespielten aufgrund von archetypischen Tendenzen hilfreich. Hier sind musikalische Archetypen zu nennen wie beispielsweise die Koppelung von Verdichtung und dynamischer Steigerung, die dynamische Balance bei komplexen Klangbildern oder die Tendenz zu Phrasierung bei der melodischen Gestaltung. Musikalische Archetypen sind nicht die einzigen Gründe eines kollektiven Beurteilungsmaßstabes, doch erscheinen sie bedeutungsvoller als angenommen.

Aspects of sound production are also important. A single note or sound is defined by its pitch, duration, dynamics, articulation, and timbre, with pitch and duration initially considered of greater relevance. Work on free group improvisation clearly focuses on bringing dynamics, articulation and timbre more strongly to the fore. Experience shows that this hierarchical change further opens up the potential of musical communication. Dynamics, timbre, and articulation are elements of the material that usually work to facilitate musical communication. Interaction becomes more direct.

Aesthetic maturity

Aesthetic maturity is a wide-ranging subject. Aesthetic originally meant "relating to perception by the senses", and perception is an extremely complex matter that brings together many different sensory and reflexive processes. These processes are experienced differently because they are tied to individuals and their own personal experiences. Together, experience and the personal filter of perception shape any one person's aesthetic stance. And because this stance, or maturity, is dependent on a range of factors, engaging with the work of free group improvisation is complex. The following statement may have some truth: the more experience of improvisation and the greater the aesthetic maturity of all the players, the greater the common understanding of the interactive creative musical process.

Personal preferences

This heading follows on directly from "aesthetic maturity". Personal preference represents an ever-present factor, the dynamic of a group process that is dependent on the personae of those involved. Precisely because the musical event is the sum total of individual, diverse and momentary decisions, a natural dynamic is always a crucial element of improvisation work.

The archetypical

When working with students at a school of music, making reference to "musical archetypes" is a very valuable undertaking. Students are often surprised at how quickly they can assess whether they enjoyed an improvisation or why they consider it to be successful. They are surprised – despite their various levels of experience and differing musical interests – that pieces are often judged similarly by different people. Analysis of what has been performed on the basis of archetypical propensities can be helpful in understanding this unanimity. Worthy of mention are musical archetypes such as the association of tonal density and an increase in dynamics, dynamic balance in complex tonal images, or the tendency to use phrase in the melodic composition. Musical archetypes do not form the sole basis for collective assessment criteria, but they appear to be more significant than is generally accepted.

6. Das Luzerner Modell, Forschungsphase II

Das Wesen der Freien Improvisation kann man zwar mit aller Bemühung zu beschreiben versuchen, doch kann dieses letztlich nur durch konkretes Ausführen und Hören erfahren werden. Dasselbe gilt auch für die Vermittlungsarbeit. Der Einblick in die Vermittlungsarbeit durch die Beschreibung der Themen gibt den Eindruck eines vielfältigen und vielschichtigen Arbeitsprozesses. Da wechseln sich spielen, Gespieltes anhören, besprechen, analysieren, neues Ansetzen, spezifische Übungen einbauen et cetera frei ab. Das kann dann allerdings von Probe zu Probe respektive von Gruppe zu Gruppe komplett anders aussehen. Der Unterrichtsgegenstand »Freie Improvisation« impliziert sozusagen eine sich stets wandelnde Vermittlungssituation.

Mit dem selbstkritischen Gedankenansatz »Das Versprechen Freie Improvisation« haben wir in Luzern unsere Forschungsarbeit gestartet. Wir haben uns die Frage gestellt, ob Freie Improvisation als Unterrichtsgegenstand überhaupt möglich ist. Da wir dies seit zweieinhalb Jahrzehnten tatsächlich tun, folgte die Frage, ob wir dem Gehalt unseres Ausgangsgedankens zumindest annähernd gerecht werden, denn »Freie Improvisation« als Pflichtkurstitel birgt doch eine gewisse Sprengkraft.

Mit der Fortsetzung unserer Forschungsarbeit in Phase II, die seit ein paar Monaten im Gang ist, wagen wir uns in gewisser Weise an eine höchst fragile Essenz. Wir haben im ersten Papier (Phase I) viele Beobachtungen, Fragen und Probleme aufgezeigt. Wir haben einen Katalog von Arbeitsmethoden aufgestellt. Das sind spezifische Ansagen, Übungen und Konzepte, welche als Ergänzung zum reflektierenden Gespräch angewendet werden. Mit fragiler Essenz meine ich hier die Dreh- und Angelpunkte des prozesshaften Geschehens. Es sind die Momente, wo Spielereignis, Reflexion, Erkenntnis und erneute lustvolle Spielunternehmung zu einer Vermittlungsbewegung führen, bei der eine bezugsdichte Matrix ineinandergreift und die gleichzeitig dem höchsten Anspruch von unvorhergesehenem Tun (Improvisation) gerecht werden kann. Wir arbeiten an einem Kompendium, das die Breite der beschriebenen Themen aufnimmt und sie mit dieser Arbeitsmatrix verflechtet. Wir wollen ein Kompendium erstellen, das nicht als Lehrmittel im üblichen Sinn verstanden wird. Wir wollen eine Schrift verfassen, die zum entsprechenden musikalischen Tun, dem Freien Improvisieren sowie zur Umsetzung auf der Ebene der Vermittlung anregt. Wir wollen unser Verständnis für diese Kunstform zum Ausdruck bringen, einer Kunstform, deren Bedeutung weit über das konkret Klingende hinausgeht.

6. The Lucerne model, research phase II

It may be possible to outline the essence of free improvisation on paper, but ultimately only actual performance and listening can really do it justice. And that is also true of our teaching; a cursory examination based on the topics we cover reveals a diverse and disparate work process that freely alternates between playing, listening, discussion, analysis, new approaches, specific exercises and much more. These aspects can also vary from rehearsal to rehearsal and from group to group. "Free improvisation" as a subject thus implies a constantly shifting teaching experience.

We commenced our research in Lucerne with the self-critical conceptual approach we call "the promise of free improvisation". We asked ourselves whether free improvisation is at all suited to being taught; as we have now been teaching it for over two decades, this was followed by the question of whether we have been at least partially true to our original idea, as an obligatory course entitled "free improvisation" can prompt a divisive response.

On continuing our research into phase II, now several months in, we are venturing towards what I would term an extremely "fragile essence". In phase I, we brought to light many observations, questions and issues. We compiled a catalog of working methods, specific instructions, exercises and ideas used to complement the post-performance discussion. In this context, the "fragile essence" is then the crux of the creative process, moments in which the musical event, reflection, understanding and renewed, pleasurable performance are mediated, in which a highly referential matrix intertwines and at the same time does justice to the highest standards of unforeseen actions (improvisation). We are working on a compendium that will cover the breadth of these topics and interweave them with this work matrix, one that is not understood as a teaching material in the conventional sense. We want to compose a work that stimulates musical activity, free improvisation and its teaching. We want to express our understanding of this art form, one whose significance extends far beyond the purely musical.

Translation into English: Oliver Dahin, Berlin

Literatur/References

Hentig, Hartmut von (2000): Kreativität: Hohe Erwartungen an einen schwachen Begriff, Weinheim: Beltz.

Mäder, Urban; Baumann, Christoph; Mejer, Thomas (2014): Freie Improvisation: Möglichkeiten und Grenzen der Vermittlung, Luzern, o.V.

Intermezzo 1

CI: Eine Krise der improvisierten Musik, wie ich sie sehe, ist, dass wir im Prinzip einen Nachholbedarf haben in der Theorie. Wir haben eigentlich kein theoretisches Feld oder nur ein sehr mangelhaftes. Daraus würde ich die Forderung schließen, dass wir uns unbedingt schonungslos einer Theorie der improvisierten Musik öffnen müssen. Ich glaube, dass wir hier einen Diskurs führen müssen, der destruktiv ist. Konstruktiv auch, aber destruktiv in dem Sinne, dass wir sehr schonungslos an dem arbeiten müssen, was ich Mythen der improvisierten Musik nennen würde. Dazu gehören für mich Begriffe wie Echtzeitmusik, Performativität, Materialität, Gestalt, Augenblicklichkeit und so weiter. Ich glaube, es wäre wichtig, uns an diesen Begriffen abzuarbeiten.

SR: Kunst und Wissenschaft sind getrennte Bereiche, und es ist wichtig und gut, dass gerade die Wissenschaft sich den Forschungsmethoden der Kunst und der künstlerischen Forschung öffnet. Aber umgekehrt muss auch die Improvisation, wenn sie mehr über sich wissen will, zulassen, dass die Wissenschaft nicht ohne Begriffe auskommt. Wir brauchen Begriffe, wir brauchen die Theorie, wir brauchen die Kälte der Wissenschaft, auch um die Hitze der Improvisation zu verstehen.

Diskussionsbeiträge von Christoph Irmer (CI) und Stefan Roszak (SR), Mai 2014

Intermezzo 1

CI: As I see it, there is a crisis in improvised music, which is that theory is basically lagging behind. In fact, we have no theoretical field or, at best, a really inadequate one. So, based on this, I think it's vital we open ourselves up mercilessly to developing a theory of improvised music. I believe that we'll have to engage in debate that is both destructive and constructive at the same time; destructive in the sense that we will have to work ruthlessly on what I would call the myths of improvised music. These include such concepts as real-time music and terms like performativity, materiality, gestalt, instantaneousness et cetera, and I think it would be important to work through these concepts.

SR: Art and science are separate areas, and it's important and right that science in particular should open itself up to the research methods of art and artistic research. On the other hand though, if improvisation really does want to know more about itself, it must also allow for the fact that science doesn't work without terminology. We need terms, we need theory, we need the coldness of science in order to also understand the heat of improvisation.

Christoph Irmer (CI) and Stefan Roszak (SR) in a public discussion, May 2014

Translation into English: Louise & Phil Loxton, GB-Wales

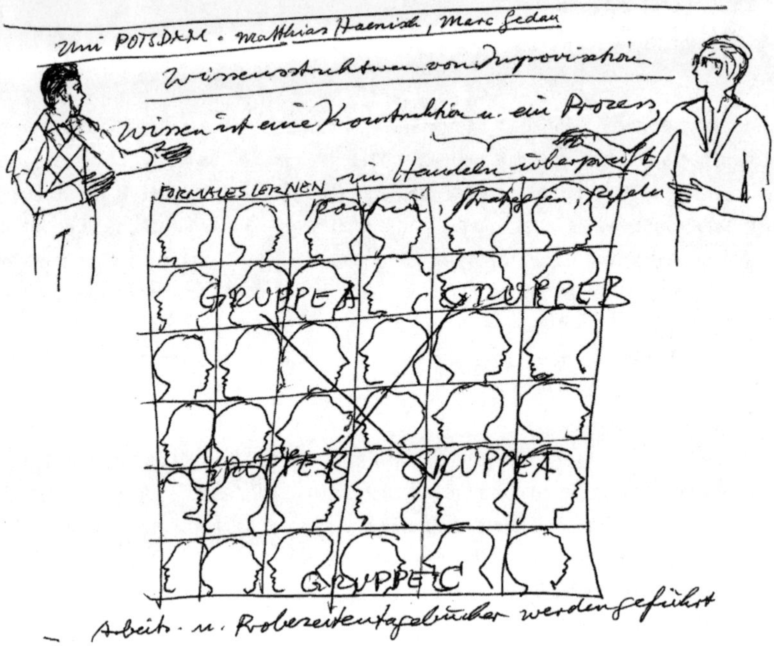
Uni POTSDAM · Matthias Haenisch, Marc Godau
Wissensstrukturen von Improvisation
Wissen ist eine Konstruktion u. ein Prozess,
im Handeln überprüft
FORMALES LERNEN
Routine, Strategien, Regeln
GRUPPE A
GRUPPE B
GRUPPE B
GRUPPE A
GRUPPE C
– Arbeits- u. Probezeitentagebücher werden geführt

Improvisierendes Wissen | Improvising Knowledge

Perspektiven einer systemisch-konstruktivistischen Improvisationsforschung | Perspectives of systemic-constructivist approach to improvisation research

---

Matthias Haenisch/Marc Godau

Einleitung

Wie lernen Improvisierende Improvisieren? Wie entwickeln sie ästhetische Urteilsfähigkeit und zugleich die Kompetenz, ästhetische Kriterien in gelingende Praxis zu übersetzen? Mit diesen Fragen beschäftigt sich das im Frühjahr 2014 angelaufene Forschungsprojekt *Improvisierendes Wissen*. Interdisziplinär zwischen Musikwissenschaft, Wissenssoziologie und Musikpädagogik angelegt, erforscht das Projekt künstlerische Lern- und Wissensformen im Kontext zeitgenössischer Improvisation. Dabei erhoffen wir uns zugleich Rückschlüsse auf grundlegendere Strukturen künstlerischen Wissens und auf Strategien kreativer Praxis.

Unser Wissensbegriff schließt vor allem an Konzepte des impliziten Wissens oder tacit knowing an.[1] Demzufolge umfasst implizites Wissen zumeist inkorporierte, überwiegend vor-reflexive Wissensformen, die als Erfahrungswissen im Vollzug der Praxis en passant erworben werden: Weder der lernende Aufbau noch das Anwenden und Weiterentwickeln impliziten Wissens müssen den Praktikern »bewusst« sein. Diese verfügen damit über Wahrnehmungs-, Entscheidungs- und Handlungsdispositionen, die sich in gelingender Praxis zeigen, aber von den Praktikern selbst oft nicht artikuliert werden können. Als Wissensphänomene gelten daher auch erlernte Fertigkeiten, Intuition und Routine sowie Problemlösungskompetenzen, praxisrelevante Orientierungs- und Deutungsmuster, aber auch Formen nicht-sprachlicher Reflexion im Sinne einer *reflection-in-action*.[2]

Vor dem Hintergrund aktueller Diskussionen zum impliziten Wissen gehen wir erstens davon aus, »dass zumindest Teile des impliziten Wissens unter bestimmten Umständen durchaus verbalisiert werden können, zum Beispiel dann, wenn sie in den Aufmerksamkeitsfokus gebracht werden«. (Büssing et alii 2002: 3) Zweitens setzen wir voraus, dass eine rekonstruktiv-hermeneutische Analyse der verbalen Aussagen von Praktikern einen Zugang zu impliziten Sinn- und Bedeutungskonstruktionen und damit zum Hintergrundwissen der Praxis ermöglicht (Kruse 2014: 369 ff.). Damit verfolgen wir das Anliegen einer verbalen Explikation und interpretierenden Rekonstruktion impliziter epistemischer Prozesse des Erfahrungslernens und praktischen Wissens Improvisierender.

Im Folgenden werden wir zunächst in das Forschungsprojekt einführen und dabei die epistemologischen und methodologischen Grundlagen sowie Forschungsgegenstand und Untersuchungsdesign erläutern. Anschließend wollen wir mit dem systemischen Interview eine unserer Erhebungsmethoden zur Exploration handlungsleitender Kategorien vorstellen und an einem Aus-

1 | Vgl.: Polanyi (1985); Collins (2010).

2 | Vgl.: Schön (1983).

Introduction

How do improvisers learn improvisation? How do they develop the ability to make aesthetic judgments and, at the same time, the competence to translate aesthetic criteria into successful practice? The research project *Improvisierendes Wissen (Improvising Knowledge)*, which began in spring 2014, addresses these questions. This interdisciplinary project integrates musicology, sociology of knowledge and music education, and researches artistic forms of knowledge and learning within the context of contemporary improvisation. We hope to draw conclusions about more fundamental structures of artistic knowledge and strategies for creative practice.

Our definition of knowledge is primarily based on the concept of implicit knowledge or tacit knowing.[1] The concept of implicit knowledge includes, for the most part, mainly pre-reflexive forms of knowledge that are obtained *en passant* during practice: the practitioner need not necessarily be consciously aware of either the development or the application and advancement of tacit knowing. Practitioners have access to perceptual, decisional and behavioral dispositions that reveal themselves during successful performance but which they themselves often cannot articulate. Therefore, learned abilities, intuition and routine are part of knowledge phenomena, as well as problem solving skills, patterns of orientation and meaning, and also those forms of non-verbal reflection in the sense of reflection-in-action.[2]

Against the background of current discourse about implicit knowledge, we assume first of all "that at least parts of implicit knowledge can certainly be verbalized under specific conditions, for example when they are made the focus of attention" (Büssing et alii 2002: 3). Secondly, we assume that a reconstructive-hermeneutic analysis of verbal statements by the practitioners can provide access to implicit sense and meaning constructions and, as such, to background knowledge of the practice (Kruse 2014: 369 ff.). We therefore pursue a verbal explication and interpretive reconstruction of implicit epistemic processes of experiential learning and practical knowledge from the improvisers.

In what follows, we will first present the research project and explain the epistemological and methodological foundations, as well as introducing the subject of research and explaining how the study was designed. Subsequently, we will introduce the systemic interview as one of our survey methods employed to explore action guiding categories and to ascertain the situative conditions for learning improvisation by looking at a sample analysis.

1 | Cf.: Polanyi (1985); Collins (2010).

2 | Cf.: Schön (1983).

wertungsbeispiel die situativen Bedingungen improvisierenden Lernens herausarbeiten.

Methodologie und Forschungsstil

Der Fragehorizont unserer Studie ist prinzipiell offen gehalten und erfordert eine explorative und flexible, zugleich systematische und kontrollierte Arbeitsweise. Mit der Grounded Theory folgen wir einer Methodologie, die weder thesengeleitet noch hypothesenprüfend vorgeht und nicht von einer vorgefassten Theorie über ihren Forschungsgegenstand ausgeht.[3] Vielmehr sollen erst innerhalb des Forschungsprozesses und unmittelbar aus dem erhobenen Datenmaterial die Konzepte und Kategorien zur Beschreibung des Forschungsfeldes gewonnen werden. Indem im Forschungsprozess auf eine Übernahme theoretischen Vorwissens über Improvisation zunächst verzichtet wird, verfolgen wir das Ziel einer im Gegenstand selbst verankerten Theorie, die nicht allseits bekannte Klischees des Improvisierens (Spontanität, Unvorhersehbarkeit, Innovativität et cetera) fortschreibt, sondern diesen Improvisationsdiskurs selbst mit zum Gegenstand der Forschung macht. Indessen gewährt der Forschungsstil der Grounded Theory eine kontinuierliche Anpassung von Fragestellungen und Methoden an die Eigendynamik des Forschungsverlaufs. Im Zuge des ständigen Vergleichs aktueller Daten mit bereits erhobenen Daten und bereits entwickelten Theoriebeständen wird die Theoriebildung vorangetrieben. In diesem iterativen Vorgehen findet eine permanente Überarbeitung und Anpassung der entstehenden Grounded Theory statt, die in künftige Datenerhebungen einfließt.

Unsere Methodologie folgt einer konstruktivistischen Programmatik.[4] Demzufolge untersucht Forschung nicht eine ihr äußerliche, unabhängige Realität, sondern konstituiert ihren Gegenstand mit. Diese Prämisse erfordert es, dass wir nicht nur Improvisationsensembles dabei beobachten, wie diese ihre Wirklichkeit musikalischer Praxis hervorbringen. Es geht vielmehr auch darum, Forschende und Forschungssetting als integrale Bestandteile des Forschungsgegenstandes mit einzubeziehen, das heißt die Interventionen, Beeinflussungen der Forschung zu beobachten und auch den Forschungsteilnehmern gegenüber ausdrücklich zu thematisieren. Insgesamt erfordert das eine im Forschungsprozess kontinuierlich mitlaufende Selbstreflexion der Forschung als Prozess der wechselseitigen Konstruktion von Erkenntnis und Erkenntnisgegenstand.[5]

3 | Vgl.: Glaser/Strauss (2010); Charmaz (2006); Clarke (2012).

4 | Vgl.: Charmaz (2006); Moser (Hrsg.) (2011).

5 | Vgl.: Breuer (2010).

Methodology and research style

Conceived as open-ended research, our study demands an explorative and flexible way of working that is, at the same time, systematic and controlled. Using *Grounded Theory*, we follow a methodology that is not logico-deductive or designed for hypothesis testing and which does not start with a predetermined theory about the object of investigation.[3] Instead, the concepts and categories for describing the research field come from within the research process and are derived from the collected data. In as far as the research process is kept free of theoretical preconceptions about improvisation, we strive for a theory that is anchored in the object itself, that does not perpetuate the well-known clichés of improvisation (spontaneity, unpredictability, innovation, et cetera) but rather makes this improvisation discourse itself part of the object of investigation. In addition, *Grounded Theory* facilitates a continual adaptation of investigation and methods used to the unique momentum of the research process. The construction of a theory takes place via the constant comparison of current data with previously collected data and elements of pre-developed theory. This iterative process creates a permanent reworking and adjustment of the emerging *Grounded Theory* that then flows into future data collection.

Our methodology follows a constructivist program.[4] This assumes that research does not investigate an independent, external reality, but rather simultaneously constructs the object of study. This premise demands that we do more than simply observe improvising ensembles as they construct their musical practice. It is much more important to establish the researchers and the research setting as integral elements of the object of study, in other words, to observe the interventions and influences of the research and to expressly discuss these with the research participants. This requires a continuous self-reflection of the research process as a reciprocal construction between knowledge and object of knowledge.[5]

Research field and object of study

In the first phase, the project concentrates on the learning processes of improvisers in the "novice stage" (Dreyfus 2004: 177-181). The selection of beginners as research participants is based on the fact that it allows the process of initial competence development to be investigated as it occurs, whereas, in the case of experts it can only be retroactively reconstructed.

3 | Cf.: Glaser/Strauss (2010); Charmaz (2006); Clarke (2012).

4 | Cf.: Charmaz (2006); Moser (Ed.) (2011).

5 | Cf.: Breuer (2010).

Forschungsfeld und Forschungsgegenstand

In seiner ersten Arbeitsphase konzentriert sich das Projekt auf Lernprozesse Improvisierender im »Novizenstadium« (Dreyfus 2004: 177-181). Die Auswahl von Anfängern als Forschungsteilnehmende hat ihren Grund darin, dass hier der Prozess beginnender Kompetenzentwicklung in actu untersucht, bei Experten hingegen nur rückblickend rekonstruiert werden kann.

Um im Anfängerstadium ein möglichst breites Spektrum sozialer Lern- und Wissensformen erfassen und voneinander unterscheiden zu können, vergleichen wir fremdinitiierte und selbstinitiierte Lernprozesse. Fremdinitiiertes Lernen kann als formales Lernen beschrieben werden, bei dem Lernzeiten und -methoden von Lehrenden beziehungsweise Anleitenden vorstrukturiert werden. Beim selbstinitiierten Lernen werden Lernziele und Lernwege von den Lernenden selbst bestimmt. Mit der Thematisierung selbstinitiierten Lernens schließen wir an Forschung zum informellen Lernen außerhalb von Bildungseinrichtungen an, die auch in der Musikpädagogik auf wachsendes Interesse stößt.[6]

Aufgrund der Fokussierung auf Anfänger im Rahmen eines komparatistischen Ansatzes erforscht das Projekt in seiner ersten Arbeitsphase improvisierendes Lernen im Feld akademischer Ausbildungspraxis. Die Entscheidung, im institutionellen Kontext universitärer Musikausbildung anstatt im nicht-institutionalisierten Bereich einer lokalen »freien« Improvisationsszene zu beginnen, hat forschungspragmatische Gründe. Universitäre Studiengänge ermöglichten es uns, größere Gruppen von Anfängern regelmäßig und über einen längeren Zeitraum zu beobachten. Im professionellen Kontext einer Improvisationsszene dagegen ist der wissenschaftliche Zugang zu Improvisationsgruppen mit einem einigermaßen einheitlichen Anfänger-Niveau weit schwieriger zu erreichen. Gleichwohl soll im Sinne eines kontrastierenden Fallvergleichs in einer späteren Arbeitsphase und auf der Grundlage eines im Projektverlauf weiterentwickelten Untersuchungsdesigns die Erforschung informeller, autodidaktischer Lernformen im Kontext nicht-institutionalisierter Szenen erfolgen.

Untersuchungsdesign

Das Untersuchungsdesign folgt unserer Überzeugung, dass implizite, verborgene Prozesse einer Praxis dadurch beobachtbar gemacht werden können, dass die Forschung in kontrolliert maßvoller Weise in die Praxis interveniert. In Anlehnung an entsprechende Erfahrungen der Ethnomethodologie gehen wir

6 | Vgl.: Green (2002); Folkestad (2006); Röbke/Ardila-Mantilla (Hg.) (2009); Godau (2015).

In order to capture the widest possible spectrum of social learning and knowledge forms and to be able to differentiate between them, we compare other-directed and self-directed processes of learning. Other-directed learning can be described as formal learning in which the learning times and methods are preconceived by the individuals who carry out the teaching or instructing. With self-directed learning, the learning goals and paths are defined by the learners themselves. By addressing the concept of self-directed learning, we draw on research of informal learning outside of educational institutions, which is of growing interest in the field of music pedagogy as well.[6]

Due to the focus on beginners in the context of a comparative approach, in the first phase the project examines how improvising is learned within the practical field of academic training. The decision to begin within the institutional context of a university music program rather than in a non-institutional, local, "free" improvisation scene was based on pragmatic considerations. University programs allow us to observe larger groups of beginners regularly and over a longer period of time. Conversely, gaining scientific access to improvising groups with a relatively uniform level of beginners is much more difficult to do within the professional context of the improvisational scene. Nevertheless, a contrasting case study will take place during a later phase with research into informal, autodidactic forms of learning in the context of a non-institutional setting. This will be done by expanding the study design during the course of the project.

Study design

The study design follows our conviction that implicit, hidden processes of a practice can be made visible through moderate, controlled intervention by the researchers. Drawing upon similar experience in ethnomethodology, we contend that the disruption of routinized communication and action associated with the practice can make otherwise tacit and unnoticed implicit background knowledge evident and recognizable.[7] For this reason, the design of our study draws upon the principles of qualitative experiments.[8] In this case, it is an explorative and adaptive form of inquiry that places less importance on repeatability and more on flexible adjustment in relation to the object of study. A qualitative experiment is more engaging than receptive forms of participatory observation, narrative interviews or group discussions, and allows for

6 | Cf.: Green (2002); Folkestad (2006); Röbke/Ardila-Mantilla (Eds.) (2009); Godau (2015).

7 | Cf.: Garfinkel (1967); Hillebrandt (2014).

8 | Cf.: Kleining (1986): *URL: http://nbn-resolving.de/urn:nbn:de:0168-ssoar-8631.* (30.05.2015); Burkart (2010).

davon aus, dass durch die Irritation des routinisierten[7] Handelns und Sprechens der Praxis das ansonsten stillschweigend und unbemerkt operierende implizite Hintergrundwissen der Akteure erkenn- und reflektierbar wird.[8] Aus diesem Grund beruht das Design unserer Studie auf Prinzipien des qualitativen Experiments.[9] Dabei handelt es sich um eine explorative und adaptive Untersuchungsform, die weniger auf Wiederholbarkeit als auf flexible Anpassung an den Untersuchungsgegenstand setzt. Stärker eingreifend als rezeptive Untersuchungsformen der teilnehmenden Beobachtung, des narrativen Interviews oder Gruppendiskussionsverfahrens, ermöglicht ein qualitatives Experiment kontrollierte Interventionen in das Untersuchungsfeld, mithin die experimentelle Exploration verborgener Praxisstrukturen.

Das erste von bisher zwei qualitativen Experimenten haben wir an einer deutschsprachigen Universität mit Teilnehmern einer wissenschaftlich-künstlerischen Lehrveranstaltung im Lehramt Musik durchgeführt. Im Sinne einer experimentellen Segmentierung des Untersuchungsfeldes wurden die Teilnehmer per Losverfahren in zwei Gruppen eingeteilt. Dadurch ermöglichten wir die unterschiedliche Perspektivierung des Gegenstands »Lernprozess« (Burkart 2010: 257): Gruppe A arbeitete während der ersten Semesterhälfte gemeinsam mit einer professionellen Musikerin der Berliner Improvisationsszene, Gruppe B arbeitete parallel unangeleitet und selbstorganisiert. In der zweiten Semesterhälfte wechselten die Arbeitsformen, so dass Gruppe A fortan selbstständig weiterarbeitete und Gruppe B von der Improvisationsmusikerin angeleitet wurde. Unabhängig von der Lehrveranstaltung bildeten freiwillige studentische Forschungsteilnehmer die Gruppe C, die über das gesamte Semester unangeleitet und selbstorganisiert probte. Auf der Semesterhälfte – vor dem Wechsel der Arbeitsformen der Gruppen A und B – stellten die Gruppen einander ihre Ergebnisse in einer Zwischenpräsentation vor. Das Semester endete mit einem öffentlichen Abschlusskonzert und einem anschließenden Abschlussexperiment, in dessen Verlauf alle Teilnehmer erneut per Losverfahren auf drei Gruppen verteilt wurden und ad hoc improvisieren sollten.

Das Setting erlaubt Komparation auf drei Ebenen: Im *synchronen Vergleich* erfolgt die parallele Beobachtung der angeleiteten und selbstständig arbeitenden Gruppen. Im *diachronen Vergleich* können die unterschiedlichen Arbeitsformen innerhalb einer Gruppe untersucht werden. Einen *Kontroll-Vergleich* gestattet die parallele Beobachtung der Gruppen A und B in Komparation mit dem Arbeitsprozess der Gruppe C.

---

7 | Zur Routine gewordenen (Anm. d. Red.).

8 | Vgl.: Garfinkel (1967); Hillebrandt (2014).

9 | Vgl.: Kleining (1986): *URL: http://nbn-resolving.de/urn:nbn:de:0168-ssoar-8631.* (30.05.2015); Burkart (2010).

controlled intervention in the research area, thus facilitating the experimental exploration of hidden structures within the practice.

The first of the two qualitative experiments which have been conducted so far we undertook at a German-speaking university with participants attending a scientific/artistic seminar as part of the Music Education program. In order to achieve an experimental segmentation of the research field, the participants were randomly divided into two groups. This provided the opportunity to differentiate the perspectivization of the object "learning process" (Burkart 2010: 257): During the first half of the semester, Group A worked with a professional musician from the Berlin improvisation scene. At the same time, Group B worked without an instructor and was self-organized. For the second half of the semester, the groups exchanged roles so that Group A worked independently and Group B was led by the improvisation instructor. Beside this, participating students volunteered to form a third group, Group C, which was independent of the seminar and practiced in a self-organized way and without any instruction throughout the entire semester. At the mid-term point – before Groups A and B exchanged their form of working – the groups presented their results during an interim presentation. The semester ended with a public concert and a closing experiment in which all participants were again randomly divided into three groups which improvised together in an ad hoc way.

The setting enables comparison to take place on three levels: the synchronous comparison is conducted by the parallel observation of the teacher-directed and self-directed groups; in the diachronous comparison, the differing work forms within each group can be examined; a control comparison is provided via the parallel observation of Groups A and B in contrast to the development process of Group C.

Data collection methods: Video Stimulated Recall (VSR) and Systemic Interviews

All rehearsals and concerts were documented using video. The aim of this was to collect rehearsal and concert data which could then be analyzed, and also to enable a comparison of the work and the learning methods employed. Furthermore, this video material was used to conduct video-stimulated recall (VSR) interviews that were carried out with the individual groups directly after the performance or rehearsal. With the video-based focus interview, we drew upon a method that has proven itself effective within different research contexts as a way to explicate social and cognitive processes that otherwise remain tacit and hidden.[9] Within the course of a VSR interview, the rehearsal and performance

9 | DiPardo (1994); Gass/Mackey (2000); Dempsey (2010).

Erhebungsmethoden: Video-Stimulated-Recall (VSR) und Systemisches Interview

Alle Proben und Konzerte wurden videographisch dokumentiert. Dieses Datenmaterial ist einerseits Gegenstand von Videoanalysen (Proben- und Aufführungsanalysen) der zu vergleichenden Arbeits- und Lernformen. Andererseits wurden diese Videos für die Durchführung von Video-Stimulated-Recall-Interviews verwendet, die jeweils unmittelbar nach den Proben beziehungsweise Aufführungen mit den einzelnen Gruppen durchgeführt wurden. Mit dem videobasierten Fokusinterview greifen wir auf ein Verfahren zurück, das sich in unterschiedlichen Forschungskontexten als Methode der Explikation sozialer und kognitiver Prozesse bewährt hat, die üblicherweise implizit und verborgen ablaufen.[10] Im VSR-Interview werden Proben- und Aufführungsvideos der Gruppen von diesen selbst kommentiert und reflektiert. Dabei werden an konkreten musikalischen Beispielsituationen ästhetische Werturteile gefällt, gemeinsame und divergierende Wahrnehmungen und Maßstäbe diskutiert, Gruppenstrukturen werden transparent, wechselseitige Erwartungen offengelegt, Ziele und Strategien formuliert und revidiert. Die Gruppen ko-konstruieren und kommunizieren praxisrelevantes Wissen, das bei einer bloßen Beobachtung von Proben und Konzerten, aber auch bei der Analyse von Probengesprächen unzugänglich bleiben würde. Dabei durchlaufen die Forschungsteilnehmer selbst einen Perspektivenwechsel. Denn während (improvisierende) Praktiker ihre Praxis *im* Tun vor allem darauf hin beobachten, *was* sie tun (Beobachtung 1. Ordnung), beobachten sie sich im Video-Stimulated-Recall-Interview dabei, *wie* sie es tun (Beobachtung 2. Ordnung). Die Auswertung der Interviews zielt mithin auf die Explikation und Rekonstruktion derjenigen Sinn- und Bedeutungszuschreibungen, die weder im bloßen Vollzug der Praxis noch im Gespräch von Praktikern »unter sich« artikuliert werden, die sich aber durch die Verschiebung des Aufmerksamkeitsfokus' beziehungsweise des Selbstbeobachtungsmodus im Interview dokumentieren und reflektieren lassen.

Um diesen Perspektivenwechsel aktiv zu unterstützen, greifen wir neben offenen Diskussionsformen unter anderem auf systemische Interviewtechniken des zirkulären Fragens zurück. Hierbei handelt es sich um Fragetechniken, die ursprünglich im Kontext systemischer Familientherapie entwickelt wurden, um Rollenmuster, Handlungs- und Kommunikationsstrukturen transparent machen zu können.[11] Über diesen spezifischen Verwendungskontext hinaus sind zirkuläre Fragen sehr gut geeignet, Strukturen sozialer Syste-

10 | DiPardo (1994); Gass/Mackey (2000); Dempsey (2010).

11 | Simon/Rech-Simon (2013).

videos are reflected upon and commented on by the groups themselves. This allows aesthetic judgments of concrete musical situations to be made, opens discussion about shared and divergent perceptions and standards, makes group dynamics more transparent, reveals reciprocal expectations and provides a space for goals and strategies to be formulated and revised. The groups co-construct and communicate practice-related knowledge that would otherwise remain untapped if other methods, for example the direct observation of rehearsals and concerts or the analysis of rehearsal discussions, were employed. This method initiates a shift in the research participants, perspectives. During the act of improvisation, the aspect that the practitioners observe most is *what* they are doing (first-order observation), whilst during the VSR interview, they focus on *how* they do it (second-order observation). The analysis of the interviews aims to explain and reconstruct the attributions of sense and meaning that would otherwise not be articulated among the practitioners during the simple execution of the performance, nor during ordinary dialog. However, with the shift in the focus of attention, or, rather, the shift into self-observation mode, these attributions can be documented and reflected upon in the interview.

In order to actively support this change in perspective, we rely upon the systemic interview techniques of circular questioning in addition to open forms of discussion. Here, we are dealing with a questioning technique that was originally developed in the context of systemic family therapy in order to help make role, action and communication structures transparent.[10] Above and beyond this specific context, circular questioning is well suited to researching the structures of social systems.[11] Systemic questioning techniques are based on fundamental assumptions of how social interactions come to be. Accordingly, each interaction starts with the condition of double contingency, in other words under the prerequisite of reciprocal indeterminacy for each partner in the interaction (Luhmann 1987: 148ff.): no one can predict the behavior of the other, and at the same time, each one remains unpredictable to the other – a situation that is of special interest when investigating the processes of improvisation.[12] Double contingency is reduced when the participants orient themselves towards each other, that is, to the observable behavior of the other. Each interaction partner directs expectations at his or her counterpart and at the same time expects that the other expects something specific from them (Luhmann 1987: 156-158). In this sense, the "structure of social systems is created out of nothing more than expectations and reflexive expectations of expectations." (Pfeffer 2004: 72). This fundamental impact is often not, or only minimally, recognized by participants (Baecker 2005: 87), but it can be made the focus of

10 | Simon/Rech-Simon (2013).

11 | Pfeffer (2004).

12 | Cf.: Haenisch (2011).

me zu erforschen.[12] Systemische Fragetechniken basieren auf grundlegenden Annahmen darüber, wie soziale Interaktion zustande kommt. Demzufolge läuft jegliche Interaktion unter den Bedingungen doppelter Kontingenz ab, das heißt unter der Voraussetzung wechselseitiger Unbestimmbarkeit der Interaktionspartner (Luhmann 1987: 148ff.): Niemand kann des Anderen Verhalten vorhersagen und ist selbst für sein Gegenüber unbestimmbar – eine Situation, die für die Erforschung von Improvisationsprozessen von besonderem Interesse ist.[13] Doppelte Kontingenz wird dadurch reduziert, dass die Beteiligten sich aneinander, das heißt am jeweils beobachtbaren Verhalten orientieren. Dabei richtet jeder Interaktionspartner Erwartungen an sein Gegenüber und erwartet zugleich, dass auch das Gegenüber Bestimmtes erwartet (Luhmann 1987: 156-158). Mithin besteht »die Struktur eines sozialen Systems [...] aus nichts anderem als aus Erwartungen und der reflexiven Erwartung von Erwartungen« (Pfeffer 2004: 72). Zwar wird diese fundamentale Wirksamkeit wechselseitigen Erwartens von Akteuren selbst oft nicht oder kaum bemerkt (Baecker 2005: 87), kann aber durch zirkuläre Fragen in den Aufmerksamkeitsfokus gebracht werden: »Wie, glaubst Du, nehmen die anderen Musiker deine Aktion wahr?«. »Was vermutest Du, wie sie das findet, was er gespielt hat?«. »Wie müsst Ihr spielen, damit die anderen sagen, es sei misslungen?«. »Was meint ihr, was die anderen Gruppen denken, was ihr über ihre Musik sagen werdet?« Entsprechende Vertiefungsfragen zielen darauf, dass Forschungsteilnehmer einander ansonsten unausgesprochene Erwartungen offen legen, mithin ein gemeinsames Wissen über die interaktionalen Bedingungen ihres Handelns erzeugen und kommunizieren.

Im Rahmen unserer Studie zielen zirkuläre Fragen einerseits auf die Identifikation der Erwartungsstrukturen und Interaktionsdynamiken innerhalb der Gruppen und damit auf die Rekonstruktion der Emergenz musikalischer Interaktion.[14] Darüber hinaus lassen sich mit systemischen Fragetechniken die spezifischen Wirklichkeitskonstruktionen der Gruppen erkunden, das heißt die ästhetischen Relevanzsysteme und handlungsleitenden Orientierungsmuster, mithin die soziale Situiertheit der Praxis.

Am folgenden Beispiel wollen wir zeigen, wie sich über die Auswertung eines systemischen Interviews erstens implizite Lernbegriffe einer Gruppe und zweitens die spezifischen Bedingungen des Lernens aus der Sicht dieser Gruppe rekonstruieren lassen. Dabei entsteht einerseits ein dichtes Gefüge von aufeinander bezogenen *Kategorien improvisierenden Lernens*, andererseits wird die spezifische *Situation improvisierenden Lernens* sichtbar, wie sie von den Praktikern beobachtet und erlebt wird.

---

12 | Pfeffer (2004).

13 | Vgl.: Haenisch (2011).

14 | Vgl.: Haenisch (2014).

attention by means of circular questions: "How do you believe the other musicians perceived your action?", "What do you suppose she thinks about what he played?", "How would you have to play in order for the others to say it was not successful?", "In your opinion, what would the other groups think you would say about your own music?" Relevant additional questions have the goal of revealing otherwise unspoken expectations held by the participants in order to create and communicate a shared knowledge of the conditions of interaction.

In the course of our study, circular questions are used to identify expectation structures and interaction dynamics within the groups in order to reconstruct the emergence of musical interaction.[13] In addition, systemic questioning techniques allow us to gain insights into the specific reality constructions of the groups; in other words, the aesthetic relevance systems and the action-guiding patterns of orientation which comprise the social situatedness of the practice.

In the following example, we wish to demonstrate how, firstly, implicit learning concepts and secondly, specific learning conditions from the group perspective can be reconstructed through the evaluation of a systemic interview. On the one hand, this creates a dense structure of inter-related *categories of improvisational learning* and, on the other, makes the *specific situation of improvisational learning* observable as it is perceived and experienced by the practitioners.

The interview chosen here took place prior to the closing concert presentation with Group B, which was teacher-directed for the second half of the semester. In the course of the conversation, the group members discussed the group's expectations regarding the upcoming concert, as well as the expected expectations of the audience which consisted of other ensembles from the project, as well as instructors from the instrumental pedagogy and music didactics department.

Categories of Improvisational Learning

The following section examines the implicit learning concept of the practice, that is to say, the question of how learning is framed by Group B and who ascribes learning to whom – or, in terms of system theory, how learning is self-referentially defined in the observed system. The data analysis allows this learning concept to be internally differentiated so that five categories of learning can be distinguished from and referenced to one another.

A. *Learning as the development of an interactional ability to improvisation* is an expectation of the group to itself. This relates to a development of the ensemble

13 | Cf.: Haenisch (2014).

Das hier gewählte Interview wurde mit der in der zweiten Untersuchungsphase beziehungsweise zweiten Semesterhälfte angeleiteten Gruppe B vor der Abschlusspräsentation geführt. Im Verlauf des Gesprächs diskutierten die Gruppenmitglieder Erwartungen an die eigene Gruppe im Hinblick auf das anstehende Konzert, ebenso auch erwartete Erwartungen des Publikums, bestehend aus den anderen Ensembles des Projekts sowie dem instrumentalpädagogischen und musikdidaktischen Lehrpersonal.

Kategorien improvisierenden Lernens

Es geht im Folgenden um das implizite Lernkonzept der Praxis, das heißt um die Frage, wie von Gruppe B Lernen aufgefasst wird und wer wem Lernen zuschreibt – systemtheoretisch formuliert: wie im beobachteten System Lernen selbstreferentiell bestimmt wird. In der Datenauswertung lässt sich dieses Lernkonzept binnendifferenziert betrachten, wodurch fünf Kategorien des Lernens unterschieden und aufeinander bezogen werden können.

A. *Lernen als Ausbildung einer interaktionalen Improvisationsfähigkeit* ist eine Erwartung der Gruppe an sich selbst. Dabei geht es um Veränderungen der Gruppe bezogen auf das gemeinsame Ensemblespiel. In diesem Prozess erwirbt die Gruppe kollektive Gestaltungsstrategien (zum Beispiel kontrastieren, imitieren, gemeinsam oder in Untergruppen spielen):

»#00:52:53-4# Interviewer: Okay, was müsst ihr machen, damit du sagst, es ist cool ( ) gewesen?
#00:52:58-8# Thomas: Ähm (3) das muss irgendwie ne Kommunikation passieren äh entweder mit allen, aber auch so in kleinen Gruppen vielleicht, dass sich gegenseitig imitiert würde oder eben kontrastiert, dass man eben merkt, die die haben jetzt zusammen gespielt und nich, nich jeder spielt einfach irgendwie. Also ja, dass dass man nich denkt, oh das klingt aber beliebig, sondern, dass man denkt, jawohl es ist ein Stück oder ein Klang, dass es irgendwie was Gemeinsames wird.«

Aufgrund ihrer Gestaltungsfähigkeiten kann die Gruppe zwar den Raum möglicher und erwünschter Interaktionsformen vorhersehen, nicht aber das konkrete erklingende Resultat, »weil ja auch wir selbst als Akteure noch nicht so richtig wissen, was wird passieren, [...] wir haben vielleicht schon irgendwie n groben Fahrplan oder was wir tun wollen.« (#00:51:56-6# Thomas). Insgesamt ist die Interaktion zukunftsoffen, allerdings wird zwischen einer vage antizipierbaren Makrostruktur (»Fahrplan«) und einer nicht-vorhersehbaren Mikrostruktur (»wie es dann klingt«) in der konkreten Ausführung unterschieden. Mit dem *Lernen als Ausbildung einer interaktionalen Improvisationsfähigkeit*

based on changes within collective music-making. In this process, the group acquires collective performance strategies (for example contrasting, imitating, playing together or in sub-groups):

"#00:52:53-4# Interviewer: Okay, what would you have to do to be able to say that was cool?
#00:52:58-8# Thomas: Um, somehow communication has to happen, um, either with everyone or maybe in smaller groups, too, when together we imitate or even contrast, so it is apparent that they, they just played together and not that everyone is just playing somehow or other. So, yeah, that you don't think, oh that sounds random but rather that you think it is a real piece or sound that somehow fits together, something collective."

Based on their creative skills, the group can predict the space of possible and desirable forms of interaction but not the concrete sound of the results, "because, yeah, even though we are the players we don't really know what will happen, [...] we have perhaps a kind of general map of what we want to do." (#00:51:56-6# Thomas). Generally, the interaction is open with regard to the future, but the concrete results can be differentiated into a macro structure ("general map") that can be vaguely anticipated and a micro structure that cannot be anticipated ("how it sounds"). *Learning as the development of an interactional ability to improvisation* does not only combine technical ability, for example structure building skills, but also different degrees and levels of predictability of musical processes. Above all, however, the interview shows that the creative skills are subordinate to a developing system of aesthetic criteria that is coordinated here by the difference "random/not random". Here, the applicability of value judgments is explained by whether or not the appropriateness or inappropriateness of specific interactions and improvisation in general is viewed as successful artistic practice.

B. *Learning as a process* is doubly conceptualized by the group, on the one hand as goal-oriented and externally observed and, on the other, as a self-observed and undirected process. At the heart of this category is the question of how and by whom learning is observed and can be evaluated with regard to creative skills.

B.1 *Learning as a goal-oriented process within an observation of the others* is an expectation of expectation, that is to say, the interviewed group expects that the other groups expect goal-oriented learning from them. It is only under this condition that others can observe the learning progress: "you have to [...] essentially define the goal ahead of time before you can even say that it is an advancement" (#00:59:58-5# Marian). As the other two groups were not present at the rehearsals of Group B and therefore do not know the goals,

verbinden sich demzufolge nicht nur handwerkliche, zum Beispiel strukturbildende Fertigkeiten sondern auch unterschiedliche Ebenen und Grade der Antizipierbarkeit musikalischer Prozesse. Vor allem aber zeigt das Interview, dass die Gestaltungsfähigkeiten einem sich entwickelnden ästhetischen Relevanzsystem unterstehen, das hier von der Differenz »beliebig/nicht-beliebig« koordiniert wird. Damit ist die Wirksamkeit von Wertmaßstäben benannt, mit denen die Angemessenheit beziehungsweise Nicht-Angemessenheit spezifischer Interaktionen und Improvisation insgesamt als gelingende künstlerische Praxis beobachtbar wird.

B. *Lernen als Prozess* wird von der Gruppe doppelt konzeptualisiert, einerseits als fremdbeobachtet zielgerichteter, andererseits als selbstbeobachtet ungerichteter Prozess. Im Zentrum dieser Kategorie steht die Frage, wie und von wem Lernen beobachtet und im Hinblick auf sich entwickelnde Fertigkeiten bewertet werden kann.

B.1 *Lernen als fremdbeobachtet zielgerichteter Prozess* ist eine Erwartungserwartung, das heißt die interviewte Gruppe erwartet, dass die anderen Gruppen von ihr zielorientiertes Lernen erwarten. Denn nur unter dieser Voraussetzung könnten die Anderen Lernfortschritte überhaupt beobachten: »Man muss [...] das Ziel quasi dafür definiert haben, dass man erst mal sagen kann, das ist ne Weiterentwicklung«. (#00:59:58-5# Marian). Da die anderen beiden Gruppen jedoch nicht bei den Proben der Gruppe B anwesend waren und daher ihre Ziele nicht kennen, können sie dementsprechend nicht beurteilen, wie und ob Gruppe B sich verbessert hat. Infolge dessen lehnt Gruppe B die Erwartungserwartung zielgerichteten Lernens ab.

Indessen schreibt Gruppe B sich selbst gar keine expliziten Lernziele zu, kann sich selbst daher auch nicht im Hinblick auf Lernen als zielgerichteten Prozess beobachten. Zielgerichtetes Lernen wird damit insgesamt ausgeschlossen. Die Gruppe kann von anderen nicht legitim beurteilt werden, ihre Selbstbeurteilung beruht dagegen auf einem komplementären, radikal prozessualisierten Lernkonzept (B.2).

B.2 *Lernen als kontinuierlicher und ungerichteter Prozess* ist eine Erwartung der Gruppe an sich selbst und die Grundlage ihrer Selbstbeurteilung. Im folgenden Interviewausschnitt geht es um die Frage, wie Weiterentwicklung zu erkennen ist. Dabei wird Lernen als fortlaufende, immerwährende Selbstveränderung bestimmt, Misserfolg und Rückschritt sind ausgeschlossen:

»#01:00:11-9# Cosima: [...] ich glaube, es gibt eigentlich keine Rückentwicklung. Es ist immer ne Weiterentwicklung, weil man sich dann auch bewusst dafür ent-

they are unable to assess how or even whether Group B has improved. As a result, Group B rejects the expectation of an expectation of goal-directed learning.

Simultaneously, Group B did not define any explicit learning goals for themselves and were therefore not able to observe themselves in the context of learning as a goal-oriented process. As such, goal-oriented learning in general is rejected. The group cannot legitimately be assessed by others, and self-assessment, by contrast, is based on a complementary, radically proceduralized concept of learning (B.2).

B.2 *Learning as a continuous and undirected process* is an expectation the group places upon itself and forms the foundation of its self-assessment. The following interview segment deals with the question of how progress can be recognized. Here, learning is viewed as a progressive, open-ended self-development which precludes failure or regression:

"#01:00:11-9# Cosima: [...] I believe there is actually no regression. It is always a progression because you then have consciously decided to go back. [...] it isn't the same point, even if perhaps you did the same thing two years ago or two months ago, it doesn't mean that you arrived at the same point, rather you can't ignore or disregard the time in between and then there is a reason why you landed BACK there [...]."

The same is not the same: even if the group observes itself whilst repeating the same practice, at the same time the group identifies a difference in the repetition, that is to say change, and all change is learning. This learning is characterized, first of all, by the fact that it is not teleological but rather proceeds openly and comprehensively. In other words, each difference is recognized as learning. Secondly, learning takes place continuously and is not threatened by stagnation or regression. This learning is a category devoid of difference: you always learn. As learning takes place constantly, it *need* not be observed, and, as no goals or criteria for learning can be set, it *cannot* be observed (Cf. B.1). This at once denies explicitly observable quality criteria and precludes the possibility of internal or external observation. This presents a discrepancy with *learning as the development of an interactional ability to improvisation*, in which we saw an effective relevance system of observable aesthetic qualities of playing (random/non-random). By contrast, learning is relegated to the unobservable with *learning as an undirected process.*

C. *With learning as the development of an ability to judge in a qualified way*, we are dealing with an expectation the group has about the audience: it is assumed that only qualified listeners with the appropriate pre-knowledge, that is to say, having listening experience and a corresponding ability to judge the performance, will

> scheidet, halt wieder zurückzugehen. [...] es ist nicht der gleiche Punkt, auch wenn man vielleicht vor zwei Jahren oder vor zwei Monaten oder so schon mal das Gleiche gemacht hat, heißt es nicht, dass man an dem gleichen Punkt ist, sondern man kann ja das Dazwischen nicht ausblenden und dann hat es halt Gründe, warum man WIEDER da gelandet ist [...].«

Dasselbe ist nie das Selbe: Auch wenn die Gruppe sich bei wiederholender Praxis beobachtet, identifiziert sie zugleich eine Differenz in der Wiederholung, das heißt Veränderung, und alle Veränderung ist Lernen. Dieses Lernen zeichnet sich erstens dadurch aus, dass es nicht teleologisch, sondern zieloffen und umfassend erfolgt, das heißt jegliche Differenz als Lernen anerkennt. Zweitens findet Lernen fortwährend statt, ist nicht durch Stagnation oder Rückentwicklung bedroht. Dieses Lernen ist eine differenzlose Kategorie: Man lernt immer. Da Lernen fortwährend erfolgt, *muss* es nicht beobachtet werden, und da keine Ziele und Kriterien des Lernens bestimmt werden, *kann* es auch nicht beobachtet werden (vergleiche B.1). Damit werden zugleich explizit beobachtbare Qualitätskriterien des improvisierenden Lernens abgewiesen und der Möglichkeit sowohl externer als auch interner Beobachtung entzogen. Mithin zeichnet sich ein Widerspruch zum *Lernen als Ausbildung einer interaktionalen Improvisationsfähigkeit* ab: Dort zeigte sich ein wirksames Relevanzsystem beobachtbarer ästhetischer Qualitäten des Spiels (beliebig/nicht-beliebig). Hier dagegen, im *Lernen als ungerichteter Prozess,* wird Lernen in die Unbeobachtbarkeit verschoben.

C. Beim *Lernen als Ausbildung qualifizierender Urteilsfähigkeit* geht es um Erwartungen der Gruppe ans Publikum: Es wird vorausgesetzt, dass nur zum Konzert erscheint, wer bereits über Hörerfahrung, damit über Urteilsfähigkeit verfügt und dadurch überhaupt erst zu einem qualifizierten Zuschauer wird. Hinsichtlich dieser Erwartung unterscheidet die Gruppe zwischen einer übergeordneten Perspektive auf das Publikum als einer Einheit und einer differenzierenden Perspektive auf eine erwartete »Individualität« einzelner Hörer.

C.1 *Lernen als Ausbildung kollektiver Urteilsfähigkeit* ist die Erwartung eines allen Publikumsanteilen gemeinsamen kollektiven Erfahrungswissens. Das heißt: vom Publikum wird erwartet, dass es vorab bereits urteilen gelernt hat und mit entsprechender Hörerfahrung zum Konzert kommt. Dieses Wissen basiert darauf, dass die Zuschauer »mindestens schon ein zwei Mal in (unverständlich), in ihrem Leben damit konfrontiert« (#00:57:48-1# Kerstin) waren. Sie »wissen ja, worauf sie sich einlassen« (#00:56:49-9# Thomas), nämlich auf »Geräuschkulisse im Orchester [...] und alles, was dazugehört. [...] Klangfarben ja und von daher denkt ich nicht, dass wir ausgebuht werden [...] in irgendeiner Form« (#00:57:57-1# Kerstin). Es

attend the concert. In terms of this expectation, the group draws a distinction between an overriding perspective of the audience as a whole, and a differentiating perspective with regard to the expected "individuality" of single listeners.

C.1 *Learning as a method to train the collective ability to judge* is the expectation of a collective experience based knowledge of the entire audience. That means: it is expected that the audience has already learned how to judge and comes to the concert already possessing the appropriate listening experience. This knowledge is based on the fact that the audience members have "been confronted with this situation at least once or twice in their life" (#00:57:48-1# Kerstin). They "know what they are getting into" (#00:56:49-9# Thomas), namely the "ambient sound and noises from the orchestra [...] and everything else. [...] Tone colors, yeah, and that's why I don't think we'll get booed [...] in any way" (#00:57:57-1# Kerstin). The audience are "people [...], that have some relationship to that" (#00:58:25-5# Kerstin). The indication of specific musical material (sounds, tone colors) shows that a knowledge pertaining to the genre is expected. The satisfaction of genre-specific expectations of expectations is a necessary condition for the possibility of aesthetic success because the audience expects collective sound improvisation and then "are not disappointed because they were hoping for a piano sonata and then here is (laughs) something completely different" (#00:56:49-9# Thomas).

C.2 *Learning as developing individual listening habits*: while the former views the audience as a whole, the individual or personal impression of the music played by the group during the concert becomes a "question of type" and a specification of an individual's aesthetic ability to judge.

"#00:56:11-2# Georg: yeah, so if, regarding good or bad, if you start from listening habits and someone, for example, really likes to always listen to loud stuff and comes to the concert and we play something totally quiet, then it could be that they find it crappy just because it was quiet and they like it loud and if we then play a loud concert then they might think, oh cool. [...] That, what each person (unintelligible) thinks is good, that's why I find it hard to say right now because we don't know, for example, if it will be loud or soft."

Stylistic differences between reductionist sound improvisation, noise and free jazz emerge during group rehearsals and provide a background against which dynamics become a differentiating criterion of improvisational style. What an individual listener expects cannot be predicted from this background and whether something is judged as being successful or unsuccessful depends on the individual's listening habits. This opens up the possibility of surprise by disappointing a listener's expectations. In terms of judgment, it follows that with

»sind Leute [...], die da'n Bezug zu haben« (#00:58:25-5# Kerstin). Dabei lässt der Hinweis auf musikalisches Material (Geräusch, Klangfarbe) vermuten, dass hier ein genrespezifisches Wissen erwartet wird. Mithin ist die Erfüllung genrebezogener Erwartungserwartungen eine Bedingung der Möglichkeit ästhetischen Gelingens, weil die Zuhörer eine kollektive Geräuschimprovisation erwarten und »dann eben nicht enttäuscht [sind], weil sie jetzt vielleicht die Klaviersonate erhoffen und dann ist aber hier (lachen) was ganz anderes« (#00:56:49-9# Thomas).

C.2 *Lernen als Ausbildung individueller Hörgewohnheiten*: Während die vorangegangene Perspektive auf das Publikum als Einheit abzielt, wird die individuelle, personale Sicht auf die von der Gruppe gespielte Musik im Konzert zur »Typenfrage« (#00:55:36-6# Cosima) und zur Spezifizierung individuell-ästhetischer Urteilsfähigkeit.

> »#00:56:11-2# Georg: Ja, also wenn, also wegen gut oder schlecht, wenn man jetzt von den Klanggewohnheiten ausgeht und ein Mensch zum Beispiel total gerne immer ganz Lautes hört und der kommt in das Konzert und wir spielen was total Leises, da kann das sein, dass er das total Scheiße findet, weil das war einfach leise, er will es aber laut und wenn wir dann aber auf einmal 'n lautes Konzert spielen, dann denkt dieser Mensch, oah geil. [...] Das, was jeder als eine (unverständlich) schön findet, so und deswegen find ich es so schwer, das jetzt zu sagen, weil wir wissen nicht, ob es laut oder leise wird zum Beispiel.«

Vor dem Hintergrund der in der Probenpraxis der Gruppen auftretenden stilistischen Differenzen von reduktionistischer Geräuschimprovisation, Noise und Free-Jazz wird Dynamik zu einem Unterscheidungskriterium improvisatorischer Stile. Was einzelne Zuschauer erwarten, kann vor diesem Hintergrund nicht vorhergesagt werden, und was als gelungen oder misslungen eingeschätzt wird, hängt von individuellen Hörgewohnheiten und -erwartungen ab. Hierdurch eröffnet sich die Möglichkeit des Überraschtwerdens als Enttäuschung von Erwartungen für Hörer. Für die Urteilsbildung folgt daraus, dass das Konzert im Hinblick auf Erwartungserwartungen an einzelne Hörer nicht als gelungen oder misslungen, sondern jeweils nur als erwartungsgemäß/-ungemäß beziehungsweise gewohnt/ungewohnt beurteilt werden kann.

In der gesamten Konstruktion dieses Lernkonzepts wiederholt sich die bereits zuvor identifizierte Abweisung von (expliziten) Werturteilen: Das Publikum als Ganzes kann als erfahrenes Publikum im Hinblick auf das Genre nicht enttäuscht werden. Differenzen innerhalb des Publikums werden mit Hörertypen erklärt. Auf diese Weise wird ein am erklingenden musikalischen Ergebnis festzumachendes Werturteil suspendiert. An die Stelle eines begründeten Werturteils zum Beispiel angesichts einer musikalischen Struk-

regard to expectations of expectations of the individual listener, the concert cannot be viewed as successful or unsuccessful, but rather only as meeting or disappointing expectations or as being familiar or unfamiliar.

Throughout the entire construction of this learning concept, the previously identified rejection of (explicit) value judgments is repeated: the audience as a whole cannot be disappointed with regard to genre. Differences within the audience are explained by listener types. In this way, any value judgment that can be placed on the results of the musical performance is suspended. In place of a valid judgment, for example one that is based on musical structure (see learning category A), a psychologizing reflection based on personal preferences is used to arrive at a judgment.

D. *Learning as transference in pedagogical contexts* is an expected expectation of the instructors. The group expects that both music education lecturers and instrumental instructors do not view improvisation as an independent artistic practice, but rather as a preparatory method for music-making in school (D.1), or as a method for expanding general musical abilities (D.2). In this expectation, the group's practice is not the aim in itself but simply provisional practice in preparation for another practice. The pedagogical purposes reveal themselves through the following systemic question, which was used in the interview: "What will the music education lecturers and instrumental instructors who are in attendance say about your music?"

D.1 *Learning as transference of improvisational expertise to the teaching of improvisation*

In relation to the expectation of expectations to the music education lecturers, the essential thing "from the aspect of pedagogy" (#00:54:28-6# Cosima) is the transferability of this music to a didactic setting because "you can do such work with kids, too, and get them excited about it and then perhaps somehow with themes" (#00:54:28-6# Cosima). This learning category includes the didactic transfer expectation that learning improvisation also fosters pedagogical competence.

A typical characteristic of improvisation is that "you don't need any special skills, so no playing techniques, you don't have to be able to play the piano or any instrument. You just have to be open to it" (#00:54:28-6# Cosima). This "being open to it" describes a kind of motivational learning requirement for a practice otherwise free of prerequisites. This gives the individual an improvisation method which they can use with groups of children. Learning in this case is a process of transformation of the practice, of the change of context from an artistic one to an educational one, from learning music in the role of student to teaching music in the role of educator.

tur (vergleiche Lernkategorie A) tritt eine psychologisierende Rückführung des Urteils auf persönliche Präferenzen.

D. *Lernen als Übertragung in pädagogische Verwendungskontexte* ist eine erwartete Erwartung an das Lehrpersonal. Die Gruppe erwartet, dass sowohl Musikdidaktiker als auch Instrumentalpädagogen das Improvisieren nicht als eigenständige künstlerische Praxis wahrnehmen, sondern als vorbereitende Methode für schulisches Musizieren (D.1) beziehungsweise als Methode der Erweiterung allgemeiner musikalischer Fähigkeiten (D.2). Die Praxis der Gruppe ist in dieser Erwartung nicht eigentliche, sondern bloß vorläufige Praxis in Vorbereitung einer anderen Praxis. Die pädagogischen Verwendungsinteressen erschließen sich über die im Interview gestellte rekursive Frage: »Was werden die anwesenden Musikdidaktiker und Instrumentalpädagogen über eure Musik sagen?«

D.1 *Lernen als Übertragung improvisatorischer Expertise in schulisches Improvisieren*

In Bezug auf Erwartungserwartungen an die Musikdidaktiker liegt das Wesentliche unter dem pädagogischen Aspekt gesehen« (#00:54:28-6# Cosima) in der Transferierbarkeit dieser Musik auf ein didaktisches Setting, weil »man so ne Arbeit auch mit Kindern machen kann und sie dafür ( ) begeistern kann und dann halt vielleicht irgendwie unter Themen« (#00:54:28-6# Cosima). Mit diesem Lernen verbindet sich die didaktische Transfererwartung, dass mit dem Lernen des Improvisierens zusätzlich Vermittlungsfähigkeiten erlernt werden.

Kennzeichnend für das Improvisieren ist, dass »man dafür keine () Fertigkeiten [braucht], also keine spieltechnischen, man muss nicht Klavier spielen können oder was auch immer, welches Instrument man nimmt. Man muss sich nur darauf einlassen« (#00:54:28-6# Cosima). Das »Sich-Einlassen« beschreibt hier eine Art motivationaler Lernanforderungen für die Begegnung mit einer ansonsten voraussetzungslosen Praxis. Dem einzelnen wird es somit möglich, über eine Methode zum Improvisieren mit Kindergruppen zu verfügen. Lernen ist hier ein Prozess der Transformation der Praxis, des Wechsels des Kontextes, von einem künstlerischen in einen didaktischen, vom Musiklernen in der Studierenden-Rolle hin zum Musiklehren in der Vermittlungsrolle.

D.2 Lernen als Übertragung improvisatorischer Expertise in andere künstlerische Praxen

Von den Instrumentalpädagogen erwartet die Gruppe, dass diese einen Lernerfolg auf handwerklich instrumentalpraktischer Ebene erwarten, »weil wir [...] neue Spieltechniken oder unkonventionelle Spieltechniken verwen-

D.2 *Learning as the transference of improvisational expertise to other artistic endeavors*

The group anticipates that the instrumental instructors will expect learning progress to occur on the practical level, that is to say, the ability to play the instrument because "we use [...] new or unconventional playing techniques" (#00:53:54-8# Georg). Above and beyond this, growth at the level of artistry is apparent in the sense of free-form creation "because we have absolutely no notated material" (#00:53:54-8# Georg). The lack of written music becomes a criterion for differentiation between interpreting existing works and improvising. The group expects less aesthetic appreciation and more interest in the pedagogical use or value from the instrumental instructors. It is assumed that they are interested in improvisation as a technique for extending general musical competence and not as an artistic practice. An expectation of an instrumental pedagogical *transference* is connected to the learning: improvisation is a means of self-development with regard to musical practice in general, and it is in this area where it really comes into its own. It is expected that interpretational skills will take precedence over improvisational ones. Simultaneously, a reduction in the value of improvisation as an independent artistic practice is expected:

"#00:51:29-7# Interviewer: Ah, yeah, ok. Let's pretend [Name of a staff member] is sitting here with us. What would he say about your, your music?
#00:51:36-0# Cosima: He would say 'Hmm, that modern stuff' (laughs)."

E. *Learning as a means of distinction* allows the group as a whole to distinguish itself both from groups A and C, as well as from the teaching staff. We have already seen such a strategy of differentiation in which assessment by the other groups was rejected (B.1). This rejection took the form of reducing the value of goal-oriented learning. A further distinction is revealed in the difference between the expectations that the group has of itself (A) and the expectations of expectations to the instructors (D), put in another way; a distinction between artistic practice and pedagogical use.

In addition to this, the unconventionality and innovation of the group's practice leads to an almost defiant self-positioning of the group within the institutional situational. What also distinguishes this group, as well as any other group in the setting, from the institutionalized conventional music practice and fixed expectations is that improvisation is "for many perhaps new, at least here in this building" (#00:54:20-0# Georg). As such, it is also expected that only a few representatives of the institute will attend the concert. Free improvisation becomes an institutionally sanctioned counter-model to institutional practice.

den« (#00:53:54-8# Georg). Darüber hinaus zeige sich ebenso ein Zuwachs auf künstlerischer Ebene im Sinne freien Gestaltens, »weil wir überhaupt gar keinen Notentext haben« (#00:53:54-8# Georg). Dabei wird die Schriftlosigkeit zum Differenzierungskriterium werkinterpretierender und improvisierender Praxis. Auch von den Instrumentalpädagogen wird weniger ästhetische Wertschätzung als vielmehr pädagogisches Verwendungsinteresse erwartet. Vorausgesetzt wird, dass sie sich für Improvisation als Methode der Erweiterung allgemeiner musikalischer Kompetenzen interessieren, nicht für die künstlerische Praxis in ihrer Besonderheit. Mit dem *Lernen* verbindet sich eine *instrumentalpädagogische Transfererwartung*: Improvisieren ist Mittel der Selbstprofessionalisierung im Hinblick auf musikalische Praxis überhaupt und erfüllt vor allem darin ihren Zweck. Erwartet wird mithin ein Vorrang interpretierender vor improvisierender Praxis. Zugleich wird die Abwertung der Improvisation als einer selbständigen Kunstpraxis erwartet:

»#00:51:29-7# Interviewer: Ah ja okay. Na nehmen wir mal an, der der [Name einer Lehrperson] sitzt hier drinne. Was wird der über eure, eure Musik sagen?
#00:51:36-0# Cosima: Ach neumodisches Zeug wird er sagen (lacht).«

E. *Lernen als Distinktionsmittel* ermöglicht es der Gruppe, sich insgesamt sowohl von den Gruppen A und C wie auch vom Lehrpersonal des Instituts abzugrenzen. Einer Strategie der Abgrenzung begegneten wir bereits in der Abweisung zielgerichteten Lernens, mit der die Bewertung durch andere Gruppen delegitimiert wurde (B.1). Eine weitere Distinktion zeigte sich in der Unterscheidung zwischen der Erwartung an sich selbst (A) und der ans Lehrpersonal gerichteten Erwartungswartung (D) als einer Unterscheidung von künstlerischer Praxis und pädagogischer Verwendung.

Darüber hinaus begründet die Unkonventionalität und Innovativität der eigenen Praxis eine widerständige Selbstpositionierung der Gruppen in der institutionellen Situation. Das, was diese Gruppe, ferner alle Gruppen von der konventionellen, erwartungssicheren Musikpraxis des Instituts unterscheidet, ist, dass Improvisation »für viele vielleicht auch neu ist so oder grad in dem Haus hier« (#00:54:20-0# Georg). Daher ist ja auch zu erwarten, dass überaus wenig Institutsangehörige zum Konzert erscheinen. Freies Improvisieren wird damit zum institutionell ermöglichten Gegenmodell institutioneller Praxis.

Die Situation improvisierenden Lernens

In unserem Auswertungsbeispiel ging es uns darum, zu zeigen, wie sich über Techniken zirkulären Fragens Erwartungen und Erwartungserwartungen der

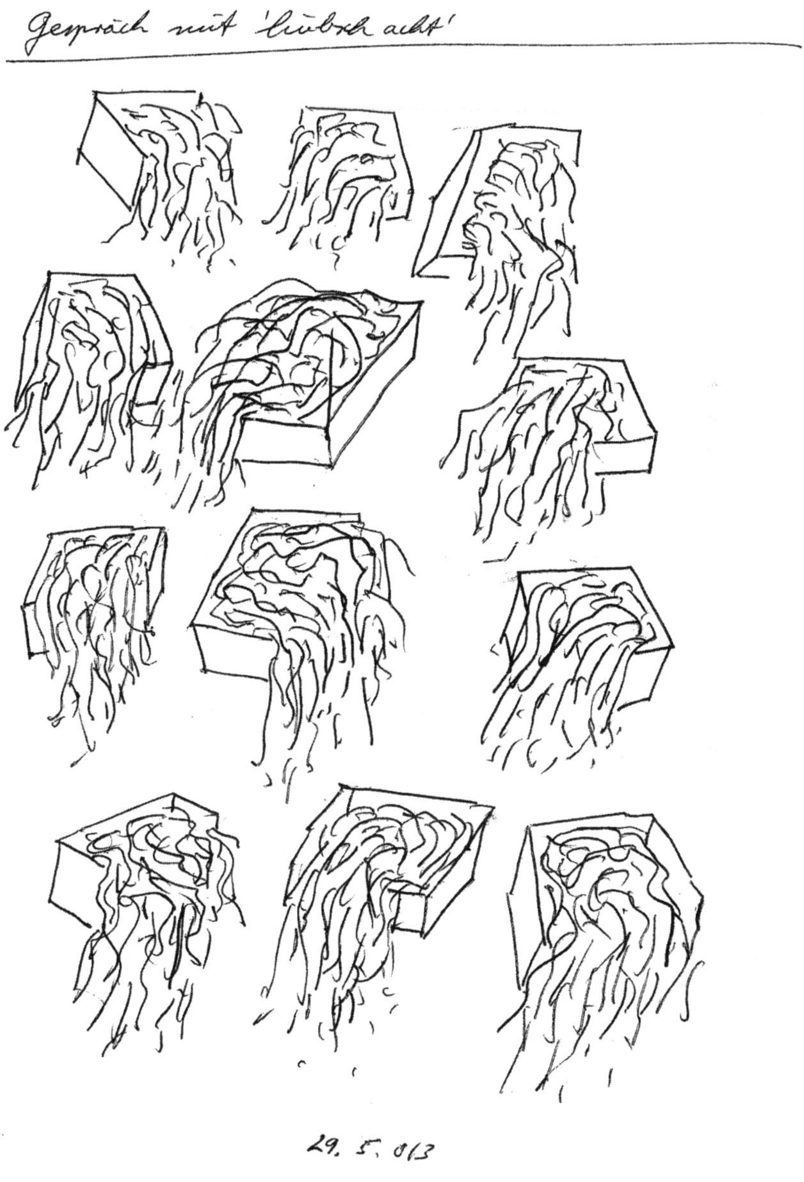
Gespräch mit 'hübsch acht'
29. 5. 013

Praxis ermitteln lassen. Auf diese Weise erhielten wir einen Zugang zu impliziten Wirklichkeitskonstruktionen des Forschungsfeldes. Dabei führt die Frage nach solchen Konstruktionen zu spezifischen Sinn- und Bedeutungszuschreibungen, das heißt zu möglichen Antworten darauf, was die eigene Praxis bedeutet, welchen Sinn das eigene Tun hat. Indessen ist die Praxis von Bedeutungskonstruktionen nicht ablösbar, sondern wird als *diese* bedeutsame Praxis überhaupt erst im kommunizierten Sinn erkennbar. Vor diesem Hintergrund verstehen wir die zuvor benannten Kategorien improvisierenden Lernens als konstitutive Bedeutungsstrukturen der Praxis.

Die am Datenmaterial entwickelten Lernkategorien geben einen ersten Aufschluss über die spezifische Lernsituation der interviewten Forschungsteilnehmer als *Situation des improvisierenden Lernens im hochschulischen Kontext.* Im Fall der Gruppe B wird das Lernen von einer professionellen Musikerin angeleitet, ist zeitlich, räumlich, methodisch vorstrukturiert, zugleich eingebettet in ein komplexes Geflecht widerstreitender institutionalisierter Erwartungsstrukturen und Praxiskonzepte. Wir wollen nun abschließend auf der Grundlage der Kategorien improvisierenden Lernens die Spezifik dieser Situation des Lernens herausarbeiten.

Im Verhältnis der Lernkategorien zueinander lassen sich drei Konfliktebenen identifizieren: Ein Konflikt in der Umwelt der Gruppe, ein Konflikt der Gruppe mit der Umwelt und ein innerer Konflikt der Gruppe. Als **Konflikt in der Umwelt der Gruppe** zeigen sich die konkurrierenden pädagogischen Konzeptualisierungen der Praxis einerseits als voraussetzungsloses Spiel mit Schülern (Musikpädagogik) andererseits als musikalische Expertise Studierender (Instrumentalpädagogik). Dass hier unterschiedliche praxisrelevante Maßstäbe wirksam werden, ist offensichtlich. Dennoch herrscht unter den beiden Institutsabteilungen aus Sicht der Gruppe Konsens im Hinblick auf die Erwartungserwartung pädagogischer Verwendung. Denn sowohl der Transfer in ein pädagogisches Setting als auch die Erweiterung der Spielfähigkeiten konzipieren, wenn auch unterschiedlichen Maßstäben verpflichtet, Improvisieren als pädagogisch motivierte Methode. Vor diesem Hintergrund entsteht ein **Konflikt der Gruppe mit der Umwelt**. Dieser zeigt sich als Widerspruch zwischen der Erwartungserwartung pädagogischer Verwendungsinteressen und der Erwartung der Gruppe an das eigene Improvisieren als selbständige Kunstform und künstlerische Expertise. Besonders deutlich tritt dieser Konflikt zwischen Musikdidaktik und Gruppe B als Differenz unterschiedlicher Praxiskonzepte hervor: Ist gelingende Improvisation eine besonders natürliche, darum jedem zugängliche Praxis, die kein oder kaum Vorwissen verlangt? Oder handelt es sich um eine kulturspezifische artifizielle Praxis, die breite Erfahrung und entwickelte Expertise erfordert? Wird nicht der behauptete Kunstanspruch der Praxis durch die Feststellung ihrer Voraussetzungslosigkeit zugleich unterminiert? Einer ähnlich konfligierenden Struktur begegnen wir schließlich im Selbstkon-

The situation of improvisational learning

In our example analysis we attempted to show how the techniques of circular questioning can help identify expectations and expectations of expectations relevant to a specific praxis. In this way, we obtain access to implicit reality constructions within the field of research. This questioning of such constructions leads us to specific sense or meaning attributions, that is to say, to possible answers as to what the individual practice means or what meaning the activity has. The practice cannot be separated from these constructions of meaning but is rather only recognizable as *meaningful* practice when it is communicated in this way. Against this background, we can understand the previously examined categories of improvisational learning as fundamental structures of meaning of the practice.

The categories of learning developed from the data offer a preliminary explanation of the specific educational situation of the research participants who were interviewed as a *situation of learning improvisation in a university context*. In the case of Group B, the learning was led by a professional musician, it was structured in terms of time, location and method, and, at the same time, embedded in a complex web of antagonistic institutionalized expectation structures and practice concepts. In conclusion, on the basis of the categories of improvisational learning we would like to reconstruct the specifics of this educational situation.

By relating the categories of learning to one another, we can identify three levels of conflict: a conflict within the group's environment, a conflict between the group and its environment and a conflict within the group itself. A **conflict within the group's environment** reveals itself as the competing pedagogical conceptualizations of the practice: on one side, school pupils playing without any prerequisites (music pedagogy) and, on the other, the expertise of music students (instrumental tuition). It is obvious that different practice-relevant standards are in effect here. Nevertheless, from the perspective of the group, both institutional departments are in agreement regarding the expectation of expectation of pedagogical purpose. Both the transference into a pedagogical setting and the extension of playing abilities conceptualize improvisation as a pedagogically motivated method, even if they are subject to different standards. This serves as a background to **the conflict between the group and its environment**. This reveals itself as the dichotomy between the expectation of expectation of pedagogical purpose and the expectation of the group regarding its own improvisation as an independent art form requiring artistic expertise. This conflict is especially apparent when considering the difference in practice concepts between Group B and the music education lecturers: is successful improvisation a natural practice open to anyone with little or no previous knowledge? Or is it a culture-specific, artificial practice that requires broad experience and the development of expertise? Would the postulated artistic demands

zept der Gruppe als **Konflikt der Gruppe mit sich selbst**. Denn einerseits artikulierte die Gruppe im Interview die Wirksamkeit ästhetischer Kriterien des Gelingens, andererseits entzog sie das künstlerische Lernen der Beobachtung und verwies die Herkunft des Urteilens an persönliche Präferenzen und Hörgewohnheiten. Dabei entsteht die paradoxale Konstruktion einer unbeobachtbaren Qualität. Die Immunisierung der Gruppe gegenüber Wertungen, vor allem gegenüber erkennbarem Lernfortschritt, scheint mithin das musikdidaktische Verwendungsinteresse eines voraussetzungslosen Musizierens zu begünstigen. Auch der von den Instrumentalpädagogen erwartete Zweifel am Status des Improvisierens als einer selbständigen Kunstpraxis wird durch die Abweisung beobachtbarer Qualität begünstigt. Wenn man den künstlerischen Anspruch der Praxis nicht beobachten kann, fällt dieser leicht der Nivellierung anheim.

Anhand des nur beispielhaft präsentierten Interviewmaterials lässt sich ein systematischer Zusammenhang dieser Konfliktebenen nicht abschließend klären. Allerdings stellen sich weiterführende Fragen. Zum Beispiel sollte eine tiefergehende Auswertung des Datenmaterials zeigen, ob die Gruppe ihren Konflikt mit der Umwelt in der Form eines Konflikts mit sich selbst reproduziert, das heißt die als widersprüchlich erlebten Erwartungen als Selbstwiderspruch internalisiert. Die Beantwortung dieser Frage ist insofern zentral, als dadurch deutlich würde, wie sich hier die spezifische Situation des institutionalisierten künstlerischen Lernens in die künstlerische Praxis einschreibt und damit divergierende Konzepte des Improvisierens zu einem widersprüchlichem Konzept vereint.

Darüber hinaus stellt sich aus übergeordneter Perspektive die Frage, ob und in welcher Weise in dieser hochschulischen Improvisationspraxis insgesamt Widersprüche pädagogischer und ästhetischer Improvisationsdiskurse reproduziert werden. So scheint es, dass mitunter auch in der improvisationspädagogischen Literatur sehr unterschiedliche Praxiskonzepte des Improvisierens zu einem einheitlichen Improvisationsverständnis zusammengefasst werden, ohne dass die Differenz dieser Praxen hinreichend deutlich würde, etwa wenn Improvisation zugleich als »ein qualitätsvolles [...] Musizieren« bezeichnet wird, welches »das Produzieren eines ganz eigenständigen, originellen Musikergebnisses« (Gagel 2010: 185) ermögliche, und damit davon ausgegangen wird, diese Praxis biete einen »niederschwellige[n], nicht durch bestimmtes Vorwissen beschränkte[n] Zugang zu einem improvisierten Musikmachen« (Ebd.).

Improvisation erforschen: Die Differenz der Praxen und die Situation des Improvisierens

Für die Beantwortung der Frage, wie Improvisierende Improvisieren lernen, ist die Berücksichtigung der Situation des Lernens und damit der Situiertheit

of the practice not be undermined by the contention that expertise is not required? A similarly conflicting structure can also be found in the self-image of the group as a **conflict within the group itself**. On the one hand, during the interviews, the group articulated the efficacy of aesthetic criteria. On the other hand, the group rejected the observation of artistic learning and attributed the source of judgment to personal preferences or listening habits. This creates the paradoxical construction of an unobservable quality. The immunization of the group against assessment, in particular against observable progress, seems to favor the didactic use of a type of music-making free from prerequisites. The expected doubt of the instrumental instructors regarding improvisation as an independent artistic practice also appears to be supported by the denial of an observable quality. If one cannot observe the artistic demands of the practice, they can easily run the risk of the artistic claim falling flat.

On the basis of the interview material presented here as an example, it is not possible to fully explain a systematic connection between these levels of conflict. We are led, however, to further questions. For example, could a deeper analysis of the data show whether or not the group reproduces their conflict with their environment in the form of a conflict with itself, that is to say, if the conflicting environmental expectations are internalized into a self-conflict? The answer to this question is central in as far as it shows how this specific situation of institutionalized artistic learning is being incorporated into the artistic practice and how divergent concepts of improvisation merge into one conflicting concept.

In addition, viewed from a higher perspective, the question arises whether or not and in what way the observed improvisation practice at the university reproduces fundamental contradictions between pedagogical and artistic improvisation discourses. It seems as though, even in pedagogical literature about improvisation, very different practice concepts of improvisation are summarized into a unified understanding of improvisation, without the differences in these concepts becoming sufficiently apparent. This is the case when improvisation is described as "a high-quality form of [...] music making" which "produces a completely self-sufficient and original musical result" (Gagel 2010: 185) while simultaneously assuming that improvised music-making offers "low barriers to entry that do not require a certain level of pre-knowledge" (ibid.).

Researching Improvisation: The Difference of Practices and the Situation of Improvising

To answer the question how improvisers learn improvisation, it is of fundamental importance to take into account the situation in which the learning takes place and therefore the situatedness of the practice and the practical knowledge. In this sense, the observation that different concepts of improvisation practice

der Praxis und des praktischen Wissens von grundsätzlicher Bedeutung. In diesem Sinne ist die Beobachtung, dass in unserem aktuellen Forschungsfeld unterschiedliche Konzepte von Improvisationspraxis wirksam sind und miteinander in Konflikt treten, für den weiteren Forschungsverlauf leitend. Denn die im Feld auftretende widersprüchliche Bestimmung der Praxis ist selbst eine Praxis des Feldes, nämlich Praxis des von uns untersuchten Hochschulsettings. Improvisieren Lernen ist demzufolge zumindest für eine Gruppe unserer Forschungsteilnehmer Lernen der Praxis unter den Bedingungen ihrer widersprüchlichen Bestimmung. Nur aufgrund der Berücksichtigung dieser situativen Bedingungen kann jeweils das, was im Forschungsfeld gelernt und gekonnt wird und schließlich als gelingende Praxis gilt, herausgearbeitet werden. In den Fokus gerät damit die Frage, wer oder was die Praxis eigentlich vermittelt. Dabei gehen wir davon aus, dass weniger einzelne Personen als vielmehr die *Situation und konkrete Vollzugswirklichkeit der Praxis* als Vermittlerin der Praxis begriffen werden muss.

Die Beobachtung der im Forschungsfeld wirksamen Konzeptualisierungen von Improvisation verpflichtet indessen zur Anerkennung grundlegender Differenzen von Improvisationspraxen. Es gibt nicht eine Praxis des Improvisierens und im Anschluss daran eine Vermittlung und Ausübung dieser Praxis in unterschiedlichen künstlerischen, sozialen Situationen, in verschiedenen ästhetischen, musikdidaktischen, instrumentalpädagogischen oder auch sozialpädagogischen, therapeutischen Vollzugswirklichkeiten. Praxen beziehungsweise deren Relevanzsysteme lassen sich von Situation und Vollzugswirklichkeit nicht trennen. Damit verbinden wir im vorliegenden Fall die Anerkennung des von uns untersuchten hochschulischen Improvisierens als eine Praxis sui generis. Improvisieren im Hochschulkontext ist nicht vorläufige, uneigentliche Praxis, sie folgt nicht dem Modell oder Muster eines anderen eigentlichen Improvisierens in anderen Situationen und Wirklichkeiten. Vielmehr muss sie in ihrer institutionellen Strukturiertheit und (möglicherweise widersprüchlichen) Eigendynamik ebenso als eigenständige Praxis verstanden werden wie jede andere Praxis auch.

In diesem Sinn ist es Aufgabe der Forschung zu untersuchen, wie Improvisation sich selbst jeweils als Improvisation definiert. Gleiches gilt für den Status des Lernens und Wissens der Praxis. Was als gelernte, gekonnte und damit gelungene Improvisation verstanden wird, unterliegt dem Relevanzsystem der jeweiligen Praxis und keinem übergeordneten, privilegierten Standpunkt der Beobachtung. Es geht nicht darum, im Wissenschaftsdiskurs auszuhandeln, was Improvisation ist und wie sie funktioniert, es geht darum, zu beobachten, wie in den Wirklichkeiten unterschiedlicher Improvisationspraxen die Auffassung dessen, was jeweils als Improvisation zu gelten hat, selbstreferentiell bestimmt wird.

are active in our current field of research and in conflict with one another is central to further research. The conflicting concepts of improvisational practice that arise in the field are themselves a practice within that field, namely how practice is conducted in the university setting that we studied. Learning to improvise is therefore, at least for one group of our study participants, learning the practice under conditions of conflicting conceptualizations. It is only when taking these situative conditions into account that we can identify what has been learned, mastered and ultimately viewed as successful practice within the area of research. This brings into focus the question of who or what the practice actually conveys. Here, we assume that it is less the certain individuals and more the *situation and the concrete environment of the practice* that need to be understood as the conveyor of the practice.

The observation of the effective conceptualizations of improvisation at work in the field requires the acknowledgement of fundamental differences in improvisational practice. There is not just one practice of improvisation which one can then execute in various artistic, social situations, or apply to different aesthetic, musically educational, instrumentally pedagogical or even socially pedagogical or therapeutic contexts. Practices and their relevance systems cannot be separated from their situation or application. With this in mind, we acknowledge the fact that improvisation in the educational context of a university is a practice sui generis. Improvisation in the university context is not a preliminary, inauthentic practice; it does not follow the model or example of another authentic improvisation in other situations or realities. It is much more important to understand it, as is the case with any other practice, as a self-contained practice within its institutional structure and its own (possibly conflicting) dynamic.

In this sense, it is the task of research to investigate how improvisation defines itself in each individual case. This applies also to the status of learning and knowledge of the practice. What is understood as learned, mastered and ultimately successful improvisation is defined by a system of relevance unique to the practice and not by a higher-level, privileged point of view. It is not about negotiating what improvisation is and how it works through scientific discourse, but rather to observe how, in the context of different improvisational practices, the definition of what counts as improvisation is determined self-referentially.

Translation into English: Tom Lynn, Berlin; Louise & Phil Loxton, GB-Wales

Bibliographie/Bibliography

Baecker, Dirk (2005): Form und Formen der Kommunikation, Frankfurt/Main: Suhrkamp.

Breuer, Franz (2010): Reflexive Grounded Theory. Eine Einführung in die Forschungspraxis, 2. Auflage, Wiesbaden-Heidelberg: VS Springer.

Bryant, Anthony; Charmaz, Kathy (Hg./Eds.) (2010): The SAGE Handbook of Grounded Theory, 2. Auflage, Los Angeles-London-New Delhi-Singapore-Washington DC-Boston: Sage Publications Ltd.

Burkart, Thomas (2010): »Qualitatives Experiment«, in: Mey, Günter; Mruck, Katja (Hg./Eds.): Handbuch Qualitative Forschung in der Psychologie, Wiesbaden-Heidelberg: VS Springer, 252-262.

Büssing, André; Herbig, Britta; Ewert, Thomas (2002): »Implizites Wissen und erfahrungsgeleitetes Arbeitshandeln«, in: Zeitschrift für Arbeits- und Organisationspsychologie 46 (1), Göttingen: Hogrefe, 2-21.

Charmaz, Kathy (2006): Constructing Grounded Theory. A Practical Guide Through Qualtitative Analysis, Los Angeles-London-New Delhi-Singapore-Washington DC-Boston: Sage Publications Ltd.

Clarke, Adele (2012): Situationsanalyse. Grounded Theory. Nach dem Postmodern Turn, Wiesbaden-Heidelberg: VS Springer.

Collins, Harry (2010): Tacit and Explicit Knowledge, Chicago, London: The University of Chicago Press.

Dempsey, Nicholas P. (2010): »Stimulated Recall Interviews in Ethnography«, in: Qual Sociol 33, Wiesbaden-Heidelberg: VS Springer, 349-367.

DiPardo, Anne (1994): »Stimulated Recall in Research on Writing: An Antidote to ›I don't know. It was fine‹«, in: Peter Smagorinsky (Hrsg./Ed.), Speaking About Writing. Reflections on Research Methodology, London und New Dehli: Sage Publications Ltd., 163-184.

Dreyfus, Stuart E. (2004): »The Five-Stage Model of Adult Skill Acquisition«, in: Bulletin of Science Technology & Society 24 (3), Sage Publications Ltd., 177-181.

Folkestad, Göran (2006): »Formal and Informal Learning Situations or Practices vs Formal and Informal Ways of Learning«, in: British Journal of Music Education 23 (2), Cambridge: Cambridge University Press, 135-145.

Gagel, Reinhard (2010): Improvisation als soziale Kunst. Überlegungen zum künstlerischen und didaktischen Umgang mit improvisatorischer Kreativität, Mainz: Schott Music Gmbh & Co. KG.

Garfinkel, Harold (1967): »Studies of the routine grounds of everyday activities«, in: Harold Garfinkel, Studies in Ethnomethodology, Upper Saddle River, New Jersey: Prentice-Hall Inc., 35-75.

Garnett, James (2014): »Has Music Happened? The ›Creative Musician‹ and the Paradox of Experiencing Music and Learning as Creative Acts«, in: Bur-

nard, Pamela (Hrsg./Ed.): Developing Creativities in Higher Music Education. International Perspectives and Practices, London, New York: Routledge, 11-22.

Gass, Susan M.; Mackey, Alison (2000): Stimulated Recall Methodology in Second Language Research. Mahwah, New Jersey, London: Lawrence Erlbaum.

Gerstenmaier, Jochen; Mandl, Heinz (2001): »Methodologie und Empirie zum situierten Lernen«, in: Schweizerische Zeitschrift für Bildungswissenschaften 23 (3), Aarau/Freiburg (CH): Schweizerische Gesellschaft für Bildungswissenschaft, 453-470.

Gibson, Barry; Hartman, Jan (2014): Rediscovering Grounded Theory, London: Sage Publications Ltd.

Glaser, Barney; Strauss, Anselm (2010): Grounded Theory. Strategien qualitativer Forschung, 3. Auflage, Bern: Huber.

Godau, Marc (2015): »Der Kontext ist die Methode. Gruppenprozesse und informelle Lernmethoden beim Musizieren von Popmusik im Unterricht«, in: Michael Ahlers (Hrsg./Ed.), Popmusik-Vermittlung. Zwischen Schule, Universität und Beruf. Theorie und Praxis der Musikvermittlung Band 14. Berlin: Lit Verlag Dr. Hopf, 203-220.

Green, Lucy (2002): How Popular Musicians Learn. A Way Ahead for Music Education. Aldershot: Ashgate.

Haenisch, Matthias (2011): »Emergenz. Zu einem theoretischen Begriff aktueller Improvisationsforschung«, in: Burkhard Beins; Christian Kesten; Gisela Nauck; Andrea Neumann (Hg./Eds.), Echtzeitmusik. Selbstbestimmung einer Szene. Hofheim: Wolke, 186-201.

Haenisch, Matthias (2014): Improvisation als System. Zur Interaktionsanalyse improvisierter Musik. Arbeitstagung der Fachgruppe Soziologie und Sozialgeschichte der Musik in der Gesellschaft für Musikforschung (GfM) an der Universität für Musik und darstellende Kunst Wien/Institut für Musiksoziologie, 23.-25. Mai 2014.

Hillebrandt, Frank (2014): Soziologische Praxistheorien, Wiesbaden-Heidelberg: VS Springer..

John, René; Henkel, Anna; Rückert-John, Jana (Hg./Eds.) (2010): Die Methodologien des Systems. Wie kommt man zum Fall und wie dahinter? Wiesbaden-Heidelberg: VS Springer.

Kleining, Gerhard (1986): »Das qualitative Experiment«, in: Kölner Zeitschrift für Soziologie und Sozialpsychologie 38, 4, VS Springer, 724-750.

Kleining, Gerhard »Das qualitative Experiment« *http://nbn-resolving.de/urn:nbn:de:0168-ssoar-8631* (30.05.2015).

Kruse, Jan (2014): Qualitative Interviewforschung. Ein integrativer Ansatz. Weinheim: Beltz Juventa.

Künkler, Tobias (2011): Lernen in Beziehung. Zum Verhältnis von Subjektivität und Relationalität in Lernprozessen. Bielefeld: transcript.

Luhmann, Niklas (1987): Soziale Systeme. Frankfurt/Main: Suhrkamp.

Moser, Sibylle (Hrsg./Ed.) (2011): Konstruktivistisch Forschen. Methodologie, Methoden, Beispiele, 2. Auflage, Wiesbaden: Deutscher Universitätsverlag.

Ochs, Matthias; Schweitzer, Jochen (Hg./Eds.) (2012): Handbuch Forschung für Systemiker, Göttingen: Vandenhoeck & Ruprecht.

Pfeffer, Thomas (2004): Das »zirkuläre Fragen« als Forschungsmethode zur Luhmannschen Systemtheorie, Heidelberg: Carl-Auer-Systeme Verlag.

Polanyi, Michael (1985): Implizites Wissen, Frankfurt/Main: Suhrkamp.

Röbke, Peter; Ardila-Mantilla, Natalia (Hg./Eds.) (2009): Vom wilden Lernen: Musizieren lernen – auch außerhalb von Schule und Unterricht, Mainz: Schott Music Gmbh & Co. KG.

Simon, Fritz B.; Rech-Simon, Christel (2013): Zirkuläres Fragen. Systemische Therapie in Fallbeispielen. Ein Lernbuch. 10. Auflage, Heidelberg: Carl-Auer-Systeme Verlag.

Spychiger, Maria (2002): »Lehrforschung, Lernforschung. Ein Blick in ihre Grundlagen und Anwendungen im Wechsel der psychologischen Paradigmen«, in: Diskussion Musikpädagogik, 2, Hamburg: Hildegard-Junker-Verlag, 3-26.

Schön, Donald A. (1983): The Reflective Practitioner: How Professionals Think In Action, London: Temple Smith.

Willke, Helmut (2011): Einführung in das systemische Wissensmanagement, 3., überarbeitete und erweiterte Auflage, Heidelberg: Carl-Auer-Systeme Verlag.

Wright, Ruth; Kanellopoulos, Panagiotis (2010): »Informal Music Learning, Improvisation and Teacher Education«, in: British Journal of Music Education 27(1), Cambridge: Cambridge University Press, 71-87.

Intermezzo 2

Seit 1999 habe ich einen wöchentlichen Workshop in London organisiert und natürlich auch anderswo. Ich habe von den Leuten, die an solchen Workshops teilnehmen, viel gelernt. Der Prozess, den wir uns dabei aneignen, ist lehrreich. Er ist oftmals paradox und erschreckend menschlich. Die Zwillings-Vorschläge für den Workshop bestehen darin, einerseits die Suche nach Klängen im Fokus zu haben, und andererseits aufmerksam dem zuzuhören, was man noch hören kann, besonders das, was von den anderen Musizierenden kommt, mit denen man Raum und allgemeine Grundsätze teilt. Dennoch legt die natürliche Tendenz nahe, dass das Erkunden des Materials (die Heuristik) oft auf Kosten von aufmerksamem Hören, Reagieren und Anpassen in Bezug auf die anderen geschieht – dem Dialogischen. Und umgekehrt.

Es gibt klare Hinweise darauf, dass eine Kombination aus der empathischen kognitiven Fähigkeit (also sozialer Intelligenz) und den technischen Mitteln, mit denen Klang erschaffen wird, die Entwicklung von Musik (vielleicht jeglicher Musik!) ermöglicht. Indem diese beiden Teile kombiniert werden, entsteht das »Best of« improvisierter Musik.

Edwin Prévost im Podiumsgespräch, Mai 2014

Übersetzung aus dem Englischen: Solveig Raschpichler, Berlin

Intermezzo 2

I have convened a weekly workshop in London since 1999, and other workshops elsewhere, of course. I have learned much from those who come to these workshops. The process we adopt is informative, often paradoxical and alarmingly human. The twin propositions for the workshop are for the musicians to focus on searching for sounds and to listen attentively to what else they hear, especially from the other musicians with whom they cohabit the space and with whom they share the general objectives. However, the natural tendency seems to reveal that exploring the material for sounds (the heurism) is often at the expense of attentive listening, responding and adapting to others – the dialogical. And, vice versa.

There are strong indications that a combination of the empathic cognitive facility (i.e. social intelligence) and the technical means of making sound prefigures the development of music (perhaps all music!). Putting these two things together is probably what makes the best of improvised music.

Edwin Prévost in a public talk, May 2014

EXPLORATORIUM Berlin 31.5.014

Alan Bern Present Time Composition (PTC)
Impulse und Cognition

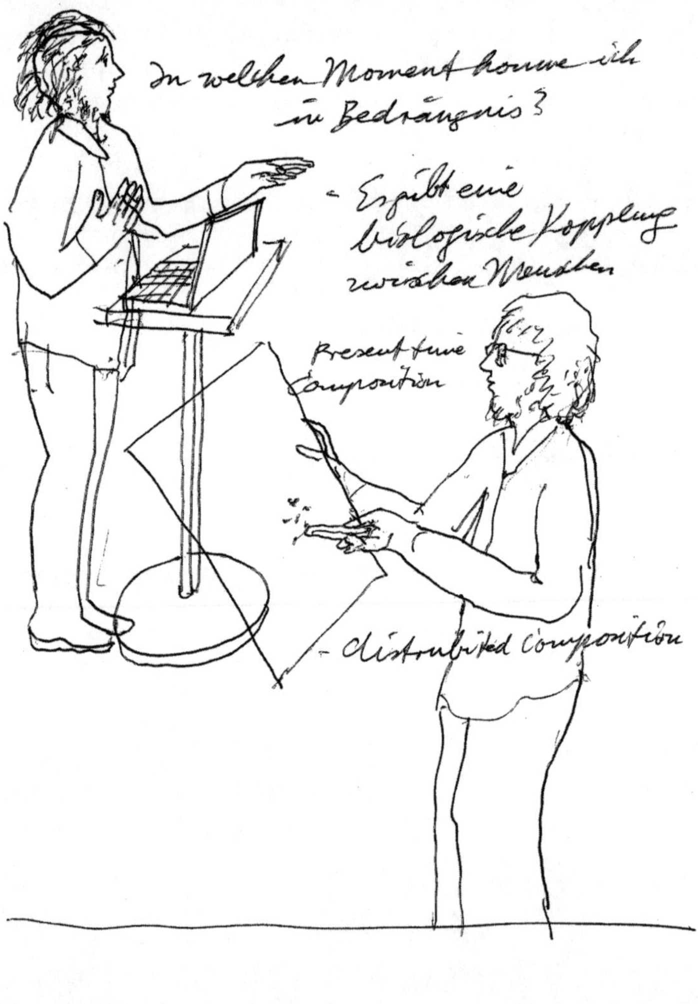

Think Fast! | Think Fast!

Einführung in die Present-Time Composition (PTC)* | An introduction to Present-Time Composition (PTC)**

Alan Bern

* Present-Time Composition und PTC sind angemeldete Schutzmarken.

** Present-Time Composition and PTC are pending trademarks.

Denken wir kurz darüber nach, wie es ist, Autofahren zu lernen. Wir müssen lernen, wie man lenkt, Gas gibt und bremst, wie man den Gang wechselt, wir müssen lernen, die Spiegel und das Tachometer zu beobachten, auf die Straßenschilder und Ampeln zu achten, die jeweilige Verkehrssituation und die Rolle, die wir darin spielen, zu erfassen, und vieles mehr. Zu Beginn des Lernprozesses sind wir uns all dieser Dinge bewusst und am Anfang überfordern sie uns, also vergessen wir den Spiegel im Blick zu behalten oder die eine oder andere Ampel zu beachten. Nach einer Weile geht es uns jedoch »in Fleisch und Blut über«, und dann fahren wir durch die Stadt, während wir essen, trinken, am Telefon oder mit unseren Mitfahrern sprechen, während wir unser Navi oder möglicherweise ein oder zwei Youtube-Videos anschauen. Es ist unglaublich, wie gut Menschen in der Lage sind, komplexe Aufgaben zu meistern, die zunächst ein hohes Maß an bewusster Aufmerksamkeit fordern, bevor diese durch Übung zu einer unbewussten Fähigkeit werden. Wenn diese Fähigkeit erst einmal existiert, erlaubt sie uns, wenn auch größtenteils unbewusst, trotzdem spontan und intelligent auf sich neu ergebende Situationen zu reagieren.

Kognitionspsychologen verwenden den Ausdruck System 1, wenn sie sich auf diese Kompetenz beziehen. In seinem wunderbaren Buch »Thinking: Fast and Slow«[1] beschreibt Daniel Kahneman System 1 als »mühelos entstehende Ausdrücke und Gefühle, welche die Hauptquellen expliziter Überzeugungen und vorsätzlicher Entscheidung von System 2 bilden« (Kahneman, dt. 2012: 33). System 2 hingegen bedeutet »wir identifizieren uns mit dem bewussten, vernünftig nachdenkenden Selbst, das Überzeugungen hat, Entscheidungen trifft und beschließt, worüber es nachdenkt und was zu tun ist« (ebd.). System 1, unbewusstes Denken, ist sehr schnell, während System 2, bewusstes Denken, im Vergleich dazu recht langsam ist. Der Hauptrichtung westlichen Gedankenguts nach wurde System 2 seit der Aufklärung mit dem Selbst gleichgesetzt, sodass beispielsweise Freuds Behauptung, es gebe ein Unbewusstes mit eigenen Gedanken und Gelüsten, die dem Bewusstsein unbekannt sind, zu Beginn des Zwanzigsten Jahrhunderts mit öffentlicher Entrüstung aufgenommen wurde.

Die Gleichsetzung des Selbst mit System 2 verstärkt die ideologische Unterscheidung zwischen Komposition und Improvisation in dem Sinne, in dem sie in westlicher Kultur überwiegend verstanden werden.

In der Tradition europäischer Klassik bedeutet Komponieren, aus musikalischen Elementen ein einzigartiges Werk zu schaffen, das schriftlich notiert ist und so von anderen Musizierenden aufgeführt werden kann. Diesem klassischen Modell gemäß sitzt der oder die Komponierende am Schreibtisch, Kla-

1 | Deutsch: Kahneman, Daniel (2012): Schnelles Denken, langsames Denken. München: Siedler Verlag.

Think for a moment about learning to drive a car. We have to learn to steer, to accelerate and to brake, to shift gears, to watch the mirrors and the speedometer, to follow the road signs and traffic lights, to understand the immediate traffic situation and our role in it, and much more. We start by being conscious of all of this, and at the beginning it is too much for us to handle, so we forget to watch the mirror, or the occasional traffic light. After a while, though, it all becomes *second nature*, and soon we are driving through the city while eating, drinking, talking on our phone and with our passengers, watching our GPS device and possibly a YouTube video or two. It is incredible how good human beings are at mastering complex tasks that take a lot of conscious attention at first and, with practice, reducing them to an unconscious ability. Once the new ability exists, it lets us react spontaneously and intelligently although largely unconsciously to novel events unfolding in time around us. Driving is of course not unique. We move through the world and keep ourselves together by acting on the basis of judgments that are cognitively highly complex and intelligent but largely unconscious.

Cognitive psychologists use the term System 1 to refer to this capacity. In his wonderful book "Thinking: Fast and Slow" Daniel Kahneman describes System 1 as "effortlessly originating impressions and feelings that are the main sources of the explicit beliefs and deliberate choices of System 2" (Kahneman 2011: 21). System 2, by contrast, is "the conscious, reasoning self that has beliefs, makes choices, and decides what to think about and what to do" (ibid.). System 1, or unconscious thinking, is very fast, whereas System 2, conscious thinking, is quite slow in comparison. The main line of Western thought since the Enlightenment has equated System 2 with the Self, so that, for example, Freud's claim that there is an unconscious with its own thoughts and desires unknown to consciousness was met with public outrage at the beginning of the 20th century.

The identification of Self with System 2 supports the ideological divide between composition and improvisation as they are commonly understood in Western culture.

In the European Art Music tradition, to compose is to use the elements of music to create a unique work, notated so that it can be performed by other musicians. The classical model of this is the composer in his or her studio, at the desk, the piano or the computer, trying things out, writing them down or recording them, revising and re-writing, and so on. Described in System 1/System 2 terms, the composer's System 1 generates musical ideas while System 2 transforms, restructures and edits them to create a coherent composition. There is constant interaction between Systems 1 and 2, but System 2 is occupied with most of the compositional planning, especially regarding form. The expectation that a new musical work have its own unique form is one of the hallmarks of European Art Music. Analysis classes are dedicated to understanding the expositions, variations, repetitions, interruptions, interventions,

vier oder Computer im Studio und probiert aus, schreibt oder nimmt auf, überarbeitet, schreibt um und so weiter.

Wendet man auf diesen Prozess die Begriffe System 1 und System 2 an, ergibt sich, dass System 1 des Komponisten oder der Komponistin musikalische Ideen entstehen lässt, während System 2 diese umformt, umstrukturiert und bearbeitet, um eine kohärente Komposition zu erhalten. Zwischen System 1 und System 2 besteht eine konstante Wechselbeziehung, doch System 2 ist mit dem Großteil der kompositorischen Planung beschäftigt – besonders im Hinblick auf die Form. Die Erwartungshaltung, dass ein neues musikalisches Werk eine eigene und einzigartige Form aufweisen müsse, ist eines der Kennzeichen klassischer Musik. Analysekurse widmen sich dem Verständnis von Expositionen, Variationen, Repetitionen, Unterbrechungen, Interventionen, Kontinuitäten und Diskontinuitäten, die Komponierende erdacht haben, um einem musikalischen Werk seine einzigartige formale Kohärenz zu verleihen.

Wenn jedoch neuartige Musikformen auf den bewussten, eher langsamen Prozessen von System 2 beruhen, dann müssten diese für eine Gruppe improvisierender Musiker unmöglich erreichbar sein. Zu jedem Zeitpunkt müsste zwischen einer Vielzahl von Ideen und Vorhaben entschieden werden, aber es gäbe weder die Zeit noch die Verfahrensweisen, um diese Entscheidungen zu treffen, bevor der Zeitpunkt bereits wieder verflogen wäre. Aus diesem Grund verlässt sich musikalische Gruppenimprovisation oftmals auf konventionelle Formen wie zum Beispiel wiederkehrende harmonische oder melodische Strukturen (Blues, Popsongs, Generalbass), die den Rahmen für Improvisationen bilden. Es sind viele Ansätze entwickelt worden, um mehr formale Freiheit und Originalität in improvisierter Musik zu erlangen, zum Beispiel strukturierte oder dirigierte Improvisation. Meines Wissens führen all diese Ansätze eine Ebene der Planung und Kontrolle in den Prozess ein, die den improvisierenden Musikern und Musikerinnen selbst die unmittelbare Verantwortung für die spontane Entwicklung einer musikalischen Form entzieht. Sie wird an eine »dritte Person« wie beispielsweise eine grafische Partitur, eine vorhergehende mündliche Abmachung oder einen improvisierenden Dirigenten delegiert, dessen individuelle Absichten den Rahmen für die Improvisierenden bilden. Viele Ansätze »freier« Improvisation geben zwar tatsächlich die Verantwortung für die musikalische Form an die Improvisierenden, die Ergebnisse folgen jedoch häufig ganz offensichtlichen Verfahren von Imitation und Kontrast, denen die Komplexität und der Einfallsreichtum, die komponierte Musik üblicherweise bietet, fehlen.

Was für Fähigkeiten würden Improvisierende benötigen, um spontan komplexe, intelligente Formen zu erschaffen, ohne auf im Voraus oder von außen vorgegebene Planungs- und Kontrollmittel zurückzugreifen, und gibt es andere Bereiche menschlicher Aktivität, in denen solche Fähigkeiten bereits Anwendung finden?

continuities and discontinuities that composers invent to give a musical work its unique, formal coherence.

But if novel musical form depends on the conscious, relatively slow processes of System 2, it should be impossible to achieve for a group of improvising musicians. At each moment, there would be decisions to make among multiple ideas and intentions, but no time nor procedure for doing so before the moment had already passed. For that reason, group music improvisation often relies on conventional forms such as a repeating harmonic or melodic structure (blues, popular songs, figured bass) that provide a framework within which improvisation takes place. Many approaches have been invented to achieve more freedom and originality concerning form in improvised music, including structured improvisation and conducted improvisation, among others. To my knowledge, all of these approaches add a level of planning and control that takes the direct responsibility for spontaneously inventing musical form away from the improvising musicians themselves and gives it to a "third party" such as a graphic score, a prior verbal agreement or an improvising conductor whose individual intentions create the framework for the improvising musicians. Various approaches to "free" improvisation do indeed give the responsibility for musical form to the improvising musicians, but very often the results reflect obvious processes of imitation and contrast which lack the complexity and inventiveness of form that composed music typically offers.

What kind of abilities would improvising musicians need to have in order to create complex, intelligent form in the moment, without resorting to prior or extrinsic means of planning and control, and are there other areas of human activity where such abilities are already in use?

Let us consider a casual conversation among a group of friends. Subjects are started, developed and elaborated, dropped, picked up and returned to in various ways, separated by interruptions or diversions. Several subjects get floated at once and interweave, the conversation is carried by different speakers or groups of speakers at different times, who return in the same or varied constellations at later points in the conversation. Different amounts of time are devoted to different subjects, with varying intensity and density. In fact, the complex form of such conversations shows many of the features that give large-scale music compositions their coherence.

We create conversational form spontaneously without prior instructions, explicit agreements or external control. Most remarkably, we negotiate the developing form of the conversation in the act of conversing itself, not by using a metalanguage to discuss the conversation. We do not, for example, say "I propose that we consider whether the remark you just made that interrupted me should cause a general change of subject and speaker, or whether I should simply speak louder and faster for a moment to show that I am giving up on neither the subject nor my role as the dominant speaker". But this is just the kind of thing a

Schauen wir uns eine formlose Unterhaltung unter Freunden an: Themen werden aufgebracht, entwickelt und ausgeführt, fallen gelassen, dann wieder aufgegriffen und auf verschiedene Weise wieder angerissen – mit Unterbrechungen und Abschweifungen dazwischen. Mehrere Themen kommen gleichzeitig auf und verflechten sich, die Unterhaltung wird zu unterschiedlichen Zeiten von unterschiedlichen Sprechern oder Sprechergruppen getragen, die in gleichen oder veränderten Konstellationen im Verlauf des Gesprächs wieder auftauchen. Es werden Zeitabschnitte von unterschiedlicher Intensität und Dichte auf die verschiedenen Themen verwendet. Die komplexe Form solcher Unterhaltungen weist tatsächlich viele der Charakteristika auf, die groß angelegten Kompositionen ihre Kohärenz verleihen.

Die Unterhaltungsform schaffen wir spontan ohne vorhergehende Anleitungen, explizite Abmachungen oder Kontrolle von außen. Vor allem handeln wir beim Unterhalten selbst aus, wie die Form der Unterhaltung sich entwickeln soll, anstatt in einer Metasprache darüber zu diskutieren. So würden wir zum Beispiel nicht sagen: »Ich schlage vor, dass wir überlegen, ob die Bemerkung, mit der du mich eben unterbrochen hast, einen grundsätzlichen Themen- und Sprecherwechsel nach sich ziehen soll oder ob ich für eine Weile einfach lauter und schneller spreche, um zu demonstrieren, dass ich weder das Thema noch meine dominante Rolle im Gespräch aufgebe.« Aber genau so etwas erwägt ein Komponist, wenn er zum Beispiel entscheidet, ob ein Trompeteneinsatz mitten in einer Streicher-Passage nur eine kurze Unterbrechung oder eine unmittelbare Überleitung zu einem neuen Abschnitt oder eine Vorwegnahme der Musik sein soll, wie sie später im Stück auftaucht. Der individuelle Komponist oder die Komponistin denkt ganz bewusst über solche Entscheidungen nach und hat auch die notwendige Zeit, damit System 2 seine Arbeit leisten kann. Aber eine Gruppe Improvisierender kann nicht innehalten, um zu überlegen und zu diskutieren, was als nächstes passieren könnte oder sollte, ohne die Musik zu zerstören. Stattdessen müssen sie praktisch sofort auf das eingehen, was gerade geschieht. Kann ihre Reaktion also mit der komplexen, informierten und überlegten Entscheidungsfindung beim Komponieren vergleichbar sein?

Zwei Beispiele der kognitiven Sportforschung können hier Aufschluss geben. Das erste wird von Jonah Lehrer in »How We Decide« (Lehrer 2009: 24-25) diskutiert. Wenn ein Pitcher (Werfer) im professionellen Baseball einen Fastball wirft, so erklärt Lehrer, steht dem Batter (Schlagmann) nicht genügend Zeit zur Verfügung, um bewusst zu entscheiden, ob er versuchen soll, den Ball zu schlagen. Dementsprechend sollte es für den Batter nahezu unmöglich sein, einen Fastball zu treffen. Dennoch gelingt es herausragenden Battern regelmäßig und mit beachtlicher Kontrolle. Wie? Dank vieler tausend mit dem Schlagen von Bällen verbrachten Stunden – so lautet die Antwort – muss der Batter nicht mehr bewusst überlegen, ob er den Ball schlagen soll. Statt-

composer considers when deciding whether, for example, a trumpet call in the middle of a string passage should be just a brief interruption, or an immediate transition to a new section, or a foreshadowing of music that arrives later in the piece, and so on. The individual composer uses conscious deliberation to make such decisions and has the necessary time for System 2 to do its work. But a group of improvisers cannot stop to deliberate and discuss what could or should happen next without destroying the music. They have to respond virtually instantly to what is going on. Can their response possibly be comparable to the complex, informed and deliberate decision-making of a composer?

Two examples from the cognitive study of sports are suggestive here. The first is discussed by Jonah Lehrer in "How We Decide" (Lehrer 2009: 24-25). As he explains, when a pitcher throws a fastball in today's professional baseball, there is simply not enough time available for a batter to consciously decide whether or not to swing before the ball has already crossed the plate.

Accordingly, it should be next to impossible for a batter to hit a fastball. But great batters do so regularly and with considerable control. How? The answer is, that thanks to many thousands of hours spent hitting baseballs, the batter no longer needs to consciously deliberate whether or not to swing. He relies instead on an extremely fast, largely unconscious impulse that has been trained or *educated* by all of his experience. In other words, the choice whether to swing or not is given over to System 1. In fact, the level of performance and tempo of baseball, like all professional sports, depend on the capacity of System 1 to react successfully to complex, changing situations with very fast, trained impulses.

There is a parallel here to the demands an improviser would have to meet to make a cognitively complex contribution to music in the moment of its creation. The baseball example suggests that this is indeed possible, but only if the improviser's System 1 is doing the work. That requires many hours of practicing the relevant, cognitively complex skills to turn them into trained impulses.

We are still left with the problem of understanding what all the other musicians are up to in each moment of an improvisation. Composers are working with their own ideas and intentions and they have the time they need to explore them. Improvisers would have to be able to recognize the musical intentions of *other* improvisers in the very moment that those intentions are being formed. Does that mean that improvisers have to be mind-readers?

As reported in the journal *Nature Neuroscience* in 2008 (Nature Neuroscience 2008: 1109-1116), an experiment was conducted in which three groups were shown videos of professional basketball players shooting baskets. The three groups were fans, coaches and other professional basketball players. The video was stopped at different points in mid-shot and the viewers were asked to predict whether the ball would go in the basket or not. As one would expect, the predictions of all three groups improved when the ball was shown closer to the basket and its full arc became obvious. But the professional basketball

dessen ist er auf einen extrem schnellen, größtenteils unbewussten Impuls angewiesen, der ihm durch seine Erfahrung antrainiert oder ihn »gelehrt« worden ist. Die Entscheidung liegt – mit anderen Worten – bei System 1. Denn in der Tat beruht das Leistungsniveau und Tempo von Baseball, wie auch aller anderen professionellen Sportarten, auf der Kompetenz von System 1, mit sehr schnellen, antrainierten Impulsen erfolgreich auf komplexe, sich verändernde Situationen zu reagieren.

Hier besteht eine Parallele zu den Anforderungen, denen Improvisierende entsprechen müssten, um einen kognitiv komplexen Beitrag zur im Entstehen begriffenen Musik zu liefern. Das Baseballbeispiel legt nahe, dass dies tatsächlich möglich ist, aber nur wenn System 1 der Improvisierenden die Arbeit macht. Dies erfordert viele Stunden, in denen die relevanten, kognitiv komplexen Fertigkeiten geschult werden, um sie in antrainierte Impulse umzuwandeln.

Dabei bleibt das Problem bestehen, dass erkannt werden muss, was all die anderen Musizierenden in jedem Moment der Improvisation vorhaben. Wer komponiert, arbeitet mit eigenen Ideen und Absichten und hat die nötige Zeit, diese zu erforschen. Wer improvisiert, müsste in der Lage sein, die musikalischen Absichten anderer Improvisierender genau im Moment ihres Entstehens zu erkennen. Bedeutet das also, wer improvisiert, muss Gedanken lesen?

Das Magazin *Nature Neuroscience* (Nature Neuroscience 2008: 1109-1116) berichtete 2008 von einem Experiment, in dessen Verlauf drei unterschiedlichen Gruppen von Testpersonen Videos davon gezeigt wurden, wie professionelle Basketballspieler Treffer erzielen. Die drei Gruppen bestanden aus Fans, Trainern und ebenfalls professionellen Basketballspielern. Die Videos wurden jeweils an unterschiedlichen Stellen mitten im Wurf angehalten, und die Zuschauer wurden aufgefordert, zu prognostizieren, ob der Ball in den Korb gehen würde oder nicht. Wie zu erwarten, waren die Prognosen besser, je näher der Ball bereits am Korb und je absehbarer somit die Flugkurve war. Die professionellen Basketballspieler waren jedoch überdies zu etwas in der Lage, was weder die Fans noch die Trainer vermochten: Sie konnten oftmals richtig einschätzen, ob der Wurf erfolgreich sein würde, bevor der Ball die Hände der Spieler überhaupt verlassen hatte! Dies dürfte niemanden überraschen, der schon einmal professionelle Basketballspiele gesehen hat. Die Spieler warten gar nicht ab, ob ein Ball zum Treffer wird, bevor sie entscheiden, ob sie es mit einem Rebound versuchen, sondern sie reagieren genau in dem Moment, in dem der Ball losgelassen wird, oder sogar davor. Dies ist ihnen möglich, weil die Entscheidung, den Ball zu werfen, nicht erst in dem Moment getroffen wird, in dem sie den Ball loslassen, sondern eher aus einer komplexen Bewertung der Gesamtsituation des Spiels hervorgeht – ein Wissen, das die anderen Spieler auf dem Feld teilen. Das bedeutet, dass die Spieler größtenteils ein Verständnis davon teilen, was gerade vor sich geht und was als nächstes pas-

players were able to do something that neither the fans nor the coaches could do: they could often predict correctly whether the shot would be successful at a point before the ball had even left the hands of the shooter! This should not surprise anyone who has watched professional basketball games. The players do not wait to see whether a shot goes in before deciding to go up for a rebound. They react at or even before the moment of release. They can do so because the intention to shoot the ball does not form at the moment the ball is released. Rather, it reflects a complex judgment about the total situation of the game, knowledge that is shared by the other players on the court. That is, the players already largely share an understanding of what is going on and expectations about what might happen next. In this shared context, a player about to shoot begins to reveal his interpretation of the situation and his intention to act through his body and movements long before he releases the ball. If this were not the case, the other players would be surprised each time someone decided to shoot the ball. Furthermore, while watching the shooter's intention unfold in time, each player can refer to his own rich history of experience in similar situations to make a comparison and predict the likelihood of success. All of this happens in the blink of an eye once again the work of System 1.

The baseball and basketball examples show that it is indeed possible to react both quickly enough and intelligently enough to keep up with a complex situation that is changing from moment to moment. The necessary abilities are on spectacular display in professional sports, but they are just as active in everyday domains such as driving, bicycle-riding, conversation and all complex activities that become *second nature* with enough practice.

Professional classical musicians today practice very hard for many years, but they are not practicing the kind of decision-making in music that would be the counterpart to decision-making in sports, conversation or driving. Most performers today practice to realize a pre-existing musical plan, the musical work, as perfectly and convincingly as possible. This process also involves both Systems 1 and 2, of course. Every performer knows how to practice to meet challenges of technique, expression or even memorization. Deliberate strategies and actions gradually give way to trained impulses as System 1 takes over from System 2. Without this capacity, it would be impossible to successfully perform most works of music. But the creative decision-making that constitutes the musical work has already been done by the composer. Performers today, including improvisers, spend very little time practicing the creative decision-making itself because they have no need to do so. We may think that playing music is cognitively more demanding than playing basketball, for example, but basketball players have an autonomy and responsibility for their decisions that musicians in our day have largely surrendered. To see this clearly, imagine that the task of the basketball player consisted in performing precisely choreographed game scripts that had been created by basketball game authors sitting at their desks.

sieren könnte. In diesem geteilten Kontext gibt ein Spieler, der kurz vor dem Wurf steht, seine Interpretation der Situation und seine Handlungsabsicht bereits lange, bevor er den Ball loslässt, über seinen Körper und seine Bewegungen zu erkennen. Andernfalls wären die Spieler jedes Mal überrascht, wenn jemand beschließen würde, den Ball zu werfen. Und während die Absicht dessen, der zum Wurf ansetzt, sich vor seinen Augen entfaltet, kann jeder Spieler auf seinen eigenen Erfahrungsschatz in ähnlichen Situationen zurückgreifen und mittels Vergleich die Erfolgswahrscheinlichkeit einschätzen. All dies geschieht blitzschnell – dank der Arbeit von System 1.

Die Baseball- und Basketballbeispiele zeigen, dass es tatsächlich möglich ist, sowohl schnell als auch intelligent genug zu reagieren, um mit einer komplexen Situation Schritt zu halten, die sich ständig verändert. Die dafür notwendigen Fähigkeiten werden im professionellen Sport auf spektakuläre Weise zur Schau gestellt, aber sie sind auch im Alltag ebenso aktiv, etwa beim Auto- oder Fahrradfahren, bei Unterhaltungen und allen komplexen Tätigkeiten, die durch ausreichend Übung »in Fleisch und Blut übergehen«.

Professionelle klassische Musiker üben heutzutage jahrelang sehr hart, doch sie üben dabei nicht die Art von musikalischer Entscheidungsfindung, die derjenigen im Sport, beim Unterhalten oder Autofahren entsprechen würde. Die meisten Interpreten üben sich heutzutage darin, einen vorher vorhandenen musikalischen Plan, das musikalische Werk, so vollkommen und überzeugend wie möglich umzusetzen. Natürlich ist sowohl System 1 als auch System 2 an diesem Prozess beteiligt. Jeder Interpret weiß, wie der Umgang mit Schwierigkeiten, die technischer Art sind oder den Ausdruck oder das Auswendiglernen betreffen, geübt werden kann. Strategien, die auf Überlegungen basieren, weichen dabei antrainierten Impulsen, während System 1 System 2 ablöst. Ohne diese Kompetenz wäre es unmöglich, die meisten Musikstücke umzusetzen. Aber die kreative Entscheidungsfindung, die das Musikstück ausmacht, ist bereits beim Komponieren geleistet worden. Heutzutage verbringen Interpreten, Improvisierende eingeschlossen, sehr wenig Zeit damit, die kreative Entscheidungsfindung an sich zu üben, weil es für sie nicht notwendig ist. Wir mögen es vielleicht für kognitiv anspruchsvoller halten, Musik zu machen als zum Beispiel Basketball zu spielen, aber Basketballspieler haben eine Autonomie und Verantwortung für ihre Entscheidungen inne, die Musiker heutzutage größtenteils abgegeben haben. Um dies zu verdeutlichen, stellen wir uns vor, dass die Aufgabe der Basketballspieler darin bestünde, präzise choreographierte Spiel-Drehbücher umzusetzen, die von Basketballspiel-Autoren am Schreibtisch erstellt worden sind.

Ich habe *Present-Time Composition* (*PTC*) als Ansatz für Solo- und Gruppenimprovisation entwickelt, um improvisierte Musik mit Charakteristika entstehen zu lassen, die wir normalerweise nur bei bewusst durchdachter, komponierter Musik erwarten würden, insbesondere bei neuartigen Formen. Die

Exploratorium
Berlin 1.6.2014
Offene Bühne
Reinhard Mario Ruth

Theorie der PTC ist stark von den Erkenntnissen der Kognitionsforschung geprägt, sowohl von den bereits erwähnten, als auch anderen. In respektvoller Parodie Freuds könnte das Motto der PTC lauten: »Wo System 2 war, soll System 1 werden.« Das heißt, an die Stelle bewusster Überlegung sollen unbewusste, aber erlernte Impulse treten.

PTC wird durch einen erfahrenen Lehrer vermittelt, der spezifische Übungen verwendet und seiner Gruppe unmittelbare, präzise Rückmeldungen gibt. Die ersten Schritte bestehen darin, dass die Schüler lernen, ihre eigenen ursprünglichsten Impulse jeglicher Art wahrzunehmen – ob musikalisch oder nicht –, damit sie diesen ohne Hemmungen zu folgen vermögen und dann entscheiden können, wann sie diesen folgen und wann nicht. In der Verbindung zu den Impulsen ankert jeder weitere Schritt dieses pädagogischen Ansatzes. Die Übungen führen zunehmend komplexe musikalische Informationen ein, und die Aufgabe der Schüler besteht auf jeder Übungsstufe darin, diese Informationen umzuwandeln: Aus Überlegungen im System 2 sollen Impulse im System 1 werden. Die Aufgabe des Lehrers ist es hierbei, jede Information nur genauso schnell einzuführen, dass die Schüler sie solcherweise verinnerlichen können. Das Lerntempo wird durch die Fähigkeit der Schüler bestimmt, freie, kreative Entscheidungen während der Improvisation zu treffen. So lange die Entscheidungen der Schüler aus System 1 hervorgehen, sind sie schnell und flexibel genug, um mit dem Musikfluss Schritt zu halten, und den anderen Musikern der Gruppe ist es mit großer Wahrscheinlichkeit möglich, diese zu spiegeln und auf sie zu reagieren, indem sie ihr eigenes System 1 einsetzen. In dem Moment, in dem es zu viele Informationen gibt, die noch nicht verinnerlicht sind, übernimmt System 2 das Steuer – das kreative Fließen im musikalischen Schaffensprozess leidet und die Kommunikation unter den Musizierenden verstummt. Das Ensemble kann und sollte diese Grenzen erkunden und versuchen, diese durch Übungseinheiten zu erweitern, die dabei helfen, die neuen Informationen zu verinnerlichen. Aber in jeder Einheit wird der Punkt erreicht, an dem eine nicht überwindbare Grenze auftaucht – das Limit wirklichen Lernens ist für die jeweilige Übungseinheit erreicht. Es kommt häufig vor, dass diese Grenze sich bereits zur nächsten Einheit aufgelöst hat oder kurz danach verschwindet, da das menschliche Lernsystem Zeit für den Prozess der Verinnerlichung benötigt.

Ich freue mich, berichten zu können, dass PTC Ensembles in Cincinnati, Antwerpen, Berlin und Weimar diese Methode weit genug verfolgt haben, um zu zeigen, dass viele Annahmen über die Begrenztheit der Improvisation im Vergleich zur Komposition falsch sind. Dennoch muss gesagt werden, dass PTC noch in den Kinderschuhen steckt. In unserer Gesellschaft wird man kaum dafür entlohnt, die Zeit und Energie für die Entwicklung der musikalischen Fähigkeiten aufzuwenden, die PTC zum Ziel hat. Niemand erhält 20-Millionen-Dollar-Verträge dafür, der weltweit wertvollste Improvisator zu

I have created *Present-Time Composition (PTC)* as an approach to solo and group music improvisation whose goal is improvised music with characteristics usually expected only of consciously deliberated, composed music, in particular novel form. The theory of PTC is strongly informed by insights from cognitive science, including those that I have mentioned here, and others. In a respectful parody of Freud, the motto of PTC could be, "where there was System 2, there shall be System 1", in other words, where there was conscious deliberation, there shall be unconscious but educated impulse. PTC is taught by an expert coach who uses specific exercises and gives immediate and precise feedback to a group of students. The first steps are for the student to learn to perceive their own most basic impulses of any kind whatsoever – musical or not – to be able to act on them without inhibition, and then to be able to choose when to act on them or not. This connection to impulse anchors every further step in the pedagogic approach. Exercises introduce increasingly complex musical information, and at each stage the task of the student is to turn this information from System 2 deliberations into System 1 impulses. The task of the coach is to present the information no faster than the student can internalize it in this way. The measure of this learning tempo is the student's own ability to make free, creative choices while improvising. As long as the student's choices are coming from System 1, they will be fast and flexible enough to keep up with the flow of music, and the other musicians in the group will have a good chance of mirroring and responding to them using their own System 1s. The moment that there is too much information not yet internalized, System 2 takes over, the creativity and flow of the music-making suffers and communication breaks down among the musicians. The ensemble can and should explore this boundary and try to expand it through practice sessions that help the new information become internalized. But at some point in each session, a boundary is always reached that cannot be crossed, that is the limit of real learning for that session. It often happens that such a boundary has already dissolved by the next session or soon afterwards, because the whole human learning system needs time for the internalization process.

I am happy to report that PTC ensembles in Cincinnati, Antwerp, Berlin and Weimar have gone far enough in this method to suggest that many assumptions about the limits of improvisation vis-à-vis composition are mistaken. But PTC is admittedly still in its baby shoes. In our society, there are few rewards for taking the time and energy to develop the musical skills that PTC has as its goals. No one gets $20 million contracts for being the league's most valuable improviser. So we are forced to imagine what kind of music-making it would be possible to develop if our values and resources were other than they are. But the inventors of soccer also had to imagine the day that there would be teams like Real Madrid and players like Lionel Messi, and they had to wait a long time for that day to come.

sein. Deswegen können wir uns nur vorstellen, was für Arten des Musikmachens möglich wären, wenn unsere Werte und Ressourcen andere wären. Aber auch die Erfinder von Fußball mussten sich den Tag vorstellen, an dem es Teams wie Real Madrid und Spieler wie Messi geben würde, und lange Zeit auf diesen Tag warten.

Übersetzung aus dem Englischen: Solveig Raschpichler, Berlin

Literatur/References

Kahneman, Daniel (2011): Thinking, Fast and Slow. New York: Macmillan, Kindle Edition.

Kahneman, Daniel (2012): Schnelles Denken, langsames Denken. Aus dem amerikanischen Englisch von Thorsten Schmidt, München: Siedler Verlag.

Lehrer, Jonah (2009): How We Decide, New York: Houghton Mifflin Harcourt.

Nature Neuroscience 11 (2008): London: Nature Publishing Group NPG, 1109-1116.

Intermezzo 3

Der nationale Wettbewerb für junge Musizierende wurde dieses Jahr (2014) in England auf junge Jazz-Musiker ausgeweitet. Ich habe mir einige der drei Hauptgewinner dieser Kategorie angehört. Der Sieger war ein 17-jähriger Saxophonist. Er war absolut hervorragend, konnte sich wohl mit jedem Spieler, den ich je gehört habe, messen, was Ton, Technik und allgemeines Verständnis von Jazz angeht. Trotzdem – er ist 17 Jahre alt! Warum schlägt er nicht über die Stränge? Warum schafft er nicht seine eigene Welt, anstatt eine idealisierte Ansicht von Jazz neu zu erfinden? Es war wunderschön gespielt, aber – meiner Meinung nach – nicht auf bedeutungsvolle Weise kreativ.

Edwin Prévost im Podiumsgespräch, Mai 2014

Übersetzung aus dem Englischen: Solveig Raschpichler, Berlin

Intermezzo 3

The national competition for young musicians in England was extended to young jazz musicians this year (2014). I just happened to listen to a couple of the three principal winners in that category. The winner was a 17 year old saxophone player. He was absolutely superb, as good as any player I have probably ever heard, with regard to tone, technique and the general understanding of jazz. However, this is a 17 year old! Why isn't he kicking over the traces? Why isn't he making his world rather than reinventing an idealized view of jazz? It was beautifully played, but it was not, in my view, creative in any meaningful sense.

Edwin Prévost in a public talk, May 2014

EXPLORATORIUM Berlin 31-5-014

Mirio Cosottini, Arezzo

EXERCISE OF RESTITUTION
Sound Invariance, graphics and improvisation

Emergency of sound
- nicht lineare improvisation
- nicht lineare music
- nicht lineare methoden
- hirarchische Kompositionen

creative

multi directional ◁ is ▷ qualitative

non consequential

- unsere Kultur hat die Qualität der TRANSFORMATION

- lineares u. nicht lineares korrespondieren

- Listening Composition, Execution

- eine Didaktik der IMPROVISATION

- du mußt hören können um LAUT zu werden

F: - 'der LAUT ist dein Arbeitsfeld'

- die Konstanz in der Wahrnehmung

F: - wenn wir improvisieren nehmen wir konstant wahr was um uns ist und was in uns ist - wir arbeiten mit der Materie um uns und in uns in der Tätigkeit.

-

Klang-Invarianz, Grafiken und Improvisation | Sound Invariance, Graphics and Improvisation

Ein Beitrag zur Methodik musikalischer Improvisation |

A contribution to the methodology of musical improvisation

Mirio Cosottini

Einführung in lineare und nichtlineare Studienmethoden

Der üblichen Methode des Musikstudiums, die ich linear nennen möchte, liegt die Idee zugrunde, dass der Schüler stufenweise ansteigende Schwierigkeitsgrade durchlaufen muss. Dieser Vorstellung nach wird der Schüler von einem Ausgangspunkt zu einem Endpunkt geführt, an dem sich Kenntnisse und Fähigkeiten verbessert haben. Im Falle der Improvisation legt die Ausgangssituation normalerweise die Ausgangsbedingungen fest, die für die Improvisation notwendig sind. Durch das Studium gewinnt der Erwerb technischer und expressiver Fähigkeiten zunehmend an Komplexität. Der Erwerb und die Perfektion der eigenen technischen und expressiven Fähigkeiten resultieren in dem Vermögen, gut zu improvisieren.

Die *lineare* Methode hat ihre Vorteile. Sie ist *progressiv*: Das heißt, dass Fähigkeiten und Kenntnisse stufenweise wachsen. Daher verringert sich die Diskrepanz zwischen dem, was wir wissen, und dem, was wir nicht wissen. Sie ist *kumulativ*: Spezifische Fähigkeiten werden in der Absicht gesammelt, musikalische Technik und Ausdruckskompetenz zu erwerben. In diesem Sinne ist sie *konstruktiv*: Unser Studium ermöglicht es uns, dem Bauwerk unseres Improvisationsvermögens einen Stein nach dem anderen hinzuzufügen. Sie ist *systematisch*: Jeder Schritt resultiert aus einer Handlung, die die jeweilige Übung mit der vorherigen verbindet. Wir haben es also mit einem Stufensystem zu tun. In anderen Worten wird jeder neue Schritt durch den vorherigen vorbereitet und übersteigt diesen in seinem Schwierigkeitsgrad. Sie hat eine *eindeutige Ausrichtung*: Der Studienverlauf führt vom Ausgangszustand eines geringen Vermögens zu einem Endzustand höheren Vermögens. Daraus folgt eine Verbesserung der Technik. Neben der erzielten Fähigkeit zu einer guten Improvisation, gewinnt man also darüber hinaus auch eine solide technische Grundlage.

Aus der linearen Studienmethode hat sich eine feste Terminologie ergeben, die dann auch zur Beschreibung von Musik verwendet wurde. Im Laufe der Zeit ist die Art, wie wir Klänge und unsere kreativen Handlungen hören, davon beeinflusst worden – wenn auch nicht nur zum Positiven.[1] So enthält der Begriff »improvisieren« im Musikunterricht eine Art »Gebrauchsanweisung«, die ihrer Natur nach linear ist. Letztlich zielt der Begriff auf das Vermögen ab, von elementaren Bauteilen aus einen musikalischen Diskurs in Echtzeit aufzubauen; die Lehrmethode beabsichtigt, dieses Vermögen schrittweise wachsen zu lassen. Daher ist es häufig der Fall, dass ein Schüler, der nie zuvor improvisiert hat und weder über Improvisationstechniken noch über theoretische

1 | Zur Bedeutung musikalischer Terminologie für das Erlernen von Musik, siehe Delalande 2013: 63.

Introduction to Linear and Non-Linear Study Methods

The basic idea of the linear method of studying music is one in which the student must undertake a gradual path through stages of increasing difficulty. This will take them from a given point to a final point at which their knowledge and skills have been improved. In the case of improvisation, the point of departure usually establishes the initial conditions necessary for improvisation. The direction which the acquisition of technical and expressive skills takes becomes increasingly complex due to the study. The outcome is an ability to improvise well, having acquired and perfected one's technical and expressive skills.

The linear method of analyzing music has its advantages: it is *progressive*, in other words, each skill and all knowledge is increased step by step. Therefore, the distance between what we know and what we do not know decreases; it is *cumulative*, specific skills are added with a view to the acquisition of technical skills and expressive competence; in this sense it is *constructive*. Our study allows us to lay one brick at a time, with the idea of building up the edifice of our ability to improvise; it is *systematic*, each step is the result of an action that connects a given exercise to the previous one. Therefore, it is a matter of levels. In other words, each new step forward is more difficult than the previous one, and is prepared for by the previous one; it is *directional*, the study time is inserted into a path so that the initial state of low competence leads to a final state of higher competence. As a result, technique is improved. Moreover, in addition to achieving the final objective, in other words, performing a good improvisation, one also gains a solid technical background.

The linear study method has resulted in the establishment of a fixed terminology which has been adapted to describe music. Over time, this has affected the way we listen to sounds and our creative acts, although not always in a positive way.[1] The term "improvise" in teaching practice contains some "instructions for use" which are linear in nature. It will eventually mean having the capacity to build a real-time musical discourse starting from elementary units; the teaching method has the aim of gradually increasing this capacity. Therefore, it is often the case that a student who has never practiced improvisation and does not know any improvisation techniques, nor possesses any theoretical knowledge, is in obvious trouble when the teacher calls on them to improvise. In fact, the student asks themselves: "what should I do?", "what should I play?" These questions are probably followed by paralysis and embarrassment; the student often refuses to play. There are many reasons for this, but one is crucial, namely the belief that with regard to improvisation, mostly

1 | For the importance of musical terminology when learning music, see Delalande 2013: 63.

Kenntnis verfügt, merklich Schwierigkeiten hat, wenn der Lehrer ihn zum Improvisieren auffordert. Er fragt sich: »Was soll ich machen?«, »Was soll ich spielen?«. Darauf folgt vermutlich eine Art Lähmung und Verlegenheit; häufig weigert sich der Schüler zu spielen. Es gibt viele Gründe dafür. Entscheidend ist sicherlich der Glaube, dass in der Improvisation hauptsächlich lineare Musik von Bedeutung sei.[2] Tatsächlich aber überschneiden sich in jedem musikalischen Phänomen Linearität und Nichtlinearität und existieren nebeneinander.[3] Bedauerlicherweise hat der Musikunterricht, und vor allem der Improvisationsunterricht, diesen Aspekt übergangen und stattdessen darauf bestanden, dass das Studium der Improvisation hauptsächlich lineare Aspekte in den Fokus nimmt.

Die Frage »Was soll ich machen?« bezieht sich auf das Problem, wie zu improvisieren sei, und ignoriert die Thematik der Nichtlinearität. Improvisieren bedeutet nicht, eine musikalische Fragestellung zu erörtern, sich einen musikalischen Erzählpfad »entlangzuschlängeln«, einer klaren Richtung zu folgen, die sich aus den Klangereignissen ergibt, oder auch systematisch darüber nachzudenken, was vorher und was nachher kommen müsste. Improvisieren bedeutet vielmehr, sich mit dem Unvorhergesehenen auseinanderzusetzen[4], mit jenen Aspekten, die nicht auf der Ebene einzelner Elemente erscheinen, sondern sich gerade aus der Gesamtheit der Ereignisse ergeben.

Das nichtlineare Studium ist auf den Klang ausgerichtet und auf die Klangeigenschaften, die im Laufe der Zeit konstant bleiben. Diese Studienart ist dann möglich, wenn wir in der Lage sind, die unveränderlichen Eigenschaften der Musik zu ermitteln. Die Konzepte der Linearität und Nichtlinearität können dabei helfen.[5] Die nichtlinearen Elemente treten als Invarianten im Musikstück auf. Beim Hören können wir diese Invarianten prüfen und lokalisieren. Die Hörweise, die für dieses Vorhaben am nützlichsten ist, wird von

---

2 | Ich habe die Gründe für dieses Missverständnis bereits in einem Artikel erklärt, Cosottini 2009: 39.

3 | Zu Beginn des zweiten Kapitels von »The Time of Music« (Kramer 1988) werden diese beiden Konzepte untrennbar verbunden und gemeinsam vorgestellt: »Nichtlinearität ist nicht nur die Abwesenheit von Linearität, sondern selbst eine strukturelle Kraft. Da diese beiden Kräfte in unterschiedlichen Kombinationen auf unterschiedlichen Ebenen der hierarchischen Struktur von Musik auftauchen, bestimmt deren Zusammenspiel sowohl den Stil als auch die Form einer Komposition«, siehe Kramer 1988: 20.

4 | Die Analogie zwischen Nichtlinearität und dem Unvorhergesehenen (Theorie komplexer Systeme) ist deutlich. Für Details dazu, siehe Reinhard Gagel (2010): »Improvisation als soziale Kunst«.

5 | Für eine Erläuterung dieser Konzepte und ihres Nutzens für die Analyse von musikalischer Improvisation, siehe Cosottini 2013: 1.

linear music matters.[2] In fact, at the heart of every musical phenomenon linearity and non-linearity overlap and coexist.[3] Unfortunately, music teaching, and, in particular, the teaching of improvisation, has neglected this aspect and has insisted that linear aspects are predominantly focused on when studying improvisation.

The question "what should I do?" focuses on the problem of practicing improvisation and ignores the non-linear issue. Improvise does not mean to "argue" a musical issue, weave a musical narrative path, follow a precise direction according to an idea of sound events, nor systematically think about what comes before and what comes after. Rather, to improvise means to deal with "emergencies" of sound,[4] those aspects that do not appear at elementary level but which occur due to the totality of events.

Non-linear study focuses on sound and sound properties that remain constant over the course of time. This type of study is possible if we are able to identify the *invariant* features of the music. To help us achieve this, the concepts of linearity and non-linearity come to our aid[5]. The non-linearity elements appear as *invariances* in the course of the musical piece. Listening is what allows us to consider these invariances and locate them. The listening type most useful for this purpose is what Kramer has called *cumulative listening,*[6] in other words, the ability to accumulate musical events in one's consciousness and "extract" certain characteristics that do not change over time. According to Kramer, this kind of listening works on *vertical time*[7] and therefore favors the present temporality over the triad of *past, present and future*. This means that the identification of

---

2 | I have explained the reasons for this misunderstanding in a previous article, Cosottini 2009: 39.

3 | At the beginning of the second chapter of *The Time of Music* (Kramer 1988), the two concepts are inextricably linked and co-presented: "Non-linearity is not merely the absence of linearity, but is itself a structural force. Since these two forces may appear in different combinations on each level of music's hierarchical structure, their interplay determines both the style and the form of a composition", see Kramer 1988: 20.

4 | The analogy between Non-linearity and Emergence (Theory of Complexity) is strong. For more details see *Improvisation als soziale Kunst* of Reinhard Gagel (2010).

5 | For an explanation of these concepts and their usefulness for the purpose of analyzing musical improvisation, see Cosottini 2013: 1.

6 | "Cumulative listening [...] is the mechanism by which we come to understand, in retrospect, the non-linear principles of a composition or passage." (Kramer 1988: 43)

7 | "[...] vertical time is a single present stretched out into an enormous duration, infinite in its potential that nonetheless feels like an instant [...]" (Kramer 1988: 55). I am currently trying to analyze this type of listening from the phenomenological point of view with respect to the concepts of retention and protention.

Kramer *kumulatives Hören*[6] genannt. Es besteht aus der Fähigkeit, musikalische Ereignisse im Bewusstsein anzuhäufen und daraus bestimmte Charakteristika zu »entnehmen«, die sich im Laufe der Zeit nicht verändern. Kramer zufolge funktioniert diese Art des Hörens in *vertikaler Zeit*[7]. Daher zieht es eine rein präsentische Zeitlichkeit der Triade von *Vergangenheit, Gegenwart und Zukunft* vor. Dies bedeutet, dass die Ermittlung von Invarianten bei der Wahrnehmung von Musik in vertikaler Zeit stattfindet, was für die Methode des kumulativen Hörens[8] typisch ist.

Nützliche Strategien zur Ermittlung musikalischer Invarianten werden in »Metodi nonlineari e improvvisazione« (Cosottini 2011: 125-28) beschrieben, die folgendermaßen zusammengefasst werden können (siehe Abbildung 1):

Abbildung 1: ©Mirio Cosottini

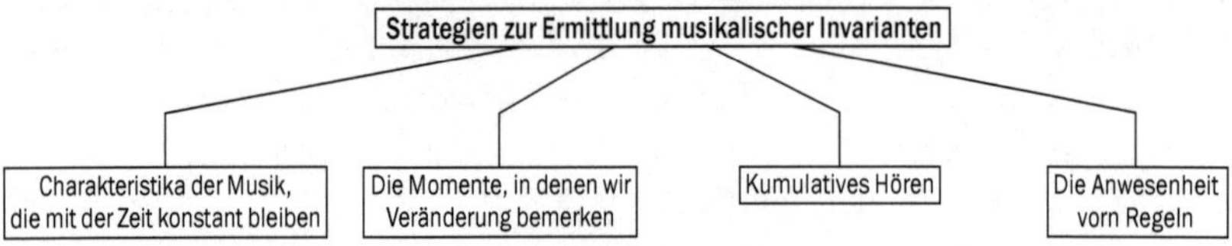

a) Ermitteln, welche Charakteristika der Musik sich mit der Zeit nicht verändern: Der Klang, der eine bestimmten Umfang hat, ein bestimmtes Register besetzt, oder eine bestimmte Dynamik hat oder eine bestimmte Geschwindigkeit beibehält, eine bestimmte Form, Körnigkeit oder Farbe hat.
b) Überprüfen, ob es Regeln (Prinzipien) gibt, die für das gesamte Stück oder einen entscheidenden Teil davon gelten.
c) Die Momente analysieren, in denen wir Veränderungen bemerken (dadurch wird das Stück vermutlich in verschiedene nichtlineare Teile unterteilt).
d) Die Ohren für kumulatives statt systematisches Hören öffnen, damit jedes musikalische Ereignis auf das Stück als Ganzes bezogen wird, anstatt nur auf die unmittelbar nachfolgenden Ereignisse.

---

6 | »Kumulatives Hören [...] ist der Mechanismus, durch welchen wir retrospektiv die nichtlinearen Prinzipien einer Komposition oder einer Passage erfassen.« Kramer 1988: 43.

7 | »[...] vertikale Zeit ist eine einfache Gegenwart, die auf eine enorme Dauer ausgestreckt wird, sie ist unendlich in ihrem Potential, das sich dennoch wie ein Moment anfühlt«, Kramer 1988: 55. Ich arbeite momentan an einer Analyse dieser Hörweise aus einer phänomenologischen Perspektive mit den Konzepten von Retention und Protention.

8 | Die Ermittlung von Invarianten ähnelt dem Prozess, den Stockhausen verwendet hat, um die »Momentform« zu ermitteln, die er in Stockhausen 1991: 63-75 beschreibt. Wie schon in Cosottini 2010 beschrieben, ist Stockhausen nur in Bezug auf den kompositorischen Prozess auf den Moment beschränkt, nicht aber in Bezug auf den improvisatorischen Prozess.

invariances in the perception of music takes place in vertical time, which is typical of the cumulative listening method.[8]

Useful strategies for identifying musical invariances are described in "Metodi nonlineari e improvvisazione" (Cosottini 2011: 25-28) and can be summarized as follows (see figure 1):

Figure 1: ©Mirio Cosottini

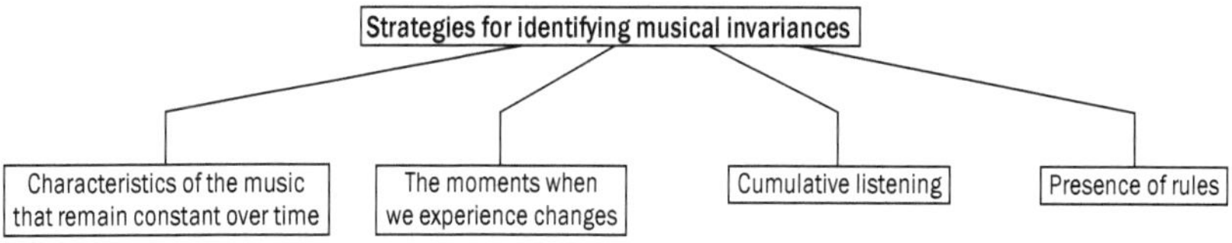

a) Identify the characteristics of the music that remain constant over time: the sound that occupies a given region, a given register, or has a certain dynamic, or maintains a given speed, has a certain shape, a certain grain, a certain color.
b) Verify the presence of rules (principles) covering the entire piece or a significant part of it.
c) Analyze the moments when we experience changes (which probably divides the piece into different non-linear parts).
d) Open your ears to cumulative listening rather than systematic listening, so as to relate every musical event to the whole rather than only to subsequent ones.

Thanks to these listening strategies, which are to some extent interdependent, we can identify *musical invariances* in a piece of music. For example, the canon "Deo gratia" by Johannes Ockeghem, arranged by Philip Legge in 2001,[9] can be listened to in a linear way, as a collection of melodic lines that intertwine and converse (in their musical logic and sequencing), or in a non-linear way, such as listening to the invariance *timbre of voices* that in their entirety create a dense sound texture. This invariance persists over time, characterizes the entire piece and is supported at all times by cumulative listening.

Once identified, invariances become the object of study through specially constructed exercises; these indicate which transformations are operating on sound in these invariances. The relationship between transformation and sound

8 | The identification of invariants is similar to the process that Stockhausen used to identify the "moment form", which he described in Stockhausen 1991: 63-75. As previously described in Cosottini (2010), Stockhausen is confined to the moment only in relation to the compositional process and not to the improvisational one.

9 | Johannes Ockeghem (1497): realization by Philip Legge in 2001 see figure 2.

Dank dieser Hörstrategien, welche in gewissem Maße voneinander unabhängig sind, können wir *musikalische Invarianten* in einem Musikstück ermitteln. Der Kanon »Deo Gratia« von Johannes Ockeghem, arrangiert von Philip Legge 2006[9], kann zum Beispiel auf lineare Weise als Ansammlung von Melodien angehört werden, die sich verflechten und unterhalten (durch ihre musikalische Logik und ihre Anordnung), derselbe Kanon kann jedoch auch auf *nichtlineare* Weise angehört werden. Dann liegt der Fokus zum Beispiel auf der Invarianz der *stimmlichen Klangfarben*, die in ihrer Gesamtheit eine dichte Klangtextur erzeugen. Diese Invariante bleibt bestehen, charakterisiert das gesamte Stück und wird stets durch das kumulative Hören bestätigt.

Abbildung 2: Deo gratia

Einmal ermittelt, werden die Invarianten dann in speziell dafür erstellten Übungen zu Studiengegenständen; diese zeigen an, welche Transformationen in diesen Invarianten auf den Klang einwirken. Das Verhältnis zwischen Transformation und Klang-Invarianz bildet das Herzstück der nichtlinearen Studienmethode von Musik[10]. Die Kenntnis solcher Transformationen und das Erlernen ihres Wirkungsspektrums hinsichtlich bestimmter Invarianten erweitert unser Vermögen, Klang zu denken, zu prüfen und zu verändern. Zusammengefasst

9 | Johannes Ockeghem 1497, Realisation von Philip Legge 2001: siehe Abbildung 2.

10 | Wie wir sehen werden, nimmt die *Complete Exercise of Restitution = ECR* sich die nichtlineare Studienmethode zu Herz (nämlich das Verhältnis zwischen Transformation und Klang-Invarianz), und erstreckt sich bis zum Hören, zur Komposition und zur Improvisation.

Figure 2: Deo gratia

invariance is at the heart of the non-linear method of musical study;[10] it is the knowledge and the assimilation of valid transformations regarding certain invariances that expands our ability to think, check and change sound.

In summary by conducting listening studies on invariant features, considering the events in their autonomy and conceiving exercises that are useful at any level of learning, non-linear study places sound at the heart of its investigations. Advantages: it is creative rather than *progressive*, in other words, it tends to perceive the outcomes as the result of a sometimes unpredictable process. For this reason it does not proceed step by step. It is *qualitative* rather than cumulative-quantitative, in other words, it tends to investigate a single event and its sound quality in depth, rather than worrying about the quantity and variety of musical events. In this sense, there is greater attention paid to the sound, and listening is characterized by its specific non-linear modality. It is *non-systematic* because it does not analyze the sound events in accordance with what went before and what will come after. In this sense it is not *hierarchical*, i.e. it does not recognize the levels between knowledge and skills. It is *multi-directional*, in other words, it does not have a single goal to aim at, but rather many goals and many possible paths to reach them.

The ability to distinguish between linear and non-linear musical elements allows us to deepen the investigation around sound and enrich it with new

10 | As we will see, the Complete Exercise of Restitution is the exercise that takes the non-linear method of study to heart (the relationship between transformation and invariance of sound), and extends it to listening, to composition and to improvisation.

lässt sich sagen, dass die nichtlineare Studienmethode Klang in den Fokus ihrer Untersuchungen rückt. Dazu führt sie Hörstudien zu invarianten Elementen durch, die die Klangereignisse in ihrer Autonomie berücksichtigen, und entwirft Übungen, die in jedem Lernstadium von Nutzen sind. Vorteile der nichtlinearen Studienmethode: Es ist weniger eine *progressive* als eine kreative Methode, die ihre Ergebnisse tendenziell aus einem zeitweise unvorhersehbaren Prozess hervorgehen sieht. Aus diesem Grunde geht sie nicht schrittweise vor. Es ist eher ein *qualitativer* als ein kumulativ-quantitativer Prozess, der darauf abzielt, ein einzelnes Ereignis und dessen Klangbeschaffenheit tiefergehend zu erforschen, anstatt sich mit der Menge und Vielzahl musikalischer Ereignisse auseinanderzusetzen. In diesem Sinne wird dem Klang mehr Aufmerksamkeit gewidmet, und das Hören zeichnet sich durch seine spezifisch nichtlineare Modalität aus. Diese Methode ist *nicht-systematisch,* weil sie die Klangereignisse nicht gemäß dem analysiert, was ihnen vorausgeht und folgt. In diesem Sinne ist sie nicht *hierarchisch,* das heißt, dass die Niveauunterschiede in Kenntnissen und Fähigkeiten für sie keine Gültigkeit haben. Sie ist *multidirektional* und hat somit kein einzelnes Ziel im Visier, sondern verfolgt mehrere mögliche Wege, um mehrere Ziele zu erreichen. Die Fähigkeit, zwischen linearen und nichtlinearen musikalischen Elementen zu unterscheiden, ermöglicht es uns, die Untersuchung rund um den Klang zu vertiefen und sie mit neuen Perspektiven anzureichern. Eine dieser Perspektiven besteht in der Gelegenheit, das Unterrichten von Improvisation im Lichte der Konzepte von Linearität und Nichtlinearität zu überdenken.

Improvisation: Eine Fallstudie

Was bedeutet es, die lineare Studienmethode auf musikalische Improvisation anzuwenden? Man stelle sich eine konkrete Fallstudie vor: Die Hauptbestandteile dieser Studie bestehen darin, 1) eine Improvisation anzuhören, 2) die Improvisation zu analysieren, 3) eine neue Improvisation zu beginnen. Wir können irgendeine Improvisation nehmen, die aufgeführt und aufgenommen wurde (eine Solo- oder Kollektivimprovisation, Jazz oder jegliches andere Genre): Denken wir über eine Weise nach, diese Improvisation zu erforschen. Die folgende Grafik (siehe Abbildung 3) stellt einen linearen Ansatz für die Untersuchung solch einer Improvisation dar:

Abbildung 3: ©Mirio Cosottini

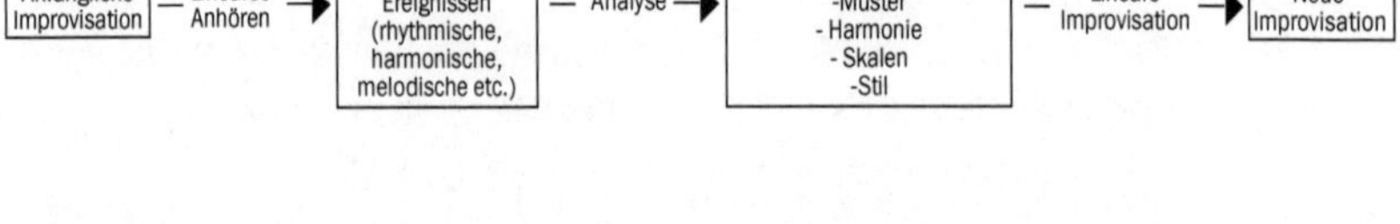

perspectives. One of these is the chance to rethink the teaching of improvisation in the light of linearity and non-linearity concepts.

Improvisation: a case study

What does it mean to apply the linear study method to musical improvisation? Imagine a concrete case study. The main steps of this study are

1. listening to an improvisation,
2. analyzing the improvisation,
3. implementing a new improvisation.

We can take any improvisation, performed and recorded (a solo, a collective improvisation, jazz or any other genre): Let us think of a way to study this improvisation. The diagram below illustrates a linear approach to the study of such an improvisation (see Figure 3):

Figure 3: ©Mirio Cosottini

The initial listening to the improvisation allows us to identify the relationship implied in the sequence of acoustic events. This is a linear type of listening because it identifies relevant relationships between events (reports, rhythmic, chordal, melody, et cetera). Then, thanks to the analysis, we can investigate these items and extract useful material for building exercises on rhythm, harmony, meter, et cetera. The results of our investigations will provide the material with which to improve our skills; then we will be able to produce a new linear improvisation. By linear improvisation I mean an improvisation based mainly on relationships between musical events in sequence rather than individual events alone.

How can we apply a non-linear method to the study of improvisation? Let us continue with the previous example, using the same improvisation.

The diagram (see Figure 4) below illustrates the application of the non-linear method to the study of such an improvisation:

Figure 4: ©Mirio Cosottini

Ein erstes Anhören der Improvisation erlaubt uns, das Beziehungssystem innerhalb der Sequenz akustischer Ereignisse zu ermitteln. Es handelt sich dabei um eine lineare Hörweise, weil sie relevante Bezüge zwischen den Ereignissen ermittelt (Beziehungen rhythmischer, akkordischer und melodischer Art). Im Anschluss können wir diese Bestandteile dann dank der Analyse untersuchen und nützliches Material zum Erstellen von Übungen zur Rhythmik, der Harmonie, des Takts et cetera entnehmen. Die Ergebnisse unserer Untersuchungen liefern das Material, mit dem wir unsere Fähigkeiten verbessern können; anschließend sind wir in der Lage, eine neue lineare Improvisation hervorzubringen. Mit dem Begriff *lineare Improvisation* beschreibe ich eine Improvisation, die in erster Linie auf den Verhältnissen zwischen musikalischen Ereignissen in ihrer Abfolge beruht anstatt lediglich auf individuellen Ereignissen.

Wie können wir eine nichtlineare Methode auf das Studium der Improvisation anwenden? Fahren wir mit der Improvisation aus dem vorigen Beispiel fort. Die folgende Grafik (siehe Abbildung 4) illustriert die Anwendung der nichtlinearen Studienmethode auf solch eine Improvisation:

Abbildung 4: ©Mirio Cosottini

Das Hören der anfänglichen Improvisation ermöglicht, Invarianten zu ermitteln, und aus diesen kann dann die neue Improvisation geschaffen werden. In diesem Falle ist das Hören kumulativ. Durch den Musiker generiert die nichtlineare Improvisation eine neue Improvisation. Mit nichtlinearer Improvisation meine ich eine Form von Improvisation, die in erster Linie auf musikalischen Ereignissen basiert, die Invarianten individuell berücksichtigt anstatt im Hinblick auf die Bezüge, die durch ihre Anordnung entstehen. Wenn das erste Hören zum Beispiel ein rhythmisches Element als Faktor zeitlicher Invarianz herausgestellt hat, dann bezieht sich die nichtlineare Improvisation in der Folge auf all diejenigen Klangfaktoren, die durch diese Invariante beeinflusst sind. Von daher hat die neue Improvisation andere musikalische Charakteristika als die vorhergehende; die rhythmischen Faktoren bleiben jedoch unverändert.

Kurzum, sowohl das Hören als auch die kreativen Prozesse unterscheiden sich also von ihren linearen Gegenstücken. Im ersten Fall hören wir darauf, wie Klangelemente untereinander in Beziehung stehen, im zweiten Fall hören wir sie auf ihren Grad an Autonomie an. Im ersten Fall führt der kreative Prozess neue Verbindungen und Beziehungen zwischen den musikalischen Elementen ein. Im zweiten Fall verändern wir die Elemente mit Rücksicht auf die Charakteristika, die konstant bleiben.

Listening to the initial improvisation leads to the identification of certain invariances, and it is thanks to these that the new improvisation can be created. Listening in this case is cumulative. Thanks to the musician, non-linear improvisation generates a new improvisation. By non-linear improvisation I mean an improvisation based primarily on musical events, invariances considered individually rather than with respect to the relationships established by their sequence. For example, if the initial listening has identified a rhythmic element as a factor of time invariance, non-linear improvisation will have to apply to all those factors of sound that are influenced by this invariance. The new improvisation will have very different musical characteristics from the previous one; however, the rhythmic factors will be invariant.

In summary (see Figure 5), both the listening and the creative processes are different to the linear ones. In the first case, we hear sound elements that are connected, in the second we listen with regard to their degree of autonomy. In the first case, the creative process establishes new connections and relationships between the musical elements. In the second, we transform the elements with respect to the characteristics which remain constant.

Figure 5: ©Mirio Cosottini

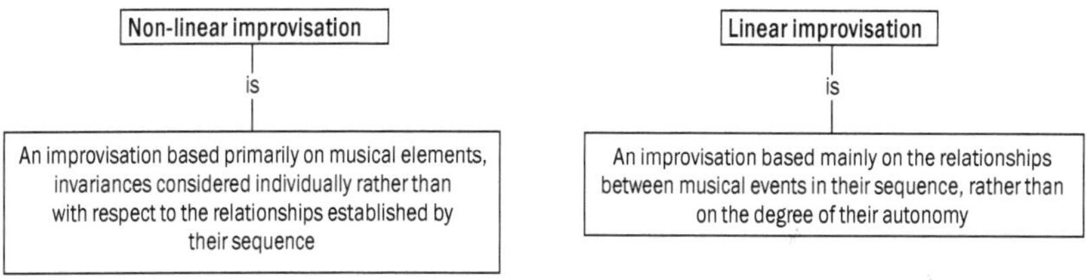

With regard to teaching improvisation, I consider it crucial to combine the linear study method with the non-linear one. This is based on the assumption that linearity and non-linearity are two co-existing and essential aspects of any musical experience. However, this goes beyond the scope of this paper.

»Complete Restitution Exercise (ECR)«[11]

The "Complete Restitution Exercise (ECR)" is the exercise that I have developed in recent years in order to apply the non-linear method of study to improvisation. It is, in fact, a system through which an unlimited number of exercises can be constructed (see figure 6).

11 | This exercise has already appeared in reduced form in Cosottini (2009).

Abbildung 5: ©Mirio Cosottini

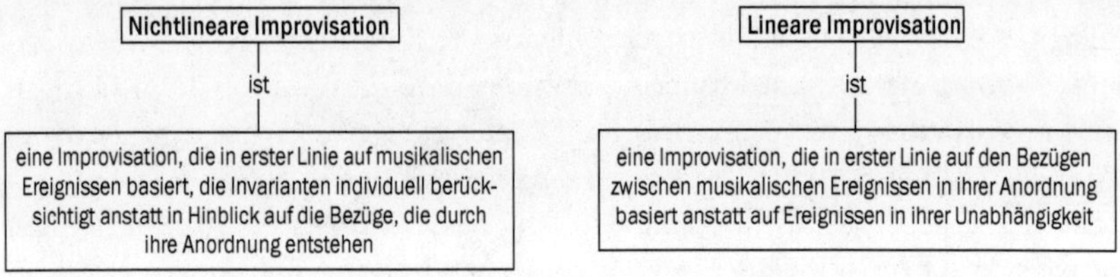

Im Improvisationsunterricht sollten beide Methoden unbedingt kombiniert werden. Dieser Ansicht liegt die Annahme zugrunde, dass Linearität und Nichtlinearität zwei nebeneinander bestehende und zentrale Aspekte jeder musikalischen Erfahrung sind. Dies führt jedoch über den Rahmen dieses Beitrags hinaus.

»Complete Restitution Exercise (ECR)«[11]

Die Übung »Complete Restitution Exercise (ECR)« habe ich in den letzten Jahren entwickelt, um die nichtlineare Studienmethode auf Improvisation anzuwenden. Es handelt sich um ein System, aus dem eine unbeschränkte Anzahl an Übungen abgeleitet werden kann (siehe Abbildung 6).

Abbildung 6: ©Mirio Cosottini

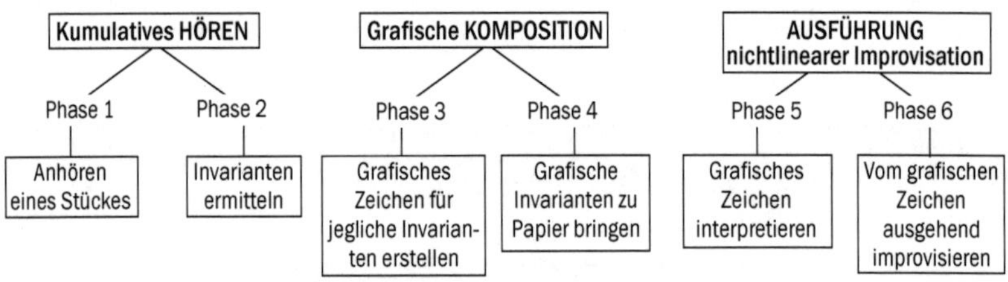

ECR baut auf den drei grundlegenden Fertigkeiten aller MusikerInnen auf: Hören, Komposition und Ausführung. Diese Fähigkeiten werden jedoch von einer ganz bestimmten Perspektive aus betrachtet: Das *Hören* stellt einen ganz bestimmten Typus dar, das *kumulative* Hören. Die *Komposition* ist auf die Verwendung des grafischen Indikators beschränkt, und die Ausführung ist auf *spezifische Symbole* für nichtlinearen Inhalt gerichtet. Daraus ergibt sich eine *nichtlineare Improvisation*, die von einem grafischen Indikator ausgeht.

ECR beginnt damit, dass das direkte Verhältnis zwischen dem Klang und seinen beständigen Merkmalen angehört und anschließend betrachtet wird.

11 | Diese Übung ist bereits in verkürzter Form in Cosottini 2009 vorgestellt worden.

Figure 6: ©Mirio Cosottini

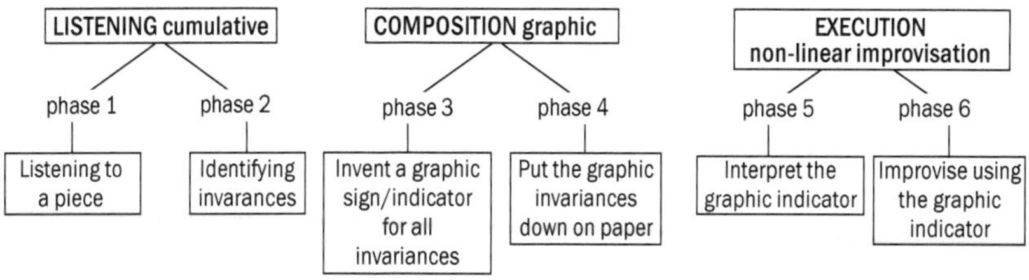

ECR is based on the three fundamental capabilities of every musician: listening, composition and execution. However, these skills are considered from a particular point of view: *Listening* is actually a special type of listening, the *cumulative* type; the *Composition* is limited to the use of the *graphic indicator;* and *Execution* is focused on *specific symbols* for non-linear content, in other words, a *non-linear improvisation* from a graphic indicator.

ECR begins with listening to and then looking at the direct relationship between the sound and its invariant features. Any piece of music can be a listening subject (phase 1), a composition or an improvisation. The listener should not focus on sound events, looking for causal relationships or sequences, rather cumulative listening must identify the invariant features of the music (phase 2). Next, we move on to the Composition, and, thanks to the use of graphic indicators, (phase 3) we can put these invariances down on paper (phase 4). Finally, during the Performance, we interpret the non-linear graphic indicators (phase 5) and execute a new non-linear improvisation.

In short, "Complete Restitution Exercise" has the characteristics of a non-linear investigation since it is based on cumulative listening, research of invariances and non-linear improvisation. It allows you to start with a piece of music which contains elements of linearity and non-linearity and to arrive at a new improvised piece after locating and "detaching" them from the original track items.

Conclusions

Music is linearity and non-linearity and, at the same time, so is musical improvisation. The study of improvisation has to take into account the contribution that it can make to the methods of linear and non-linear study. For the purpose of teaching improvisation, it is desirable to take into account both methods of study, and this tends to lead to their integration. What a linear approach allows you to acquire can, thanks to a non-linear approach, be investigated and enriched anew. Conversely, the degree of awareness of sound and its properties that characterize the non-linear approach can be enhanced, thanks to the linear approach that enables the enrichment of the discursive and narrative aspect of music.

Jedes Musikstück – eine Komposition oder eine Improvisation – kann zum Thema des Hörens werden (Phase 1). Es geht nicht darum, Klangereignisse auf der Suche nach kausalen Bezügen oder Anordnungen zu fokussieren, sondern vielmehr im kumulativen Hören die invarianten Merkmale der Musik herauszuhören (Phase 2). Als nächstes beschäftigen wir uns mit der Komposition, wobei wir – dank der Verwendung grafischer Indikatoren (Phase 3) – die Invarianten auf Papier festhalten können (Phase 4). Und schließlich folgt die Umsetzung: Wir interpretieren die nichtlinearen grafischen Indikatoren (Phase 5) und führen eine neue, nichtlineare Improvisation aus.

Kurz, eine »Complete Restitution Exercise« weist die Charakteristika einer nichtlinearen Untersuchung auf, da sie auf kumulativem Hören, der Suche nach Invarianten und nichtlinearer Improvisation basiert. Sie erlaubt, von einem Musikstück auszugehen, das Elemente von Linearität und Nichtlinearität enthält, die wir lokalisieren und aus dem ursprünglichen Kontext herauslösen können. So gelangen wir zu einem neuen improvisierten Stück.

Schlussfolgerungen

Musik ist Linearität und Nichtlinearität und dasselbe gilt für musikalische Improvisation. Das Studium der Improvisation muss seinen Beitrag zu den Methoden des linearen und nichtlinearen Studiums leisten. Wer Improvisation unterrichtet, sollte beide Studienmethoden in Betracht ziehen, wodurch sie tendenziell allmählich integriert werden. Was eine lineare Herangehensweise zu erreichen ermöglicht, kann mittels einer nichtlinearen Herangehensweise untersucht und neu angereichert werden. Umgekehrt kann das ausgeprägte Bewusstsein für Klang und seine Eigenschaften, das einen nichtlinearen Ansatz charakterisiert, durch den linearen Ansatz gesteigert werden, da dieser die diskursiven und narrativen Aspekte von Musik bereichert.

ECR reiht sich in die Übungen zum Studium nichtlinearer Improvisationsarten ein. Sie ermöglicht Lernenden, die konstant bleibenden Eigenheiten einer Musik herauszuhören, diesen einen grafischen Indikator »zuzuteilen« und dann aufs Neue zu improvisieren. Der Improvisationsprozess ist außerdem nichtlinear, weil er sich nicht dafür interessiert, musikalische Ereignisse in ihrer zeitlichen Ordnung oder ihren konstanten Beziehungen zu untersuchen, sondern eher in ihrer Autonomie.

ECR ermöglicht es Musizierenden, Improvisation zu üben und dabei mentale Blockaden zu vermeiden und Ausdrucksprobleme zu überwinden; die Übung ermöglicht angstfreie Improvisation, regt die Kreativität an und weckt Neugier auf den Klang.

Übersetzung aus dem Englischen: Solveig Raschpichler, Berlin

ECR is one of the exercises for studying non-linear types of improvisation. It allows the student to listen to the properties of the music which are constant, to "assign" them a graphic indicator and then improvise once again. The improvisation process is also non-linear because it is not interested in investigating musical events, their temporal order or their constant relationships, but rather in their autonomy.

ECR allows the musician to practice improvisation, avoiding mental blocks and overcoming problems with expression; it enables improvisation without fear, instead stimulating creativity and curiosity about the sound.

Bibliographie/Bibliography

Aebersold, Jamey (2000): Jazz Handbook, Jamey Aebersold Jazz, 11.

Bergstrøm-Nielsen, Carl (2002): Experimental Improvisation Practise and Notation 1945-1999. An annotated Bibliography. *URL: http://www.intuitive-music.dk/intuitive/cfavlit.htm*

Baker, David (1988): How to Play BeBop 1: For All Instruments, California/USA: Alfred Publishers & Co.

Bartolini, Donatella (2002): »La frammentazione del senso musicale: l'apprendimento strumentale tra linearità e complessità«, in: Anna Maria Freschi (Hrsg./Ed.): Insegnare uno strumento, Turin: EDT, 43-63.

Coker, Jerry; James Casale; Gary Campbell; Jerry Greene (1982): Patterns for Jazz, Alfred Music Publishing.

Cosottini, Mirio (2009): »Non-linearità per aprirsi all'improvvisazione musicale«, in: Musica Domani, EDT n. 151, 39-41.

Cosottini, Mirio (2010): »Studio del silenzio«, in: contesti nonlineari«, De Musica, Seminario Permanente di Filosofia della Musica. *URL: http://users.unimi.it/~gpiana/XIV/casottini.htm*

Cosottini, Mirio; Pisani, Alessio (2011): »Metodi nonlineari e improvvisazione«, in: Musica Domani, EDT, n. 158, 25-28.

Cosottini, Mirio (2013): »Five Improvisations: aspetti nonlineari di un'improvisazione«, in: Ontologie Musicali, Aisthesis, Vol 6, Special Issue, 155-172.

Delalande, François (2013): La musica è un gioco da bambini, Franco Angeli, übersetzt von G. Curti.

Gagel, Reinhard (2010): Improvisation als soziale Kunst: Überlegungen zum künstlerischen und didaktischen Umgang mit improvisatorischer Kreativität, Mainz: Schott Music.

Globokar, Vinco (1979): Individuum – Collectivum, Milano: Edizioni Unicopli.

Hearle, Dan (1983): Scale for Jazz Improvisation: A Practice Method for All Instruments, California/USA: Alfred Music.

Kramer, Jonathan (1988): The Time of Music, New York: Schirmer Books.

Mathez, Jean-Pierre (1977): Vienna Instrumental Method, Wien: Universal.

Meyer, Leonard B. (1961): Emotion and Meaning in Music, Chicago: University of Chicago Press.

Nozick, Robert (2003): Invarianze: La struttura del mondo oggettivo, Roma: Fazi Editore.

Ockeghem, Johannes (1497): »Deo gratia«, arranged by Philip Legge (2001), Choral Public Domain Library.

Prati, Walter (2010): All'improvviso: Percorsi d'improvvisazione musicale, Milano: Auditorium.

Sarath, Ed (2010): Music Theory Through Improvisation: A New Approach to Musicianship Training, London: Routledge.

Stockhausen, Karlheinz (1991): »Moment-forming and Moment«, in: Stockhausen on Music, Lectures & Interviews, New York: Marion Boyars Publishers Ltd.

Berlin 30.5.014

Konzert 2: Neumann – Phillips – Prévost – Shibolet

Andrea Neumann – Innenklavier, Elektronik
Barre Phillips (USA/F) – Kontrabass
Eddie Prévost (GB) – Perkussion, Schlagzeug
Ariel Shibolet (ISR) – Saxophon

INTERMEZZO 4

BP: Ich denke, dass die Betrachtung von Musik in einem gemeinschaftlichen Sinne – das nennen wir dann Ästhetik oder Ethik – sich verändern wird, wenn die Leute sich selbst verändern. Es ist kein bewusster Wandel: »Jetzt verändern wir uns alle«. Es kommt von innen und ist demokratisch.

EP: Der verstorbene britische Ethnomusikologe John Blacking[1] wies – mit Bezug auf seine Erfahrung von Musik in Südafrika – darauf hin, dass Musik oft eine Vorstellung davon innewohnt, in welche Richtung sich die politische Lage bewegt, bevor diese Politik sich verfestigt. Das impliziert, dass kreative Menschen oft eine Vorahnung von der Situation haben, ohne sich dessen wirklich bewusst zu sein. Genau mit diesem Gefühl des Unbekannten und der Unsicherheiten haben wir es in explorativer Musik zu tun. Dennoch ist dieses intuitive Gefühl mysteriös. Es ist eine ganz normale menschliche Reaktion. (Obwohl sie in unserer momentanen westlichen Bildungsphilosophie nicht ausreichend ermutigt wird.) Die Weise, wie wir Unsicherheiten auflösen, prägt soziale (und möglicherweise politische) Klimata.

Barre Phillips (BP) und Edwin Prévost (EP) im Podiumsgespräch, Mai 2014

Übersetzung aus dem Englischen: Solveig Raschpichler, Berlin

---

1 | Blacking, John (1995): Music, Culture and Experience, selected papers, Chicago: University of Chicago Press.

Intermezzo 4

BP: I think that the consideration of music in a group sense, which we would then call an aesthetic or an ethic, will change its own self, when the people themselves are changing. It's not a conscious change: "now we're all changing". It comes from the inside, and it's a democratic process.

EP: The (late) British ethnomusicologist John Blacking[1] – regarding his experience of music in South Africa – suggested that music very often has a sense of where things are going politically, before the politics get hardened. This implies that creative people often have a presentiment about the situation of which they are not fully aware. It is this sense of the unknown and the uncertainties we are dealing with in an exploratory music. However, this intuitive sense is mysterious. It is a very normal human reaction. (Although one not sufficiently encouraged in our current Western educational philosophy.) How we resolve uncertainties creates social (and possibly political) atmospheres.

Edwin Prévost in a public talk, May 2014

---

1 | Blacking, John (1995): Music, Culture and Experience, selected papers, Chicago: University of Chicago Press.

Rogerio Costa, Universität of Sao Paulo

- Eintauchen in den Klang oder ihn bauen?
- Technologien u. neue Arten des Hörens
- Den Klang aufbauen: die empirische Synthese instrumentaler freier Improvisation

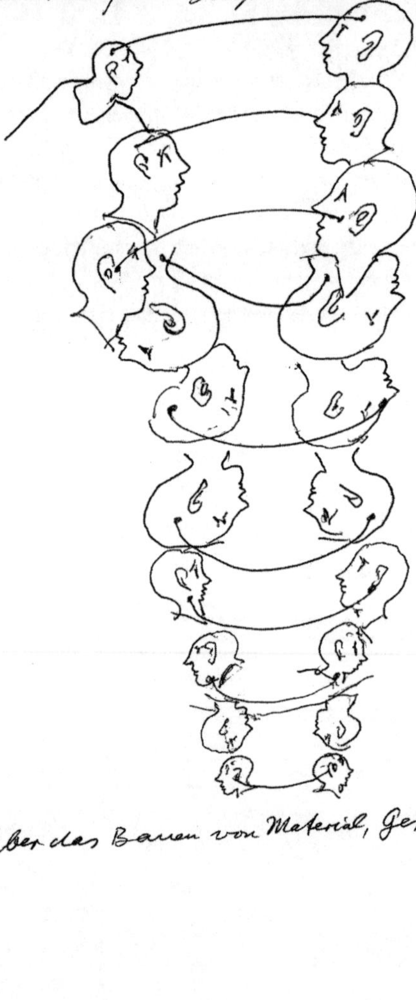

- über das Bauen von Material, Gestalt und „Sprache"

Improvisation, Klang, Körper und neue Technologien | Improvisation, Sound, Body and New Technologies

Rogério Costa

Übersicht

Dieser Artikel diskutiert das Verhältnis der Praxis freier Improvisation zu neuen Paradigmen des Hörens und zeitgenössischer Komposition, die auf der Idee basieren, Klang zu schaffen, indem die abstrakte Idee musikalischer Noten überwunden wird. In diesem Zusammenhang werden Freie Improvisation sowie die Ausweitung und Erschließung der Klangdimensionen nicht nur als Symptome verstanden, sondern auch als entscheidende Kraftfelder, die auf bestimmte Weise – genauso wie andere kreative Trends des 20. und 21. Jahrhunderts – zu den bedeutsamen Veränderungen in den Verfahrensweisen zeitgenössischer Musik beitragen. Infolge dieser Veränderungen werden die Grenzen zwischen Klang und Geräusch überwunden. In diesem Zusammenhang werden auch einige Themen aufgegriffen und diskutiert, die mit der Nutzung von Live-Elektronik zusammenhängen und das Problem von Klangcharakteristik und Körperlichkeit sowie den Aufbau geeigneter Aufführungstechniken in den Fokus nehmen.

Freie Improvisation – Definitionen

»Die Emanzipation des akustisch vorgestellten Klanges aus seiner vergleichsweise untergeordneten Funktion in der alten Musik gehört zu den Errungenschaften der musikalischen Entwicklung in unserem Jahrhundert. Anstelle der alten, tonal bezogenen, konsonanten und dissonanten Klang-Auffassung ist heute die unmittelbar empirisch-akustische Klang-Erfahrung zwar nicht in den Mittelpunkt gerückt, aber doch an den Schlüsselpunkt des musikalischen Erlebnisses.« (Lachenmann 1996: 1)

Zu allererst ist es notwendig, festzustellen, dass die sogenannte Freie Improvisation kein Stil und auch kein kompositorischer Trend ist. Vielmehr handelt es sich um eine experimentelle, empirische und kollektive musikalische Praxis, die sich nicht einer bestimmten ästhetischen Tendenz direkt verschreibt, sondern stattdessen mit verschiedenen zeitgenössischen musikalischen Verfahrensweisen im Dialog steht. Außerdem sollte darauf hingewiesen werden, dass es sich bei der freien Improvisation nicht um eine geografisch begrenzte musikalische Erscheinungsform handelt und dass sich Musiker, die sich dieser Praxis widmen, in mehreren Ländern Europas, den Vereinigten Staaten und verschiedenen lateinamerikanischen Ländern finden, einschließlich Brasiliens, das derzeit eine sehr vielfältige und aktive Szene hat. Das wichtigste Ziel der freien Improvisation ist es, kreative, interagierende und kollektive Prozesse, nicht aber abgeschlossene Werke, live zu erzeugen. Daher müssen die Kriterien zur Analyse und zum Verständnis von Improvisation andere sein als die zur Untersuchung von Kompositionen. In unserem Verständnis basiert Freie Improvisation auf

Abstract

This article discusses the relationship between the practice of free improvisation and the new paradigms of listening and contemporary composition, which are based on the idea of achieving sonority by overcoming the abstract idea of musical notes. In this context, free improvisation and the expansion and valorization of the sound dimension are perceived, not only as symptoms, but also as crucial lines of force that contribute in a specific way, along with other creative trends of the twentieth and twenty-first centuries, to the significant changes in contemporary musical practices. As a result of which, the boundaries between sound and noise are surmounted. In this context, some issues involved in the use of live electronics which focus on the issue of sonority, physicality and on the creation of appropriate performance techniques are also reported on and discussed.

Key words: free improvisation, contemporary music, aesthetics of sonority, new technologies, live electronics.

Free improvisation – definitions

"The emancipation of sound, from an acoustic perspective, which traditionally had a subordinate role in music, is an essential element in terms of the evolution of music in our century. By replacing the old sonorous concept linked to the tonal reference of consonance and dissonance, empirical and immediate experience of sound has today become, if not necessarily central to the musical experience, certainly a key part of it." (Lachenmann 2009: 36)

To begin the discussion, it is necessary to say that so-called free improvisation is not a style or a compositional trend. It is rather an experimental, empirical and collective musical practice that does not submit directly to any specific aesthetic tendency, but instead converses with a number of contemporary musical practices. It should also be pointed out that free improvisation is not a geographically constricted musical manifestation and that it is possible to find musicians who are dedicated to this type of practice in several countries in Europe, the United States and several Latin American countries, including Brazil, which currently has a very diverse and active scene. The main goal of free improvisation is to generate creative, interactional and collective processes in real time, as opposed to finished works. Therefore, the criteria for analyzing and understanding improvisation must be different from those used for composition. In our understanding, free improvisation is founded on:

a) the idea of a process through which intentional creative instrumental actions are carried out by the participating musicians;

a) der Idee eines Prozesses, in dem intentionale und kreative instrumentale Aktionen durch die teilnehmenden Musiker durchgeführt werden;
b) verstärktem Hören und Interaktion in Echtzeit der Erschließung des Klangphänomens, das als dynamischer Prozess gedacht wird, und
c) der anschließenden Eingliederung von Geräuschen (oder dem, was noch nicht als musikalisch betrachtet wird).

All diese Merkmale sind Folgen einer empirischen, experimentellen und konkreten Praxis (zeit- und ortspezifisch), die unabhängig von jeglicher vorgeformten musikalischen Sprache ist. Und da es in der freien Improvisation keine Interpreten gibt, partizipieren alle Musizierenden bewusst als kreative Künstler in einer interaktiven Praxis.

In den Klang eintauchen oder den Klang aufbauen?

»Leben innerhalb des Klanges: Leben, das auf den Klang selbst fokussiert – gelegentlich auf Kosten der Beziehungen zwischen den Klängen – oder auch Leben, das sich für die Beziehungen interessiert, die sich innerhalb des Klanges ergeben, kann dazu verleiten, den Klang als „Subjekt" zu betrachten. In diesem Fall wäre er kein Objekt, also eine geschlossene Einheit, die sich uns zur Betrachtung darbietet und die man von außen manipulieren kann: Stattdessen würden wir durch ihn bearbeitet. In diesem Sinne erweitert der Fokus auf den Klang, der in der gegenwärtigen Musik sichtbar wird, die organizistische Metapher von Musik – Musik wird als wachsende Pflanze wahrgenommen. Diese hat Teile des 19. Jahrhunderts dominiert und wird nun mit einer unerwarteten Dimension ausgestattet: Der Klang würde eine eigene „Innerlichkeit" besitzen. Im Klang zu sein, mit dem Klang zu verschmelzen, von Klang umgeben zu sein, in das Zentrum des Klanges zu reisen, in den Abgrund des Klanges zu sinken usw. werden die neuen Metaphern, die Komponisten und Zuhörer gleichsam inspirieren.« (Solomos 2012: o. S.)

Diese Metapher des Eintauchens, die der Musikologe Makis Solomos einführte, könnte auf eine gewisse Passivität hinweisen, obwohl sie gleichzeitig den konkreten, dynamischen und energetischen Aspekt von Klang im Gegensatz zum statischen und abstrakten Konzept der Note bewahrt. Um die Vorstellung von Klang als Objekt abzulehnen, wird dieser hier fast als autonomes Phänomen oder als lebende und unabhängige Einheit (als Subjekt) betrachtet, in die Musizierende oder Zuhörer »eintauchen« müssen, um ihre Abläufe zu entdecken.

In der freien Improvisation ist Klang weder Objekt noch Subjekt. Einerseits existiert Klang nicht im Voraus. Er wird während der Aufführung generiert, bearbeitet und zu einem empirischen kreativen Prozess geformt. Andererseits offenbart der Klang in ebendiesem Prozess seine Materialität, seine Trends,

b) enhanced listening and interaction in real time;
c) valorization of the sound phenomenon, in terms of it being a dynamic process, and the subsequent incorporation of noise (or what is not "yet" considered musical).

All these characteristics are consequences of an empirical, experimental and concrete practice (time and space specific) that does not rely on any pre-established musical language. Moreover, since there are no "interpreters" in free improvisation, all musicians intentionally participate as creative artists in an interactive practice.

"Diving" into sound or building sound?

"Life inside the sound: one that focuses on the sound itself, often at the expense of relationships between sounds, or one that focuses on sounds' internal relationships, can result in it being viewed as a 'subject'. In this case it would not be an object, a closed entity to be held in front of us that could be manipulated from the outside: instead, we would be worked out by it. In this sense, the focus on sound that can be seen in recent music extends the organicist metaphor - music is perceived as a growing plant - which dominated part of the nineteenth century, and provides it with an unexpected dimension: the sound would possess 'interiority'. Being in the sound, to emerge in sound, to be surrounded by sound, traveling to the center of the sound, sinking into the abyss of sound, etc. have become the new metaphors that inspire both composers and listeners." (Solomos 2012: no page reference)

This metaphor of immersion presented by musicologist Makis Solomos, despite retaining the concrete, dynamic and energetic aspect of sound, as opposed to the static and abstract concept of note, may suggest a certain passivity. In order to refute the idea of sound thought as an object, sound is presented here almost as an autonomous phenomenon or as a living and independent entity (a subject) in which the musician or listener must "dive" into, in order to discover its processes.

In free improvisation, sound is neither an object nor a subject. On the one hand, sound does not previously exist. During a performance it is generated, manipulated and molded into an empirical creative process. At the same time, during that same process, sound reveals its materiality, its trends, potentialities and internal energies that ultimately give rise to this creative process. Therefore, what we have here is a complex configuration process: sound is created and creates its ways in a dialectical assemblage with the musician who produces it.

Solomos also makes reference to this later on in the same text:

Potenziale und inneren Energien, die letztendlich diesen kreativen Prozess erschaffen. Wir finden daher einen komplexen Gestaltungsprozess vor: Klang wird erschaffen und erschafft seine Wege in einem dialektischen Zusammentreffen mit dem Musiker, der diesen erzeugt.

Solomos nimmt später im selben Text Bezug auf diese Frage:

»Von Debussy, der uns in klangliche Mikrozeit wirft, bis zu der zeitgenössischen „mikro-klanglichen" oder mikrotonalen Musik haben zahlreiche Komponisten das Bild vom Innenleben des Klanges sichtbar gemacht: Anton Webern, Varèse [...] Alois Haba, Luigi Nono, Karlheinz Stockhausen, Pierre Henry, François Bayle, Gérard Grisey, Tristan Murail, Jonathan Harvey, Horacio Vaggione, Barry Truax, Luca Francesconi, Pascale Criton [...]. Zwei Musiker, Scelsi und Xenakis, gehören jedoch zu denen, die die Metapher mit der meisten Kraft und Überzeugung realisiert haben.« (Ebd.)

In diesem Zitat bezieht sich Solomos auf Komponisten, die gewissermaßen von der Metapher des Eintauchens in den Klang geleitet waren. So betont Scelsi zum Beispiel ausdrücklich seine Reise zum Zentrum des Klanges, und dass seine Kompositionen generell aus seinen Improvisationen resultieren (mit Hilfe seiner Komponistenkollegen in Partituren geschrieben und festgehalten). Im Gegensatz dazu verfolgt Xenakis das Ziel, die Klänge und ihr Fortschreiten von Ton zu Ton durch eine Granular-Synthese aus deren kleinsten Bestandteilen aufzubauen und zu bearbeiten. Also benutzt er neben anderen Hilfsmitteln Wahrscheinlichkeitsrechnung und komplexe mathematische Operationen.

In der freien Improvisation wird der Klang als Folge von absichtsvollen, empirischen und zumeist interaktiven instrumentalen Handlungen erschaffen und bearbeitet. Dabei erfolgt das Gefühl des Eintauchens in den Klang zeitgleich mit dem Empfinden der Klangerschaffung. Wie detailreich dieser Prozess ist, variiert stark. Das bedeutet, dass die an der Aufführung teilnehmenden Musiker sich in detaillierte Prozesse, die sich einem reinen (molekularen) Klang nähern, einbringen können sowie gleichzeitig in eher molare Prozesse, abgegrenzte und identifizierbare Figuren, Gesten oder Klangfragmente von Ausdrucksweisen ins Spiel bringen. Wenn in diesem Zusammenhang elektronische Verarbeitung in Echtzeit benutzt wird, dann steigt der Komplexitätsgrad des Aufführungsumfeldes und damit auch die Möglichkeit, tiefer in reinen und deterritorialisierten Klang einzutauchen.

In diesem Sinn lässt sich sagen, dass Freie Improvisation ein komplexer Prozess ist, der bezüglich des verwendeten Materials verschiedenste Ebenen der Ausarbeitung beinhalten kann. Aber die Tatsache, dass die Musiker während einer Aufführung immer in direktem Kontakt mit der Klangproduktion in all ihrer Komplexität stehen, gibt dieser Praxis ihren spezifischen Charakter und ist verbunden mit der Idee der Körperlichkeit, die uns beispielsweise an das Konzept der *musique concrète instrumentale* von Helmut Lachenmann

"Since Debussy, which plunges us into acoustic sonorous micro time, to the contemporary 'micro sonorous' or microtonal music, numerous composers have illustrated the metaphor of the inner life of sound: Anton Webern, Varèse [...] Alois Hába, Luigi Nono, Karlheinz Stockhausen, Pierre Henry, François Bayle, Gérard Grisey, Tristan Murail, Jonathan Harvey, Horacio Vaggione, Barry Truax, Luca Francesconi, Pascale Criton [...]. However, two musicians, Scelsi and Xenakis, remain among those who have realized the metaphor with more power and conviction." (Ibid.)

In this quote, Solomos is referring to composers who were, to some extent, guided by this metaphor of diving into the sound. Scelsi, for example, explicitly mentions his journey to the center of the sound and the fact that his compositions (written and fixed in scores with the help of his Italian composers) result, in general, from his improvisations. On the other hand, Xenakis, through granular synthesis, aims to build and manipulate the sounds, and the sonorous flow from their smallest particles. Thus, to realize his compositional projects, he uses, among other resources, probabilistic numerical calculations and complex mathematical operations.

In free improvisation, construction and manipulation of sound is due to intentional, empirical and, in general, interactive instrumental acts. During free improvisation, the feeling of sound immersion is simultaneous to the sensation of sound production. The degree of detail within this process varies widely. This means that the musicians involved in performance can both engage in detailed processes, approaching a pure (molecular) sound and in more molar processes that bring into play more complex, defined and identifiable figures, gestures or sound fragments of idioms. In this context, when electronic processing is used in real time, the degree of complexity of the performance environment increases, as does the possibility of a deeper dive into pure and deterritorialized sound.

In this sense, it is possible to say that free improvisation is a complex process that can incorporate various levels of elaboration with regard to the materials used. However, the fact that in a performance the musicians are always in direct contact with making sound in all its complexity gives this practice a specific character related to the idea of physicality that reminds us, for example, of Helmut Lachenmann's concept of *musique concrète instrumentale*. This is especially so when he says that the act of composing involves the idea of building sound from an emphasis on the possible relationship of the musician with his instrument and that with regard to contemporary music, empirical and immediate experience of sound undoubtedly occupies a key position.

erinnert. Dies gilt besonders, wenn er sagt, dass der Akt des Komponierens auf der Idee beruht, Klang zu generieren, indem die mögliche Beziehung zwischen Musiker und Instrument betont wird, und dass empirische und direkte Erfahrung von Klang zweifellos eine Schlüsselposition in der zeitgenössischen Musik einnimmt.

Technologie und neue Hörweisen

Laut Gérard Grisey

»ermöglicht die Elektronik seit einigen Jahren ein mikrophones Hören von Klang. Das Innere des Klanges selbst, das jahrzehntelang von makrophonen musikalischen Verfahrensweisen verdeckt wurde, liegt endlich frei, um bewundert zu werden. Darüber hinaus ermöglicht uns der Computer zum allerersten Mal, Klangfarben-Felder zu adressieren und die Kompositionen sehr detailliert zu analysieren. Die Erschließung dieses neuartigen, erweiterten Klangfeldes, das noch unberührt ist, hat neue Hörweisen geprägt: Endlich ist es möglich, das Innere des Klanges zu erforschen, indem man seine Dauer ausdehnt und sich in verschiedenen Tempi vom Makrophonen zum Mikrophonen bewegt.« (Grisey 1991: 352)

Grisey bezieht sich hier im Besonderen auf elektronische Synthese, die für elektro-akustische Musik und instrumentale Synthese charakteristisch ist, also eines der kompositorischen Verfahren spektraler Musik (insofern sie das Klangspektrum als wichtigste Vorlage zur Komposition benutzt). Freie Improvisation bezieht sich nicht ausdrücklich auf eines dieser Verfahrensmodelle. Trotzdem verhält sich der Ansatz des bewussten, mikrophonen Hörens von Klang, das im Gegensatz zum makrophonen Hören steht, analog zum Gegensatz molekular/molar. Es eignet sich von daher perfekt als Vergleich zwischen freier Improvisation und idiomatischer Improvisation und verweist auf die schon erwähnten Konzepte von der Befreiung des Klanges und dem Eintauchen in den Klang.

Ein besonders interessanter Aspekt von Griseys Überlegungen zu kompositorischen Verfahren spektraler Musik bezieht sich auf den »Aufbau von synthetischen Klangfarben«. Der Ansatz von Grisey ist in dem folgenden Text klar definiert:

»Es ist wichtig, aus diesen mehrfachen Bearbeitungsverfahren (instrumentale Synthese) zu schlussfolgern, dass der instrumentale Ursprung zugunsten einer vollständig erfundenen synthetischen Klangfarbe verschwindet, die nicht von den Instrumenten vorgegeben ist. Tonstufe und Klangfarbe sind daher gleichzeitig vermischt und Instrumentierung im traditionellen Sinne wird zu einem veralteten Konzept.« (Grisey 1991: 353)

Technology and New Ways of Listening

According to Gérard Grisey,

"For the last few years, electronics have enabled sound to be listened to microphonically. The interior of the sound itself that was hidden for centuries due to essentially macrophonic musical practices is finally free for us to admire. Moreover, the computer allows us to address timbre fields and analyze compositions in great detail, something which was unprecedented until today. Gaining access to this new, still virgin, upgraded sound field, has determined new ways of listening: it is finally possible to explore the inside of a sound, by extending its duration and journey from the macrophonic to the microphonic via variable speeds." (Grisey 1991: 352)

Here, Grisey refers specifically to electronic synthesis, characteristic of electroacoustic music and instrumental synthesis, which is one of the compositional procedures of spectral music (in that it takes the sound spectrum as the main model for composition). Free improvisation does not explicitly relate to any of these models or procedures. However, the idea of an intentional, microphonic hearing of sound, as opposed to macrophonic listening, is analogous to molecular/molar opposition. It is thus perfectly suited to be used as a comparison between free improvisation and idiomatic improvisation, and refers to the ideas already mentioned: emancipation of sound and sound immersion.

A particularly interesting aspect of Grisey's reflections on spectral music's compositional procedures relates to the "construction of synthetic timbres." Grisey's approach is clearly defined in the following text:

"It is important to realize from these multiple treatments (instrumental synthesis) that the instrumental source disappears in favor of a completely invented synthetic timbre, rather than being given a priori by the instruments. Pitch and timbre are therefore compounded simultaneously and instrumentation in the traditional sense becomes an outdated concept." (Grisey 1991: 353)

As well as the procedures used by Xenakis on granular synthesis, the kind of compositional process (instrumental synthesis) described by Grisey, which is characteristically used in spectral music, depends on thorough and rigorous analysis and planning. In this case, the sounds synthesized by instrumental combinations result from meticulous calculations based on spectral analysis and specific formal designs of each composer. On the other hand, in electroacoustic music, obtaining the synthetic tones through additive or subtractive synthesis also depends on the software used, the type of sampling, et cetera.

Regarding the use of new technologies for analyzing or composing music, another aspect to be considered is that the immersion in sound can be

So wie die Verfahren, die Xenakis zur granularen Synthese benutzt, basiert die Art des Kompositionsprozesses, den Grisey beschreibt (die instrumentelle Synthese) und der typischerweise in der spektralen Musik Verwendung findet, auf gründlicher und rigoroser Analyse und Planung. In diesem Fall resultieren die von instrumentalen Kombinationen synthetisierten Klänge aus äußerst genauen Berechnungen auf der Grundlage spektraler Analyse und spezifischer formaler Designs jedes einzelnen Komponisten. Andererseits hängt bei elektro-akustischer Musik das Erlangen der synthetischen Töne durch additive oder subtraktive Synthese auch von der eingesetzten Software, dem Typus das Samplings und so weiter ab.

Bezüglich der Anwendung neuer Technologien zur Analyse oder Komposition von Musik ist ein weiterer Aspekt zu berücksichtigen: Sie erlauben nämlich ein tieferes detaillierteres Eintauchen in den Klang. Da die Komposition in rein elektro-akustischer Musik (sowohl bei der Klangverarbeitung als auch im Synthetisierungsprozess) zeitversetzt erfolgt, unterscheidet sich diese von der freien Improvisation, bei der elektronische Verarbeitung in Echtzeit erfolgt. Der Grund dafür ist, dass die in der freien Improvisation für Echtzeitbearbeitung eingesetzten Softwares (MAX, PD und andere) noch immer nicht in der Lage sind, die technische Qualität (Samplingquote, Geschwindigkeit und so weiter) eines zeitversetzten Synthese- beziehungsweise Verarbeitungsprogramms zu erreichen. Daher kann man sich bei komponierter elektro-akustischer Musik tiefergehend mit den molekularen Klangdetails befassen (sowohl den ursprünglichen und konkreten als auch den synthetisierten). Trotzdem ändert das bei der Freien Improvisation nichts an der grundlegenden Veränderung, die im Paradigma des Hörens laut Grisey stattgefunden hat: »Das Innere des Klanges selbst, das jahrzehntelang von makrophonen Musikpraxen verdeckt wurde, liegt endlich frei, um bewundert zu werden.« (Grisey 1991: 252)

Den Klang aufbauen: Die empirische Synthese instrumentaler freier Improvisation

In der freien Improvisation erreicht man so etwas wie eine instrumentale Synthese letztlich durch empirische Verfahren während der Aufführung. Und unter diesem Aspekt ist die Freie Improvisation, wie wir gesehen haben, der spektralen Musik sehr ähnlich. Trotzdem bleiben eine »synthetische« Klangfarbe oder »synthetischer« Klang in der freien Improvisation immer eine Entdeckung, ein Ergebnis der konkreten Interaktion der Performenden. Dies ist der Fall, weil die sich ständig ändernden Ergebnisse der Aufführung unvorhersehbar sind, denn in der kollektiven Performance ist das Unerwartete und das Unkontrollierbare Teil des Umfeldes.

deemed to be deeper (in the sense of detail). Pure electroacoustic music is different from free improvisation with electronic processing in real time, due to the use of the composition in deferred time (both in the processing of sounds and the synthesis processes). This is because the software used in free improvisation for real-time processing (MAX, PD, and others) still falls short of the technical quality (sampling rate, speed, etc.) of a synthesis or processing program in deferred time. Therefore, in composed electroacoustic music, it is possible to address the molecular details of sound (both pre-existing and concrete, as well as the synthesized ones) in a more profound way. However, in free improvisation, this does not affect the fundamental change that takes place in the paradigm of listening as quoted by Grisey at the beginning of his text: "The interior of sound itself, that which was hidden for many centuries of musical practice, i.e. essentially macrophonic, is finally free for our appreciation." (Grisey 1991: 252)

Building the Sound: The Empirical Synthesis of Instrumental Free Improvisation

In free improvisation, a sort of instrumental synthesis is eventually achieved by empirical means during the performance. In this respect, as we have seen, free improvisation is similar to spectral music. However, in free improvisation, "synthetic" timbre or sound is always a discovery, a result of the empirical interaction between the performers. This is because the ever-changing results of the performance are unpredictable, since in collective performance the unexpected and uncontrollable are part of the environment.

However, free improvisation is not limited to this type of procedure which is based only on microphonic sound, as the gestural and figural material that permeates the performances is often, by its very nature, macrophonic. This means that free improvisation, as already explained above, not only works with microscopic, molecular and essential materials (such as in sine wave or granular synthesis), but also with molar materials which originate in idioms or systems of organization (such as tonality). During the performance they are reworked, fragmented and transformed into various elements (sometimes even very close to a molecular level).

This is because the sound of acoustic instruments is too complex to be considered molecular and the empirical combination of the various instruments in an improvisational performance can result both:

a) in relatively homogeneous flows, which are compact and cohesive, and where individual instrument sounds vanish in favor of a new timbre, thus merging into a real instrumental synthesis, where, as Grisey would say, "the in-

Freie Improvisation ist jedoch nicht auf diese Verfahrensweise begrenzt, die sich nur auf mikrophonen Klang stützt, denn das gestische und figürliche Material, das in die Performance einfließt, ist oft von Natur aus makrophon. Das bedeutet, dass Freie Improvisation, wie bereits erklärt, nicht nur mit mikroskopischen, molekularen und wesentlichen Materialien funktioniert (wie in der abgeschnittenen Sinuskurve oder in der granularen Synthese), sondern auch mit molaren Materialien, die aus Idiomen oder Organisationssystemen (wie zum Beispiel Tonalität) stammen. Diese Materialien werden während der Aufführung umgearbeitet, fragmentiert und in verschiedene Elemente transformiert (manchmal sogar fast bis in die molekulare Ebene).

Dies liegt daran, dass der Klang der akustischen Instrumente zu komplex ist, um als molekular zu gelten, und die empirische Kombination der verschiedenen Instrumente in einer Improvisationsperformance zwei Folgen haben kann:

a) einen relativ gleichbleibenden Fluss, dicht und geschlossen, wo individuelle instrumentale Klänge zugunsten einer neuen Klangfarbe in den Hintergrund treten und so in einer echten instrumentalen Synthese verschmelzen, in der, wie Grisey sagen würde, »der instrumentale Ursprung zugunsten einer vollständig erfundenen synthetischen Klangfarbe verschwindet, die nicht von den Instrumenten vorgegeben war« (Grisey 1991: 253);
b) heterogene Strukturen, die klar aufgeteilt sind und in denen die Klangfarben der Instrumente kenntlich bleiben, die ihre Molarität und spezifische Territorialität in Erinnerung rufen. Natürlich bilden diese beiden Beispiele Extreme, ideale Punkte in der Abstufung von molekular zu molar.

Dass die Instrumente territorialisiert sind, ist für die Freie Improvisation nicht unbedingt ein Problem, da sie einen Raum musikalischen Denkens und Handelns erschafft, in dem das Entscheidende die Kontinuität des interaktiven Klangflusses ist, der sich metaphorisch auf die Konzepte von Spiel und Konversation stützt. Natürlich kann das Überwinden des Idiomatischen, Molaren, Makrophonen und das Suchen nach dem molekularisierten Klang, das durch erweiterte Techniken und ein tiefes, reduziertes und mikrophones Hören umgesetzt wird (siehe Pierre Schaeffer, Pauline Oliveros et cetera), eine wichtige Strategie sein, um die Wucht und Beständigkeit des akustischen Flusses zu erhalten. Aber es ist möglich, das gleiche Ergebnis mit Hilfe anderer Strategien der Deterritorialisierung, Reterritorialisierung, Collage und Bricollage zu erhalten. Diese werden durch klare makrophone Materialien (molar und territorialisiert) gestützt. Also kann sich, selbst wenn die Klangfarben der Instrumente erkennbar bleiben und sie den Bezug zu ihrer Territorialität aufrecht erhalten, das dynamische Ergebnis des Klangflusses richtig und mit vitaler Energie entfalten.

strumental source disappears in favor of a completely invented synthetic timbre rather than being given a priori by the instruments." (Grisey 1991: 253);

b) in heterogeneous textures, which are clearly segmented, where the timbres of the instruments remain identifiable, evoking their molarities and specific territoriality. These two extreme examples represent ideal limits of gradations ranging from the molecular to the molar.

Therefore, the fact that the instruments are territorialized is not necessarily problematic for free improvisation, as it builds an environment of musical thought and action, where what matters is the continuity of interactive sound flow, which is metaphorically based on the ideas of game and conversation. Of course, overcoming the idiomatic, molar and macrophonic, and searching for molecularized sound – implemented through extended techniques and deep, reduced and microphonic hearing (to quote Pierre Schaeffer, Pauline Oliveros, et cetera) – can be an important strategy for maintaining power and consistency of interactive sonic flow. However, it is possible to achieve this same result through other strategies, such as deterritorialization, reterritorialization, collage and bricollage. These are supported by clearly macrophonic materials (molar and territorialized). Thus, even when the timbres of the instruments remain identifiable and related to their territoriality, the dynamic result of sound flow can unfold properly and with vital energy.

In musical practice that is based on sound and aims to achieve molecularization and deterritorialization, even strongly territorialized instruments (such as traditional and folk instruments) can be addressed in a renewed way. Regarding this meticulous work of deconstruction and reconstruction of the usual sound of instruments, it is worth quoting again the composer Helmut Lachenmann (here cited by Didier Guigue):

"I speak sometimes of a new virginity of sound: the sound as a conventional experience, as a known element, always comes tainted, loaded with conventions and ultimately, impure. The work of the composer is to create a context that can remain intact; intact in terms of a new aspect; untangling that which was exposed to the surface to bring light to that which was hidden, thus allowing a purer experience. This does not only mean to do something, but rather to always avoid and resist." (Guigue 2007: 94)

Nevertheless, regarding this idea of deterritorialization of sound, we must clarify that the idea of molecularization and microphonic hearing does not necessarily produce music of homogeneous textures or music which is based on metaphors of sound phenomena, such as the idea of dynamic or spectral envelope, et cetera Microphonic hearing simply opens the way to music that is based on the construction, manipulation and transformation of sound but not submitted to the abstract logic of the note. In this context, for example, the

Man kann sich in musikalischer Praxis, die auf Klang basiert und auf Molekularisierung und Deterritorialisierung abzielt, mit stark territorialisierten Instrumenten (wie traditionelle und volkstümliche Instrumente) auf neue Weise befassen. Zu dieser akribischen Arbeit der Dekonstruktion und Rekonstruktion des normalen Klanges von Instrumenten ist es sinnvoll, noch einmal den Komponisten Helmut Lachenmann zu zitieren (zitiert nach Didier Guigue):

> »Ich spreche manchmal von einer neuen Unberührtheit von Klang: Der Klang als konventionelle Erfahrung, als bekannter Bestandteil, begegnet uns immer als unrein, mit Konventionen beladen und letztendlich schmutzig. Die Arbeit des Komponisten ist es, ein Umfeld zu schaffen, das unversehrt bleiben kann, unversehrt unter einem neuen Aspekt. Zu entwirren, was der Oberfläche ausgesetzt war, um ans Licht zu bringen, was versteckt war, und so eine reinere Erfahrung zu ermöglichen. Und das bedeutet nicht nur etwas zu tun, sondern immer zu vermeiden und zu widerstehen.« (Guigue 2007: 94)

Bezüglich dieser Idee einer Deterritorialisierung des Klanges müssen wir trotzdem klarstellen, dass die Idee von Molekularisierung und mikrophonem Hören nicht notwendigerweise Musik produziert, die homogene Strukturen aufweist oder auf Metaphern von Klangphänomenen basiert, wie zum Beispiel dem Konzept der dynamischen oder spektralen Hüllkurve. Das mikrophone Hören öffnet einfach nur den Zugang zu Musik, die auf der Konstruktion, Manipulation und Transformation von Klang basiert, sich aber nicht der abstrakten Logik der Note unterworfen hat. In diesem Zusammenhang entsteht zum Beispiel die Faszination für die Eigenschaften der konkreten Klänge und/oder die Lust, neue Klänge zu erschaffen und sie in Klangobjekten, Oberflächen und neuen Strukturen zu vereinen. In diesem Zusammenhang ist es möglich, in der freien Improvisation ursprünglich molare Materialien (Fragmente idiomatischer Gesten) zu verwenden, vorausgesetzt sie unterlaufen den Prozess der Deterritorialisierung und Molekularisierung.

Daher muss ergänzt werden, dass Freie Improvisation nicht vollständig oder ausschließlich von dem Konzept des Klanges getragen wird, aber sicherlich das Idiomatische überwindet, indem sie letztlich Fragmente ihres Materials und Verfahrens integriert und diese als wirkende Kräfte einsetzt. Das Vokabular (Klangmaterial) und die Syntax (organisatorische Verfahren) wohnen freier Improvisation inne, und das Klangmaterial kann darin mehr oder weniger mikroskopisch (molekular) sein. Außerdem ist es wichtig, die dynamischen und verfahrenstechnischen Dimensionen der Anordnungen zu betonen. Improvisation leistet einen Beitrag zu Bewusstwerdungsprozessen von Klangeigenschaften und deren Möglichkeiten, generiert, manipuliert und kontrolliert zu werden.

fascination with the qualities of concrete sounds and/or the desire to create new sounds and compound them into objects, textures and new structures arises. In this context, it is possible to use materials that were originally molars (fragments of idiomatic gestures) in free improvisation, provided they undergo the process of deterritorialization and molecularization.

Therefore, it must be said that free improvisation is not supported fully or exclusively by the idea of sound, but that it surely surmounts idioms, eventually integrating fragments of its materials and procedures and incorporating them as one of its possible agents. In free improvisation, the "vocabulary" (sound material) and the "syntax" (organizational procedures) are immanent and these sound materials may be more or less microscopic (molecular). It is also important to emphasize the procedural and dynamic dimension of these assemblages. In any case, improvisation contributes to the processes of becoming aware of the concept of material and the possibility of this being created, manipulated and controlled.

"That is why the material proliferates or, more accurately, everything tends to become material. Tonal music perceived control as domination, and, for this reason, its material, which was 'watched closely' was very limited. By contrast, in the twentieth century, control of the material was synonymous with its proliferation. Adorno writes that 'The release of the material increases the possibility of it being technically controlled at the same time.' This proposal was reversed: refocusing on the material. The wealth of twentieth century music materials did not arise from a simple search for renewal in which materials would continue to be treated as in the past (that is, via a rule such as language or syntax). This refocusing resulted in an acute awareness of the concept of material and the possibility of it being controlled." (Solomos 2013: 285)

On building the material, the shape and the "language"

Also with respect to the question of material, it is possible to say that, as much as in other musical manifestations of the same period of history, in free improvisation:

"[...] material is not sound matter: it is not given by nature; it tends to be entirely composed and constructed. This is certainly the case with electronic music that makes use of synthesis of sound. However, it is also the case with 'advanced instrumental music' where the sound matter (natural sound) that is produced by the instruments, is not a material but simply a starting point that the latter (the material) transmutes." (Ibid.)

This is exactly what happens in free improvisation: sound – sound matter – produced by the instruments (from the most territorialized to the most molecular-

»Darum verbreitet sich das Material stark oder, genauer gesagt, alles tendiert dahin, Material zu werden. Tonale Musik begriff Kontrolle als Beherrschung und darum war ihr Material, »stark überwacht«, sehr begrenzt. Im Gegensatz dazu war die Kontrolle von Material im 20. Jahrhundert gleichbedeutend mit seiner Verbreitung. ›Mit der Befreiung des Materials‹, schreibt Adorno, ›steigt gleichzeitig die Möglichkeit, technisch kontrolliert zu werden.‹ Dieser Vorschlag wurde durch die Neuausrichtung auf das Material umgekehrt. Der Reichtum des musikalischen Materials des 20. Jahrhunderts entstand nicht aus einer schlichten Suche nach Erneuerung, in der die Materialien weiter wie in der Vergangenheit bearbeitet würden (durch eine Sprache oder Syntax, also eine Vorschrift). Stattdessen resultierte diese Neuausrichtung in einem akuten Bewusstsein des Konzeptes des Materials und der Möglichkeit, es zu kontrollieren.« (Solomos 2013: 285)

Über den Aufbau des Materials, der Form und der Sprache

In Bezug auf die Frage des Materials lässt sich auch sagen, dass so wie in anderen musikalischen Erscheinungsformen derselben historischen Periode in der freien Improvisation:

»[...] Material nicht mehr die Klangsubstanz ist: Es ist nicht naturgegeben, stattdessen neigt es dazu, vollständig komponiert und konstruiert zu sein. Dies ist zweifellos bei der elektronischen Musik der Fall, welche die Klang-Synthese nutzt. Aber es ist auch bei der Instrumentalmusik mit erweiterten Spieltechniken der Fall, wo die den Instrumenten eigene Klangsubstanz (ihr natürlicher Klang) nicht auch das Material ist, sondern lediglich einen Ausgangspunkt bildet, der vom Letzteren (dem Material) umgewandelt wird.« (Ebd.)

Genau das passiert in der freien Improvisation: Klang – Klangsubstanz – von Instrumenten produziert (von den am stärksten territorialisierten bis zu den am stärksten molekularisierten, von den unpassendsten, lauten und komplexen bis zu den „saubereren“, harmonischen, fast sinusförmigen) wird während der Aufführung in Material verwandelt. In diesem Fall, wie Solomos konstatiert:

»[...] ist das Material nicht länger die Grundlage des musikalischen Aufbaus. Vollständig komponiert kann es nicht unbedingt von anderen Entwicklungsstufen von Sprache und Form unterschieden werden, welche in der tonalen Musik als Charakteristika des Aufbaus anerkannt waren [...]. Die Neuausrichtung auf das Material und seine Erweiterung bedeutet nicht, dass Sprache und Form verschwinden, sondern dass sie allmählich aufhören, von der materiellen Ebene unterscheidbar zu sein.« (Ebd.)

ized, from the most incongruous, noisy and complex to the "cleaner", harmonious, almost sinusoidal) is transmuted into material during the performance. In this case, as Solomos states:

"[...] the material is no longer the basis of musical building. Entirely composed, it cannot necessarily be distinguished from the other stages of language and form, which tonal music used to recognize as the characteristics of building [...] refocusing on the material and its proliferation does not mean that the language or form disappear but rather they gradually cease to be distinguishable from the material level." (Ibid.)

Thus, in this sense, the idea that the shape is formed from the inside out, as in a biomorphic metaphor, is appropriate to describe both the compositions, which Solomos referred to as "advanced", as improvisation performances. In free improvisation the situation is even more extreme because the material does not exist as such (there are no pre-prepared materials). It is constructed; composed from the interventions of the performers in real time. Furthermore, it is the interactive and experiential process that brings these materials that shape the sound stream into play. Therefore, any sound matter produced by a musician (be it a sound, a figure, a texture or a gesture), only acquires its musical "sense" in the interactive flow of the performance that outlines a form. Moreover, in this sense, it can be said that in free improvisation the "vocabulary" (sound material) and the "syntax" (organizational procedures) are immanent.

Free Improvisation and New Technologies: Hybrid Machines

Let us now examine the use of electronic processes in real time in free improvisation performances. In this context, a musician who uses an acoustic instrument and electronic processing in real time is responsible for a kind of "hybrid machine (acoustic and digital) of creative performance" that can be summarized in the following formula:

... musician + acoustic instrument + digital instrument (microphone + interfaces + computer + patch + speakers) + performance environment = ...

In this "machine" there is a complex coupling. In the case of the acoustic instrument, according to Aden Edens, cited by Thor Magnusson (Magnusson 2009: 168), "the instrument becomes an extension of the body, and trained musicians are, through incorporated knowledge that is primarily non-conceptual and tacit, able to express themselves through this". In the case of digital instruments there is another type of relationship that could be designated as hermeneutic:

Daher ist der Gedanke angemessen, dass die Form in diesem Sinne von innen heraus biomorph gebildet wird, um sowohl die Kompositionen, die Solomos als »erweitert« bezeichnet, als auch Improvisationsperformances zu beschreiben. In der freien Improvisation ist die Situation sogar noch extremer, weil das Material als solches nicht existiert (es gibt kein vorbereitetes Material). Es wird konstruiert und von Performenden durch ihre Interventionen in Echtzeit komponiert. Darüber hinaus ist es der interaktive und auf Erfahrung basierende Prozess selbst, der diese Materialien, die den Klangfluss formen, ins Spiel bringt. Also erwirbt jede Klangsubstanz, die von einem Musiker produziert wurde (sei es ein Klang, eine Figur, eine Struktur oder eine Geste), ihren musikalischen »Sinn« im interaktiven Fluss der Performance, der ihre Form umreißt. Und in diesem Sinne kann gesagt werden, dass in der freien Improvisation das »Vokabular« (Klangmaterial) und die »Syntax« (organisatorische Vorgehensweisen) immanent sind.

Freie Improvisation und neue Technologien: Hybride Maschinen

Lassen Sie uns jetzt die Verwendung elektronischer Prozesse in Echtzeit bei Aufführungen der freien Improvisation untersuchen. In diesem Zusammenhang ist der Musiker, der ein akustisches Instrument und elektronische Verarbeitung in Echtzeit anwendet, verantwortlich für so etwas wie eine »hybride Maschine (akustisch und digital) der kreativen Performance«, die in folgender Formel zusammengefasst werden kann:

... Musiker + akustisches Instrument + digitales Instrument (Mikrophon + Interfaces + Computer + Patch + Lautsprecher) + Umfeld der Performance = ...

In dieser »Maschine« gibt es eine komplexe Verkupplung. Denn in dem Fall des akustischen Instrumentes »wird das Instrument zu einer Erweiterung des Körpers, durch welche ausgebildete Musiker in der Lage sind, sich selbst durch eingearbeitetes Wissen, das hauptsächlich nicht-konzeptionell und implizit ist, auszudrücken«, so Aden Edens, wie er von Thor Magnusson (Magnusson 2009: 168) zitiert wird. Im Fall des digitalen Instruments besteht eine andere Art von Verhältnis, das als hermeneutisch bezeichnet werden könnte:

»[...] das hermeneutische Verhältnis unterscheidet sich in dem Sinn, dass hier das Instrument nicht eine Erweiterung des Körpers darstellt, sondern dass es vielmehr ein dem Körper äußerliches Werkzeug ist, dessen Informationen wir interpretieren müssen (daher hermeneutisch). Dieses Instrument kann als Text betrachtet werden, etwas, das wir lesen müssen, wenn wir es verwenden [...]. Im Gegensatz zum Körper des akustischen

"[...] the hermeneutic relationship differs in the sense that here the instrument is not an extension of the body, but rather a tool external to the body whose information we have to interpret (thus hermeneutic). This instrument can be seen as a text, something we have to read during our use of it [...] As opposed to the body of the acoustic instrument, the digital instrument does not resonate; it contains few latent mysteries and holds little hidden expressive potential that can typically be derived from the materiality of the acoustic." (Ibid.)

In order to reflect on the above issues from a practical perspective, I shall describe, review and analyze an environment prepared for free soloist improvisation performances and which incorporates electronic processing in real time. Reflections on the operation of this acoustic-digital coupling can also be found here, both on a more specialized level, with regard to the technologies involved, and at the level of physicality, with regard to the preparation of an "instrumental" technique specific and appropriate to the functioning of this "hybrid performance machine".

Brane~: technical features

Brane~ is the name of the patch developed in Pure Data[1] (PD) by Alexandre Porres[2] that I have used in my free improvisation solo saxophone performances (see figure 1). Here are some informal notes on the patch features that are controlled through a midi pedal like this (see figure 2):

Pedal number:

1. Total reset of sound processing.
2. Record.
3. Stop recording.
4. Play/stop playing.

1 | Pure Data is a programming environment in which it is possible to structure applications (patches) for electronic interaction in real time. From a broader viewpoint, it is a graphical programming environment for audio and video which is used as the interactive composition environment, as a synthesizing station and as a live audio processing environment. It was originally developed by Miller Puckette and, because it is an open source project, there are a large amount of developers working on extensions to the program.

2 | Alexandre Porres. Musician, composer and researcher, has a master's degree in Composition/Creative Processes at UNICAMP (2008) and a PhD in the area of Sonology/Computer Music at USP. He was a researcher in CIRMMT/McGill in 2010. Areas of Interest:
- Creation, Performance and Improvisation in Contemporary Music and New Media
- Music and Technology (Production Sonora, Computer Music and Electroacoustic Music)
- Sound Perception (Source: Lattes platform).

Instruments hallt das digitale Instrument nicht nach, es enthält nur wenige verborgene Mysterien und wenig verstecktes Ausdruckspotential, welches üblicherweise aus der Materialität des Akustischen abgeleitet werden kann.« (Ebd.)

Um die obigen Themen aus einer praxisnahen Perspektive zu reflektieren, werde ich ein Umfeld für solistische Improvisationsaufführungen, die elektronische Verarbeitung in Echtzeit beinhalten, beschreiben, prüfen und analysieren. Hier finden sich auch Reflexionen zum Ablauf dieser akustisch-digitalen Verkupplung. Diese Reflexionen erfolgen zum einen auf einer auf die beteiligten Technologien spezialisierten Ebene; und zum anderen auf der Ebene der Körperlichkeit im Hinblick auf die Bereitstellungen einer »instrumentalen« Technik, die speziell auf das Funktionieren dieser »hybriden Performance-Maschine« ausgerichtet ist.

Brane~: Technische Merkmale

Brane~ ist der Name des Patches, das für Pure Data[1] (PD) von Alexandre Porres[2] entwickelt wurde (siehe Abbildung 1) und das ich für meine Improvisations-Soloauftritte mit dem Saxophon benutzt habe. Hier sind einige informelle Kommentare zu den Funktionen des Patches, die durch eine Midi Fußleiste wie diese bedient werden (siehe Abbildung 2):

Pedal Nummer:
1. Komplettrückstellung der Klangverarbeitung
2. Aufnahme
3. Aufnahme beenden
4. Wiedergabe/Wiedergabe stoppen

---

1 | Pure Data ist eine Entwicklungsumgebung, mit deren Hilfe Applikationen (Patches) für elektronische Interaktion in Echtzeit strukturiert werden können. Aus einem größeren Blickwinkel betrachtet, ist es eine grafische Entwicklungsumgebung für Audio und Video, die als interaktive Kompositionsumgebung, als Synthetisierstation und Echtzeit-Audio-Verarbeitung benutzt wird. Ursprünglich war sie von Miller Puckette entwickelt worden. Weil es ein Open Source Projekt ist, gibt es einen großen Pool von Entwicklern, die an Erweiterungen des Programms arbeiten.

2 | Alexandre Porres, Musiker, Komponist und Forscher erwarb 2008 einen Master in Komposition/kreative Prozesse an der UNICAMP und einen Doktortitel im Feld Sonologie/Computer Musik an der USP. 2010 war er Forscher am CIRMMT/Mc Gill. Interessensgebiete: Kreation, Performance und Improvisation in der zeitgenössischen Musik und in den Neuen Medien – Musik und Technologie (Produktion Sonora, Computer Musik und Elektroakustische Musik) – Klangwahrnehmung (Quelle: Lattes platfom).

5. Playback from beginning of buffer.
6. Total reset of sound processing (almost identical to pedal 1, the only difference is that after it is activated, playback will proceed without stopping at the buffer limit).
7. Reverse playback direction.
8. Freeze playback.
9. Harmonize 1.
10. Harmonize 2.

Figure 1: Brane~ on the computer screen. ©Rogério Costa

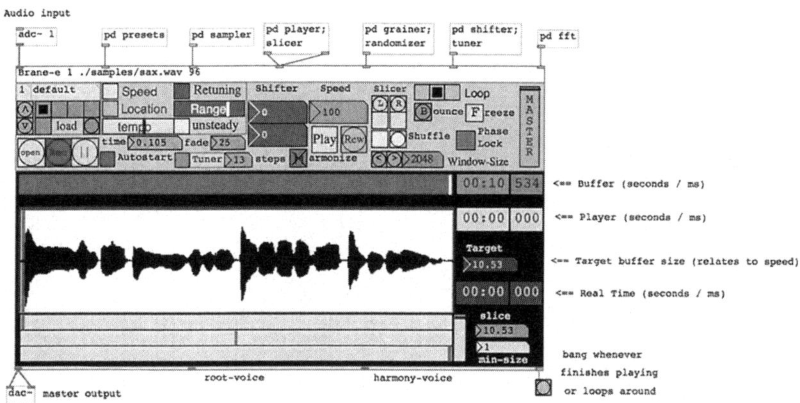

Figure 2: Midi pedal. ©Rogério Costa

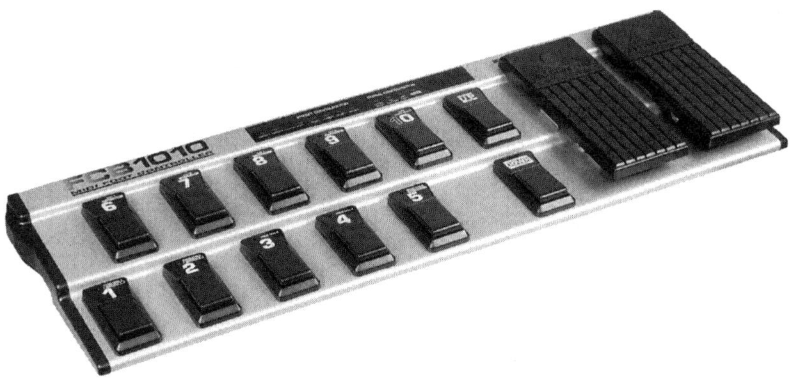

Other features in addition to those described above, which are operated by the expression pedal (the right side of the equipment) and which can be applied to the reproduction of samples, are:

5. Wiedergabe ab Anfang des Zwischenspeichers
6. Komplettrückstellung der Klangverarbeitung (fast identisch mit Pedal 1 mit dem einzigen Unterschied: nach dem Aktivieren fährt die Wiedergabe fort, ohne am Limit der Zwischenspeicherkapazität zu stoppen)
7. Wiedergabe rückwärts spielen
8. Pause
9. Harmonieren 1
10. Harmonieren 2

Abbildung 1: Brane~ auf dem Computerbildschirm. ©Rogério Costa

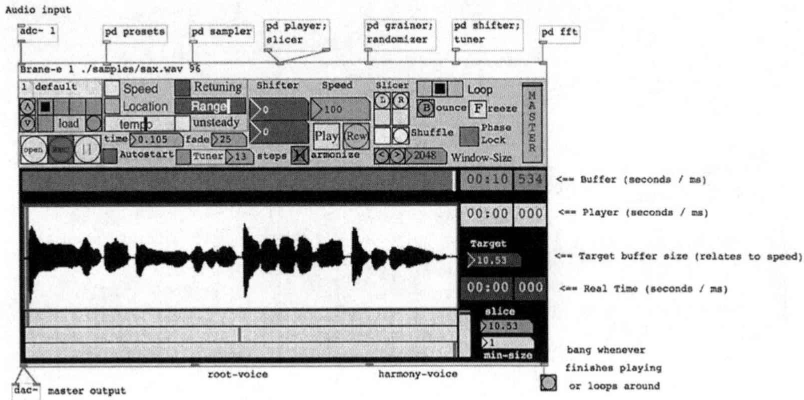

Abbildung 2: Midi Fußleiste. ©Rogério Costa

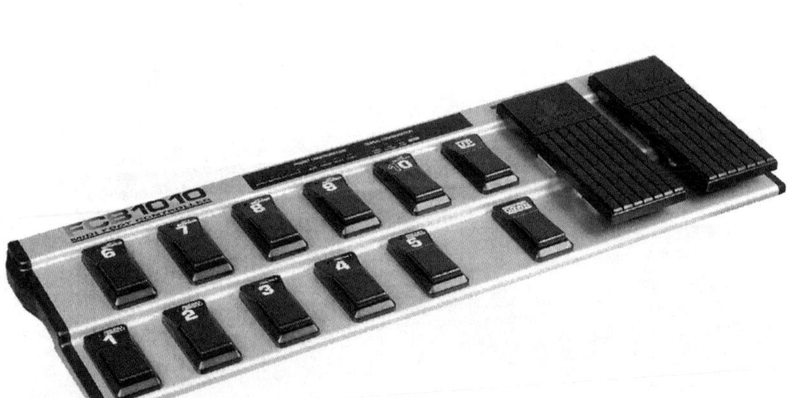

Neben den oben beschriebenen gibt es folgende weitere Funktionen, die durch die Expression Pedale (rechte Seite des Gerätes) bedient werden und zur Wiedergabe der Samples benutzt werden können:

a) transpositions and glissandos;
b) changes of speed and direction. There are also many possible combinations of processes such as: 1. triggering the freeze pedal (freezing playback) at a point on the sample and applying glissandos and/or transposition to the resulting sound; 2. reproducing the sample from a given point and applying different processing during playback (glissandos, transpositions, speed changes, harmonization, et cetera);
c) applying a loop in a fragment of the recorded sample (for this, the musician must stop playing and work directly with the mouse in the gray bar at the bottom of the patch image on the screen). It is also possible to create a contrapuntal texture with recorded and reproduced material and live performance, or by deleting the sample and starting the recording again.

Specific techniques for performances with live electronics

First of all, the performer must develop a specific technique that incorporates the use of the pedal and enables processing control during the performance. What is more, this technique can only be developed by practicing, through rehearsals and performances. Therefore, it is necessary to study this new hybrid instrument in order to simultaneously manage traditional and extended acoustic instrument techniques – linked to the idea of pure physicality – and the hermeneutic relationship with the digital instrument. In the latter case, it is necessary to understand how the electronic processing implemented by the patch in PD works and its relationship to physical actions on the pedal.

This learning ranges from very basic knowledge, such as knowing the functions of the various pedal commands to being able to control them competently with the feet in order to combine them creatively with instrumental actions. Controlling the electronic processes using the pedal generates a new body dimension, adding to the physicality present in an instrumental performance. In my experience with this "hybrid machine performance", I have endeavored to create a specific technique that allows me to go deeper into the sound flow construction processes through interaction between the instrumental techniques with electronic devices. To the extent that I can record and transform the saxophone sounds in real time, I can also invent, construct and empirically combine the sounds in an interactive process, from the inside out, molecularly. As a result, I am able to expand my sonorous repertoire from the limited universe of sounds that can be produced by the saxophone. As such, I have at hand a kind of super-saxophone synthesizer.

a) Transpositionen und Glissandi;
b) Veränderungen von Geschwindigkeit und Richtung. Es gibt auch viele mögliche Prozesskombinationen wie 1. Pausetaste auslösen (Pause der Wiedergabe) an einem Punkt im Sample und Glissandi und/oder Transpositionen an dem resultierenden Klang anwenden; 2. das Sample ab einem gegebenen Punkt wiederholen und unterschiedliche Verarbeitungsweisen während der Wiedergabe anwenden (Glissandi, Transpositionen, Veränderungen der Geschwindigkeit, Harmonisierung, et cetera);
c) einen Loop innerhalb eines Fragmentes des Samples anwenden (dafür muss der Musiker aufhören zu spielen, um direkt mit der Mouse an dem grauen Balken am unteren Ende der Patchabbildung auf dem Bildschirm zu arbeiten). Man kann auch eine kontrapunktische Textur mit aufgenommenem und abgespieltem und live erzeugtem Material schaffen oder einfach das Sample löschen und erneut mit der Aufnahme beginnen.

Spezielle Techniken für Performances mit Live-Elektronik

Zuallererst muss der Performende eine spezielle Technik entwickeln, die den Gebrauch der Fußleiste beinhaltet und es ermöglicht, die Verarbeitung während der Performance zu kontrollieren. Und diese Technik kann nur auf praktische Weise entwickelt werden – durch Proben und Auftritte. Also ist es notwendig, sich mit diesem neuen hybriden Instrument zu befassen, um einerseits die traditionelle und erweiterte akustische Instrumentaltechnik zu beherrschen – die mit der Idee einer reinen Körperlichkeit verbunden ist – und dabei andererseits auch das hermeneutische Verhältnis mit dem digitalen Instrument. Im letzteren Fall ist es notwendig, die elektronische Verarbeitung, die durch das Patch in PD zur Anwendung gebracht wird, in Beziehung zu den physischen Aktivitäten an der Fußleiste zu verstehen.

Dieser Lernprozess reicht von sehr elementarem Wissen, wie der Kenntnis der Funktionen der verschiedenen Pedale bis zur Fähigkeit, diese sicher mit den Füßen zu kontrollieren, um sie auf kreative Weise mit den instrumentalen Aktivitäten zu kombinieren. Die Kontrolle elektronischer Prozesse durch den Gebrauch der Fußleiste erzeugt eine neue körperliche Dimension, die zu der ohnehin vorhandenen Körperlichkeit einer instrumentalen Performance hinzugefügt wird. Aus meiner Erfahrung mit dieser »hybriden maschinellen Performance« habe ich mich bemüht, eine spezielle Technik zu kreieren, die es mir ermöglicht, mich durch Interaktion zwischen instrumentalen Techniken und elektronischen Geräten tiefer in die Konstruktionsprozesse des Klangflusses zu versenken. In dem Maß, in dem ich die Saxophonklänge in Echtzeit aufnehmen und verändern kann, kann ich die Klänge in einem interaktiven Prozess auch von innen heraus molekular erfinden, konstruieren und empirisch

29.5-014

kombinieren. In der Folge kann ich mein Klangrepertoire von dem begrenzten Universum von Klängen, die mit einem Saxophon erzeugt werden können, erweitern. So habe ich eine Art Super-Saxophon-Synthesizer zu Verfügung.

Der Fluss der Performance

Während einer solchen Performance ist es möglich, so etwas wie einen Dialog mit den aufgenommenen Klängen in einer Art »Duett mit den Klängen der Vergangenheit« (verarbeitet oder nicht) aufzubauen. Und für diesen Typus kreativen Vorgehens, in dem das Kurzzeitgedächtnis genutzt wird, könnte sich der Performende, um sich auf das Klangmaterial, das in Echtzeit erschaffen wird, zu beziehen, beispielsweise auf die Verfahrensvorschläge (imitieren, kontrastieren, integrieren, zögern und etwas anderes tun) des Komponisten und Improvisatoren Vinko Globokar stützen, die dieser in dem Text »Réagir« (Globokar: 1971) vorgestellt hat. Eine weitere interessante Möglichkeit ist der Dialog mit dem Sonogramm, das auf dem Bildschirm des Computers für den Interpreten sichtbar ist und so als eine Art Partitur funktioniert, die graduell aufgebaut wird und Pfade, Kurse, Transformationen et cetera aufzeigen kann. Auf Grundlage des »Lesens« dieser »Partitur« und des genauen und sorgfältigen Anhörens des Geschehens, ist es möglich, die umfassenden Aspekte der Performance auf vereinfachte Weise zu kategorisieren. Zum Beispiel als: Pointillismus (dünn oder dick), strukturell (verschiedene Dichten mit sich verändernden Graden von Harmonie und Disharmonie), gestisch (visuelle Metaphern, Grafik, Gestalt, Gebärden mit einem Beginn, einer Mitte und einem Ende) et cetera.

Im Allgemeinen basiert die Performance immer auf dem Gespeicherten. Was in Echtzeit produziert wird, bleibt im Zwischenspeicher erhalten und kann später wieder genutzt werden. Wichtig ist, dass in diesem Patch der Speicher begrenzt ist, was sich im grafischen Interface zeigt: Wenn der Cursor das Ende ganz rechts erreicht hat, ist es nicht mehr möglich weiter aufzuzeichnen. In diesem Fall kann man entweder mit zuvor aufgenommenem Material weiterarbeiten (es wiedergeben) oder neues Material produzieren beziehungsweise aufnehmen (und dafür das alte Material löschen). Das Material im Zwischenspeicher kann von verschiedenen Zeitabschnitten aus reproduziert werden (durch das Patch verarbeitet oder unverarbeitet). Wenn das Playback das Ende des Zwischenspeichers erreicht, beginnt es automatisch erneut am Anfang. So ist es möglich, mit den Klängen, die vom Instrumentalisten in Echtzeit produziert werden, einen »verformten Kanon« zu spielen (grundsätzlich »zweistimmig«).

Bezüglich der Anzahl der Ebenen gibt es drei Möglichkeiten: akustisches Solo, elektronisches Solo (verarbeitet oder nicht), elektronisch-akustisches Du-

THE PERFORMANCE FLOW

During this kind of performance, it is possible to establish a sort of dialog with the recorded sounds in a kind of "duet with the sounds of the past" (processed or not). For this type of creative operation in which short-term memory is used, the performer may, for example, base their operation on the procedure proposals created by composer and improviser Vinko Globokar in his text "Réagir" (Globokar 1970) (imitate, contrast, integrate, hesitate and do something different) in order to relate to the sound materials that are being created in real time. Another interesting possibility is the dialog with the sonogram that, being visible to the interpreter on the computer screen, can function as a kind of score that is built gradually and may suggest pathways, advances, transformations, et cetera Based on the "reading" of this "score" and detailed and careful listening to the events, it is possible to categorize, in a simplified manner, the global aspects of the performance flow. For example: pointillism (thin or thick), textural (varying densities, with varying degrees of harmonicity or inharmonicity), gestural (visual metaphors, graphic, gestalt, gestures with a beginning, middle and end), et cetera.

In general terms, the performance is always based on memory. What is produced in real time remains saved in the buffer to be re-used. Importantly, in this patch, the buffer has a storage limitation that is visible in the graphical interface: when the cursor reaches the end at the far right, it is not possible to record any more. In this case, the alternatives are to work with the previously recorded material (playing it back), or to produce and record new material (therefore deleting the earlier material). The material in the buffer can be reproduced (processed or unprocessed by the patch) at various points of time. If the playback reaches the end of the buffer, it automatically restarts from the beginning. It is possible to create "deformed canons" (basically "two voices") with the sound that is produced in real time by the instrumentalist.

In terms of the number of layers, there are three possibilities: acoustic solo, electronic solo (processed or unprocessed) and electronic acoustic duet. In some specific settings it is possible to create the sensation of three or more voices, for example using the harmonizer. Alternatively, one can create a texture composed of a "duo" (sax live + buffer) using the highest register of the saxophone, creating an additional layer with the so-called differential sounds. It is possible to create homogeneous textures (retaining the unity of the acoustic sound materials + electronics) or heterogeneous textures (with a maximum of two different materials: one on the acoustic layer, one on electronics). Sound materials used in performances can be described in more microscopic terms, such as consisting of:

a) "clean" continuous sounds, well-defined in terms of frequency (tonic), in the various regions and with varying degrees of dynamics and "allure" (vibrato, non vibrato, oscillating, et cetera);

ett. In bestimmten Settings ist es außerdem möglich, den Eindruck von drei oder mehr Stimmen zu kreieren, indem beispielsweise die Harmonisierungsfunktion benutzt wird. Wahlweise ist es auch möglich, eine Textur zu schaffen, die sich aus einem Duett zusammensetzt (Saxophon live mit Zwischenspeicher), indem das höchste Register des Saxophons verwendet wird, und so eine weitere Ebene mit den sogenannten Differenzialklängen zu kreieren. Möglich sind homogene (Erhalt der Einheit des akustischen Klangmaterials und der Elektronik) oder heterogene Texturen (mit höchstens zwei verschiedenen Materialien: einem auf der akustischen und einem auf der elektronischen Ebene). Klangmaterialien, die bei Aufführungen genutzt werden, können durch eine eher mikroskopische Terminologie beschrieben werden, dazu gehören:

a) »saubere« anhaltende Klänge, die bezüglich ihrer Frequenz (Grundton) und den verschiedenen Räumen und nach unterschiedlichem Grad von Dynamik und Reiz (Vibrato, Non-Vibrato, schwingend usw.) klar definiert sind;
b) unharmonische Klänge: Luftklänge (anhaltend und durch dynamische Variationen moduliert), Klappenanschläge (kurze Klänge mit geringer Resonanz, mit sich verändernden Dynamiken und mit oder ohne festgelegter Taktfrequenz);
c) Veränderungen in der Klangfarbe und in »unsauberen« Tönen: extrem scharfe Stimmenklänge und Grundtöne, Frullatos (Flatterzunge), Bisbigliando, Slap Tongue, Tongue Ram;
d) Harmonie: Multiphonics;
e) Polyphonie oder Kombinationen des Obigen, zum Beispiel: Töne mit begrenzter Frequenz + Klappenanschläge + Atemgeräusche.

In eher makroskopischen Begriffen kann gesagt werden, dass es mehr molare und territorialisierte Materialien gibt (Sprachfragmente in der Form von Gesten oder rhythmisch-melodischen Figuren) und mehr molekular deterritorialisierte Materialien (Geräusch, Texturen, »reine Klänge«). Besonders mit Hilfe elektronischer Verfahren ist es möglich, unwahrscheinliche Sinnzusammenhänge hervorzubringen, indem selbst die am meisten territorialisierten Klänge denaturiert werden.

Ein Problem, das in einigen Performances auftaucht, betrifft das Verhältnis zwischen akustischem und elektronisch verarbeitetem Material. Letzteres hört sich manchmal wie eine Karikatur des akustischen Klanges an, da die Verfahren in den Transpositionen und den zeitlichen Veränderungen zu offensichtlich hervortreten. Es ist möglich, diese zu »maskieren«, indem die Klänge stimmiger aufeinander bezogen und gemischt werden. Eine Strategie dafür bestünde zum Beispiel darin, mit akustischen Klängen zu arbeiten, die ziemlich homogen sind und deren Beschaffenheit den entstehenden verarbeiteten Klängen ähnelt (zum Beispiel Multiphonics, also Spaltklang; hohe Fre-

b) inharmonic sounds: air sounds (continuous and modulated by dynamic variations), percussion using the keys (short sounds, with little resonance, with varied dynamics and with or without frequency settings);
c) timbre variations and "dirty" notes: super sharp, voice sounds + tonic sounds, frullatos, bisbigliandos, slap tongue, tongue ram;
d) harmony: multiphonics;
e) polyphony or combinations of the above, for example: notes with a defined frequency + key clicks + breath sounds.

In more macroscopic terms it can be said that there are more molar and territorialized materials (language fragments in the form of gestures or rhythmic-melodic figures) and more molecular deterritorialized materials (noise, textures, "pure sounds"). Electronic processing in particular makes it possible to "denature" even the most territorialized sounds, thus creating improbable contexts.

One problem that arises in some performances concerns the relationship between acoustic and electronically processed material. The latter, on some occasions, sounds like a caricature of the acoustic sound, since the processes are very evident in the transpositions and time modifications. It is possible to mask these results, making the sounds relate and blend together more consistently. One strategy for this would be, for example, to use acoustic sounds which are more or less homogeneous, and which may have a quality closer to that of the processed sounds generated (for example: multiphonics, super high frequencies, a "continuous jet" of short notes, key clicks, et cetera) and that blend into a more textural sound flow.

Steps can be taken to manage the transitions between different types of materials, when one wants to stop the reproduction and start a new recording. It is possible to prepare for this transition in some way, for example, by recording, close to the end of the sample, in pianissimo and adding the same type of sound material, so that, when resuming a new recording, the electroacoustic cut is not noticeable. Another strategy to create novelty is to fill the buffer (recording) up to a certain point with specific sound material, whilst retaining the reproduction of this material. Then record new material that will fill the rest of the buffer. So there will in effect be three successive situations: 2 layers (acoustic and electronic) with the same type of material, the coexistence of the old and new material and finally a new texture composed of two layers of new material.

The idea of always using materials that have been created previously (including the possibility of viewing their graphical representations) makes it possible to listen and modify "old" sound ideas in real time. The idea of creating a dialog with the past is one rich in promise. Of course, the possibilities are limited to the features implemented in the patch. Nevertheless, current ideas are always fed by the memory of previous actions. Furthermore, the sound material may be thought of metaphorically as something "solid" or "malleable"

quenzen, ein »konstanter Fluss« von kürzeren Tönen, Klappenklicks et cetera). Diese würden einen stärker strukturierten Klangfluss ergeben.

Weitere Vorkehrungen könnten beim Übergang zwischen unterschiedlichen Materialtypen an der Stelle getroffen werden, an der man die Wiedergabe stoppen und eine neue Aufnahme beginnen möchte. Es ist zu einem gewissen Maße möglich, diesen Übergang vorzubereiten, indem man zum Beispiel gegen Ende eines Samples im Pianissimo aufnimmt und denselben Materialtyp anfügt, sodass der elektro-akustische Schnitt bei Beginn einer neuen Aufnahme nicht bemerkbar ist. Eine weitere Strategie, etwas Neues zu erschaffen, besteht darin, den Zwischenspeicher (Aufnahmen) bis zu einem bestimmten Punkt mit einem speziellen Klangmaterial zu füllen und gleichzeitig die Wiedergabe dieses Materials fortzuführen. Dann kann neues Material aufgenommen werden, das den Rest des Zwischenspeichers auffüllt. Demnach ergeben sich drei aufeinander folgende Situationen: zwei Ebenen (akustisch und elektronisch) mit demselben Materialtyp, das Nebeneinander des alten und neuen Materials und letztlich die neue Struktur, die aus zwei Ebenen neuen Materials besteht.

Der Ansatz, immer mit Materialien zu arbeiten, die zuvor produziert worden sind (einschließlich der Möglichkeit ihre grafischen Repräsentationen zu betrachten), ermöglicht es, diese anzuhören und »alte« Klangideen in Echtzeit zu verändern. Das Konzept, mit der Vergangenheit einen Dialog zu führen, ist sehr vielversprechend. Natürlich sind die Möglichkeiten auf die Features begrenzt, die das Patch enthält. Dennoch werden die aktuellen Ideen durch die Erinnerung der vorherigen Handlungen genährt. Darüber hinaus könnte man sich das Klangmaterial metaphorisch als etwas »Festes« oder »Geschmeidiges« vorstellen, das Plastikmaterial insofern ähnelt, als dass es auf viele Weisen geformt werden kann. Hier begegnen wir wieder der zuvor erläuterten Idee von der Integration von Material, Form und »Sprache« in einen immanenten Prozess.

Schlussfolgerungen

In der freien Improvisation besteht der molekulare und »unberührte« Klang als ersehnter, utopischer Horizont, da er sich durch sein Potential für molare Konditionierung (territorial, idiomatisch, sozial, stilistisch, instrumental, historisch, geografisch et cetera) von den Musikern während des dynamischen Flusses (solo oder kollektiv) in einer interaktiven Performance aufbauen und verändern ließe. Eine Strategie, um dieses Ziel zu erreichen, ist die Intensivierung des Hörens – ich erinnere hier an die Konzepte des reduzierten Hörens von Pierre Schaeffer und des tiefen Hörens von Pauline Oliveros – mit dem Ziel, intentional auf die akustischen Qualitäten des Klanges zu fokussieren, die als vormusikalisch und als kontextbefreites Material betrachtet werden. Der

resembling plastic material that can be shaped in many ways. Here, again, we have the previously explained idea of integration between material, shape and "language" in an immanent process.

Conclusion

In free improvisation, the molecular, "virgin" sound, with its potential for molar conditioning (territorial, idiomatic, social, stylistic, instrumental, historical, geographical, et cetera), ready to be built and molded by the musicians' instrumental actions during the dynamic flow in an interactive performance (solo or collective) is a desired utopian horizon. One strategy for achieving this objective is the enhancement of listening (I recall here Pierre Schaeffer's concept of reduced listening and Pauline Oliveros' deep listening) with the goal of focusing intentionally on the acoustic qualities of sounds, considered as pre-musical and decontextualized material. The use of new technologies provides greater insight into the molecular properties of sound (envelope, spectrum, grain, et cetera) and into procedures for manipulating sound. As Gérard Grisey said: "[...] electronics have enabled sound to be listened to microphonically. The interior of the sound itself that was hidden for centuries due to essentially macrophonic musical practices is finally free for us to admire" (Grisey 1991: 252). However, all this does not exclude the work of deterritorialization of molar sound by an act which, according to Lachenmann, can "create a context that can remain intact; intact in terms of a new aspect" (Guigue 2007: 94). This is because, as I say in my doctoral thesis (Costa 2003: 16), I imagine that it is possible:

"[...] to think of free improvisation as a possible way to achieve musical pragmatism, open to infinite variation in terms of the fact that systems and languages no longer impose their abstract grammars but rather surrender to a fruitful creation, a time in pure state, not causal, not hierarchical, not linear. Through free improvisation we think we can achieve 'this secret, neutral language with no constants. Everything is via indirect discourse, where the synthesizer and the instrument speak as much as the voice and the voice plays as much as the instrument.'" (Deleuze; Guattari 1997: 40)

Gebrauch neuer Technologien bietet größere Einsicht in die molekularen Eigenschaften von Klang (Tonumfang, Spektrum, Granularität et cetera) und in die Verfahren der Klangbearbeitung. Nach Gérard Grisey »ermöglicht die Elektronik seit einigen Jahren ein mikrophones Hören von Klang. Das Innere des Klanges selbst, das jahrzehntelang von makrophonen Musikpraxen verdeckt wurde, liegt endlich frei, um bewundert zu werden.« (Grisey 1991: 252). Aber all das schließt die Arbeit der Deterritorialisierung von molarem Klang durch einen Akt ein, der nach Lachenmann »ein Umfeld [...] schaffen [kann], das unversehrt bleiben kann, unversehrt unter einem neuen Aspekt« (Guigue 2007: 94). Aus diesem Grund, um meine Doktorarbeit (2003: 16) zu zitieren, ist es denkbar

> »durch Freie Improvisation eine musikalische Pragmatik als möglich zu denken, die insofern für unendliche Variationen offen ist, als die Systeme und Sprachen nicht länger ihre abstrakte Grammatik aufzwingen, sondern sich einer fruchtbaren Gestaltung, einer Zeit in reinem Zustand, nicht ursächlich, nicht hierarchisch, nicht linear ergeben. Wir gehen davon aus, ›dass wir durch freie Improvisation diese geheime, neutrale Sprache ohne Konstanten, verwirklichen können. Alles erfolgt in einem indirekten Diskurs, in dem der Synthesizer und das Instrument wie die Stimme sprechen, und die Stimme genauso spielt wie das Instrument.‹« (Deleuze; Guattari 1997: 40)

Übersetzung aus dem Englischen: Solveig Raschpichler, Berlin

Literatur/References

Costa, Rogério Luiz Moraes (2003): O músico enquanto meio e os territórios da livre improvisação, Dissertation, Brasil: PUC-SP.

Costa, Rogério Luiz Moraes (2012): »Free Improvisation and the Philosophy of Gilles Deleuze«, in: Perspectives of New Music, New York: Band 49, 2-16.

Deleuze, Gilles; Guattari, Félix (1997): Mil Platôs: Capitalismo e Esquizofrenia, Vol. 2, São Paulo: Band 34.

Grisey, Gérard (1991): »Structuration des timbres dans la musique instrumental«, in: Jean-Baptiste Barrière; Christian Bourgois (Hg./Eds.), Le Timbre: Métaphore pour la composition, Paris: Editeur Ircam, 352-385.

Globokar, Vinko (1970): »Réagir«, in: Musique en jeu 1, Paris: Edition du Seuil, 70-77.

Globokar, Vinko (1971): »Vom Reagieren«, in: Melos 2, Jg. 38, 59-62.

Guigue, Didier (2007): »Serynade e o mundo sonoro de Helmut Lachenmann«, in: Revista Opus, Band 13, Nr. 2, São Paulo: Editora da Anppom.

Lachenmann, Helmut (1996): »Klangtypen der neuen Musik«, in: Häusler, Josef (Hrsg./Ed.), Musik als existentielle Erfahrung, Wiesbaden: Breitkopf & Härtel, 1-20.

Lachenmann, Helmut (2009): »Typologie sonore de la musique contemporaine«, in: Ecrits et entretiens, Genf: Contrechamps Editions.

Magnusson, Thor (2009): »Of epistemic Tools: Musical Instruments as Cognitive Extensions«, in: Organized Sound, Vol. 14, issue 02, August 2009, Cambridge: Cambridge University Press, 168-176.

Solomos, Makis (2012): »Deux visions de la vie intérieur du son: Scelsi et Xenakis«, in: Filigrane, Revue de Musique, Esthétique, Science et Société, Band 15, Paris: Edition Université Paris 8. *URL: http://revues.mshparisnord.org/filigrane/index.php?id=504*

Solomos, Makis (2013): De la musique au son, l'émergence du son dans la musique des XXe – XXIe siècles, Rennes: Presses Universitaires de Rennes.

INTERMEZZO 5

Ich denke, dass wir im improvisatorischen Moment, im Augenblick des praktischen Spiels, immer zugleich Zukunftshorizonte eröffnen. Es ist nicht nur ein Bewahren von etwas und ein Erinnern oder auch Vergessen, sondern es ist auch ein Vorwegnehmen. Dieses Vorwegnehmen hat seine eigenen Probleme, und so befinden wir uns auch immer auf den Schnittstellen zwischen dem, was kommt, und dem, was gerade gewesen ist. Dieser Balanceakt im Augenblick ist gar nicht zur Sprache zu bringen, beziehungsweise er boykottiert das, was man zur Sprache bringen möchte: die Kommunikation. Es gibt eigentlich keine Kommunikation im Augenblick, aber es gibt natürlich die Kommunikation über den Augenblick, und in dieser Spannung müsste man weiter diskutieren.

Diskussionsbeitrag von Christoph Irmer, Mai 2014

Intermezzo 5

I think that in the improvisational moment, which is to say in the very moment of practical performance, we are also always opening up future horizons. It's not just about preserving something and remembering or even forgetting, but rather it is also an anticipation. This anticipation brings with it its own problems, and so we actually find ourselves always at the interface between that which is coming and that which has just passed. This balancing act in the moment cannot be voiced, or rather it blocks that which one is trying to articulate, that is communication. There is, in fact, no communication in the moment itself, but there is, of course, communication about the moment, and in this conflict, I think, we ought to discuss things further.

Christoph Irmer in a public discussion, May 2014

Translation into English: Louise & Phil Loxton, GB-Wales

Berlin 30.5.014

Corinna Eikmeier, Uni f. Musik u. darstellende Kunst, Wien

Improvisieren mit einem improvisierenden Körper

Improvisation als Arbeitsmethode

In die Gegenwart kommen

Forschungsansatz

Qualitative Heuristik

Improvisatorische Versuchsreihen
+
Dokumentationsform über
- Hörbeispiele und Experimente

Die Spiegelneuronen funktionieren

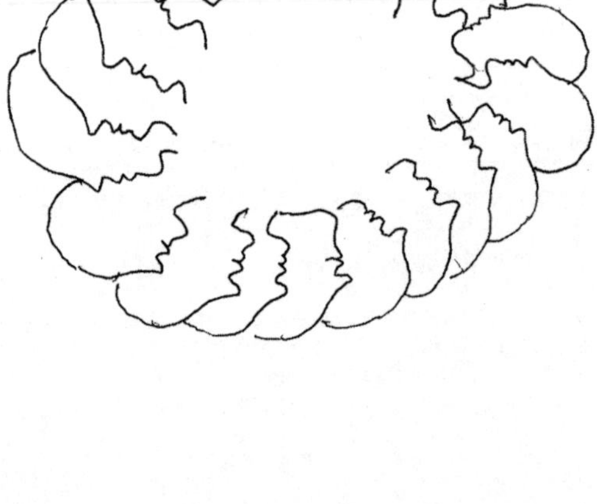

Improvisieren mit einem improvisierenden Körper | Improvisation with the Improvising Body

Corinna Eikmeier

1. Ausgangsbeobachtungen

Die klassische Musikausbildung steht in der Instrumentalpädagogik im westlichen Kulturkreis im Vordergrund und wird größtenteils durch Interpretation und Reproduktion vermittelt. Ein beachtlich hoher Prozentsatz der professionellen Musiker leidet unter Beschwerden des Bewegungsapparates. Als Prävention wird von renommierten Musikermedizinern die ergänzende Beschäftigung mit Körpertechniken empfohlen. Vertreter der somatischen Lernmethoden spezialisieren sich auf die Arbeit mit Musikern. Während meiner Lehrtätigkeit im Fach Feldenkrais[1] an einer Musikhochschule beobachte ich, dass viele klassisch ausgebildete Musiker die Erfahrungen aus Feldenkrais-Stunden nicht auf ihr Instrumentalspiel anwenden können. In Feldenkrais-Stunden wird eine »improvisatorische Bewegungsqualität« erforscht und scheinbar lassen sich gradlinig eingeübte Bewegungsmuster nicht einfach verändern.

Die Beschreibungen des Körpergefühls beim Improvisieren ähneln jedoch den Beschreibungen von Empfindungen, die viele Menschen nach Feldenkrais-Stunden haben. Die gleichen Personen erinnern ihre Bewegungsempfindungen beim Interpretieren eher negativ. Die technischen Spielbewegungen können nicht allein ausschlaggebend hierfür sein, sondern die innere Einstellung beim Musizieren, die Wahrnehmung, das Hören und die Bereitschaft, sich ganz auf die gegenwärtige Situation einzulassen, tragen offensichtlich dazu bei.

2. Fragestellungen

In vielen Studien über Musikermedizin und Musikphysiologie wird die Frage nach den Unterschieden zwischen den verschiedenen Arten der Musizierpraxis nicht gestellt. Für das im Folgenden beschriebene Forschungsprojekt waren diese Unterschiede in der Musizierpraxis und Auffälligkeiten beim Improvisieren bereits in den ersten Beobachtungen relevant. Aus diesem Grunde wurde das Improvisieren zum Untersuchungsgegenstand. Beim Improvisieren sind Tugenden gefordert, die für jede andere Musizierpraxis ebenso wichtig, beim Improvisieren jedoch unabdingbar sind. Der Terminus der »improvisatorischen Handlungsweise«, der ebenso in interpretierender Musizierpraxis Anwendung finden kann, wurde definiert.

Von den Ausgangsbeobachtungen wurden die folgenden zentralen Fragestellungen abgeleitet:

1 | Fortlaufende Lehrveranstaltung in den Gruppenstunden »Bewusstheit durch Bewegung« und in Einzelstunden »Funktionale Integration« für Studierende aller Studiengänge an der Hochschule für Musik, Theater und Medien, Hannover.

1. Background

The practice of learning instruments in Western culture center on classical training and is largely taught through models of interpretation and reproduction. A significant percentage of professional musicians suffer from disorders of the locomotor system, and preventive techniques favored by leading music therapists focus on expanding movement patterns. In addition, proponents of somatic learning frequently specialize in working with musicians. In the course of teaching the Feldenkrais[1] method at a school of music, I observed the fact that many classically trained musicians are not able to apply the knowledge gained in Feldenkrais sessions to performance on their instrument. Feldenkrais aims to release "improvisational movement" and often reveals that directly acquired habits of movement are not easy to change.

However, descriptions of corporeal sensation when improvising are similar to the accounts of the emotions many people feel after Feldenkrais sessions. The same individuals recall their sensations of movement during performance in a largely negative light. This cannot be due alone to the purely technical movements which playing involves; personal attitudes, perception, listening and a willingness to fully submit to the moment also appear to be key contributing factors.

2. Issues

The question "How do the various kinds of music-making differentiate from one another?" is not even posed in many music-therapy and music-physiology studies. During my present project, initial observations have already shown the relevance of differences in musical practice and anomalies to improvisation. Improvisation thus came to the fore as the subject of my investigation: it demands skills that are important for all kinds of music-making, but which are, in fact, absolutely indispensable for spontaneous music. The term "improvisational action" – which may also be applied to the interpretation of pre-existing music – has acquired new and concrete meaning.

The following key research questions were identified from the initial observations:

- Which specific actions are of relevance to improvisation?

---

1 | An on-going course of group sessions on "Awareness through Movement" and individual sessions on "Functional Integration" for students of all disciplines at the Hanover University of Music, Drama and Media.

- Welche spezifischen Handlungsweisen sind für das Improvisieren bedeutsam?
- Welche Wechselwirkung gibt es zwischen den spezifischen improvisatorischen Handlungsweisen und der Bewegungsqualität beim Musizieren.

Bezogen auf die Feldenkrais-Methode:

- Welche der improvisatorischen Handlungsweisen werden in der Feldenkrais-Methode implizit mit behandelt?
- Welche Vergleichsmöglichkeiten lassen sich zwischen den in der Feldenkrais-Methode angewendeten Lernstrategien und den improvisatorischen Handlungsweisen erkennen?

3. Forschungsprozess

Sowohl Improvisation als auch die Feldenkrais-Methode lassen sich auf Grund der extrem hohen Komplexität mit naturwissenschaftlichen beziehungsweise quantitativen Messverfahren nicht befriedigend untersuchen. Das Forschungsdesign entwickelte sich im Verlauf des Forschungsprozesses auf improvisatorische Weise. Die Forschungsmethodologie lehnt sich an die Qualitative Heuristik an. Als methodische Variationen wurden Forschungsgespräche, Introspektion und insbesondere das »qualitative Experiment« angewendet.

Phase 1 (detaillierte Ausführungen siehe Kapitel 5)

Zunächst kamen in Forschungsgesprächen Experten der Improvisation zu Wort. Daraus wurde die improvisatorische Handlungsweise abgeleitet und definiert. Es stellte sich heraus, dass die Gesprächspartner zur Wechselwirkung zwischen ihrem improvisatorischen Verhalten und ihren Bewegungsempfindungen nur sehr allgemeine Aussagen machen konnten. Bewegungen werden nicht geplant, sondern einfach ausgeführt und sie funktionieren dann erstaunlich gut.

Phase 2 (detaillierte Ausführungen siehe Kapitel 6)

Durch eine Analogie zwischen der Feldenkrais-Methode und der Improvisation wurde die »improvisatorische Bewegungsqualität« definiert und gezeigt, dass in der Feldenkrais-Methode auf einer Metaebene improvisatorische Tugenden geübt werden.

Phase 3 (detaillierte Ausführungen siehe Kapitel 7)

Im dritten Schritt wurde Improvisation und Bewegung in den qualitativen Experimenten in insgesamt 16 verschiedenen Versuchsanordnungen kombiniert. Das qualitative Experiment findet, wie auch andere qualitative Forschungsan-

- What kinds of interactions exist between specific improvisational actions and the quality of movement in music-making?

Regarding the Feldenkrais method:

- Which improvisational actions are implicitly covered by the Feldenkrais method?
- What comparisons may be drawn between the learning strategies applied in the Feldenkrais method and improvisational actions?

3. The research process

Due to their extreme complexity, neither improvisation nor the Feldenkrais method lend themselves to adequate analysis using scientific or quantitative principles. The research method employed here evolved in an improvisational way during the course of the research process, drawing its methodology from qualitative heuristics. Research discussions, introspection and in particular the "qualitative experiment" were used as methodological variations.

Phase 1 (explained in more depth in section 5)

Initially, experts on improvisation took the lead in research discussions, helping to identify and define improvisational actions. It became clear that the speakers were only in a position to make very general statements regarding the interaction between their improvisational conduct and their sensations of movement. Movements are not planned; they are simply carried out and work surprisingly well.

Phase 2 (explained in more depth in section 6)

An analogy between the Feldenkrais method and improvisation helped to define the "improvisational quality of movement" and revealed that meta-level improvisational skills are practiced under the Feldenkrais method.

Phase 3 (explained in more depth in section 7)

In what were termed qualitative experiments, improvisation and movement were combined in a total of 16 different experimental settings. Similar to other qualitative approaches, the qualitative experiment deliberately dispenses with randomized, controlled conditions (Burkart 2010: 252-62).

The experiments began with a free improvisation. Depending on the personal interests of the participants, and also to satisfy my curiosity, I then selected which of 16 experimental set-ups would be used as the introduction. The changes consisted of locomotor coordination tasks. Changes in the participants' improvisations were then observed.

sätze, bewusst nicht unter randomisierten, kontrollierten Bedingungen statt. (Burkart 2010: 252-262)

Die Experimente begannen mit einer freien Improvisation. Anschließend habe ich je nach Interesse der Versuchsteilnehmer und aufgrund meiner Neugier entschieden, welche der 16 Versuchsanordnungen als Einstieg gewählt wurde. Die Veränderungen bestanden in Aufgaben zur Bewegungskoordination. Zu beobachten waren die Veränderungen in den Improvisationen der Teilnehmer.

In der Auswertung der Experimente wurden die Grenzen der Sprache deutlich. Die Personen waren häufig so involviert in ihr Spiel, dass sie sich nicht verbal äußern konnten. An diesem Punkt wurden Aspekte von künstlerischer Forschung einbezogen. Die Hörbeispiele der Improvisationen wurden selber zum Teil der Forschung. (Klein 2010: 25-28)

4. Die Rolle der Forscherin

Die Rolle der Forscherin bedarf einer gesonderten Reflexion. Die Motivation das Projekt durchzuführen, entstand aus persönlichen Erfahrungen direkt aus dem Feld. Eine scheinbar neutrale Perspektive war durch mein Vorwissen und meine persönliche Betroffenheit nicht möglich. Aus diesem Grund wurden die folgenden Perspektiven bewusst eingenommen und reflektiert: Durchführung der Experimente mit einer Dokumentation in einem Introspektionstagebuch, Teilnahme an den Experimenten auf Augenhöhe mit den Versuchspersonen, Auswertung der Daten teilweise mit bewusst gesetztem zeitlichen Abstand, der implizite Einfluss der künstlerischen und pädagogischen Aktivitäten, die indirekt den Dokumentationsprozess des Projektes geprägt haben.

5. Phase 1: Die improvisatorische Handlungsweise

Metaphorisch wurde Improvisation wie folgt als *Autopoiesis* in der Gegenwart definiert.

Rahmenbedingungen der Improvisation

Die Situation wird durch einen vorher bestimmten Ort und Zeitpunkt für die Improvisation geschaffen.

Die Art der Situation wird bestimmt, zum Beispiel Konzert-, Proben- oder Unterrichtssituation.Es wird geklärt, ob der Improvisation Konzepte oder Vorgaben zugrunde liegen sollen.

The limits of language became obvious when evaluating the experiments. Participants were frequently so involved in their playing that they could not express themselves verbally. Aspects of artistic research were incorporated here. The examples of improvisation themselves became part of the research process (Klein 2010: 25-28).

4. The role of the researcher

The role of the researcher demands separate attention. My interest in the project arose directly from my personal experience in the field. My prior knowledge and personal involvement ruled out an ostensibly neutral perspective. The following perspectives were therefore deliberately adopted and considered: conduct the experiments and document them in an introspection diary; participate in the experiments with the subjects on an equal footing; evaluate part of the data only after a defined period of time has elapsed; the implicit influence of artistic and educational activities indirectly affect the project documentation process.

5. Phase 1: improvisational actions

Improvisation was metaphorically designated a form of autopoiesis as follows.

Improvisational framework

A setting for improvisation is created with a predetermined time and place.

The type of setting is defined; for example concerts, rehearsals or teaching situations. A decision is taken as to whether the improvisation is based on specific ideas or instructions.

Components of the improvisation

The following components are interlinked and affect the creative artistic process of improvisation:

- The musician (including his or her instrument/voice) who has taken a conscious decision to employ improvisation as a form of art
- The music and its rules (irrespective of a chosen style)
- The other players in an ensemble, if the improvisation is not performed alone
- The venue, to the extent that it is incorporated in the improvisation

Komponenten der Improvisation

Die folgenden Komponenten sind miteinander vernetzt und wirken in den künstlerischen Entstehungsprozess der Improvisationen hinein:

- Der Musizierende (einschließlich seines Instrumentes beziehungsweise der Stimme), der sich bewusst zur Improvisation als Kunstform entschieden hat.
- Die Musik mit ihren eigenen Gesetzmäßigkeiten (unabhängig von einem festgelegten Stil).
- Die Mitspieler eines Ensembles, sofern es keine Soloimprovisation ist.
- Der Spielort, sofern er in die Improvisation eingebunden wird.

Indirekte Komponenten der Improvisation

- Anwesenheit des Publikums
- Geräusche, die ungeplant von außen eindringen und von den Spielern in die Improvisation integriert werden (zum Beispiel Vogelgezwitscher oder ein aufdringliches Handyklingeln). Derartige akustische Inspirationen werden erst dann als Teil der Improvisation betrachtet, wenn sie von den Spielern aufgenommen und weiterentwickelt werden und nicht aus dem Grunde ihrer schlichten Existenz.

Pertubationen

Vergleichbar mit der Natur ist auch die Improvisation als Autopoiesis Störungen und Gefahren ausgeliefert. Störungen – wie zum Beispiel Vermeidung von Fehlern, Planung und Kontrolle, Angst vor Schwierigkeiten oder der Wunsch ein Erfolgserlebnis zu wiederholen – bringen die Spieler mental aus der Gegenwart in andere Zeitebenen. Die Reproduktion von Erfolgserlebnissen bringt sie in ihren Gedanken in die Vergangenheit. Fehlervermeidung und technische Kontrolle bringen sie mental in die Zukunft.

Wahrnehmung als Klebstoff

Eine authentische Wahrnehmung der Gegenwart hält die Komponenten der Improvisation wie ein Klebstoff zusammen. Jede Störung schwächt die Wahrnehmung und führt dazu, dass sich die Handlung weniger auf den Moment beziehen kann.

Gegenwart als Lebensraum

In der Gegenwart sind alle Komponenten der Improvisation verbunden. Nur unter diesem Umstand kann das Unvorhersehbare auftauchen. Unvorhersehbar ist nur, was für den konkreten Moment einmalig ist. Die Improvisation wird unter diesen Umständen zu einem Spiel ohne äußeren Zweck. Die Zeit gehört allein dem improvisatorischen Prozess.

Indirect components of the improvisation

- Presence of an audience
- Sounds that enter the performance from outside and are integrated into the improvisation by the players (for example a birdsong or a ringing mobile phone). These acoustic phenomena are only considered elements of the improvisation if they are incorporated into the work by the players, not by virtue of their mere existence.

Perturbation

As with nature, improvisation as autopoiesis is subject to disruption and danger. Problems such as planning and control, avoidance of mistakes, fear of difficulty or the desire to repeat a former success mentally displace the players from the present moment: reproducing previous successes casts their minds back into the past, while avoiding mistakes and technical control causes them to think of the future.

Perception as the binding agent

Authentic perception of the present is the glue that holds the components of the improvisation together. Every problem or disruption dilutes perception and mitigates the ability of the performer to respond to the moment.

Living in the present

Every component of the improvisation is interwoven with the present. Only then can the unpredictable happen. The unpredictable comprises only that which is unique to the specific moment. In this context, improvisation becomes a performance with no external purpose. Time serves only as the vehicle for the improvisational process.

6. Phase 2: Improvisational Quality of Movement

The criteria for "improvisational quality of movement" were identified on the basis of optimum movement as described by Moshé Feldenkrais. Spontaneity is only possible if actions, and therefore movements too, are reversible. A movement is reversible if it can be halted, reversed or transformed into another movement at any moment. Reversibility is always accompanied by lightness; a reversible action must be free of external motivation. The following criteria for optimum movement produce reversibility:

- Neutral starting position
- Dynamic balance

6. Phase 2: Die improvisatorische Bewegungsqualität

Die Kriterien für die »improvisatorische Bewegungsqualität« wurden aus dem von Moshé Feldenkrais beschriebenen Optimum abgeleitet. Spontaneität ist nur möglich, wenn die Handlungen und mit ihnen auch die Bewegungen umkehrbar sind. Eine Bewegung ist dann umkehrbar, wenn sie in jedem Moment gestoppt, zurückgeführt oder in eine andere Bewegung verwandelt werden kann. Umkehrbarkeit wird immer von Leichtigkeit begleitet. Eine umkehrbare Handlung muss frei von Fremdmotivationen sein. Die nachstehenden Kriterien für optimale Bewegung führen zu Umkehrbarkeit:

- Neutrale Ausgangsposition
- Dynamisches Gleichgewicht
- Proximale Unterstützung aller Bewegungen
- Koordination von Becken und Kopf: Becken ist Motor und Kopf ist Teleskop
- Ausgeglichene Muskelspannung. Die Muskeln arbeiten im Verhältnis zu ihrer Größe.
- Flexible Atmung

Analogien zwischen Improvisation und Feldenkrais-Methode

- Es herrscht ein Forschungsgeist im Tun selber.
- Die Situationen fordern eine kreative Problemlösung.
- Befreiung von Werturteilen ist die Voraussetzung für Entwicklung.
- Die Qualität des Tuns ist wichtiger als das Ziel.
- Authentische Wahrnehmung trägt die Prozesse.
- Die Sensibilität für kleine Unterschiede ermöglicht Qualität.
- Die kritische Auseinandersetzung mit Gewohnheiten ist wichtig, damit sich das Lernen und Handeln auf die gegenwärtigen Situationen beziehen kann.
- Die Akzeptanz von Einschränkungen ist die Voraussetzung für einen kreativen Prozess innerhalb des gesetzten Rahmens.
- Sprache innerhalb kreativer Prozesse beruht auf der Problematik, dass sich die Gegenwart durch die Errungenschaft des Sprechens nicht einfangen lässt. Entweder wird bereits vorher Gedachtes reproduziert oder es wird aus einer Distanz auf Vergangenes zurück geblickt. Häufig entstehen verallgemeinernde Aussagen, die sich nicht auf die konkrete Situation beziehen.
- »Fehler« werden neutral wahrgenommen und werden so zu neuen Impulsen.
- Pertubationen durch Fehlervermeidung, Angst, Vorplanung und ausschließlich kognitive Denkprozesse behindern den Bezug zur gegenwärtigen Situation.

- Proximal support of all movements
- Coordination of pelvis and head: the pelvis is the motor, the head the telescope
- Balanced muscle tension: the muscles work in relation to their size
- Flexible breathing

Analogies between improvisation and the Feldenkrais method

- There is an investigative spirit in the act of doing.
- The situation demands creative problem-solving.
- Freedom from value judgment is the prerequisite to growth.
- The quality of what is done outweighs the goal.
- Authentic perception underlies the processes.
- Awareness of minor differences produces quality.
- Critical engagement with habits is important and allows learning and acting to relate to situations in the present.
- Accepting limitations is a condition of the creative process within the set framework.
- Language within creative processes addresses the problem that the present cannot be captured by the act of speaking. Previous thoughts are reproduced, or speakers look back to previous situations with the benefit of hindsight. Generalizing statements that do not relate to the specific situation are frequently heard.
- "Mistakes" are perceived impartially and transformed into new stimuli.
- Perturbation due to the desire to avoid mistakes, fear, planning and exclusively cognitive thought processes inhibit a connection to the present situation.
- Actions may relate to the present if they are reversible. In other words: they can be halted, reversed or transformed into different actions.
- Preparedness for action at any time and in any direction permits decisions in the present and their direct translation into action.
- Organic learning is never to be externally directed. Distracting the learner from their undirected action which is firmly rooted in the present is highly disruptive and extremely disconcerting.

7. Phase 3: Results from the qualitative laboratory[2]

Aspects of improvisational quality of movement confront improvisational action in the qualitative laboratory. Four hypothetical laboratories were set up with the following research subjects:

---

2 | 49 experiments were conducted in the qualitative laboratory with 16 experimental set-ups. These were divided into four thematic blocks, each called laboratories.

- Die Handlungen können sich auf die Gegenwart beziehen, sobald sie umkehrbar sind, das heißt, dass sie zu stoppen oder zurückzunehmen sind oder in eine andere Handlung verwandelt werden können.
- Handlungsbereitschaft in jedem Moment in jede Richtung ermöglicht Entscheidungen in der Gegenwart und deren unmittelbare Umsetzung in Aktion.
- Das organische Lernen darf unter keinen Umständen von außen gesteuert werden. Es ist extrem störanfällig und wird unterbrochen, sobald der Lernende aus seinem zielungebundenen, in der Gegenwart verhafteten Tun herausgebracht wird.

7. Phase 3: Aus dem qualitativen Labor[2]

Im qualitativen Labor wurden Bewegungsaspekte der improvisatorischen Bewegungsqualität mit der improvisatorischen Handlungsweise konfrontiert. Es gab insgesamt vier fiktive Laborräume mit den folgenden Themen:

1. Muskelspannung
2. Dynamisches Gleichgewicht
3. Impulse
4. Atmung

Im Folgenden wird aus jedem Laborraum ein Beispiel präsentiert.

Laborraum 1

Versuchsanordnung – Käfer/Boot

Die Aufgabe bestand darin, einen imaginären Käfer oder ein Boot auf der Horizonthöhe zu beobachten und dabei den Kopf und die Augen gleichmäßig zu bewegen. Die Bewegung sollte unabhängig vom musikalischen Ausdruck immer weitergehen.

Beispiel

Die Versuchsperson ist ein zwölfjähriger Junge. Er gehört zu den Versuchspersonen, die keine Worte finden, und somit muss die Musik die Ergebnisse transportieren. Beim Hören der Dokumentation ist deutlich, wie sich die Bewegung und der musikalische Ausdruck zusammenfügen. Das Stück ähnelt einem

---

2 | Im qualitativen Labor fanden 49 Experimente mit 16 Versuchsanordnungen statt, die in vier Themenblöcke, sogenannte Laborräume aufgeteilt waren.

1. Muscle tension
2. Dynamic balance
3. Stimuli
4. Breathing

Below, one example from each laboratory is listed.

Laboratory 1

Experimental set-up – beetle/boat

The task consisted of observing an imaginary beetle or boat on the horizon while moving eyes and head evenly. The required movement had to continue irrespective of the musical expression.

Example

The subject is a boy of twelve, one of the experimental subjects who does not speak. The results must therefore be conveyed by the music. The audio sample clearly reveals how movement and musical expression cohere. The piece resembles a slow funeral march. Synchronization of expression and movement was frequently observed in the experiments. For the subsequent free improvisation, the subject employs considerably more daring experimental timbres.[3] The courage to try out new possibilities was observed in many examples from all the experimental set-ups.

Laboratory 2

Experimental set-up – dynamic playing position

The experimental set-ups in this laboratory were relatively simple. The subjects were asked to alter their playing position and then improvise freely.

Example

Immanent "moments of magic" occurred with notable frequency in this laboratory. Having adopted new positions, the subjects clearly revealed a greater willingness to react without hesitation, producing sudden reversals in the formal sections and abrupt endings. There did not appear to be any thought processes involved at the interface between action/reaction and the unpredictability of these moments of magic.

3 | See Experiment 12 phases 4 and 5. Audio samples E12 Phase 4 and E12 Phase 5 can be found at *http://forschung.corinna-eikmeier.de*

langsamen Trauermarsch. Eine Synchronisation von Ausdruck und Bewegung war in den Experimenten häufig zu beobachten. In der darauffolgenden freien Improvisation verwendet die Versuchsperson wesentlich mutiger experimentelle Klangfarben.[3] Der Mut, neue Möglichkeiten zu erproben, war in vielen Beispielen verteilt über alle Versuchsanordnungen zu beobachten.

Laborraum 2

Versuchsanordnung – dynamisches und stabiles Gleichgewicht

Die Versuchsanordnungen in diesem Laborraum waren vergleichsweise einfach. Die Versuchspersonen wurden gebeten, ihre Spielposition zu verändern und in der veränderten Position frei zu improvisieren.

Beispiel

Unmittelbare »magische Momente« traten in diesem Laborraum auffällig oft auf. Die Personen waren offenbar durch die veränderten Positionen verstärkt bereit, ohne Verzögerungen zu reagieren, wodurch plötzliche Wendepunkte der Formteile und plötzliche Schlüsse entstanden. Es schienen keine Denkprozesse zwischen dem Handeln und Reagieren und der Unvorhersehbarkeit dieser magischen Momente zu stehen.

Die Versuchsperson ist die älteste Teilnehmerin der Experimente. Sie ist 83 Jahre und sehr energiegeladen. Im Beispiel sitzt sie mit einer Pobacke auf einem Stuhl. In der Improvisation ist exemplarisch deutlich eine Tendenz zu plötzlichen Wendepunkten und Schlüssen zu hören. Dieses Phänomen trat in diesem Laborraum besonders gehäuft auf. Zudem beschreibt die Versuchsperson ein für sie vollkommen neues, unvorhergesehenes Gefühl:

»That was the first time, that I felt my heart beating. [...] it is probably trigging some places, where I love to be on my Cello. I love certain parts of the sounds. It is a special exiting kind of thing. [...] Emotionally I was closer to the parts of my Cello. The sound parts. The sound parts, that I like so much.« [4]

Laborraum 3

Versuchsanordnung – der Motor

In den Experimenten haben sich die Versuchspersonen Körperteile ausgesucht, von denen aus sie ihre Bewegungen gesteuert haben. Teilweise waren es pro-

---

3 | Vgl. Experiment 12 Phase 4 und 5. Hörbeispiele: E12 Phase 4 und E12 Phase 5 unter *http://forschung.corinna-eikmeier.de*.

4 | Vgl. Experiment 24 Phase 2, Hörbeispiel E24 Phase 2 unter *http://forschung.corinna-eikmeier.de*.

The subject is the oldest participant in the experiments. She is 83 years old and highly energetic. In the example, she sits with just one buttock on the chair. A clear tendency to employ sudden reversals and abrupt endings can be heard in the improvisation. The phenomenon occurs particularly frequently in this laboratory. The subject also describes what she experiences as a completely new, unexpected emotion:

"That was the first time that I felt my heart beating. [...] It is probably triggering some places where I love to be on my cello. I love certain parts of the sounds. It is a special, exciting thing. [...] Emotionally, I was closer to the parts of my cello. The sound parts. The sound parts that I like so much."[4]

Laboratory 3

Experimental set-up – the motor
In these experiments, the subjects chose parts of their bodies which they then used to control their movements. These were sometimes proximal areas such as the pelvis, navel or the spine. At other times, they were distal, less accessible parts, such as an earlobe or a little toe.

The musical task ran thus: the stimuli for musical actions were to be set in motion from the feeling from a body part and its concomitant potential for movement.

Example
The subject is a professional opera singer. She has no prior experience of improvisation. At the start of the experiment, she says that she is thrilled and also a little nervous about the improvisation scenario. Over two hours, she gradually discovers her improvisational skills. The experiments in this laboratory made an important contribution to this process. One particular improvisation is examined here more closely by way of example. The subject allows all stimuli to come from her navel. She realizes that she usually goes through a wide range of preparation before singing. Here, song unexpectedly flowed out of her of its own volition. She is surprised to have effortlessly mastered a technical challenge that, mere seconds earlier, she had not even given thought to. Neither did she have to make any particular effort; she simply felt the energy without actively having to produce it.

The audio sample clearly demonstrates how she sustains long notes with extreme ease.[5]

---

4 | See Experiment 24 phase 2. Audio sample E24 phase 2 can be found at *http://forschung.corinna-eikmeier.de*.

5 | See Experiment 1 phase 3. Audio sample E1 Phase 3.4 can be found at *http://forschung.corinna-eikmeier.de*.

ximale Regionen, wie Becken, Bauchnabel oder Lendenwirbelsäule. Teilweise waren es auch sehr distale, schwerer zugängliche Körperteile, wie zum Beispiel ein Ohrläppchen oder ein kleiner Zeh.

Die musikalische Aufgabenstellung war folgendermaßen: Die Impulse für die musikalischen Aktionen sollten aus dem Gespür für den gewählten Körperteil und damit auch aus den Bewegungsmöglichkeiten angestoßen werden.

Beispiel
Die Versuchsperson ist professionelle Opernsängerin. Sie hat keine Vorerfahrung in Improvisation. Zu Beginn des Experiments äußert sie, dass sie aufgeregt sei und auch ein wenig Stress mit der Improvisationssituation habe. In dem zweistündigen Experiment entdeckt sie Schritt für Schritt ihre improvisatorischen Fähigkeiten. Die Experimente dieses Laborraums sind dabei ein Baustein. Exemplarisch soll hier eine bestimmte Improvisation näher beleuchtet werden. Die Versuchsperson lässt alle Impulse vom Bauchnabel kommen. Sie stellt fest, dass sie gewöhnlich eine ganze Palette an Vorbereitungen zum Singen trifft. In diesem Fall funktionierte das Singen für sie unerwartet von selber. Sie ist überrascht, dass ihr eine technische Herausforderung, an die sie Sekunden vorher noch nicht gedacht hatte, mühelos gelang. Zudem brauchte sie sich nicht anzustrengen, sondern sie spürte einfach die Kraft ohne sie produzieren zu müssen.

Im Hörbeispiel ist deutlich zu hören, wie sie mit einer Selbstverständlichkeit die langen Töne spannt.[5]

An diesem Beispiel wird der folgende Zusammenhang exemplarisch deutlich: Durch die Aufgabe wird die Wahrnehmung auf eine körperliche Empfindung gelenkt. Dadurch verstärkt sich die Handlung in der Gegenwart. Die Gewohnheit, Technik zu kontrollieren, wird schwächer und sie singt mit ihrem ganzen Selbst präsent und ausdrucksstark.

Laborraum 4

Versuchsanordnung – paradoxe Atmung
Der Versuchsanordnung liegt die bekannte Feldenkrais-Lektion »Paradoxe Atmung« zu Grunde, in der die Atembewegungen von Unterbauch und Brustkorb als Wippbewegung unabhängig von der Atmung erforscht werden.

Beispiel
Die Versuchsperson hatte zur Zeit des Experiments eine Überlastungsverletzung (Tennisellenbogen). Sie ließ sich mit viel Zeit auf die Versuchsanordnung ein. Die Wippbewegung zwischen Bauch und Brustkorb war ihr sehr

5 | Vgl. Experiment 1 Phase 3 Hörbeispiel E1 Phase 3.4 unter *http://forschung.corinna-eikmeier.de*.

This example perfectly illustrates the premise of the experiment: the task focuses the mind on corporeal perception, propelling the action into the present. Her habit of controlling technique recedes, brings her to sing expressively and with full presence, utilizing her entire being.

Laboratory 4

Experimental set-up - paradoxical breathing
The experimental set-up is based on the well-known Feldenkrais technique of "paradoxical breathing", in which the respiratory movements of the lower abdomen and rib cage are explored as a rocking movement independent of breathing.

Example
At the time of the experiment, the subject was suffering from a strain injury (tennis elbow). She invested a great length of time in the experiment. The rocking movement between the stomach and rib cage was new to her and at first she could only do it slowly. Her interest in mastering this movement appeared to increase during the course of the experiment. After we had experimented without the cello, with movement and vocalization, for an hour in a range of positions, she could not resist reattempting to perform the movement. Following a short break, I suggested she employ the movement whilst playing the cello. We added the voice and, for the moment, disregarded artistic considerations. The result was several wild, forceful episodes. The subject – acting cautiously due to the pain in her elbow – increasingly allowed energy to flow through her. Her elbow stopped hurting. She expressed her feeling when playing as follows:

"It's as if I'd taken drugs (laughter). And it was lovely to see that my body remembered how to play the cello. I feel seriously injured, and when I then play the cello, I feel out of it. But this flow and the energy took me back to a place where I could remember how to play."[6]

Implicit knowledge allows her to play without fearing for her injury. She no longer needs the control she has developed as protection. The energy she finds for wild, noisy improvisation is not derived from muscle exertion, as that would not have been possible in her medical state.

6 | See Experiment 26 at *http://forschung.corinna-eikmeier.de*.

fremd und sie konnte sie zunächst nur langsam ausführen. Während des Experiments schien sie immer mehr Interesse daran zu gewinnen, diese Bewegung zu finden. Nachdem wir über eine Stunde ohne Cello in verschiedenen Positionen mit der Bewegung und der Stimme experimentiert hatten, konnte sie fast nicht mehr aufhören, die Bewegung immer wieder auszuprobieren. Nach einer kurzen Pause schlug ich ihr vor, die Bewegung beim Cellospielen zu benutzen. Wir nahmen die Stimme hinzu und ließen für den Moment künstlerische Ansprüche außen vor. Es entstanden mehrere wilde, kraftvolle Episoden. Die Versuchsperson, die durch die Schmerzen im Ellenbogen vorsichtig war, ließ mehr und mehr die Kraft durchfließen. Ihr Ellenbogen schmerzte dabei nicht mehr. Sie konnte ihr Spielgefühl verbalisieren:

»Es fühlt sich an, wie wenn ich Drogen genommen hätte. (Gelächter). Und es war sehr nett, dass mein Körper sich erinnert hat, wie man Cello spielt. Ich fühle mich so verletzt und wenn ich dann das Cello spiele, dann fühle ich mich neben der Spur. Aber dieser Fluss und die Kraft haben mich zurück in ein Stadium geworfen, wo ich mich erinnern konnte.«[6]

Ein implizites Wissen erlaubt es ihr, ohne Furcht vor ihrer Verletzung zu spielen. Die Kontrolle, die sie als Schutz aufgebaut hat, braucht sie nicht mehr. Die Kraft, die sie für die wilde und laute Improvisation zur Verfügung hat, hat nichts mit Muskelanstrengung zu tun, denn das wäre zu der Zeit für sie nicht möglich gewesen.

8. Überblick über die Ergebnisse[7]

Die Auswertung der insgesamt 49 qualitativen Experimente, von denen hier beispielhaft vier dargestellt wurden, ergab, dass durch Verstärkung einzelner Aspekte der improvisatorischen Bewegungsqualität Merkmale der improvisatorischen Handlungsweise stärker wurden. In Beispielen, in denen das verbale Datenmaterial die Veränderungen nicht befriedigend transportieren kann, wurden die oben genannten Hörbeispiele als Datenmaterial einbezogen. In der künstlerischen Form lassen sich Vergleiche zwischen ersten Improvisationen zu signifikanten Unterschieden in Stil und Ausdruck der Probanden im Verlauf eines Experiments erkennen.

6 | Vgl. Experiment 26 unter *http://forschung.corinna-eikmeier.de*.

7 | Einen detaillierten Einblick ist der in Kürze erscheinenden Buchform dieser Studie zu entnehmen: Sie wird 2016 unter dem Titel »Bewegungsqualität und Musizierpraxis. Zum Verhältnis von Feldenkrais-Methode und musikalischer Improvisation« im Musikautorenverlag Burkhard Muth (ISBN 978-3-929379) erscheinen.

8. Overview of Results[7]

Evaluation of the 49 experiments showed that qualities of improvisational action improve as aspects of improvisational quality of movement are refined. For those samples where verbal data do not satisfactorily convey the transformation, the data set has been represented as audio samples. In terms of artistic form, comparisons between initial improvisations and significant stylistic and expressive differences among the subjects in the course of an experiment were observed.

Below is a summary of the trends that were observed:

The boundaries coalesce between players, music and communication in the ensemble. This creates a state of "freedom", both described by the improvising musicians in their general observations, as well as strongly felt during the experiments. There is no room for control in this state of "freedom".

- The players are ready to act with full immediacy. This was shown by the fact that stimuli were directly translated into music.
- Many unexpected and extremely precise reversals were enacted in the unhesitant, immanent actions.
- Many improvisations grew in a highly organic manner.
- When addressing musical parameters, fine differentiation was observed, particularly in secondary parameters such as timbre, articulation or agogic accents.
- Customary musical vocabulary was frequently supplemented by new timbres and techniques when the progress of the improvisation demanded it.
- The voice leading became more autonomous. Synchronization of movement tasks with the music's moods and tempi created homophony of expression and quality of movement.
- Polyphony of music and movement presented a challenge that produced freer action in the experimental process.
- The partly unusual and confusing experimental set-ups prevented playing techniques from being "properly" controlled. In many cases, it was precisely this loss of control that had a positive impact on the technique.

Translation into English: Oliver Dahin, Berlin

---

7 | A more in-depth description will be featured in a book about this study, to be published shortly. The book "Quality of movement and musical performance. The relationship between the Feldenkrais method and musical improvisation" will be published in 2016 by Burkhard Muth (ISBN 978-3-929379).

Zusammengefasst ließen sich die folgenden Tendenzen beobachten:

Die Grenzen zwischen Spieler, Musik und Kommunikation im Ensemble verschmelzen. Dadurch entsteht der Zustand der »Auflösung«, der von improvisierenden Musikern in allgemeinen Reflexionen beschrieben wird und während der Experimente verstärkt erlebt wurde. In diesem Zustand der »Auflösung« hat Kontrolle keinen Platz.

- Die Spieler sind unmittelbar handlungsbereit. Dies zeigte sich daran, dass Impulse unmittelbar musikalisch umgesetzt wurden.
- In den unverzögerten, unmittelbaren Aktionen entstanden viele unerwartete Wendepunkte, in zeitlich hoher Präzision.
- Im Umgang mit den musikalischen Parametern war vor allem bei sekundären Parametern wie Klangfarbe und Artikulation oder Agogik ein differenzierter Umgang zu beobachten.
- Das gewohnte musikalische Vokabular wurde häufig durch neue Klangfarben und Spieltechniken erweitert, sofern die Entwicklungen der Improvisationen dazu herausforderten.
- Die Stimmführungen wurden autarker. Durch die Synchronisation von Bewegungsaufgaben mit den Stimmungen und Tempi der Musik entstand eine Homophonie zwischen Ausdruck und Bewegungsqualität.
- Polyphonie zwischen Musik und Bewegung war eine Herausforderung, die im Prozess der Experimente zu freierem Handeln führte.
- Durch die teilweise ungewohnten und verwirrenden Versuchsanordnungen war es nicht mehr möglich die Spieltechnik »ordentlich« zu kontrollieren. Häufig hatte gerade dieser Kontrollverlust eine positive Auswirkung auf die Spieltechnik.

LITERATUR/REFERENCES

Burkart, Thomas (2010): »Qualitatives Experiment«, in: Mey, Günter; Mruck, Katja (Hg./Eds.), Qualitative Forschung in der Psychologie, Wiesbaden: Springer VS-Verlag, 252-262.

Eikmeier, Corinna: Forschungsdokumentation *http://forschung.corinna-eikmeier.de*

Klein, Julian (2010): »Was ist künstlerische Forschung?«, in: Stock, Günter (Hrsg./Ed.), Gegenworte 23, Wissenschaft trifft Kunst, Berlin-Brandenburgische Akademie der Wissenschaft: Akademieverlag, 25-28.

Intermezzo 6

In meinem Forschungsprozess mit den Versuchsteilnehmern war die Versprachlichung ein ganz großes Problem. Deshalb habe ich erstmal mit mir selber angefangen zu experimentieren, wie ich das, was ich erlebe, beschreiben kann. Für mein Projekt war es wichtig, die Musik und den Menschen, der sie macht, zusammen zu sehen. Ich konnte also nicht nur über die Musik reden, sondern es ging immer auch darum, wie sich derjenige bewegt, wie er seine Bewegung organisiert. Der Mensch musste mitreflektiert werden. Für die Experimente mit mir selbst dachte ich: Wenn dir etwas auffällt, schreibst du es auf. Aber der Prozess des Aufschreibens ist so weit weg vom Tun, dass da schon tausend Gedanken dazwischen stehen, die das wieder auf eine ganz andere Ebene bringen. Und dann hat es nichts mehr mit dem zu tun, was ich wirklich vorher gefühlt oder wahrgenommen habe. Deshalb habe ich etwas anderes ausprobiert. Wenn mir irgendetwas auffiel, habe ich es laut ausgesprochen und alles aufgenommen. Das war ein ganz interessanter Weg, einfach die Erlebnisse direkt zu sprechen. Auch das ist nochmal ein Schritt, etwas in Sprache zu fassen. Man geht jedes Mal raus aus dem Improvisieren. Aber ich habe dabei irrsinnig viel gelernt über mein eigenes Spiel.

Diskussionsbeitrag von Corinna Eikmeier, Mai 2014

Intermezzo 6

In the course of my research I found that the participants had a big problem with putting things into words. This was the reason I started off experimenting and trying out different ways to describe my own experience. For my project it was really important to see the music and the people who make it as one entity. So I couldn't just speak about the music, instead it was also about how somebody moves, how they organize their movement. It was necessary to reflect on the person too. For the experiments with myself, my thoughts were: as something occurs to you, write it down. But the process of writing is actually so far away from that of the action itself that you have time to think a thousand other thoughts which take you to a totally different level and then it doesn't have anything to do with what I was really feeling or perceiving beforehand. So then I took another step. If something occurred to me I would voice it immediately and record it. This was a very interesting process, just saying directly what I was experiencing out loud. This too is a way to capture something in language. Every time you find yourself departing from improvising. But this way I learned a massive amount about my own playing.

Corinna Eikmeier in a public discussion, May 2014

Translation into English: Louise & Phil Loxton, GB-Wales

EXPLORATORIUM Berlin 31-5-014

LARA FRISCH

Improvisation

Improvisierte Musik und die Unwahrscheinlichkeit der Kommunikation

Improvised music and the Improbability of Communication

- In der Zusammenarbeit ... um den gemeinsamen kreativen Prozess
- Plattform für gemeinsames Schaffen
- kaum offene Konflikte, die Gruppe war konsensorientiert
- die kollektive Orientierung wurde eingehalten
- 'Verständigung' über Metaphern
- durch zu viele musikwissenschaftliche Begriffe wurde die 'Kommunikation' zu steif
- Metaphern und Begriffe die 'verschleiern' offen sind. Der Gegenstand wird mit Metaphern beschrieben
- die Metaphern schaffen einen Konsens
- ?: weil sie offen sind für unterschiedliche Assoziationen

Improvisierte Musik und die Unwahrscheinlichkeit der Kommunikation | Improvised Music and the Improbability of Communication

Lara Frisch

Vorwort

Eine neue Studie der John Hopkins University in Baltimore hat ergeben, dass die Gehirne gemeinsam improvisierender Musiker wie bei einem Gespräch arbeiten (ohne Verfasser: Melodische Unterhaltung 2014: 14). Der Hirnforscher Charles Limb und sein Forschungsteam haben dies herausgefunden, indem sie erfahrene Jazz-Musiker einer funktionellen Magnetresonanztomographie (fMRT) unterzogen, während diese auf einem eigens gebauten Keyboard spielten[1]. Dabei fand das Team heraus, dass besonders die Hirnareale angeregt wurden, die für den Satzbau, also die Syntax zuständig sind (ebd.).

Improvisierte Musik wird oft mit einem Gespräch oder einer Unterhaltung verglichen (u.a. Berliner 1994, Monson 1996, Sawyer 2001). Diese Meinung wird nicht nur von Hirnforschern und Musikwissenschaftlern geteilt, sondern auch von vielen Musikern. Speziell im Bereich der Beschreibung improvisierter Musik scheint die Analogie zur Sprache äußerst beliebt zu sein.

Um mehr über die Prozesse hinter dieser Analogie herauszufinden, wird dieser Text kurz erläutern, welche Rolle der verbalen Kommunikation im Rahmen improvisierter Musik bisher zugeordnet wurde und was für Charakteristiken diese aufweist. In einem weiteren Schritt wird dann nach der Systemtheorie Niklas Luhmanns versucht, zu erklären, was geschieht, wenn Konflikte oder Widersprüche auf verbaler Ebene entstehen, und ob diese den Prozess der improvisierten Musik beeinflussen.

Kommunikation und improvisierte Musik

Es gibt viele verschiedene Ebenen von Kommunikation im Kontext der improvisierten Musik. Darunter befinden sich unter anderem die musikalische, die physische und die verbale Ebene. In seinem Buch »Hear and Now« behauptet Peter Wilson, dass die musikalische Ebene, als Konzept der Kommunikation, alles umschließt, was an klanglichen Interaktionen innerhalb einer Gruppenimprovisation zustande kommt: vom banalen Echo bis zur gegenseitigen Induktion oder dem kollektiven Weben eines gemeinsamen Klang-Teppichs (Wilson 1999: 13-14). Dabei kann es passieren, dass die improvisierte Musik Formen der Kommunikation, wie zum Beispiel der des Gesprächs, annimmt[2].

Die zweite Ebene, die innerhalb improvisierter Musik oft als Kommunikation beschrieben wird, ist als die physische bekannt. Dies beinhaltet die Kör-

1 | Die Pianisten spielten »trading fours«, eine Art Improvisation, bei der sich zwei Musiker nach jeweils vier Takten abwechseln (ebd.).

2 | Wie die Studie von Limb bezeugt, wo bei der »musikalischen Unterhaltung«, Hirnregionen angeregt werden, die für die Syntax verantwortlich sind.

Preface

A recent study at John Hopkins University in Baltimore found that the brains of musicians jointly engaged in improvisation function as if in mutual conversation (without author: Melodische Unterhaltung 2014: 14). Brain researcher Charles Limb and his team made this discovery using functional magnetic resonance imaging (fMRI) to track the brain activity of experienced jazz musicians whilst in the act of playing on a specially created keyboard.[1] In particular, the study found heightened activation in areas of the brain associated with sentence construction, in other words, syntax (ibid.).

Improvised music is often compared to a conversation or discussion (for example Berliner 1994, Monson 1996, Sawyer 2001), an opinion shared not only by brain researchers and musicologists, but also by many musicians themselves. The analogy to language is especially common in descriptions of improvised music.

In exploring the processes behind this analogy, this essay briefly explains the aspects of verbal communication generally assigned to improvised music, together with their characteristics. Niklas Luhmann's systems theory is then applied to a description of what happens when conflicts or contradictions occur on a verbal level, and whether they influence the process of improvised music.

Communication and improvised music

Many different levels of communication exist in improvised music, including musical, physical and verbal strata. In "Hear and Now", Peter Wilson claims that the musical level, as a communicative concept, encompasses everything that occurs within the interaction of sounds during a group improvisation: from the straightforward echo to the mutual inducement or the collective weaving of a common soundscape (Wilson 1999: 13-14). This may cause improvised music to assume forms of communication not dissimilar, for example, to conversation.[2]

The next level frequently described in terms of communication in improvised music involves physical characteristics, such as body language, facial expressions and the musicians' physical interaction. Sociology's increasing exploration of improvisation as a creative action (Joas 1996, Figueroa-Dreher 2012, Kurt 2012) is worthy of note in this context.

The verbal level usually occurs before and/or after the improvisation, although this does not mean that it is not part of the process. Ingrid Monson,

1 | The pianist played "trading fours", a type of improvisation in which musicians participate in back and forth instrumental exchanges, four bars in duration (ibid.).

2 | As Limb's study corroborates, showing activation of areas in the brain associated with syntax during "musical discussion".

persprache, die Gestik, die Mimik und die physische Interaktion der Musiker. Dabei wird die Improvisation in der Soziologie immer mehr als kreatives Handeln thematisiert (Joas 1996, Figueroa-Dreher 2012, Kurt 2012).

Die verbale Ebene der Kommunikation findet meist vor und/oder nach dem Improvisieren statt. Dies bedeutet jedoch nicht, dass sie nicht auch einen Teil des Prozesses darstellt. Ingrid Monson, die ihr Buch »Saying Something« unter anderem auch der Sprache und Kommunikation im Kontext des Jazz gewidmet hat, behauptet, dass das verbal-ästhetische Bild[3] die kollaborative und kommunikative Qualität der Improvisation betont (Monson 1996: 2). Viele Jazz-Ausdrücke wie *jitterbugs, cat* oder *ickey,* gehören genauso zur Geschichte des Jazz wie die Musik. Der Jazz-Jargon bestand deswegen nicht nur aus der Musik, sondern auch aus den Gesprächen und dem Austausch der Musiker untereinander.

Der Fokus dieses Textes soll jedoch weniger auf dem geschichtlichen Aspekt der verbalen Kommunikation liegen, sondern vielmehr auf deren Charakteristik und Gebrauch innerhalb improvisierter Musik.

Charakteristiken der verbalen Kommunikation im Kontext improvisierter Musik

Die verbale Kommunikation, wie sie im Rahmen improvisierter Musik auftaucht, ist in ihrer Form dem musikalischen Gegenstand nahe, dem sie entspringt. So entwerfen Ensembles, die schon längere Zeit zusammen spielen, ihre eigene Art der Kommunikation. Während meiner Studie[4], die sich mit der Gruppenkommunikation improvisierender Ensembles befasst, hat sich herausgestellt, dass diese nicht nur Einsichten in die Lern- und Arbeitsprozesse der einzelnen Ensembles gibt, sondern auch spezifisch auf die individuellen Anliegen und die Bedürfnisse der Ensembles angepasst ist. Hinzugefügt werden muss, dass diese Gruppenkommunikation zudem sehr kontext- und situationsabhängig ist. Die Kontextabhängigkeit der Gruppenkommunikation ist durch den geschichtlichen Rahmen der Musikszene gesetzt, während die Situationsabhängigkeit durch die Einzigartigkeit der Ensembles gegeben ist.

Erstaunlicherweise trifft dies sogar auf Ensembles zu, die sich zum ersten Mal in einer gewissen Konstellation zusammentun, um gemeinsam zu musi-

3 | Aus dem Englischen »this verbal aesthetic image«.

4 | Der Titel meiner Dissertation an der *Bauhaus Universität Weimar* lautet: »Welchen Einfluss besitzt die Gruppenkommunikation auf den kreativen Prozess improvisierender Ensembles?« Es ist eine Studie, die die unterschiedlichen Merkmale der Gruppenkommunikation im künstlerischen Schaffensprozess improvisierender Ensembles untersucht.

who dedicates part of her book "Saying Something" to language and communication in jazz, asserts that the verbal aesthetic image underscores the collaborative and communicative quality of improvisation (Monson 1996: 2). Many jazz terms such as *jitterbugs*, *cat* or *ickey* are just as important in jazz as the music itself. Jazz jargon thus arose, not purely from the notes, but also from the conversations and discussions between the musicians themselves.

This essay, however, focuses less on the historical aspect of verbal communication than on its characteristics and use in improvised music as a practiced art form.

Characteristics of Verbal Communication in Improvised Music

Verbal communication, as it occurs in improvised music, assumes a form closely resembling the musical object from which it emanates. This can clearly be seen in ensembles that have developed their own form of communication over many years of playing together. In the course of research for my doctoral dissertation,[3] which examines group communication within improvising ensembles, it became apparent that analysis of this communication not only opens up insights into the learning and working methods of individual ensembles, but is also closely related to their individual concerns and needs. It must further be stated that this group communication is also contextual and situational: the contextuality arises from the historical nature of the music scene, while its situational dependency relates to the uniqueness of the ensemble.

Surprisingly, this is even true of ensembles that come together for the first time in a specific grouping to make music. Although less emphasis is placed on establishing a common form of communication in such contexts, there are, nevertheless, indications that the members of these new ensembles do try to communicate with one another using a common vocabulary.

Another feature of communication in improvised music is the coinage and use of verbal imagery. This is found not only in personal accounts of musical experience, but also moulds the ensemble's group discussion. In a series of interviews conducted for his book "Improvisation", Derek Bailey observed that almost all musicians prefer to discuss improvisation in "abstract" terms (Bailey 1980: 11). They often resort to metaphor and analogy to describe their work. Im-

3 | The title of my doctoral dissertation at the *Bauhaus University Weimar* is "Welchen Einfluss besitzt die Gruppenkommunikation auf den kreativen Prozess improvisierender Ensembles?" It investigates the various qualities of group communication within the creative artistic process of improvising ensembles.

zieren. Obwohl der Fokus in diesen Kontexten weniger auf dem Etablieren einer gemeinsamen Art der Kommunikation liegt, gibt es doch Anzeichen dafür, dass die Mitglieder dieser neuen Ensembles versuchen, sich anhand eines gemeinsamen Vokabulars zu verständigen.

Ein weiteres Merkmal der Kommunikation im Rahmen improvisierter Musik ist das Benutzen und Gestalten von verbalen Bildlichkeiten. Diese finden sich nicht nur in den persönlichen Beschreibungen über die individuelle musikalische Erfahrung wieder, sondern prägen auch den Gruppendiskurs von Ensembles. Schon Derek Bailey bemerkte in einer Reihe von Interviews, die er für sein Buch »Improvisation« führte, dass fast alle Musiker vorzogen, Improvisation in »abstrakten« Begriffen zu diskutieren (Bailey 1980: 11). Dabei greifen Musiker oft zu Metaphern oder Analogien, wenn es um die Beschreibung ihrer Tätigkeit geht. Der Improvisations-Musiker Fritz Hauser vergleicht zum Beispiel Freie Improvisation mit Bergsteigen:

> »Die Vorbereitungen sind wichtig, man kann dabei fast alles in den Griff bekommen: Man kann den Körper trainieren, man kann die Ausrüstung bereit stellen [...] alle Eventualitäten abschätzen und trotzdem: Wenn es dann losgeht und man in früher Morgenstunde die Hand auf den Fels legt [...] dann macht das Ganze nur Sinn, wenn Instinkt und Reaktionsvermögen, Erfahrung, Neugier und Wachsein gleichzeitig da sind. Ganz im Sinne von: Erfolg ist, wenn Vorbereitung und Gelegenheit zusammen kommen.« (Hauser in Nanz 2011: 28)

Es scheint, als wären es die Interaktionsmuster zwischen den Musikern, die immer wieder zur Kommunikations-Analogie führen. Auch im Jazz und im Free Jazz wurde die Musik oft als Konversation beschrieben. In seinem Buch »Thinking in Jazz: The Infinite Art of Improvisation« hat der Musikethnologe Paul Berliner ein ganzes Kapitel danach benannt (»The Collective Conversation and Musical Journey«) und bemerkt, dass Jazz-Musiker zwei Lieblings-Metaphern haben, wenn es um das Beschreiben von Jazz geht:

> »[...] the two metaphors favored among musicians are, firstly to compare group improvisation to a conversation that players carry on among themselves in the language of jazz, and secondly, to equate the experience of improvising to going on a demanding musical journey«. (Berliner 1994: 348)

Wie schon Fritz Hausers Beispiel gezeigt hat, heben die meisten Analogien oder Metaphern die Prozesshaftigkeit der improvisierten Musik hervor und enthalten Referenzen bezüglich der Vorbereitung, Balance und Intuition. Hinzu kommt, dass die Metaphern und Analogien oft eine körperliche und geistige Aktivität beschreiben, in der es um die situative Bestimmtheit des Augenblicks geht: also um das Anpassen der Handlung an den Moment.

provising musician Fritz Hauser, for example, compares free improvisation to mountain climbing:

"Preparation is crucial and ensures you can get the hang of almost anything: you can train the body, you can get your equipment ready [...] account for all eventualities, but when you finally get started and feel the rock under your hands in the early hours [...] it only really works when instinct and reactions, experience, curiosity and vigilance come together. In a nutshell, success is what happens when preparation and opportunity converge." (Hauser 2011: 28)

It appears as if the communication analogy stems from the patterns of interaction between musicians; jazz and free jazz have also frequently been described in terms of conversations. In his book "Thinking in Jazz: The Infinite Art of Improvisation", ethnomusicologist Paul Berliner uses this idea as a chapter title ("The Collective Conversation and Musical Journey") and notes that jazz musicians have two favourite metaphors to describe their music:

"[...] the two metaphors favoured among musicians are, firstly, to compare group improvisation to a conversation that players hold among themselves in the language of jazz, and secondly, to equate the experience of improvising to going on a demanding musical journey." (Berliner 1994: 348)

As the example given by Fritz Hauser shows, the majority of analogies and metaphors highlight the linear processes of improvised music and reference preparation, balance and intuition. They also often describe a physical and mental activity concerning the situational force of the present, in other words, how specific actions are adapted to the moment.

Derek Bailey also comments on "Some Comparisons between Intuitive and Scientific Descriptions of Music" by Thomas Clifton, who asserts:

"The question is not whether the description is subjective, objective, biased or idiosyncratic, but very simply; whether or not the description says something significant about the intuited experience. So that the experience itself becomes something from which we can learn and, in so doing, learn about the object of that experience as well [...]." (Clifton quoted in Bailey 1980: 11)

In Clifton's view, describing musical processes is one part of making music. What he disregards, however, is that personal ("subjective") description of these processes may also provide insights into individual experience. This is particularly relevant to ensembles, as the metaphors used in such descriptions typically serve to analyze/express a common creative process. Within any one ensemble, it is not unusual for one of the musicians to use a metaphor whose meaning

Derek Bailey machte zudem auch eine Anmerkung zu Thomas Cliftons »Some Comparisons between Intuitive and Scientific Descriptions of Music«, in der dieser behauptet:

»Die Frage ist nicht, ob eine Beschreibung subjektiv oder objektiv, von einer besonderen Neigung oder von Ressentiments getragen ist, sondern ganz einfach, ob sie etwas Signifikantes über die intuitive Erfahrung aussagt, so dass diese Erfahrung ihrerseits zu etwas wird, das wir in Erfahrung bringen können, um so auch etwas über ihren Gegenstand zu erfahren [...].« (Clifton in Bailey 1980: 11)

Für Clifton ist die Beschreibung musikalischer Prozesse ein Teil des Musikmachens. Was er jedoch nicht beachtet, ist, dass das persönliche (Clifton sagt subjektiv) Beschreiben dieser Prozesse auch Einblicke in die individuellen Erfahrungswelten gewähren kann. Dies ist besonders relevant im Rahmen von Ensembles, da die Metaphern, die während dieser Beschreibungen aufkommen, meist der Beobachtung bzw. der Reflektion eines gemeinsamen Schaffens dienen. Innerhalb eines Ensembles passiert es oft, dass eine Metapher von einem Musiker initiiert, und dabei ihr Sinnesinhalt erst durch die Gruppe konstruiert wird. Hinzu kommt, dass Metaphern auch die Kohäsion[5] von Gruppen bzw. Ensembles beeinflussen können (Owen 1985: 415). Dementsprechend unterstützt der verbale Prozess der Selbst- und Fremdreflektion mittels Metaphern die gruppendynamischen Vorgänge innerhalb von Ensembles. Dies ist besonders relevant im Rahmen einer Kollektiv-Improvisation, bei der es unter anderem um das Nacharbeiten von Schaffensprozessen geht. Das Benutzen von Metaphern in solch einem Kontext, verhilft der Gruppe zu einer gemeinsamen Sprache, die die Kohäsion der Gruppe bzw. des Ensembles weiter bestärkt.

Demzufolge bestehen die Charakteristiken der verbalen Kommunikation in der Improvisation unter anderem aus dem Beschreiben von Situations- und Interaktionsprozessen, die innerhalb der Musik passieren. Hinzu kommt, dass die Kommunikation eines Ensembles nicht nur dessen Situation, sondern auch dessen Kontext wiederspiegelt. In diesem Zusammenhang wird oft nach Metaphern und Analogien gegriffen, da diese eine Form der Kommunikation ermöglichen, die sich mit dem musikalischen Gegenstand befasst, und dessen weitere Entwicklung besonders innerhalb von Ensembles, sprachlich weiter fördert. Dementsprechend geht es in den Musikbeschreibungen, welche eine Analogie oder Metapher zur Sprache besitzen, weniger um ein einvernehmliches Verstehen, sondern eher um ein gemeinsames Schaffen.

5 | Gruppenkohäsion aus dem Englischen group-cohesiveness: »[T]he result of all those forces acting upon members to remain in or to leave the group«. (Shaw in Owen 1985: 415)

Berlin 1·6·2014
Offene Bühne
Marion Timi Eiko Max

Um sich jetzt ein genaueres Bild über die Kommunikation innerhalb von improvisierenden Ensembles zu machen, wird sich nun der Kommunikationstheorie von Niklas Luhmann zugewandt.

Niklas Luhmann und Kommunikation

Die Systemtheorie von Luhmann basiert auf der Annahme, dass ein System die Differenz darstellt zwischen sich und der Umwelt (Luhmann 2010: 66 in Horster 2013: 4). Das Beziehen dieser Grenze und ihr Erhalt beruhen auf einer von den Biologen Humberto R. Maturana und Fransisco J. Varela konzipierten Organisationsart genannt *Autopoiesis*. Der Begriff Autopoiesis leitet sich vom altgriechischen *autos* »selbst« und *poiein* »machen« ab. Maturana und Varela gingen davon aus, dass Lebewesen autopoietische Systeme sind, die sich durch ihr ständiges Selbsterzeugen charakterisieren (Maturana/Varela 1984: 50).

Was ist Kommunikation?

Die Kommunikation nach Luhmann ist eine autopoietische Operation, die soziale Systeme erzeugen, um sich zu erhalten. Demzufolge ist die Autopoiesis der Kommunikation selbstherstellend und setzt voraus, dass nur die Kommunikation kommunizieren kann. (Luhmann 1995/3: 113) Im Rahmen dieses Beitrags werden nun Kollektiv-Improvisationen als soziale Systeme gesehen, auch wenn diese nur einmalig zusammenkommen. Diese Systeme können sich durch unterschiedliche Ebenen der Kommunikation erhalten. Im Rahmen dieses Artikels wird sich nur auf die verbale Kommunikation und deren möglichen Einfluss auf die musikalische Ebene konzentriert.

Die Kommunikation funktioniert anhand einer Synthese dreier Selektionen: Information, Mitteilung und Verstehen. Diese Synthese vollzieht sich in drei Schritten: Zuerst soll die Selektion der Information von der Selektion der Mitteilung differenziert werden, damit die Kommunikation zustande kommt (Dieckmann 2004: 22). In einem zweiten Schritt soll die Auswahl der Mitteilung entschieden werden, die der Übertragung der Information dient, was zum Beispiel schriftlich oder flüsternd geschehen kann (Kneer; Nassehi 1993: 81). In einem dritten Schritt kann das Verstehen eintreten, welches die Differenz zwischen dem Informationswert des Inhalts und dessen Gründen markiert (ebd.). Der Mechanismus der Synthese hat die Funktion, die Anschlussfähigkeit der Kommunikation zu sichern. So müssen die unterschiedlichen Selektionen immer eine Möglichkeit zum Anschluss geben, sonst kann sich die Kommunikation nicht weiterführen.

is then explicitly constructed by the group. Metaphors may also impact on the cohesiveness[4] of groups and ensembles (Owen 1985: 415). As such, the verbal process of reflecting on the self and the other using metaphors bolsters the group dynamic within ensembles. This is particularly relevant to collective improvisation, which in part involves the reworking of creative processes. Using metaphors in these contexts helps the group to develop a common language that further cements group/ensemble cohesion.

Thus, the characteristics of verbal communication in improvisation partly consist of the description of the situational and interactive processes that occur within the music. An ensemble's communication further reflects not only the situation, but also the context at hand. Metaphors and analogies are frequently used because they enable a form of communication that engages with the musical object and linguistically aids its development, especially in ensembles. As a result, descriptions of music that contain linguistic analogies or metaphors are less about consensual understanding than a common basis for creativity.

In order to obtain a more detailed picture of communication within improvising ensembles, I now turn to the work of Niklas Luhmann.

Niklas Luhmann and communication

Luhmann's systems theory is based on the hypothesis that a system is defined by the boundary between itself and its environment (Luhmann 2010: 66). The identity and maintenance of this boundary draws on a form of organisation theorized by biologists Humberto R. Maturana and Francisco J. Varela as *autopoiesis*, a term derived from Ancient Greek *autos* ("self") and *poiein* ("do"). Maturana and Varela see living organisms as autopoietic systems characterized by constant self-generation (Maturana; Varela 1984: 50).

What is communication?

Luhmann considers communication to be an autopoietic process that social systems employ to maintain themselves. Autopoiesis of communication is thus self-creating and assumes that only communication can communicate (Luhmann 1995/3: 113). This paper henceforth views collective improvisations, even if only on a one-off basis, as social systems that can be sustained using various levels of communication. Only verbal communication and its potential impact on the musical level is considered.

---

4 | "[T]he result of all those forces acting upon members to remain in or to leave the group." (Shaw 1985: 415)

1. Kommunikation als Unwahrscheinlichkeit

Die Kommunikation ist für Luhmann höchst unwahrscheinlich und somit riskant (Luhmann 1995/3: 119). Dies wird nach folgenden drei Kriterien begründet: Erstens nach dem Verstehen als Vollzug einer Einheit der Kommunikation, zweitens nach dem Erreichen des Empfängers und drittens nach dem Erfolg der Kommunikation, also deren Anschlussgültigkeit. Das Hindernis des Verstehens beruht auf der Annahme, dass es sehr unwahrscheinlich ist, voll und ganz verstanden zu werden. Diese Annahme stammt daher, dass Luhmann auf die Trennung und Individualisierung von Bewusstseinssystemen hinweist (Jahraus 2001: 78). So ist die Kommunikation zwischen zwei Menschen unwahrscheinlich, da beide unter anderem individuelle psychische Systeme haben, deren Definition von Sinn beispielsweise komplett verschieden sein kann (ebd.).

Hinzu kommt auch als zweites Hindernis das Erreichen des Adressaten. Es ist demzufolge sehr unwahrscheinlich, dass eine Kommunikation gleichzeitig mehrere Personen in einer gleichen Situation erreicht (ebd.). So kann man eine Kommunikation beispielsweise aufgrund einer räumlichen Situation nicht hören, weil es zu laut ist oder man die Kommunikation zu spät hört.

Es kann natürlich auch passieren, dass die Kommunikation zwar gehört und verstanden, aber nicht angenommen wird. Dies wäre dann das dritte Hindernis der Kommunikation. Systemtheoretisch bedeutet das Verweigern einer Kommunikation, dass diese nicht den entsprechenden Direktiven, Ebenen, Kognitionen und dem Denken des eigenen Verhaltens entspricht (ebd.: 79).

2. Kontingenz

Gemäß Luhmann unterliegt jede Art von Kommunikation einer Kontingenz. Der Begriff geht zurück auf Parsons Begriff »contingent on«, also »abhängig sein von« und stellt dar, was eine Komplementarität zweier Akteure offenlegt, die gegenseitig ihr Handeln davon abhängig machen, wie der andere handelt (Esposito in Horster 2013: 50). Luhmann entwickelt dies weiter, indem er diese doppelte Kontingenz mit zwei »black boxes« vergleicht, die füreinander intransparent bleiben, aber voneinander abhängig sind, und dies sogar wissen (ebd.). Demzufolge manifestiert sich die doppelte Kontingenz in der Kommunikation dadurch, dass Kommunikationen in Abhängigkeit zueinander erstellt werden. Es ist dieser Mechanismus, der die zukünftigen Anschlüsse einer Kommunikation ermöglicht. Obwohl Luhmann diese Kontingenz als eine Ordnung darstellt, scheint sie von einer ungleichen Natur zu sein, die die Kommunikation stabiler aussehen lässt, sie aber noch unwahrscheinlicher macht. Die Balance zur Stabilität kann nur gehalten werden, indem zwei Systeme sich vertrauen (Dieckmann 2004: 22). Erst dann ist eine Systembildung und dessen Erhalt möglich.

Communication works as a composite of three functions – information, articulation and understanding – synthesized in three steps. Information must first be differentiated from its articulation so that communication is possible (Dieckmann 2004: 22); the form of articulation used to convey the information comes next and could be, for example, writing or whispering (Kneer/Nassehi 1993: 81); understanding, noting the difference between the informational value of the content and its motives comes last (ibid.). The mechanism of the synthesis works to ensure the continuity of communication. The various different functions must therefore always enable a way of progressing if communication is to be maintained.

1. Communication as Improbability

Luhmann sees communication as highly improbable and thus risky (Luhmann 1995/3: 199). He justifies this stance on the basis of three criteria: understanding as the "performance" of a unit of communication, its ability to reach the recipient and the success of communication, in other words, its continuity. The barrier to understanding is based on the assumption that being fully understood is extremely unlikely. This notion arises from Luhmann's separation of individualization and awareness systems (Jahraus 2001: 78). Communication between two individuals is therefore improbable because both have their own psychological systems whose definition of meaning, for example, may be completely different (ibid.).

The situation is compounded by the second barrier; the ability of what is communicated to reach the recipient. It is thus highly improbable that communication can be received simultaneously by several people in the same setting (ibid.). A message may not be heard due to spatial aspects, for example if it is too loud or what is said is heard too late.

Of course, it is possible for communication to be heard and understood, yet not received. This is the third barrier to communication. Within this system theory, the refusal to receive communication means it does not match the rules, levels, cognition and thought processes in the individual's behavior (ibid.: 79).

2. Contingency

According to Luhmann, all types of communication are subject to contingency. The term indicates the complementarity of two individuals, each of whose actions are dependent on those of the other (Esposito 2013: 30). Luhmann goes further by comparing this double contingency with two "black boxes" that remain opaque to each other but are interdependent and even aware of this fact (ibid.). Double contingency thus manifests itself in communication as a form

Daraus folgt, dass die Kommunikation sozialer Systeme nicht auf Verstehen beruht, sondern auf dem Ermöglichen von Anschlüssen durch Vertrauen.

3. Kommunikation als Konflikt

Nun stellt sich die Frage: Wenn man sich sowieso nicht versteht, wie kann es dann möglich sein, in Konflikt zu geraten?

Ein Konflikt entsteht im luhmannschen Sinne dann, wenn einer Kommunikation widersprochen wird (Luhmann 2012: 530). Mit anderen Worten ausgedrückt, ein Konflikt ergibt sich beim Kommunizieren eines Widerspruchs. Der Widerspruch stellt ein Ereignis von unbestimmtem Anschlusswert dar, das die Kommunikation und somit das System ausarbeiten soll. Da der Anschlusswert unbestimmt ist, kann es passieren, dass mit dem kommunizierten Widerspruch eine Situation entsteht, die die Kommunikation immer mehr in Richtung Konflikt steuert.

Das Gefährliche am Konflikt ist, dass er sich zu einem System entwickeln kann, dessen Hauptinklusionsfaktor (das heißt, der Hauptfaktor, der seine Autopoiesis steuert) die Gegnerschaft ist. Dies bedeutet, dass es jeden und alles als Gegner betrachtet. Hinzu kommt, dass das Konflikt-System sich wie ein Parasit an einem anderen System bildet (ebd.: 531). Die destruktive Kraft des Konflikt-Systems liegt in dessen Fähigkeit, das Gast-System (zum Beispiel Freundschaft) zu absorbieren, indem es alle Aufmerksamkeit und Ressourcen beansprucht (ebd.: 533).

Wenn man den Konflikt im Luhmannschen Sinne versteht, kann es durchaus vorkommen, dass ein Konflikt, der auf der verbalen Ebene entsteht, zu einem Konflikt auf der musikalischen Ebene führen kann. Der Grund hierfür besteht darin, dass der Konflikt ein Gast-System beansprucht hat, dessen Kommunikation es sich unter anderem langsam zu Eigen macht, um sich so weiter zu entwickeln. Paul Berliner berichtet von einem Fall, bei dem die Musiker keinen anderen Ausweg sahen, als sich mitten im Konzert auf der Bühne an die Gurgel zu gehen (Berliner 1994: 430).

Jedoch gibt es auch Anzeichen dafür, dass die kommunikative Form des Konfliktes in der Musik übernommen wird. So scheint es manchmal, als würden Musiker musikalisch in Konflikt treten. Speziell im Free Jazz gibt es Beispiele dafür, wie Musiker – meist in Duo-Konstellationen (unter anderem auch einige Konzerte von Dizzy Gillespie und Max Roach) – in konfliktähnliche Situationen geraten. Dies würde bedeuten, dass die improvisierte Musik auch die Kommunikationsform des Konflikts annehmen könnte. Als Folge dessen würde nicht nur der destruktive Faktor des Konflikts benutzt werden, um etwas Gemeinsames zu gestalten, sondern es gäbe ein konkretes Anzeichen dafür, dass die musikalische und die verbale Kommunikation innerhalb des Systems improvisierter Musik sich beeinflussen könnten. Ob dies als Methode der

of dependency (Esposito 2013: 30): it is this mechanism that enables the future continuity of any communicative act. Although Luhmann presents this contingency as social order, the latter appears to be a paradox that helps stabilize communication whilst actually making it more improbable. The balance of stability can only be maintained if two systems trust each other (Dieckmann 2004: 22), enabling the formation and survival of these systems.

It follows that communication in social systems is based not on understanding but on the enablement of continuity through trust.

3. Communication as conflict

This logically gives rise to a key question: how is it possible to have conflict if we cannot understand each other?

In Luhmann's theory, conflict arises when communication is contradicted (Luhmann 2012: 530). In other words, conflict arises when a contradiction is communicated. A contradiction serves to disrupt the continuity of the communication and should enable the communication, and also the system, to be worked out. The communicated contradiction may give rise to a situation that leads the communication into ever deeper conflict.

The danger of a conflict is that it may turn into a system whose defining characteristic factor (in other words, that which controls its autopoiesis) is antagonism. This means it sees everyone and everything as an opponent. The conflict system further impacts on another system in the manner of a parasite (ibid.: 531). The destructive force of the conflict system resides in its ability to absorb the host system (for example friendship) by consuming all attention and resources (ibid.: 533).

If we view conflict as depicted by Luhmann, it is highly possible that a conflict arising on the verbal level may lead to a conflict on the musical level. This is because the conflict has laid claim to a host system whose communication it appropriates for its own development. Paul Berliner relates the case of musicians who, during a concert, saw no other alternative than to go for each other's throats (Berliner 1994: 430).

There are, however, also indications that the communicative form of conflict is also present in music. Musicians sometimes appear to engage in performance rivalry, for example in free jazz, where they usually play in duos resembling a conflict situation (for example concerts given by Dizzy Gillespie and Max Roach). This would mean that improvised music can also take on the communicative form of a conflict. As a result, it is not only the destructive component of conflict that is used in joint creation; there is then also concrete evidence that musical and verbal communication can influence each other within the system of improvised music. Whether this constitutes a method of conflict resolution is a separate issue that is not considered further here.

Konflikt-Resolution gelten soll, ist eine andere Frage, die in diesem Beitrag nicht beantwortet werden soll.

Folglich geht es in der Kommunikation nach Luhmann nicht darum, sich voll und ganz zu verstehen, sondern Anschlüsse zu ermöglichen. Die Situation des Konflikts hindert dies nicht, sondern macht sie sich gemäß ihrer eigenen Funktionen zu Eigen. Das Problematische am Konflikt besteht jedoch darin, dass es ab einem gewissen Stadium kein gemeinsames Schaffen mehr gibt, da der Konflikt alles zu übernehmen droht. Die verbale Kommunikation wie sie im Kontext von Jazz, Free Jazz, und improvisierter Musik beschrieben wurde, ist ein sehr dynamischer Prozess von gestalterischer Natur. Dies gilt besonders im Bereich der Kollektiv-Improvisation, wo persönliche Beschreibungen nicht nur den Inhalt der Musik wiedergeben, sondern auch gruppendynamische Prozesse reflektiert werden. Der Gebrauch von Metaphern in diesen Beschreibungen ermöglicht es der Gruppe, mittels eines gemeinsamen Bildes einen Kontext zu erschaffen, indem das Anpassen der kollektiven Handlung immer wieder neu reflektiert wird. So gab es in meiner Studie[6] immer wieder Beispiele, in denen Ensembles versuchten, mittels gemeinsam entwickelter Metaphern einzelne schwierige Situationen zu meistern. Ein Ensemble gestaltete die Metapher einer »Welle«, um die musikalische Interaktion der einzelnen Mitglieder besser verbildlichen zu können und so eine komplizierte Situation zu überwinden.

Die Ensembles meiner Studie wählen somit eine Form der Kommunikation, die sich auf den musikalischen Spielprozess konzentriert, und nicht die aufkommenden interpersonellen Auseinandersetzungen thematisiert. Obwohl die Gruppenkommunikation generelle Merkmale aufweist, ist sie doch sehr einzigartig, da sie gewisse Muster und Metaphern hervorbringt, die den einzelnen Ensembles eigen sind.

Dabei ist dies besonders relevant im Kontext improvisierter Musik, wo es meines Erachtens mehr darum geht, etwas mit anderen zusammen zu (er) schaffen. Im Rahmen dieses Textes, der sich mit dem Erforschen des Prozesses hinter der Analogie zur Sprache beschäftigt hat, scheinen sich somit beide Kommunikationen sehr zu ähneln, da beide Ebenen durch ihre vielfältige Anschlussfähigkeit charakterisiert sind. Bei der verbalen Kommunikation manifestiert sich diese Anschlussfähigkeit anhand der Überfülle von Metaphern und Analogien. Die musikalische Kommunikation scheint in diesem Zusammenhang eher Gebrauch von unterschiedlichen Gesprächsformen, wie Konflikten oder Diskussionen, als Anschlusscharakteristik zu nehmen. Dies sind jedoch nur einige von vielen Möglichkeiten, wie beide Ebenen im komplexen und zugleich faszinierenden Prozess der improvisierten Musik wechselwirken.

---

6 | Siehe oben.

Communication as described by Luhmann is thus not a question of complete understanding but a method of enabling continuity. A conflict situation does not hinder continuity but appropriates it on its own terms. The problematic nature of conflict resides in the fact that joint creativity becomes impossible beyond a certain point because the conflict threatens to overwhelm the whole. Verbal communication, as described in jazz, free jazz and improvised music contexts, is an extremely dynamic creative process, especially in collective improvisation, where individual descriptions not only reproduce the music's content but also reflect group dynamics. The use of metaphors in these descriptions allows the group to employ a common image to create a context by continuously rethinking the collective action. My dissertation[5] outlines many examples in which ensembles attempted to master difficult situations through the use of jointly constructed metaphors. One of them used the metaphor of a "wave" to better illustrate musical interaction among its members and thus master a difficult situation. The ensembles I looked at thus chose a form of communication that focuses on the musical performance process and does not explore questions of interpersonal conflict. Although group communication reveals general characteristics, it is still highly individual because it yields certain patterns and metaphors specific to each of the ensembles.

This is of particular relevance to improvised music, which in my opinion is more a matter of creating and working together with others. The aim of this paper, engaging with the process underlying the analogy to language, has thus been to characterize both types of communication as comparable in their diverse potential for continuity. In verbal communication, this continuity comes to the fore with an abundance of metaphors and analogies. Musical communication, in this context, appears to use different forms of dialog such as conflict or discussion as a means of continuity. These, however, are just some of the many ways in which the two levels interact in the complex and fascinating process of improvised music.

Translation into English: Oliver Dahin, Berlin

5 | See above.

Literatur/References

Bailey, Derek (1980): Improvisation. Kunst ohne Werk, Frankfurt: Wolke.

Berliner, Paul (1994): Thinking in Jazz. The Infinite Art of Improvisation, London: University of Chicago Press.

Dieckmann, Johann (2004): Luhmann-Lehrbuch, München: Wilhelm Fink Verlag.

Esposito, Elena (2013): »Doppelte Kontingenz«, in: Horster, Detlef (Hrsg./Ed.) (2013): Niklas Luhmann. Soziale Systeme. Berlin: Akademie Verlag.

Figueroa-Dreher, Silvana K. (2012): »Wann und weshalb ist Improvisation kreativ?«, in: Göttlich, Udo; Kurt, Ronald (Hg./Eds.) (2012).

Göttlich, Udo; Kurt, Ronald (Hg./Eds.) (2012): Kreativität und Improvisation. Soziologische Positionen. Wiesbaden: Springer VS.

Hauser, Fritz (2011) »Fragen über Fragen«, in: Nanz, Dieter A. (Hrsg./Ed.): Aspekte der Freien Improvisation in der Musik, Hofheim: Wolke.

Horster, Detlef (Hrsg./Ed.) (2013): Niklas Luhmann. Soziale Systeme. Berlin: Akademie Verlag.

Jahraus, Oliver (2001): Niklas Luhmann: Aufsätze und Reden, Stuttgart: Philipp Reclam jr.

Joas, Hans (1996): Die Kreativität des Handelns, 4. Auflage, Frankfurt am Main: Suhrkamp.

Kneer, Georg; Nassehi, Armin (1993): Niklas Luhmanns Theorie Sozialer Systeme, München: Wilhelm Fink Verlag.

Kurt, Ronald (2012): »Improvisation als Grundbegriff, Gegenstand und Methode der Soziologie«, in: Göttlich, Udo; Kurt, Ronald (Hg./Eds.) (2012).

Luhmann, Niklas (1995): Soziologische Aufklärung 3. Soziales System, Gesellschaft, Organisation, Opladen: Westdeutscher Verlag.

Luhmann, Niklas (1995): Soziologische Aufklärung 6. Die Soziologie und der Mensch, Opladen: Westdeutscher Verlag.

Luhmann, Niklas (2012): Soziale Systeme. Grundriss einer allgemeinen Theorie, Frankfurt am Main: Suhrkamp.

Luhmann, Niklas (2010): Einführung in die Systemtheorie. Dirk Baecker (Hrsg.) 6. Auflage. Heidelberg: Carl Auer Verlag. In: Horster, Detlef (Hrsg./Ed.) (2013): Niklas Luhmann. Soziale Systeme. Berlin: Akademie Verlag.

Maturana, Humberto R.; Varela, Francisco J. (1984): Der Baum der Erkenntnis. Die Biologischen Wurzeln des menschlichen Erkennens, Berlin: Goldmann Verlag.

Monson, Ingrid (1996): Saying Something. Jazz Improvisation and Interaction, Chicago: Chicago University Press.

O.V.: »Melodische Unterhaltung: dpa«, in: Gehirn und Geist. Das Magazin für Psychologie und Hirnforschung, Nr. 5. 2014, 14.

Owen, William Foster (1985): »Metaphor Analysis of Cohesiveness in Small Groups«, in: Small Group Behavior. Vol. 16. Number 3. August Edition. London: Sage Publications Inc. 415-424.

Sawyer, Keith R. (2001): Creating Conversations. Improvisation in Everyday Discourse, New York: Hampton Press.

Shaw, M. E. (1976): Group dynamics: The psychology of small group behavior. New York: Mc-Graw-Hill. In: Owen, William Foster (1985): Metaphor Analysis of Cohesiveness in Small Groups. In: Small Group Behavior. Vol. 16. Number 3. August Edition. London: Sage Publications Inc. 415-424.

Wilson, Peter N. (1999): Hear & Now. Gedanken zur Improvisierten Musik, Hofheim: Wolke.

Intermezzo 7

MS: Gibt es für Euch Kriterien, die »gute« improvisierte Musik ausmachen?

BP: Die Kriterien für meine Wertschätzung gelten für aufgenommene Musik genauso wie für Live Musik. Die Frage ist: Fühle ich, dass die Person, die musiziert, zu mir durchdringt oder höre ich nur die intellektuellen Ideen, das technische Beherrschen oder andere »erlernte« Dinge? Erreichen mich beim Hören seine Schwingungen in seinem Material?

MS: Du möchtest die Person hinter der Musik spüren.

BP: Ganz genau. Und so kann es mir mit jeder Art von Musik gehen.

EP: Ich kann Barres Einstellung nachempfinden. Aber ich würde den Fokus gerne auf die Idee des Erkundens ausrichten. Für mich ist Musik nicht so interessant, außer sie hat diese Qualität. Normales Material ist »auf die Präsentation ausgerichtet«. Etwas, woran im Vorhinein gearbeitet worden ist und das den Musikern bekannt ist, bevor sie spielen. Vielleicht zählt das zu den intellektuellen Ideen und dem Beherrschen des Instruments, worauf Barre sich bezogen hat. Das sehen wir fast alle so. Es ist vielleicht eine Frage des Grades. Wenn der musikalische Prozess jedoch nicht von einem erforschenden Ethos durchzogen ist, dann werden die Ergebnisse schal. Für einen improvisierenden Musiker ist ständiges Erkunden vielleicht die einzige Art, neues Material zu entwickeln. Wenn ich von »Musik« spreche, meine ich damit eine »Aktivität«, die Menschen einzigartig ist. Etwas, das für ihre Menschlichkeit

Intermezzo 7

MS: Are there criteria for what you would call "good" improvised music?

BP: Well, the criteria for my appreciation apply to recorded music as well as live music. The question is: do I feel that person who is playing the music coming through to me or am I just listening to intellectual ideas, technical mastering or other "learned" things? Am I hearing-receiving his vibration in his material?

MS: You want to feel the person behind the music.

BP: Yes, yeah yeah. And I can get that from any and all kinds of music.

EP: I can sympathize with Barre's sentiment. But I would like to shift the emphasis back to the idea of exploration. For me, music is not so interesting unless it's got this quality. The usual material is "presentational". Something that has been worked on beforehand and is essentially known to the musicians before they play anything. These (perhaps) are the intellectual ideas and mastery of the instrument to which Barre refers. I guess most of us do this. Maybe it is a question of degree. However, if the musical process is not laced with an investigatory ethic, the resultant sounds will become stale. For an improvising musician, constant exploration is perhaps the only way to develop new material. So, when I use the word "music" I mean it as an "activity" unique to human beings. Something that is fundamental to their humanity. That's what I'm looking for instead of "received wisdom". This is the domain of the classicist. Formal music (classical, folk or popular), which I would suggest probably arose in an "exploratory" fashion, has, arguably, become self-contained – an

entscheidend ist. Danach suche ich anstatt nach »tradiertem Wissen«. Das liegt im Bereich der Klassizisten. Formale Musik (Klassik, Folk oder Pop), von der ich meine, dass sie auf erforschende Weise entstanden ist, ist selbstständig geworden – eine blendende Reflexion der vorherrschenden kulturellen Mores – und kann nur innerhalb ihrer selbst ohne Bezug auf ein weiteres kreatives, menschliches Programm beschrieben werden. Ich suche nach der Zukunft.

Matthias Schwabe (MS), Barre Phillips (BP) und Edwin Prévost (EP)
im Podiumsgespräch, Mai 2014

Übersetzung aus dem Englischen: Solveig Raschpichler, Berlin

almost blinding reflection of the prevailing cultural morés – and can be explained only within itself without reference to a wider creative human programme. I'm looking for the future.

Matthias Schwabe (MS), Barre Phillips (BP) and Edwin Prévost (EP)
in a public talk, May 2014

29.5.014

Improvisation – Performativität – Ästhetik | Improvisation – Performativity – Aesthetics

Von der Performance musikalischer Improvisation zur Improvisationsästhetik | From performing musical improvisation to aesthetics of improvisation

---

Mathias Maschat

Das hier beschriebene methodologische Prisma, um Improvisation in den Blick zu nehmen und zu erforschen, besteht in der Verbindung der Begriffe *Performativität* und *Ästhetik*. Bei derartigen terminologischen Operationen stellt sich die Frage, wie gut sich Begriffe von einer Disziplin in eine andere übertragen lassen und wie sich Begriffe innerhalb dieses Prozesses verändern. Teils lässt sich allerdings ohnehin beobachten, dass ein tatsächlicher begrifflicher Ursprung vielfach nur schwer auszumachen ist und Begriffe beinahe selbstverständlich in ganz unterschiedlichen Kontexten gebraucht werden. Es sind in mancher Hinsicht die Verdienste der Kulturwissenschaften beziehungsweise der *cultural studies*, durch welche gelegentlich auch künstlich gezogene Fächergrenzen sowie als dahingehend festgeschrieben verhandelte Begriffszugehörigkeiten obsolet erscheinen. Mieke Bal beispielsweise spricht in diesem Zusammenhang von »wandernden Begriffen« (Bal 2006: 7-27), den *traveling concepts*[1]. In ihrem Verständnis sind Begriffe insgesamt keine feststehenden Entitäten, sondern fortwährendem Wandel unterlegen (ebd.: 11ff). Umso mehr betont sie die Notwendigkeit eines präzisen und seriösen Umgangs mit ihnen, so dass sie dadurch zugleich einen »operationale[n] Wert« (ebd.: 11) erhalten. Um dies zu erreichen, warb sie nicht nur für eine Anwendung der Begriffe, sondern vielmehr für deren »Konfrontation mit den kulturellen Objekten« (ebd.); eindringlich plädierte sie dafür, dass »man niemals bloß ›theoretisieren‹, sondern dem Objekt stets die Möglichkeit geben sollte, Widerworte zu geben« (ebd.: 18). Grob gesprochen, bezeichnete sie diese Praxis als »Kulturanalyse« (Bal 2006) und der Rückschluss liegt auf der Hand, dass man den hier erhobenen Anspruch, Theorie und Praxis im Wechselspiel zu kontextualisieren und zu untersuchen, mit Bal gesprochen als »Improvisationsanalyse« oder als »Analyse von Improvisationskultur« bezeichnen könnte.[2] Vorausgeschickt sei nun, dass die Forderung beziehungsweise die Notwendigkeit der konkreten Anwendung der Theorie auf die Praxis an dieser Stelle keine Einlösung findet, geht es doch im Zusammenhang der methodologischen Konzeption zunächst um eine Kombinatorik von Diskursen, um überhaupt das Feld abzustecken, in welchem die Ästhetik von Improvisation verhandelt werden kann.[3]

---

1 | Fechner-Smarsly, Thomas; Neef, Sonja: »Kulturanalyse. Zur interdisziplinären Methodologie Mieke Bals«, in: Bal 2006: 342.

2 | Es ist klassischerweise das Feld der Musikanalyse, welches streng am Gegenstand arbeitet, um dadurch konkrete Untersuchungsergebnisse zu erzielen. Im Hinblick auf die Analyse von zeitgenössischer Improvisationsmusik sind die Beiträge der Musikanalyse bisher rar gesät, was nicht zuletzt in der Flüchtigkeit und gleichzeitigen Komplexität von Improvisation begründet liegt. Vergleiche hierzu zum Beispiel: Holtsträter 2014. *URL: http://www.act.uni-bayreuth.de/de/archiv/201405/01_editorial_05_Holtstraeter/index.html* (05.06.2015).

3 | Eine explizite Anwendung von Begriffen auf die Praxis findet sich in: Maschat 2012. *URL: http://edoc.hu-berlin.de/kunsttexte/2012-2/maschat-mathias-5/PDF/maschat.pdf* (05.06.2015).

The methodological prism that is described here with which to view and investigate improvisation is comprised of the combination of the terms *performativity* and *aesthetics*. This kind of terminology raises the question of how well terms from one discipline can be transferred to another and how they are altered during this process. To a certain extent, it can be observed that the precise origin of meaning of a term is difficult to pinpoint and that terms are almost naturally used in widely differing contexts. To some degree it seems that *cultural studies* have rendered both the sometimes artificial boundaries between disciplines, and the assumption that the application of terminology is inflexible, obsolete. Mieke Bal, for example, talks about *traveling concepts*.[1] In her opinion, concepts are not of themselves fixed entities, but rather subject to constant change (Bal 2006: 11ff). She therefore places great emphasis on the necessity of dealing with terms precisely and respectfully, so that they retain their "operational value" (ibid.: 11). In order to achieve this, she argues not just for the use of terms but rather for their "confrontation with cultural objects" (ibid.); she pleads the case that we "should never simply 'theorize' but rather always give the object the opportunity to disagree" (ibid.: 18). Roughly speaking, she terms this practice "cultural analysis" (Bal 2006), and it therefore seems natural to call the claim raised here to investigate and contextualize the interplay of theory and practice "improvisation analysis" or "analysis of improvisation culture".[2] It is important to mention here that the challenge or necessity of concretely applying theory to practice is not met in this case. In the context of methodological conception it is instead about identifying a combination of approaches in order to define the context in which the discussion about the aesthetics of improvisation can take place.[3]

Combining the terms *performativity* and *aesthetics* in the context of improvisation seems to have become feasible at least since the formulation of the concept: *Aesthetics of the Performative*.[4] The goal and intention is to enable by this means statements about aesthetically relevant characteristics of musical impro-

---

1 | Fechner-Smarsly, Thomas; Neef, Sonja: "Kulturanalyse. Zur interdisziplinären Methodologie Mieke Bals", in: Bal 2006: 342.

2 | It is traditionally the domain of music analysis which focuses exclusively on the object in order to obtain concrete research results. With regard to the analysis of contemporary improvised music, the contribution of music analysis to date is relatively scant owing to the transient and complex nature of improvisation. Compare for example: Holtsträter 2014. *URL: http://www.act.uni-bayreuth.de/de/archiv/201405/01_editorial_05_Holtstraeter/index.html* (05.06.2015).

3 | An explicit application of terms relating to the practice of improvisation can be found in: Maschat 2012. *URL: http://edoc.hu-berlin.de/kunsttexte/2012-2/maschat-mathias-5/PDF/maschat.pdf* (05.06.2015).

4 | Compare in essence: Fischer-Lichte 2004; Mersch 2002.

Die Verbindung der Begriffe *Performativität* und *Ästhetik* auch im Kontext von Improvisation erscheint spätestens seit der Formulierung einer *Ästhetik des Performativen*[4] plausibel. Ziel und Intention ist es, auf diesem Weg Aussagen über ästhetisch relevante Charakteristika von musikalischer Improvisation zu erlangen. Wichtig ist es dabei zunächst zu vermerken, dass hier unter Ästhetik weniger eine Theorie der sinnlichen Wahrnehmung in der Nachfolge Baumgartens verstanden wird, wenngleich auch dessen Hervorhebung der Bedeutung ästhetischer Erfahrung im Kontext musikalischer Improvisation und improvisatorischer Forschung einen geeigneten Ankerpunkt bildet. An Stelle dessen wird der Terminus vor einem phänomenologischen und diskursanalytischen Hintergrund schlicht als Philosophie der Kunst verstanden. Übertragen auf den Kontext der Improvisation bedeutet das dementsprechend, über eine philosophische Theorie der Kunst der Improvisation nachzudenken. Der hierfür entwickelte und auch in der Parallelführung zu bestehender Improvisationstheorie weiterhin zu entfaltende Begriff ist der der *Improvisationsästhetik*[5].

Zunächst stellt sich in diesem Zusammenhang die Frage, worauf eine solche Ästhetik abzielen und was für eine Relevanz ihr zukommen könnte. Es war der Musikwissenschaftler Peter Niklas Wilson, der explizit nach der Möglichkeit einer »genuinen Ästhetik der Improvisation« fragte, nach »eine[r] Ästhetik, die das Spezifische von Improvisation als positive Qualität zu fassen in der Lage ist, nicht, wie so oft geschehen, lediglich als Defizienz, als Abwesenheit des Textes, als Archaik, als Vor-Form heutiger Kunst« (Wilson 1999: 27). Aus seiner Formulierung und Fragestellung spricht bereits die Problematik, dass das Thema Improvisation in der musikästhetischen Debatte – mit der historischen und systematischen Musikwissenschaft als Bezugsgrößen – bislang eher kurz gekommen ist. Zwar wurde das Selbstverständnis der Musikästhetik auch von innen heraus immer wieder befragt, beispielsweise von Klaus-Ernst Behne, der ihre ausschließend-verengte Sicht auf »so genannte Kunstmusik« und vor allem ihre ideologisierte Fixierung auf das »im Werk Objektivierte« in der Nachfolge von Adorno, Dahlhaus und Eggebrecht als Irrwege benennt. (Behne 1997: 1011f) Auch ihre tendenzielle Hermetik und Selbstbezüglichkeit (Tadday 2004) sowie ihr überwiegend normativer Ansatz (Kneif 1971) wurden kritisiert. Aber dessen ungeachtet ist festzustellen, dass diese Problematiken bis heute ungebrochen bestehen, indem in der einschlägigen, auch lexikalischen Literatur zur Musikästhetik nach wie vor eine Orientierung primär an den Werken der sogenannten »abendländischen Kunstmusik«[6] zu beobachten

4 | Vergleiche im Wesentlichen: Fischer-Lichte 2004; Mersch 2002.

5 | Den Terminus verwendet ebenfalls Roland Borgards, der den Begriff im Kontext einer literarischen Improvisationsästhetik ins Feld führt: Borgards 2007; Borgards 2009.

6 | Zur Problematik dieser Sammelbezeichnung vergleiche zum Beispiel: Hentschel 2012.

visation. It is important to note that by saying *aesthetics* it is less a theory of sensory perception as per Baumgarten that is meant – even though his emphasis on the significance of aesthetic experience in the context of musical improvisation and improvisation research offers a suitable foundation for such a theory. By contrast, when we consider aesthetics in terms of phenomenology and discourse analysis, the term is merely understood as philosophy of art. However, if we transfer this to the context of improvisation, it means thinking about a philosophical theory of the art of improvisation. The term developed for this, which is still to be further developed, also in a parallel consideration of existing improvisation theory, is *aesthetics of improvisation*.[5]

In this context, we are immediately confronted with the question of what such aesthetics aspire to and what relevance they can achieve. It was the musicologist Peter Niklas Wilson who explicitly asked about the possibility of "genuine aesthetics of improvisation", about the existence of "aesthetics that are equipped to frame the specifics of improvisation as positives, rather than, as is often the case, deficiencies, lacking in text, archaic, just a preliminary form of art as we know it today" (Wilson 1999: 27). Due to these questions we are confronted with the problem that improvisation itself is underrepresented in the debate on music aesthetics, if we take historical and systematic musicology as benchmarks. The self-image of music aesthetics has frequently been called into question from within, for example by Klaus-Ernst Behne, who resisted the exclusive and narrow view of "so-called art music" and considered in particular the ideological fixation on that which was "objectified in the work", as per Adorno, Dahlhaus and Eggebrecht, to be the wrong path (Behne 1997: 1011f). The tendency towards hermeticism and self-reference (Tadday 2004), as well as the taking of a predominantly normative approach (Kneif 1971) have also been criticized. However, even without this criticism, it can be seen that problems still remain, such as an orientation which tends toward "occidental art music"[6] and which can be observed in the primary and lexicological literature on music aesthetics. Research into musical aesthetics does not seem to consider or extend to popular music or music from cultures outside of what can be classed as "European", "Western" or "Occidental". Responsibility for these areas has been largely given over to pop music research or ethnomusicology. It is the same with improvisation, which does not even appear as a keyword

5 | In German I use the compound noun and neologism *Improvisationsästhetik*; by merging the terms *improvisation* and *aesthetics* to a single word, it is possible to explicitly underline the new conceptual approach and its entity as an aesthetical concept. Roland Borgards uses the term as well and introduced the term to the field in the context of aesthetics of improvisation in literature: Borgards 2007; Borgards 2009.

6 | For more information on the problems associated with this collective labeling, see for example: Hentschel 2012: 251-257.

ist. Weder Populäre Musik noch die Musik von Kulturen jenseits des als »europäisch«, »westlich« oder »abendländisch« Zusammengefassten scheinen aus Sicht musikästhetischer Forschung von besonderer Relevanz zu sein. Der Zuständigkeitsbereich hierfür ist weitgehend in die Popmusikforschung sowie in die Musikethnologie verlagert. Ebenso verhält es sich mit der Improvisation, die in mancher einschlägigen, als Überblickswerk angelegten Veröffentlichung zur Musikästhetik nicht einmal als Schlagwort auftaucht. Hintergrund hierfür ist sicherlich in erheblichem Umfang die Tatsache, dass es sich bei Improvisationen nicht um Werke im traditionellen Sinn handelt, die gegenüber ephemeren Kunstformen zumeist als prioritär erachtet werden. Dies wurzelt in einer insgesamt seit Ende des 18. Jahrhunderts zu beobachtenden Verdrängung improvisationsbasierter Bühnenkunst, die mit den spezifischen ästhetischen Diskursen der Zeit einhergeht und in einer Unterscheidung zwischen hoher und niedriger Kunst, zwischen E und U, mündet (Landgraf 2011: 7). »Das Ewige wird vom Ephemeren getrennt, das Festgeschriebene vom Flüchtigen und das Ideale und Universelle vom bloß Gegenwartsbezogenen und Partikularen.« (Ebd.; Übersetzung durch M.M.) Eine Folge davon ist, dass auch heute noch die vielfach zu beobachtende Verlagerung musikästhetischer Sinnebenen vom Textualen hin zum Performativen nur allmählich ins Bewusstsein dringt. Nach wie vor lenken werkästhetische Kategorien die wissenschaftliche Auseinandersetzung mit Musik, wenngleich im Rahmen der musikwissenschaftlichen *Performance Studies* ein Paradigmenwechsel eingeleitet worden ist. Nun ist es offenkundig, dass Ästhetiken, die sich primär an Vorstellungen von Werk, Inhalt und Form orientieren, als geeignete Annäherung an improvisierte Musik nur eingeschränkt in Betracht zu ziehen sind; denn Improvisation bewegt sich weitgehend jenseits dessen, was mit einem werkästhetisch orientierten Blickwinkel wahrzunehmen ist. Die Frage ist also, was sich für Alternativen bieten,[7] um ein Phänomen in seiner Ästhetik zu beschreiben, das nicht festgeschrieben und definiert, sondern wandelbar und flüchtig auftritt. Als geeigneter Anknüpfungspunkt bietet sich in erster Linie der performative Charakter von Improvisation an.[8] Damit ist zunächst einmal jene Tatsache gemeint, dass Improvisation nicht jenseits ihrer Aufführung existiert und nur im Zuge ihrer aktualen Produktion in spezifischen Live-Situationen prozessual in Erscheinung tritt. Sie ist nicht die konkrete Repräsentation einer im Voraus erdachten Komposition oder eines umzusetzenden Konzepts und bezieht sich in ihrer Umsetzung nicht auf ein mit einem Titel versehenes Musikstück. Dies bedeutet, dass der Aufführung einer Improvisation eine besondere Rolle zukommt, denn verglichen mit einer

7 | Verwiesen sei in diesem Zusammenhang auf: Sanio 1999.

8 | Der Performance-Charakter von Improvisation wird bei Nettl und Russell (1998) schon in der Titelgebung besonders hervorgehoben: In the Course of Performance. Studies in the World of Musical Improvisation.

in some prominent publications which are said to feature overviews of music aesthetics. The reason for this is largely due to the fact that improvisation does not deal with works in the traditional sense, which are usually considered as primary, when compared to more ephemeral art forms. This is rooted in the displacement of improvisation-based performance that can be traced back to the end of the 18th century and which fits to the specific aesthetic discourse of the time and leads ultimately to the differentiation between "high" and "low" art, between "serious music" and "entertainment music" (Landgraf 2011: 7). "[...] separating the eternal from the transitory, the fixed from the fleeting, the ideal and the general from the actual and the particular – improvisation is suppressed by 'official' aesthetic considerations" (ibid.). The result of this is that even today in music, the frequently observed shift in aesthetic levels of meaning from textual to performative only penetrates the consciousness slowly. Even though a paradigm shift has been initiated by *Performance Studies* in the context of musicology, the scientific understanding of music is still guided by categories which determine the aesthetics of the work. It should be obvious that aesthetics which are mainly oriented toward notions of work, content and form can only be of limited use when considering the aesthetics of improvised music. Improvisation goes beyond what is perceptible in terms of the aesthetics of the work. The question is what alternatives[7] are available to describe the aesthetics of a phenomenon that is not predefined or notated, but rather malleable and transient. A useful starting point is the performative character of improvisation.[8] Here, we are talking about the fact that improvisation does not exist outside of its performance and is only created during its actual production within a specific live situation. It is not the concrete representation of a previously thought out composition or of a concept which is to be implemented. Furthermore, it does not refer to a piece of music decorated with a title. This means that the act of performing an improvisation takes a special role, as the performance, compared to a composition, is its only way of existing, whereas compositions also exist as medial notation. With this in mind, it is vital, in the case of improvised music, to pay special attention to the performance situation. As "terms [...] are never used with exactly the same meaning" (Bal 2006: 13), it seems prudent to briefly elucidate the fundamental understanding of performativity,[9] to ask how the term *performativity* is related to performances, and ultimately to query how far performativity can be connected to improvisation or, rather, to its aesthetics. Put simply, the term *performativity* refers to the

7 | In this context see: Sanio 1999.

8 | The performance character of improvisation is highlighted even in the title of Nettl and Russell (1998): In the Course of Performance. Studies in the World of Musical Improvisation.

9 | Overviews of the topic are: Fischer-Lichte 2012; Hempfer and Volbers 2011.

Komposition ist die Aufführung ihre einzige Existenzweise, wohingegen Kompositionen auch eine Existenz als mediales Notat zukommt. Somit erscheint es vor diesem Hintergrund unerlässlich, der Aufführungssituation im Fall von improvisierter Musik besondere Aufmerksamkeit zu widmen. Nachdem »Begriffe [...] nie in genau dem gleichen Sinn verwendet« (Bal 2006: 13) werden, erscheint es angeraten, das hier zugrundeliegende Verständnis von Performativität[9] in aller Kürze zu skizzieren, zu fragen, wie sich der Begriff *Performativität* zu Aufführungen verhält und schließlich, inwiefern Performativität mit Improvisation beziehungsweise zu deren Ästhetik in Verbindung zu setzen ist. Einfach beschrieben, bezieht sich der Begriff *Performativität* auf den Aufführungscharakter von Kulturen. Er betont die »Selbstbezüglichkeit von Handlungen und ihre wirklichkeitskonstituierende Kraft« (Fischer-Lichte 2012: 29) – im Gegensatz etwa zum Begriff der *Theatralität*, der eher auf die Darstellung oder Inszenierung etwas vorgängig konkret Gegebenen abzielt. (Ebd.) Auch wenn schon im Theater Max Reinhardts und den Anfängen der Theaterwissenschaft um Max Herrmann wesentliche Veränderungen zu verzeichnen waren, erfuhren Momente des Performativen besondere Relevanz im Zuge des umfangreich diskursivierten Paradigmenwechsels vom Werk zum Ereignis, der auch als *performative turn* oder als »performative Wende« bezeichnet wird.[10] Die wesentlichen Bezugnahmen sind diesbezüglich vor allem die Umbrüche in der Kunst der 1960er Jahre; als Stichworte wären zu nennen: John Cage und das *Untitled Event*, Happening, Performance Art et cetera. Auf der Suche nach den Ursprüngen der performativen Wende kommt John Cage eine besondere Rolle zu. Erika Fischer-Lichte hält diesbezüglich fest, dass in »der Musik [...] der Performativierungsschub bereits in den frühen 50er-Jahren mit den ›Events‹ und ›Pieces‹ von John Cage ein[setzte]«.[11] An anderer Stelle schildert sie das von Cage initiierte und konzipierte *Untitled Event*, das 1952 am Black Mountain College stattgefunden hat. Sie spricht im Zusammenhang mit diesem »bemerkenswerte[n] Ereignis der Theatergeschichte der westlichen Kultur« von der »›Entdeckung‹ des Performativen« (Fischer-Lichte 2002: 277). Ihre Darstellung wurzelt in der Fokussierung derjenigen Elemente, die ihr für eine »künftige Theorie des Performativen« (ebd.) von Relevanz erschienen, zum Beispiel die Inszenierung einer Situation der Unbestimmtheit, die Intermedialität und die Verteilung der auktorialen Verantwortlichkeiten auf mehrere Individuen. Ihrer Ansicht nach stand im *Untitled Event* »die performative Funktion [im] Vordergrund« (ebd.:

9 | Überblicksdarstellungen zum Thema sind: Fischer-Lichte 2012; Hempfer und Volbers 2011.

10 | Mersch 2002: 157-244 (III. Vom Werk zum Ereignis. Zur »performativen Wende« in der Kunst); Fischer-Lichte 2002; Fischer-Lichte 2004.

11 | Fischer-Lichte 2004: 24. Genannt werden an dieser Stelle aus dem Bereich der Musik jedoch auch Karlheinz Stockhausen, Dieter Schnebel und Mauricio Kagel.

performance characteristics of cultures. It highlights the "self-referentiality of actions and their ability to constitute reality" (Fischer-Lichte 2012: 29) – as opposed, for instance, to the term *theatricality* which is rather focused on the presentation or staging of something concrete and pre-existing (ibid.). Although significant changes had already been seen in theater with Max Reinhardt as well as in the origins of theater studies centered around Max Herrmann, aspects of the performative took on particular relevance as a result of the extensively discussed paradigm shift from work to event that is also known as the *performative turn.*[10] The main references concerning this matter are especially the changes within art of the 1960s; notably: John Cage and the *Untitled Event,* Happening, Performance Art, et cetera. In terms of trying to locate the origins of the performative turn, John Cage plays a special role. Erika Fischer-Lichte writes that in "music, the push toward performatization began in the early 1950s with the 'events' and 'pieces' of John Cage".[11] Elsewhere, she describes the *Untitled Event,* initiated and conceived by John Cage, which took place in 1952 at Black Mountain College. In connection with this "remarkable event in the history of theatre in the western culture" she speaks about the "'discovery' of the performative" (Fischer-Lichte 2002: 277). Her argument is focused on the elements that seem to be significant for a "future theory of the performative" (ibid.), for example the creation of a situation of indeterminacy, the intermediality and the sharing of authorial responsibility among several individuals. In her view, the *Untitled Event* brought "the performative functions to the forefront" (ibid.: 300), which generated "opposition to contemporary theatre" (ibid.: 279) by "dissolving artifacts [like existence as works] into concrete performed actions" (ibid.: 286). For the *Untitled Event* it can overall be considered as characteristic that the concrete event has only been generated situationally during its performance and that the process, the structure and the artistic material are often largely unforeseeable. According to this, the artistic results articulated themselves as event-based rather than work-based.[12]

With eventness, an essential feature of performativity or of performances in the context of "dissolution of artistic boundaries" (Fischer-Lichte 2004: 29) is alluded to. There are, however, a few other characteristics described in performativity theory that seem particularly relevant to improvisation.[13] The following are especially noteworthy: the auratic, meaning the unique, special or

10 | Mersch 2002: 157-244 (III. Vom Werk zum Ereignis. Zur "performativen Wende" in der Kunst); Fischer-Lichte 2002; Fischer-Lichte 2004.

11 | Fischer-Lichte 2004: 24. Here, from the field of music, Karlheinz Stockhausen, Dieter Schnebel and Mauricio Kagel are mentioned, too.

12 | This aspect is explained by Dieter Mersch who likewise discusses John Cage as an important source: Mersch 2002.

13 | Discussed in detail, see: Maschat 2012.

300), wodurch ein »Gegensatz zum zeitgenössischen Theater« (ebd.: 279) hergestellt wurde, indem »Artefakte [wie etwa Werkhaftigkeit] in Handlungsvollzüge auf[gelöst wurden]« (ebd.: 286). Als charakteristisch kann insgesamt angesehen werden, dass sich das konkrete Ereignis erst während seiner Aufführung situativ gestaltete und der Ablauf, die Struktur oder das künstlerische Material oft weitgehend unvorhersehbar waren. Die künstlerischen Ergebnisse artikulierten sich dementsprechend weniger werk-, sondern eben ereignishaft.[12]

Mit dem Ereignishaften ist eine wesentliche Eigenschaft von Performativität beziehungsweise von Aufführungen in jenem Kontext der »Entgrenzung der Künste« (Fischer-Lichte 2004: 29) benannt. Jedoch gibt es noch einige weitere Charakteristika, die in der Performativitätstheorie beschrieben worden sind und die bezogen auf Improvisation besonders relevant erscheinen.[13] Zu nennen sind: Das Auratische, also das Einzigartige, Besondere oder Originale von Aufführungen; die Betonung von Präsenz, worunter verschiedene Aspekte fallen, so die Hervorhebung des Unmittelbaren und Gegenwärtigen gegenüber dem Reproduktiven, der Vorrang des phänomenal Erscheinenden gegenüber dem hermeneutisch Sinnhaften, die Intensität und Absolutheit des Erlebnisses oder auch die auf die Rezipierenden überspringende Ausdruckskraft und starke Wirkung der Produzierenden; mit dem bereits benannten Aspekt des Unvorhersehbaren steht des Weiteren das Phänomen der Emergenz in enger Verbindung, worunter ein Strukturbildungsprinzip zu verstehen ist, das jenseits des konkret Kontrollierbaren eine bestimmte Eigendynamik in Aufführungsprozesse implementiert; außerdem sind in dieser Reihe noch die Faktoren der Materialität sowie der Körperlichkeit zu ergänzen – Aspekte, die eine wesentliche Rolle spielen, wenn es um die performative Hervorbringung von Klang und seine Formung sowie Strukturierung geht.[14] Erörtert und diskursiviert worden sind viele dieser Punkte im Kontext philosophischer Ästhetik: Zu verweisen ist diesbezüglich insbesondere auf die *Ästhetiken der Performance*[15] beziehungsweise *der Präsenz*[16] von

12 | Diesen Aspekt führt vor allem Dieter Mersch aus, der ebenfalls John Cage als wichtige Bezugsgröße diskutiert: Mersch 2002.

13 | Ausführlich hierzu vergleiche: Maschat 2012.

14 | Einige dieser Punkte leuchten bereits in Wilsons (1999) Überlegungen zu einer Ästhetik improvisierter Musik auf, so zum Beispiel die grundsätzliche Performanz des »Gestischen« (S. 27-36), die Präsenz des »Im-Hier-und-Jetzt-Seins« und der »Fokussierung auf den Augenblick« (S. 31), der »Aura des Sakralen« in der »rituellen Geste« (ebd.), die »Entgrenzungserfahrungen« und »›liminoiden‹ Phänomene« (S. 33) sowie die Emergenz des »interaktive[n] Prozeß[']« und der »Übersummativität von Improvisation« (S. 35).

15 | Charles, Daniel: Esthétiques de la Performance (1983). Auf Deutsch erschienen als: Ästhetiken der Performance (1989).

16 | Ebd.: 64. Weitere Anknüpfungspunkte zu Präsenz und Präsenzästhetik sind: Bohrer 1981; Gumbrecht 2004; Gumbrecht 2012; Kolesch 2001; Nancy 1993; Seel 2000.

original aspects of a performance; the emphasis on presence, which has different aspects such as the focus on the immediate and present, as opposed to the reproductive, the predominance of the phenomenologically appearing over the hermeneutically meaningful, the intensity and absoluteness of the experience and also the expressiveness that is transmitted to the recipients and the strong effect of the performers; the phenomenon of emergence is closely connected to the previously mentioned aspect of the unforseen, which should be understood as a principle of creating structure that implements, within performance processes, its own dynamic beyond the concretely controllable; this list should also contain materiality and physicality – factors that play an essential role in the performative generation of sound and its formation and structuring.[14] Many of these points have been discussed and debated in the context of philosophical aesthetics as in *aesthetics of performance*[15] or *of presence*[16] by Daniel Charles, Dieter Mersch's *aesthetics of the event* (2002) and Erika Fischer-Lichte's *aesthetics of the performative* (2004). Once there are *aesthetics of the performative,* it follows, as improvisation is deeply rooted in the performative, the presentive and the eventive, that there must be *performative aesthetics of improvisation*: it seems only natural, then, to refer to these as *aesthetics of improvisation.*

In keeping with the argumentation presented above regarding relevance and use, this description may not just be viewed as a term but rather as "an approach that brings together interrelated terms into something more than just concepts, in fact the skeleton of a theory" (Bal 2006: 19). Just as we lack access to one consistent definition of aesthetics of the work and just as we are rather dependent on incrementally collecting single characteristics and relating them to each other (Goehr 2007), there are also different aspects that combine to form a complete picture of aesthetics of improvisation: aesthetics of improvisation are aesthetics of presence highlighting immediacy, being in the moment and being embedded in the situation, physical/auratic presence and negation of the representational. Aesthetics of improvisation are

14 | Several of these points can already be seen in Wilson's (1999) thoughts on the aesthetics of improvised music, for example the fundamental performance of the "gestural" (p. 27-36), the presence of the "being here and now" and the "focus on the moment" (p. 31), the "aura of the sacred" in the "ritual gesture" (ibid.), the "experience of debordering" and "liminoid phenomena" (p. 33), as well as the emergence of the "interactive process" and of "improvisation as more than the sum of its parts" (p. 35).

15 | Charles, Daniel: Esthétiques de la Performance (1983). Published in German as: Ästhetiken der Performance (1989).

16 | Ibid.: 64. Additional starting points for presence and the aesthetics of presence can be found in: Bohrer 1981; Gumbrecht 2004; Gumbrecht 2012; Kolesch 2001; Nancy 1993; Seel 2000.

Daniel Charles, auf Dieter Merschs *Ereignisästhetik* (2002) und wiederum auf Erika Fischer-Lichtes *Ästhetik des Performativen* (2004). Nachdem es also zum einen eine *Ästhetik des Performativen, der Präsenz, des Ereignisses* gibt und zum anderen Improvisation wesentlich im Performativen, im Präsentischen, im Ereignishaften wurzelt, lässt sich schlussfolgern, dass es auch eine *performative Ästhetik von Improvisation* geben muss: Es liegt nahe, eine solche als *Improvisationsästhetik* zu bezeichnen.

Anschließend an die eingangs aufgeworfene Fragestellung nach der Relevanz und dem Nutzen, ließe sich diese Bezeichnung nicht nur als Begriff verstehen, sondern überdies hinaus als »ein Ansatz, bei dem sich zusammenhängende Begriffe [...] summieren und zu etwas mehr werden als bloßen Begriffen, nämlich zum Gerippe einer Theorie« (Bal 2006: 19). Ähnlich wie wir über keine konsistente Definition von Werkästhetik verfügen und eher darauf angewiesen sind, einzelne charakteristische Momente additiv zusammenzutragen und aufeinander zu beziehen (Goehr 2007), sind es auch beim Improvisationsästhetischen verschiedene Aspekte, die in ihrer Kombination zu einem Gesamtbild führen: Improvisationsästhetik ist eine Ästhetik der Präsenz, indem in ihr Unmittelbarkeit, Momentaneität und Situationsbezogenheit, Wachheit für den Augenblick, physisch-auratische Anwesenheit und Negation des Repräsentationalen exponiert sind. Improvisationsästhetik ist Performativitätsästhetik, indem die in ihrem Modus hervorgebrachte Musik innerhalb des Performativen entsteht – mit Emergenz als autopoietischem Formungs- und Strukturbildungsprinzip sowie Körperlichkeit und Materialität als maßgeblichen Evokatoren der klingenden Resultate. Improvisationsästhetik wurzelt zudem im Ereignisästhetischen, indem die performativen Energien das musikalische Geschehen auf ein Niveau des Ereignishaften transzendieren und damit Planbarkeit und Konstruierbarkeit ins Wanken bringen. In einer zuspitzenden Opposition zu Werkhaftem beziehungsweise »Vorkomponiertem«[17] lässt sich resümieren: Präsenz statt Repräsentation, Ereignis statt Werk, Aura im Sinne von Originalität und Einmaligkeit anstelle von Reproduktion, Emergenz des Klingenden statt dessen vorab entwickelte Konstruktion, Qualitäten des (konkret) Materialen statt des (abstrakt) als Timbrekombinatorik Inszenierten, körperlicher Eigensinn statt bloßer Disziplinierung des Körpers. Mit der Konturierung des Improvisationsästhetischen gegenüber dem Werkästhetischen werden veränderte Paradigmen ins Bewusstsein gerückt, welche die originären Qualitäten von Improvisation in den Mittelpunkt stellen, anstatt Im-

17 | Da auch Improvisation gelegentlich als eine Form des Komponierens angesehen wird, schlägt Bruno Nettl zur Unterscheidung die Formulierung *precompositions* vor, um damit die Erschaffung von Musik vor ihrer klanglichen Umsetzung zu bezeichnen: Nettl, Bruno: »Introduction: An Art Neglected in Scholarship«, in: Nettl und Russell 1998: 1-23, hier 5.

aesthetics of the performative as the music created in this mode is brought out via the performative – with emergence as an autopoietic principle generating form and structure, as well as physicality and materiality functioning as leading evocators of the resulting sounds. Aesthetics of improvisation are further rooted in aesthetics of the event as the peformative energies transcend the musical activity to a level of eventness, thus shaking the foundations of calculability and constructability. To illustrate the opposition to the work-based or "precomposed"[17], it can be summarized: presence rather than representation, event rather than work, aura – in the sense of originality and uniqueness – as opposed to reproduction, emergence of the music instead of its pre-developed construction, qualities of the (concrete) material rather than the (abstract) staging of timbre combinations, self-determinacy of the body instead of merely discipling it. Giving aesthetics of improvisation contours other than those of work-based aesthetics, brings different or altered paradigms into play by bringing salient qualities of improvisation into focus rather than investigating improvisation using notions of the elaborated and the orderly smoothed-off. Aesthetics of improvisation do not negate the diversity of composition and improvisation, but rather apply the relevance of the principles of composition to free playing. That which is potentially composed in improvisation is performatively modified and reordered in the swirl of eventness, thus giving space to the unforeseen, based upon the etymological root of improvisation. There can be no doubt that the chosen musical material and the structure it is given play a meaningful role in the aesthetic result. However, it is obvious that the essential constituents of improvised music cannot be made perceptible with just a narrow view of material and structure and that its layers of meaning in terms of aesthetic practice cannot be fully unveiled. Within the act of reception, meaning is generated more by holistic factors such as presence, aura or eventness of the immediate experience of the music, rather than through common elements in the presentation and analysis of music, such as material, form or parameter.

Furthermore, a viewpoint based on aesthetics of improvisation allows music which is very different in terms of the resulting sound or the artistic self-conception, but that is still based on or implying improvisation, to be viewed from a similar perspective, even though in each case the emphasis can vary significantly. The following are aspects of the concepts presented here. They provide brief, ideal-typical, but non-specific examples:

---

17 | As improvisation is also at times considered a form of composition, Bruno Nettl suggests the term *precompositions* to differentiate music created prior to its realization in sound: Nettl, Bruno: "Introduction: An Art Neglected in Scholarship", in: Nettl and Russell 1998: 1-23, here 5.

provisationen entlang an Vorstellungen des Ausgearbeiteten und planmäßig Geebneten zu untersuchen. Improvisationsästhetik negiert dabei nicht die Diversität von Komposition und Improvisation, aber sie bezieht die Relevanz des Prinzips Komposition für das freie Spiel mit ein. Dabei wird das an Improvisationen potentiell Komponierte im Strudel des Ereignishaften performativ modifiziert und neu geordnet, wodurch das etymologisch in der Improvisation fundierte Unvorhersehbare seinen Raum erhält. Ohne Frage haben das gewählte musikalische Material sowie dessen Strukturierung allergrößte Bedeutung für das ästhetische Resultat. Dennoch ist es offenkundig, dass das jeweils Essentielle der Konstituenten improvisierter Musik mit einem verengten Blick auf Material und Struktur nicht wahrnehmbar gemacht werden kann und ihre Bedeutungsschichten als ästhetische Praxis damit nicht vollständig freigelegt werden. Bedeutung stellt sich im Akt der Rezeption vielmehr über ganzheitliche Faktoren wie Präsenz, Aura oder Ereignishaftigkeit des unmittelbaren Musikerlebnisses her als über für gewöhnlich in Darstellungen und Analysen von Musik berücksichtigte Elemente wie Material, Form oder Parameter.

Weiterhin ermöglicht eine improvisationsästhetische Sichtweise, dass im klingenden Resultat und künstlerischen Selbstverständnis ganz unterschiedliche, aber dennoch auf Improvisation beruhende oder sie implizierende Musiken aus einem ähnlichen Blickwinkel betrachtet werden können, wenn auch die jeweils anteilige Gewichtung deutlich variieren kann. Im Folgenden seien einige Aspekte des hier Dargelegten anhand von idealtypischen, aber nicht weiter spezifizierten Beispielen kurz und verallgemeinernd veranschaulicht:

1. Eine leise, von Pausen durchsetzte Improvisation bezieht ihre Intensität weniger aus einer impulsiven Körperlichkeit Klangereignisse evozierender Gesten, dafür umso mehr aus der spannungsreichen Präsenz einer konzentrierten und nur minimal variierenden Transformation von Geräuschqualitäten. Zugleich kann aber auch eine direktere, impulsive Körperlichkeit einen hohen Grad an Präsenz erzielen, wohingegen auch das präzise und aufmerksame, aber beinahe unsichtbare Verändern des Fingerdrucks im stillen Spiel die Klangvariabilität entscheidend steuern kann und somit das Paradigma des Körperlichen die Musik entscheidend beeinflusst.
2. In einer tendenziell freien Improvisation können sich ebenso auffallend emergente Momente ereignen wie in einer vorkomponierten Struktur, die nur ansatzweise mit Improvisation operiert.
3. In einem charakteristischen Free Jazz-Setting kann die Erfahrung des Auratisch-Einmaligen und -Originalen ebenso erlebt werden wie in einem Echtzeitkompositions-Umfeld.
4. Ein improvisiertes Noise-Konzert kann in vergleichbarer Weise die Materialität von amplifizierten Alltagsobjekten ausloten wie es ohne Verstärkung in einem frei improvisierenden Trio vonstattengeht.

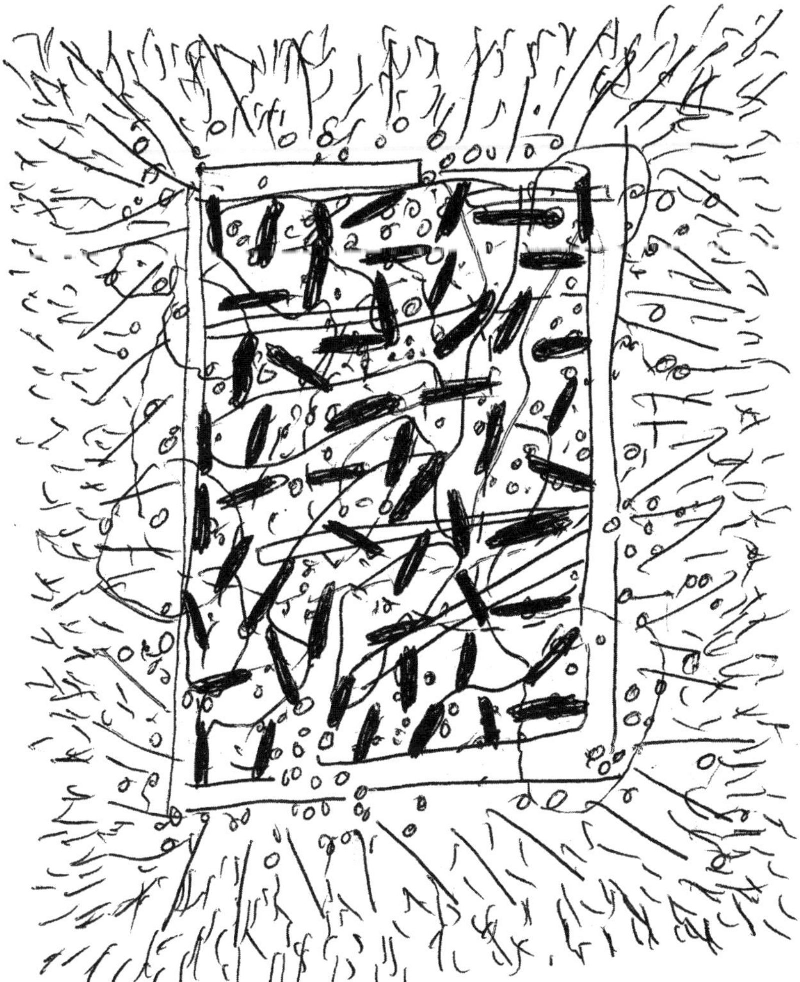

29.5.014

5. Und im Kontext elektroakustischer Improvisation kann die phänomenale Vorführung sinnlicher Klanglichkeit ebenso auf die reine Präsenz außergewöhnlicher Soundqualitäten abzielen wie das Solospiel eines mit Zirkularatmung, Obertönen und Spaltklängen operierenden Saxofonisten.

Improvisationsästhetik realisiert sich jenseits streng dichotomischer Sichtweisen auf Komposition und Improvisation auf ähnliche Weise in ganz unterschiedlichen Praxen der improvisationsbezogenen, zeitgenössischen Stile und schöpft in hohem Maß aus den hier angedeuteten Momenten. Damit ist sie eine zwar nicht allgemeine, aber doch vielseitig anwendbare ästhetische Theorie, die das ästhetische Phänomen nicht durch ihre eingeengte Perspektive einebnet, sondern es in seiner jeweilig individuellen Modifikation betrachtet. Vor der Folie dezidierter Vorbereitung durch die Erarbeitung eigener Spieltechniken, die aus der Erinnerung und in der fortwährenden Rekombination und Erweiterung durch bisher Ungekanntes gespeist werden, verlässt sich aktuelle Improvisationsmusik in größtmöglicher Weise auf die performative Kraft und ihr Vermögen zur Präsentifikation im Improvisationsereignis. Sie lebt im Modus des Improvisationsästhetischen.

1. A soft improvisation, punctuated by periods of rest, draws its intensity less from the impulsive physicality of the gestures evoking sound events, but more from the thrilling presence of a concentrated and hardly varying transformation of sound qualities. However, at the same time, a more direct, impulsive physicality can achieve a high degree of presence, whereas the precise and attentive but barely perceptible change in finger pressure in silent play can have a decisive influence on the sound variability, so that the paradigm of physicality affects the music directly.
2. Strikingly emergent moments are as likely to occur in tendentially-free improvisation as they are in a precomposed structure that only allows for a small amount of improvisation.
3. The auratic, unique and original can be experienced in a typical free jazz setting, as well as in a real-time composition environment.
4. An improvised noise concert can explore the materiality of amplified everyday objects just as well as a freely improvising trio without amplification.
5. And in the context of electroacoustic improvisation, the phenomenal demonstration of sensual sonority can aim to create the pure presence of exceptional sound qualities, just like the solo performance of a saxophonist using circular breathing, overtones and multiphonics.

Aesthetics of improvisation are realized beyond strict dichotomic views of composition and improvisation. They do this in a similar way in different improvisation-based and contemporary styles of music practice and draw significantly upon characteristics such as those mentioned here. Admittedly, this precludes the theory of aesthetics from being deemed a general one, however, it is still a widely applicable one; a theory that does not crush aesthetic phenomena into a narrow perspective but rather views them in terms of their respective modifications. With a background of thorough preparation achieved through the development of personal playing techniques, which is a combination of memory and a continuous expansion fed by new input, contemporary improvised music relies in the broadest possible sense on performative power and its capacity for creating presence in the form of an improvisation event. The music lives in the realm of aesthetics of improvisation.

Translation into English: Tom Lynn, Berlin; Louise & Phil Loxton, GB-Wales

Bibliografie/bibliography

Bal, Mieke (2006): Kulturanalyse. Fechner-Smarsly, Thomas; Neef, Sonja (Hg./Eds.), Frankfurt a. M.: Suhrkamp. Darin: »Wandernde Begriffe, sich kreuzende Theorien. Von den *cultural studies* zur Kulturanalyse«, 7-27. Sowie: Fechner-Smarsly, Thomas; Neef, Sonja: »Kulturanalyse. Zur interdisziplinären Methologie Mieke Bals«, 335-371.

Behne, Klaus-Ernst (1997): »Musikästhetik. III. Musikalische Urteilsbildung«, in: Finscher, Ludwig (Hrsg./Ed.): Die Musik in Geschichte und Gegenwart, Sachteil Bd. 6, Kassel: Bärenreiter, Sp. 998-1012.

Bohrer, Karl Heinz (1981): Plötzlichkeit. Zum Augenblick des ästhetischen Scheins, Frankfurt a. M.: Suhrkamp.

Borgards, Roland (2007): »Literatur und Improvisation. Benjamins ›Auf die Minute‹ und die Geschichte der literarischen Improvisationsästhetik«, in: Barner, Wilfried et alii (Hg./Eds.): Jahrbuch der deutschen Schillergesellschaft, Göttingen: Wallstein, 268-286.

Borgards, Roland (2009): »Improvisation, Verbot, Genie. Zur Improvisationsästhetik bei Sonnenfels, Goethe, Spalding, Moritz und Novalis«, in: Dauss, Markus; Haekel, Ralf (Hg./Eds.): Leib/Seele – Geist/Buchstabe. Dualismen in der Ästhetik und den Künsten um 1800 und 1900, Würzburg: Königshausen & Neumann, 257-268.

Charles, Daniel (1983): »Esthétiques de la Performance«, in: Encyclopaedia Universalis, Bd. Création et Culture, Paris: Société d'édition *Encyclopædia Universalis* S.A., 197-210.

Charles, Daniel (1989): »Ästhetiken der Performance«, in: Ders./Id.: Zeitspielräume. Performance, Musik, Ästhetik, Berlin: Merve, 25-85.

Fischer-Lichte, Erika (2002): »Grenzgänge und Tauschhandel. Auf dem Wege zu einer performativen Kultur«, in: Wirth, Uwe (Hrsg./Ed.): Performanz. Zwischen Sprachphilosophie und Kulturwissenschaften, Frankfurt a. M.: Suhrkamp, 277-300.

Fischer-Lichte, Erika (2004): Ästhetik des Performativen, Frankfurt a. M.: Suhrkamp.

Fischer-Lichte, Erika (2012): Performativität. Eine Einführung, Bielefeld: transcript .

Goehr, Lydia (2007): The Imaginary Museum of Musical Works. An Essay in the Philosophy of Music, Oxford: Oxford University Press.

Gumbrecht, Hans Ulrich (2004): Diesseits der Hermeneutik. Die Produktion von Präsenz, Frankfurt a. M.: Suhrkamp.

Gumbrecht, Hans Ulrich (2012): Präsenz, Frankfurt a. M.: Suhrkamp.

Hempfer, Klaus W.; Volbers, Jörg (Hg./Eds.) (2011): Theorien des Performativen. Sprache – Wissen – Praxis. Eine kritische Bestandsaufnahme, Bielefeld: transcript.

Hentschel, Frank (2012): »Modularisierte Musikgeschichte«, in: Danielczyk, Sandra et alii (Hg./Eds.): Konstruktivität von Musikgeschichtsschreibung. Zur Formation musikbezogenen Wissens, Hildesheim: Olms, 241-260.

Holtsträter, Knut (2014): »Editorial 2014/5: Improvisierte Musik analysieren und deuten«, in: Act – Zeitschrift für Musik & Performance, Heft 5: Improvisierte Musik analysieren und deuten, Bayreuth: Universität Bayreuth. *URL: http://www.act.uni-bayreuth.de/de/archiv/201405/01_editorial_05_Holtstraeter/index.html* (05.06.2015).

Kneif, Tibor (1971): »Musikästhetik«, in: Dahlhaus, Carl (Hrsg./Ed.): Einführung in die systematische Musikwissenschaft, Laaber: Laaber, 133-169.

Kolesch, Doris (2001): »Ästhetik der Präsenz: Theater-Stimmen«, in: Früchtl, Josef; Zimmermann, Jörg (Hg./Eds.): Ästhetik der Inszenierung, Frankfurt a. M.: Suhrkamp.

Landgraf, Edgar (2011): Improvisation as Art. Conceptual Challenges, Historical Perspectives, New York: Continuum.

Maschat, Mathias (2012): »Zur Performativität zeitgenössischer Improvisation«, in: kunsttexte.de/auditive_perspektiven, Ausgabe 2.2012 (Mai): Haenisch, Matthias (Hrsg./Ed.): Improvisation. Theorie – Praxis – Ästhetik. *URL: http://edoc.hu-berlin.de/kunsttexte/2012-2/maschat-mathias-5/PDF/maschat.pdf* (05.06.2015).

Mersch, Dieter (2002): Ereignis und Aura. Untersuchungen zu einer Ästhetik des Performativen, Frankfurt a. M.: Suhrkamp.

Nancy, Jean-Luc (1993): The Birth of Presence, Stanford: Stanford University Press.

Nettl, Bruno; Russell, Melinda (Hg./Eds.) (1998): In the Course of Performance. Studies in the World of Musical Improvisation, Chicago: The University of Chicago Press.

Sanio, Sabine (1999): Alternativen zur Werkästhetik. John Cage und Helmut Heißenbüttel, Saarbrücken: Pfau.

Seel, Martin (2000): Ästhetik des Erscheinens. Frankfurt a. M.: Suhrkamp.

Tadday, Ulrich (2004): »Musikalische Körper – körperliche Musik. Zur Ästhetik auch der populären Musik«, in: de la Motte-Haber, Helga; Tramsen, Eckhard (Hg./Eds.): Musikästhetik, Laaber: Laaber, 395-407.

Wilson, Peter Niklas (1999): Hear and Now. Gedanken zur improvisierten Musik, Hofheim: Wolke.

Berlin 30.5.014
SOUP
Schlagzeug
Bläser
grün
TEXT
STREICHER
rot
gelb
zupfinstrumente
orange
weiß
TEXTE
ANDERE
Reinhard Gagel
und Matthias Schwabe dirigieren die SOUP, freie Improvisation
für viele Spieler, m.a. Gesang, Sprache, Instrumente
Jede Farbe in Zuordnung zu einer Spielerinnengruppe
FK. am Tageslichtprojektor. Textgruppe liest aus der Seminar-
diskussion: Sprüche/Widersprüche, Zitate, mit eigenen
Zeichen vom EXPLORATORIUM

Die SOUP – Schnittstelle des Symposiums | The SOUP – Interface of the Symposium

Reinhard Gagel

Das Symposium war ein Nacheinander verschiedener Präsentationsformen: Vorträge und Diskussionen am Vormittag, Offene Bühne am Mittag, Workshops und Seminare am Nachmittag und Konzerte am Abend[1]. Unsere spezielle Idee war, diese verschiedenen medialen Ebenen – Sprechen, Diskutieren, Spielen, Zuhören – bewusst als ein Aufeinandereinwirken zu gestalten. Im Zentrum unseres Programms schufen wir deshalb einen Zeitpunkt, an dem alle diese Stränge zusammenkommen konnten. Dies sollte in Form einer gemeinsamen Performance geschehen. Wir nannten sie SOUP. Der Name hat eine improvisatorische Tradition: als SOUP bezeichnete die Gruppe *Musica Elettronica Viva (MEV)* eine Musik-Performance, die im Herbst 1968 in Rom stattfand. Alvin Curran schreibt als Mitmusiker Jahre später über die kulinarisch-musikalische Namensgebung:

»Suppe ist etwas Grundlegendes. Die besten Suppen ergeben sich in der Regel einfach. Ein alter Knochen, etwas Selleriegrün, alles Vergessene, Beiseitegelegte, Erinnerte, Übriggebliebene, Lächerliche kann zu Suppe werden. Suppe ist irgendwas, Suppe ist alles. Alles, was sie braucht, ist Notwendigkeit, Spiel und inspirierte Improvisation, wie bei gelungenem Kochen überhaupt.« (Curran 2000: 50)

Er listet im Folgenden die Zutaten auf, die *MEV* in ihrem römischen Studio zusammenstellten: verschiedenste Klang- und Geräuscherzeuger, Instrumente, Kochgeräte (!), Medien und technische Geräte. Sie wurde dann mit ebenfalls anwesenden Zuhörern *verquirlt*, »bis aus allem eine harmonische Mischung entsteht, die nicht mehr von den Klängen unterscheidbar ist, die sie erzeugen oder hören. Langsam zum Kochen bringen und zwei bis drei Stunden simmern lassen« (ebd.). Es sollte also in einer langen Garzeit eine Entmaterialisierung der Klänge stattfinden, eine Art Umschlagen in eine neue Qualität. Die *MEV*-SOUP war ein musikalisches Happening.

Suppe haben wir als reizvolle Metapher gesehen und die SOUP als Methode für ein konkretes Zusammenwirken von Theorie und Praxis genommen. Herausgekommen ist ein künstlerisch-wissenschaftliches Projekt in Form eines Happenings. Das geschah folgendermaßen: Am Nachmittag der beiden Symposiumstage sollten Musiker, die die Workshops von Ariel Shibolet und Barre Phillips besucht hatten, und die Wissenschaftler, die Vorträge gehalten hatten, als Musiker oder Sprecher auf die Bühne kommen. Die Musik sollte in Großbesetzung improvisatorisch entstehen und mit dem Verlesen beziehungsweise performativen Sprechen von Texten (Vorträge, Diskussionsprotokolle, Zitate) durchmischt werden. Im Vorfeld entschieden wir, »unsere« SOUP nicht dem Anarchischen der *MEV*-SOUP zu überlassen. Die Suppe bekam also ein Rezept und wurde dann folgendermaßen angekündigt und organisiert:

1 | Siehe Festivalablauf auf Seite 403.

The symposium consisted of different presentation formats that took place consecutively throughout the event: lectures and discussions in the morning, open stage sessions at lunchtime, workshops and seminars in the afternoon, and concerts in the evening.[1] It was our idea to consciously include different types of media – speaking, discussing, playing and listening – in order to create an environment in which these elements could have an impact on one another. The main aim of our program was to create a specific moment in time when all of these strands would come together. This took the form of a collective performance, which we called SOUP. This title has a history with regard to improvisation: SOUP was the name given to a performance by the group *Musica Elettronica Viva (MEV)*, which took place in Rome in autumn 1968. Alvin Curran, who was part of this group, wrote many years later about the culinary aspect behind the musical name:

"Soup is fundamental. The best soups usually just happen. An old bone, some celery tops, anything forgotten, discarded, remembered, leftover or ridiculous can become a soup. Soup is anything. Everything. Necessity, play and inspired improvisation are its only requirements - as in all good cooking." (Curran 2000: 50)

He then lists the ingredients which *MEV* put together in their studio in Rome: a wide variety of vessels to create sound and noise, instruments, cooking equipment (!), media and technical equipment. The players are gradually blended with the listeners, "until all becomes a harmonious mixture, indistinguishable from the sounds they make or hear. Bring to a boil slowly and simmer for two to three hours" (ibid.). Over such a long period of cooking time a dematerialization of sounds takes place, a kind of transformation into a new quality. The *MEV* SOUP was a groundbreaking musical happening.

We saw soup as an appealing metaphor and utilized SOUP as a method to establish concrete cooperation between theory and practice. What resulted was an artistic-scientific project in the form of a musical happening. It took the following format: during the afternoons of the two-day symposium, musicians who had attended Ariel Shibolet's and Barre Phillips' workshops, and scientists who had given speeches came together on stage. Within this large gathering, music should occur improvisationally and be blended with the reading or performing of texts (lectures, discussion notes, quotations). Prior to this, we decided that we did not want our 'SOUP' to be at the mercy of the anarchistic *MEV* SOUP. Therefore, our soup was made to a recipe and was organized and introduced as follows:

1 | See the festival program on page 403.

»*Die SOUP* ist eine 45minütige gemeinsame Performance mit den Elementen Musik, Text, Bewegung und Bild. Hier sollen die Stränge des Jubiläums zusammenlaufen und Beteiligte an den Workshops, den Konzerten und den Vorträgen und Seminaren gemeinsam ein improvisiertes mehrmediales Werk schaffen. Mit dabei sollen 24 Mitwirkende sein. Publikum ist erwünscht.

Die SOUP ist grundsätzlich ergebnisoffen und unvorhersehbar. Was und wie jemand spielt, spricht, liest, sich bewegt, entsteht grundsätzlich aus dem Moment. Wir haben dennoch ein paar Regeln vorbereitet, an denen sich der Ablauf und Besetzungen orientieren sollen.

- Mitspieler sollten sich um 17 h in Saal 1 einfinden, eine spätere Teilnahme ist nicht möglich. Die explo-SOUP ist für 24 Spieler ausgelegt.
- Jeder Mitspieler erhält eine Karte, die eine Farbe, und eine Form auszeichnet. Diese drei Eigenschaften dienen zur Bildung von temporären Teil-Ensembles. Es gibt sechs Farben und vier Formen, das heißt, Farben sind immer Quartette und Formen Sextette.
- Die SOUP wird gesteuert von zwei »Promptern«. Sie halten die genannten Karten gut sichtbar hoch und lenken somit die Besetzungen.
- Sie geben heterogene und homogene Instrumentenbesetzung vor.
- Außerdem soll es gelesene Texte (Karte TEXT) und eventuell kurze Gespräche (Karte TALK) geben und eine Aufforderung, mit anderen die Karte zu tauschen, damit man in einem neuen Ensemble spielt: CHANGE CARDS
- Beginn (die ersten 5 Minuten) als gemeinsame »Reinigung« = wenig tun, hören, Klänge aus der Stille, sich einstimmen.«[2]

Man sieht: wir haben »Ordnungsinstanzen« vorgegeben. Das lag am Doppelcharakter als Prozess und Performance. Wir wollten die Kommunikation in gewisse Bahnen lenken – 24 adhoc mitspielende Mitwirkende haben es schwer, ihr Spielen selbst zu organisieren – und eine transparente Durchmischung von Klang, Text und Bewegung erreichen. Das konnten wir durch Variationen der Besetzungen – Gruppen nach ähnlichen Instrumenten, heterogene Gruppen nach Zufall und Sprecher – erzielen, die von den beiden sogenannten Promptern[3] während der Performance auf den Karten angezeigt wurden. Die dahinterstehende qualitative Vorstellung war die einer durchhörbaren Ordnung. Allerdings: Welche Strukturen im Detail entstanden, wie und wohin sie sich letztlich entwickelten, war nicht vorgeplant. Das blieb dem Verlauf überlassen.

Die SOUPs waren im Grunde ein künstlerisch-wissenschaftliches Projekt in breiter Öffentlichkeit. Sie verbanden Theoretisches mit Musikalischem in

2 | Spielregel der SOUP, auf Handzetteln an die Teilnehmer verteilt am 30. und 31.5.2015 im *exploratorium berlin.*

3 | Der Begriff »Prompter« stammt aus dem Cobra-Konzept von John Zorn. Prompter in den SOUPS im *exploratorium* waren Reinhard Gagel und Matthias Schwabe.

"*SOUP* is a collective performance lasting 45 minutes; it is comprised of music, text, movement and images. It brings together the different elements of the festival so that the participants of the workshops, concerts, lectures and seminars can create an improvisational multi-media work. There should be 24 contributors and the event should be open to the public.

What comes out of SOUP should be open and unpredictable. What and how someone plays, speaks, reads, moves is dependent upon the moment. Nevertheless, we have prepared a few ground rules for the process and the participants.

- Contributors should meet at 5pm in Hall 1; it is not possible to take part if you arrive late. SOUP is limited to 24 performers.
- Every performer receives a card that has a color and a shape on it. These elements serve to create temporary part-ensembles. There are six colors and four shapes, colors are for quartets and shapes are sextets.
- SOUP is guided by two "prompters". They hold the aforementioned cards up, so that they are clearly visible, and use them to direct the participants.
- They stipulate whether the instrument combinations are homogenous or heterogeneous.
- In addition, there should be texts which are read (with the word TEXT on them) and perhaps short conversations (cards with the word TALK on them). Participants should be asked to exchange cards so that they play in different ensembles (CHANGE CARDS).
- The beginning (the first 5 minutes) should be a collective "cleansing" = do little, listen, tune in, let sounds evolve from the silence."[2]

As you can see, we have stipulated "a system of rules". This is due to the dual nature of the event – process and performance. We wanted to steer the communication in certain directions – 24 participants, playing in an ad hoc way, find it difficult to organize themselves – and we wanted to achieve a transparent blend of sound, text and movement. This we were able to do by varying the constituent parts of the ensembles – groupings according to similar instruments, heterogeneous groupings created randomly and other groupings containing speakers. All this information was on the cards which were displayed by the two prompters during the performance.[3] The qualitative intention behind this performance was order, which was clearly audible. However, the exact nature of the structures which occurred and how, and to what extent, they developed was not planned in advance. This was down to how events unfolded.

---

2 | The ground rules of SOUP were written on handouts that were given to the participants on 30th and 31st May 2015 at the Berlin *exploratorium*.

3 | The SOUP prompters at the *exploratorium* were Reinhard Gagel and Matthias Schwabe.

einem performativen Rahmen. In der SOUP wurden ästhetische Beziehungen zwischen Menschen und heterogenen Elementen geschaffen, die sich aus der spezifischen Situation ergaben. Wie wird ein Text über Improvisation wahrgenommen, wenn er im Kontext von dem gelesen wird, was er beschreibt? Wie wird Sprechen musikalisch? Wie wird improvisierte Musik erlebt, wenn in ihr Texte über das Improvisieren aufscheinen? Wie wird Musik theoretisch? Das sind im Grunde ästhetische Fragen, die auch Bewertungen ins Spiel bringen: Kann das gewählte Verfahren zu einem sinnlich schlüssigen Ergebnis führen, obwohl alle Elemente sehr unterschiedlicher Art sind? Macht das Zusammenwirken einen Sinn, für mich persönlich oder als allgemeine Erkenntnis? Man liebt die Suppe gerade wegen der Variationsbreite ihrer Zutaten, die jedoch *eine* spezifische Geschmacksrichtung ergibt. Für den italienischen Philosophen Alessandro Bertinetto ist das Kochen eine Kunst, die über das Biologische hinaus auch zu ästhetischen Bewertungen herausfordert. Er sieht die *ars culinaria* mit der *Improvisation* in engem Zusammenhang: »Als Geschmackskunst bietet die *ars culinaria* ... den exquisiten Zusammenhang von Improvisation, Experiment und Ästhetik als kritische Geschmackstheorie.« (Bertinetto 2011: 13)

Er sieht das Kochen voller improvisatorischer Verfahrensweisen und lässt eine spezifisch improvisatorische Ästhetik erkennen:

> »[...] Die *ars culinaria* ist Experiment als kontrollierte Freiheit, die in unterschiedlichen Graden experimentell sein kann und unsere Bewertungskräfte herausfordert. Ihre Voraussetzung ist dieselbe ›Sensibilität für das Situative‹, das heißt dieselbe ›Achtsamkeit auf das Spezifische der Situation‹, die für die Improvisation erforderlich ist. In der *ars culinaria* kann man sowohl inventiv als auch spontan sein, mehr oder weniger passend auf unvorhergesehene Situationen reagieren, mehr oder weniger experimentell vorgehen.« (ebd.)

Diese in Bertinettos Worten aufscheinende Ästhetik liegt nicht nur im Ergebnis, sondern vor allem in der Verfahrensweise selbst. Das Spezifische der Situation erfordert eine achtsame und sensible Reaktion, sei es am Kochtopf oder in der SOUP als Happening. Ohne das ergibt sich Mischmasch, eine formlose Masse, ohne Geschmack und Sinn. Die SOUP ist eine soziale und situationsbezogene Handlung: Man wirkt zusammen an einem »Topf«. Sie wird von einer ästhetischen Grundhaltung geleitet, die daraus besteht, dass sich alle in jeder Phase des Gesamtverlaufes den Fragen stellen müssen: »Was passt zu der Struktur, die gerade geschieht? Worauf achte ich und wie handle ich der Situation gemäß?«

Man konnte unsere Suppe allerdings nicht essen. Man hatte (hoffentlich) einen gewissen Genuss beim Mitmachen und Zuhören. Die improvisatorischen SOUPs des Symposiums waren ephemer und einmalig. Sie waren in gewisser

The SOUPs were basically an artistic-scientific project which took place in public. They brought together the theoretical and the musical within a performative framework. In SOUP, aesthetic relationships between people and heterogeneous elements were created. These relationships arose from specific situations. How is a text perceived improvisationally when it is read in the context of that which is being described? How can speaking be musical? How is improvised music experienced when texts about improvisation appear within it? How does music become theoretical? Fundamentally, these are questions of aesthetics that also bring the concept of evaluation into play: can the process chosen lead to a sensual and coherent conclusion, despite the fact that the various elements involved are all very different? Does this collaboration make sense, either to me personally or in general? One loves soup because of the variation of its ingredients, which ultimately give it one specific flavor. For the Italian philosopher Alessandro Bertinetto cooking is an art which goes beyond the biological and demands an aesthetic evaluation. He perceives culinary art as being closely associated with improvisation: "Culinary art offers an exquisite combination of improvisation, experimentation and aesthetics; it is a critical theory of taste." (Bertinetto 2011: 13)

He sees cooking as being full of improvisational practices and recognizes specific improvisational aesthetics within these:

> "[...] *Culinary art* is an experiment in controlled freedom; it is experimental to varying degrees and challenges our ability to evaluate. The prerequisities for this are the same 'sensibility towards the situative', the same 'paying attention to the specifics of the situation' that are demanded by improvisation. In culinary art one can be inventive and spontaneous, react to unforeseen situations as little or as much as one wishes and proceed in an experimental way." (Ibid.)

What appears in Bertinettos description is not only to be found in the results but also in the processes themselves. The specifics of the situation demand attention and a sensitive reaction to sounds, texts and players, be that in the saucepan or, in the case of SOUP, the happening. Without this, there is only a mishmash, a shapeless mass without taste or sense. SOUP is a social and a situational action: people work together around one "pot". They are guided by a basic aesthetic attitude, one that stipulates that at every phase of the process questions must be asked: What fits to the structure that is occuring? What should I take into account and how do I manage the situation?"

Of course, one cannot eat our soup. Hopefully, one received a certain enjoyment from participating and listening. The improvisational SOUPs of the symposium were ephemeral and unique. They were in a certain way paradoxes, as after the cooking nothing remained. By contrast, Bertinetto points out the limited performative character of cooking: "Unlike improvisation as a pro-

Weise paradox: nach dem Kochen war nichts mehr übrig. Bertinetto weist auf den beschränkten performativen Charakter des Kochens hin:

»Anders als die Improvisation als Prozess, und dem Experiment ähnlich, ist die Kochkunst zwar nicht ausschließlich performativer Natur, da ihre Produkte vom produktiven Prozess unterschieden sind und nach dem Ende desselben erlebt werden.« (Bertinetto 2011: 13)

Er sieht in allem Experimentellen und Ephemeren aber auch konservierende Aspekte: der Genuss der Zuschauer und audiovisuelle Aufzeichnungen ergeben das Gericht:

»Werden nun nicht nur der Prozess der improvisatorischen Tätigkeit, sondern auch deren Resultate, das sind die audiovisuellen Aufnahmen, berücksichtigt, so exemplifiziert die *ars culinaria* den experimentalen/experimentellen Charakter der improvisatorischen Praxis sehr gut [...].« (ebd.)

Wir haben die SOUP aufgezeichnet und so dem Verschwinden vorgebeugt. Und wir haben lange überlegt, wie wir das Gericht servieren sollen und einem Buch beifügen können. Schriftlich allein jedenfalls lässt sich unsere SOUP nicht angemessen veröffentlichen. Man kann Rezepte und Kochkritiken auch nicht essen. Wir können aber auch am tatsächlichen Prozess niemanden mehr teilhaben lassen. Er ist vergangen.

Wir sehen SOUP auch als ein allgemeines Prinzip von Anordnung und Verbindung. SOUP ist Happening und Methode. Im Situativen verbinden sich Elemente und Menschen auf spezifische Weise miteinander. Sie nehmen Beziehungen auf, verlassen sie aber auch sofort wieder. Sie agieren überraschend, anarchisch, unverständlich, dann wieder logisch, einleuchtend, aufklärend. Sie sind präsent, echt, ästhetisch wahrnehmbar, lebendig. Eine Präsentation im Internet mit seinen Möglichkeiten vielfältiger Verbindungen von Hören, Lesen und Anschauen scheint uns dafür am besten geeignet. Auch andere Elemente des Symposiums – zum Beispiel auch Konzertmitschnitte – werden wir in die Internet-SOUP aufzunehmen. Wir haben eine Software[4] gefunden, mit der wir den Charakter der Aufhebung von Grenzen zwischen Musizieren und Sprechen und dem Finden neuer Bezüge wirklich darstellen können. Vielleicht lösen wir damit die Konzeption der SOUP auch in der Präsentation im Netz ein und können mehr Menschen daran teilhaben lassen.

Die Internet-SOUP ist zu finden über *http://exploratorium-berlin.de/improvisation-erforschen-improvisierend-forschen/*.

---

4 | Mehr dazu unter *URL: http://www.taswir-institute.org.*

cess but similar to it as an experiment, the art of cooking does not only possess a performative nature, as its products are differentiated from the productive process and after the end is reached, are still capable of being experienced." (Bertinetto 2011: 13)

He sees aspects of preservation in both the experimental and ephemeral; the enjoyment of the spectators and audiovisual recordings create the dish:

"If we do not only consider the process of improvisational activities, but also their results - the audiovisual recordings, then culinary art exemplifies the experimental nature of improvisational practice extremely well [...]." (Ibid.)

We have recorded SOUP and thereby prevented it from disappearing entirely. Moreover, we have thought long and hard about how we can serve up the dish and add it to a book. We cannot publish our SOUP adequately if we just write about it. After all, one cannot eat recipes or cooking reviews. At the same time, we can no longer bring anyone into the actual process. It is in the past.

We perceive SOUP as being a general principle of organizing and combining. SOUP is event and methods. It is a situative combining of elements and people with one another in a specific way. These establish relationships but then immediately break them again. These combinations act surprisingly, anarchically, unintelligibly, then logically, obviously and enlighteningly. They are present, honest, aesthetically perceivable and lively. A presentation in the internet with its myriad of possible combinations for hearing, reading and showing seems to be best suited to convey this. We will take other elements of the symposium – also the live recordings – and put them into the Internet SOUP. We have found software[4] with which we can clearly demonstrate the characteristic of overstepping limits and finding connections between music, speaking and movement. Perhaps by presenting it online we can realize our conception with regard to SOUP and allow even more people to share in it.

The internet SOUP can be found at *http://exploratorium-berlin.de/improvisation-erforschen-improvisierend-forschen/.*

Translation into English: Louise & Phil Loxton, GB-Wales

4 | Atlas-Software; see *URL: https://www.taswir-institute.org.*

Literatur/References

Curran, Alvin (2000): »Improvisationspraxis und Musica Elettronica Viva«, in: Musiktexte 86/87, Zeitschrift für neue Musik, Köln: Verlag MusikTexte.

Bertinetto, Alessandro (2011): »Improvisation und Experiment«, in: Experimentelle Ästhetik. VIII. Kongress der Deutschen Gesellschaft für Ästhetik, Düsseldorf: Kunstakademie Düsseldorf 4.-7.10.2011/4th-7th October 2011.

http://exploratorium-berlin.de/improvisation-erforschen-improvisierend-forschen/

Exploratorium Berlin 30.5.014

- der Mensch als Person muß mit bedacht werden
  mitreflektiert werden — 'PERSONA'
  ↓
  Maske
- das Oszillieren im Machen und Reflektieren
- 'Abgrund' zwischen den Personen
- 'The point of no return'
- wir brauchen die Kälte der Wissenschaft um die Hitze der Improvisation zu verstehen
- die Grauzone der 'Kommunikation'

AKTION (SOUP) 30.5.014

- Stille zu Beginn

Why do we improvise?

Eddie Prevost

Bewußtsein für

– technical intelligence
– social intelligence
+
wir müssen zu
+
Empathy zurückfinden

– the searching sound

wie suche ich?

– wir müssen zurück zum menschlichen Element

– Beherrschung des Instrumentes verbunden mit reflektierender Offenheit in der Improvisation

– wir benötigen eine neue Ethik in der Musik

– welche Erkenntnisspuren liegt in der Erforschung von Klang und was bedeutet das Geräusch / / Klangereignis?

– es geht nicht um ein REINVENTING (WIEDER/NEUERFINDUNG) um eine nochmalige ERFINDUNG

– die Musik eilt immer wohin die Gesellschaft sich entwickelt

– ich gebe eine freie Atmosphäre vor, eine Atmosphäre, die einen nicht in irgendeine Richtung zwingt
: laßt Euch fallen, keine Ängste entwickeln
–

Exploratoria | Exploratoria

Edwin Prévost

> »Wenn ihr uns stecht, bluten wir nicht?
> Wenn ihr uns kitzelt, lachen wir nicht?
> Wenn ihr uns vergiftet, sterben wir nicht?«
> WILLIAM SHAKESPEARE: DER KAUFMANN VON VENEDIG, AKT 3, SZENE 1

ERSTE NATUR

Unsere primären Reaktionen sind biologisch. Lebende Organismen suchen nach Material, um Wachstum zu erzeugen und zu erhalten. Jeder unserer Sinne verleiht diesem Gebot eine Dimension. Die *erste Natur* entwickelt sich zu einer Ansammlung von Reaktionen, die durch Erinnertes wächst. Die Erfolgswahrscheinlichkeit dafür, an einem bestimmten Ort Nahrung zu finden, wird durch die Erinnerung an frühere ähnliche Orte, an denen das gelungen ist, gesteigert. Dies ist ein grundlegendes Beispiel für technische Intelligenz.

Hören ist reaktiv. Klänge zu erzeugen ist adaptiv. Zuhören (als reflexive Erweiterung der Hörfähigkeit) ist ebenfalls adaptiv. Klänge zu erzeugen verändert die Welt. Echoortung. Klänge werden ausgesandt, um die Umrisse des Fledermaus-Universums auszumessen. Die Spezies der Zwergfledermäuse erfasst ihre Existenz über Klänge.[1] Durch die Herausbildung dieser Fähigkeit erhielt sie eine evolutionäre Nische, in der sie gedeihen konnte. Zwergfledermäuse verwenden Klänge auch, um miteinander zu kommunizieren. Erweiterung von Klangtechnik.

Unsere prähistorischen Vorfahren entwickelten stimmliche Klangerzeugung aus reaktiven (und vielleicht unfreiwilligen) Ausrufen vor Angst, als Warnung und als Ermunterung anderer. Klänge sind zu Werkzeugen geworden. Imitation und Verstärkung. Mimesis. Viele Vogelgesänge haben für menschliche Ohren eine musikalische Qualität. Dabei sind sie natürlich keine Musik. Vogelgesang hat sich in komplizierte Abfolgen von Warnrufen, territorialen Behauptungen und Paarungsmelodien entwickelt: Es sind artentypische Liedkomplexe entstanden. Qualifiziert sich so ein Klang-Schauplatz als »Vogelkultur«? Olivier Messiaen hat Transkriptionen von Vogelgesang in viele seiner Kompositionen eingebaut.[2] Dies bezeugt die komplexe Schönheit von Vogelgesang (für das menschliche Ohr). Aber natürlich ist Messiaens »Ästhetik der Imitation« Teil menschlicher Kultur.

---

1 | Nicht alle Fledertiere sind blind. Vielleicht ist die Sicht durch geringe Verwendung geschwächt. Indem sie nachts jagen, vermeiden Fledertiere die Konkurrenz mit anderen fliegenden Tieren – Vögeln.

2 | So zum Beispiel die Sammlung von 13 Klavierstücken »Catalogue d'oiseaux«, die 1958 fertig gestellt wurde, und »La fauvette des jardins« von 1970.

> "If you prick us do we not bleed?
> If you tickle us do we not laugh?
> If you poison us do we not die?"
> William Shakespeare: The Merchant of Venice,
> Act 3, Scene 1

First nature

Our primary responses are biological. Living organisms search for material to generate and sustain growth. Each of our senses lends a dimension to this imperative. *First nature* develops into a congregation of responses augmented by remembered undertakings. Success in finding fruit in a particular place is reinforced by remembering places similar to an earlier location. This is a fundamental example of technical intelligence.

Hearing is reactive. Making sounds is adaptive. Listening (as a reflective extension of the faculty of hearing) is also adaptive. Making sounds changes the world. Echolocation. Sounds are emitted to measure the contours of the bat universe. The microbat species gains a hold upon existence through sound.[1] Developing this faculty gave them an evolutionary niche in which to flourish. They also use sounds to communicate with each other. Sound technique extension. Our prehistoric forebears developed voice sound-making from the reactive (and perhaps involuntary) squeals of fear, warning and encouragement to others. Sounds became tools. Imitation and amplification. Mimesis. Many bird songs are musical to human ears. It is not music, of course. Bird song has developed into complicated series of warning cries, territorial claims and courtship melodies: making species oriented song complexes. Does such a location of sound qualify as "bird culture"? Olivier Messiaen incorporated transcriptions of birdsong into many of his compositions.[2] This is testament to the complexity (for human ears) in the beauty of bird song. But, of course, Messiaen's "aesthetic of imitation" is part of human culture.

Likewise, humans developed a highly aggregated series of socially meaningful sounds. We categorize these, most commonly, as language and music. When does the shift from the instinctive occur? What promotes it?

"He spoke about music in its pre-cultural state, when song had been a howl across several pitches, [when] musical performances must have had a quality something like free recitation; improvisation. But if one closely examined music, and in particular its

---

1 | Not all bats are blind. Perhaps sight is diminished through reduced use. Bats, by hunting at night thus avoid competition with other flighted animals – birds.

2 | For example, the collection of thirteen pieces for piano "Catalogue d'oiseaux", completed in 1958, and "La fauvette des jardins" of 1970.

Auch Menschen haben eine umfangreiche Sammlung sozial bedeutungsvoller Klänge entwickelt. Wir unterteilen diese für gewöhnlich in Sprache und Musik. Wann erfolgt die Verlagerung weg vom Instinktiven? Wodurch wird sie befördert?

»Er sprach von den vor-kulturellen Zuständen der Musik, als noch der Gesang ein Heulen über mehrere Tonstufen weg gewesen sei; [dass] der Musikübung vielmehr etwas frei Rezitierendes, Improvisatorisches eigen gewesen sein müsse. Beobachte man aber die Musik, und gerade auf ihrer letzterreichten Entwicklungsstufe, genau, so merke man ihr die heimliche Lust an, in diese Zustände zurückzukehren.«[3]

Zweite Natur

Wenn diese kurze Charakterisierung der *ersten Natur* überzeugend ist, dann zieht sie die Betrachtung einer *zweiten Natur* nach sich. Diese ist in menschlichen Angelegenheiten ein vertrauteres Konstrukt. Der Logik nach lässt die *zweite Natur* natürlich auf eine *erste Natur* schließen. Wir spielen oft auf die *zweite Natur* an, wenn wir bei jemandem (normalerweise bewundernd) eine Mühelosigkeit im Umgang mit erlernter Technik bemerken. Nicht selten hört man, dass diese als instinktiv bezeichnet wird. Dies gilt nur insofern, als die Mühelosigkeit so natürlich wirkt, dass sie instinktiv scheint. In Wirklichkeit ist sie jedoch erlernt und stark kulturell beeinflusst. Daraus ergibt sich ein trügerisch naturalistischer Status. Wir erkennen die Qualitäten der zweiten Natur an. Ein Gespür für Sprachen, begabte Footballer, junge Mathematiker, jugendliche Virtuosen am Klavier. Diese Attribute (oft als angeboren angesehen) stehen eigentlich mit der unterliegenden Kultur in Einklang. Sie hängen mit so alltäglichen Dingen wie Ernährung, Unterkunft, Religion, gesellschaftlichen Normen und sogar Unterhaltung zusammen. Natürlich sind sie alle kulturell bestimmt. Diesen assoziativen kulturellen Zuordnungen werden von unterschiedlichen menschlichen Zusammenkünften unterschiedliche Prioritäten zugeschrieben. Innerhalb einer Kultur werden diese Dinge als »normal« akzeptiert, und zwar ohne die nötige intellektuelle Reflexion: Man geht oft davon aus, dass sie universal gültig sind. Die Auseinandersetzung mit anderen Kulturen bringt daher einen Kontrast der Werte hervor. Einen Konflikt mit unserer Auffassung von Normalität. Nicht in einer qualitativen Hinsicht besser zu sein – wenn dies auch keine seltene Reaktion ist. Und vielleicht liegt hier die Wurzel von Rassismus und sozialer Diskriminierung.

3 | Mann, Thomas: Doktor Faustus, Frankfurt: Fischer Taschenbuch Verlag, S. 88-89.

most recently achieved stage of development, one noticed the secret desire to return to those conditions."[3]

Second nature

If this brief characterization of *first nature* is persuasive, it leads to a review of a *second nature*. This is a more familiar construct in human affairs. Logically, of course, *second nature* infers *first nature*. We often allude to second nature when we notice (usually with admiration) a person's facility with learned technique. It is not unusual to hear it described as instinctive. This holds only as far as the facility seems so natural that it *appears* to be instinctive. It is, in reality, learnt and with a strong cultural bias. This gives it a deceptive naturalistic status. We acknowledge second nature qualities. The flair for languages, gifted footballers, youthful mathematicians, juvenile virtuoso pianists. These attributes (often considered innate) are culturally aligned. They cluster together with familiar everyday things: diet, shelter, religion, social *mores* and even entertainment. They are, of course, all culturally bound. These associative cultural groupings differ in priority from one human assembly to another. Internally, each culture accepts such things as 'normal' and, without due intellectual reflection, they are often thought of as universal. Confronting other cultures is therefore a contrast of values. A conflict with our sense of normality. Not in a qualitative sense of being better – although this is not an unusual response – and is perhaps the root of racialism and social discrimination.

Second nature in music is unconsciously nurtured from our cultural cradle. The social-economic situation into which we are born. For children, vocal cadences become familiar before the linguistic essence of the sounds become clear. Inflection and tone convey meaning. An infant (or even a dog) knows when it is being scolded. Is this where much of the meaning of music is situated? If so, then our musical universe is wider – and impinges upon our being – more than conventional musical appreciation usually allows. Primitive *first nature* responses have more of a hold on our psyche than we might care to admit.

Given the emotional affect sounds have upon us, it cannot be surprising that developing human intelligence – in becoming aware of such effects – began to emulate sounds and investigate natural acoustic properties. Within the relative confinement of social groups sound worlds developed to reflect a growing familiarity and preferences. How much continued sonic investigation might ensue probably depended (and maybe still depends) upon the social and economic forces it supports.

---

3 | Mann, Thomas: Doctor Faustus, London: Vintage Books, 1997: 70.

Die *zweite Natur* in der Musik wird von unserer kulturellen Wiege aus genährt. Die sozial-ökonomische Situation, in die wir geboren werden. Bevor sich ihnen die linguistische Essenz von Klängen erschließt, sind Kinder mit stimmlichen Kadenzen vertraut. Tonfall und Ton vermitteln Bedeutung. Ein Kleinkind (oder sogar ein Hund) weiß, wann mit ihm geschimpft wird. Liegt hier ein Großteil der Bedeutung von Musik? Wenn ja, dann ist unser musikalisches Universum weitreichender – und wirkt mehr auf unser Wesen ein – als es die konventionelle Würdigung von Musik normalerweise zugibt. Die primitiven Reaktionen, die der *ersten Natur* angehören, haben einen größeren Einfluss auf unsere Psyche, als wir gerne zugeben möchten.

In Anbetracht der emotionalen Wirkung, die Klänge auf uns ausüben, überrascht es nicht, dass die Entwicklung menschlicher Intelligenz – durch die Bewusstwerdung solcher Wirkungen – begann, Klänge nachzuahmen und natürliche akustische Eigenschaften zu erkunden. Innerhalb der jeweiligen Beschränkung sozialer Gruppen haben sich Klangwelten entwickelt, die eine zunehmende Vertrautheit und Vorlieben widerspiegeln. Wie viel kontinuierliche akustische Erkundung folgte, hing vermutlich (und hängt vielleicht immer noch) von den sozialen und ökonomischen Kräften ab, die sie unterstützte.

Die Chinesen der Antike nahmen eine Wechselbeziehung zwischen Klang und Geschmack, Farbe und Atmosphäre wahr. Wahrsager, die militärischen Befehlsgebern zugeordnet waren, konnten angeblich die Stimmung des Feindes erkennen, indem sie den Klängen der Pfeifen auf dem Schlachtfeld zuhörten, und so den Schlachtverlauf vorhersagten – Sieg oder Niederlage. (Needham 1997: 135/6)

Klang hat in menschlichen Angelegenheiten eine Bedeutung, die über das Instinktive oder Reaktive hinausgeht. Überlegen wir, was Thomas Mann mit seiner Rückkehr zu einem »Heulen über mehrere Tonstufen weg« intuitiv erkannt hat.

DRITTE NATUR

Improvisierte Musik, und besonders jene, die formale Harmonik und musikalische Konventionen meidet, wird als naiv und primitiv angesehen. Thomas Manns »Heulen« ruft eine Rückkehr zu ursprünglicheren Reaktionen, als sie in formeller westeuropäischer Musik gepflegt werden, hervor. Der historische Status eines musikalischen Schamanen wurde von der Zivilisation eingeschränkt. In westlicher Kultur wird dieses Konzept eines starken, naturnahen Vermittlers zwischen Menschen und deren Umwelt nicht unterstützt. Diese Rolle wurde zugunsten »des Komponisten« verworfen, der nun unser

Exploratorium
Fritz Hauser
Jean Laurent Sasportes
Berlin 31.5.014
FK.

ausgewiesener, musikalischer Forscher ist.[4] Das Spielfeld für diese kulturelle Form der Entdeckung wird von unseren didaktischen, marktbezogenen und habituellen Reaktionen abgesteckt. Improvisation gilt hier als Wirkungsraum von Exzentrikern. Die Idee, die Welt neu (und ständig) zu erkunden, wird den meisten Menschen verwehrt. Es wird durch Vertreter für uns übernommen. Wir sind dazu verdammt, Musik zu konsumieren, anstatt an ihrer Erzeugung und an einer besonderen Art von Verständnis teilzuhaben.

»Unser Leben lang erzeugen die konventionellen Verfahren unserer Zeit überall die Erwartung von sorgfältig und klar präsentierten, verfügbaren Fertigprodukten. Ebendiese Verfahren erlauben selten einen konzentrierten Blick auf die Launen, wechselnden Probleme und den unbequemen Reichtum des Erkundens an sich. Üblicherweise ist ein großer Teil des Entwicklungsvorgangs versteckt, aufbereitet oder unsichtbar; erst nach Abschluss des Entwicklungsprozesses wird ein Produkt der Öffentlichkeit präsentiert, fein geschliffen zur nachträglichen Anerkennung: in vielfacher Weise wiedererkennbar, reproduzierbar und als Endprodukt oder Tonaufnahme zustimmungsfähig.«[5]

Thomas Mann betrauert die Denaturierung der Menschheit, ihren Verlust der technologischen Prozesse *zweiter Natur.* Seymour Wrights Eingriff geht in Richtung einer Erklärung von Manns Plädoyer und bietet mögliche Lösungen an. Die meisten Menschen wissen, welche Klänge Musik sein sollen. Zuhören. Das Taktile ist außerdem wichtig. Die feinsinnigsten Musiker entwickeln ein Gefühl für die Bedeutsamkeit des Materials und bewundern das Auftauchen von Klängen aus allem Möglichen. Es ist das trügerische (und vielleicht abträgliche) Mysterium der zweiten Natur, dass unser Bewusstsein sich zu Formalität verhärtet. Kreativität ist flüchtig und zuweilen illusorisch.

In der Kultur ist Konservatismus einschränkend. Während unsere gesellschaftlichen Institutionen Aufbewahrungsorte für Wissen und technische Informationen sind, eignen sie sich weniger gut für die Förderung von Innovation.

John Blacking bemerkte:

---

4 | Partituren in offener Form scheinen Musizierenden kompositionelle Zusammenarbeit anzubieten. Dies erfolgt meistens in grafischer oder in Prosaform. Sie fordern vom Musizierenden die Ausarbeitung eines vorgeschlagenen Schemas, um musikalisches Material zu erfinden. Diese Strukturen lenken Musiker (meiner Erfahrung nach) vom akustischen Material und der persönlichen Auseinandersetzung mit den anderen Musizierenden ab.

5 | Wright, Seymour (2011): CD-Notes, in: Allum, Jennifer; Prévost, Eddie: Penumbrae, Matchless Recordings MRCD79.

The ancient Chinese perceived a correlation of sound with flavor, color and atmosphere. Diviners attached to military commanders reputedly could tell the mood of the enemy by listening to the sound of pipes on the battlefield. Foretelling the course of battle – victory or defeat. (Needham 1997: 135f)

Sound has a significance in human affairs beyond the instinctive or the reactive. Let us consider what Thomas Mann intuited with his return to "a howl across several pitches".

Third nature

Music improvised, and especially the forms eschewing formal harmonic and musical conventions, is seen as naive or primitive. Thomas Mann's "howl" elicits a return to more fundamental responses than are nurtured in formal Western European music. The historical status of a musical shaman has been contained by civilization. A strong naturalistic medium between human beings and their environment is not fostered in Western culture. This has been rejected in favor of "the composer" as our designated musical explorer.[4] Our educational, market and habitual responses confine the arena for this cultural form of discovery. Improvisation is considered as the domain of eccentrics. The idea of newly (and constantly) exploring the world is essentially denied to most people. It is done for us by proxy. We are suffered to be consumers of music rather than participants in its making and appreciation.

"Everywhere, the orthodox systems of our times anticipate the careful and clear presentation of ready-worked-out on-tap outcomes, throughout our lives. Said systems seldom afford focused vantage on the vagaries, protean problems, the awkward wealth, of investigation itself. Generally, the on-goings of development are hidden, edited or simply unseen; what has been developed over time is rendered public, honed for appreciation after the fact, variously knowable, reproducible and endorsable qua final product or record."[5]

Thomas Mann mourns humankind's denaturing. Humanity's loss in *second nature's* technological progress. Seymour Wright's intervention moves towards an explanation of Mann's plea and offers possible solutions. Most know what

4 | Open form scores appear to offer musicians compositional collaboration. Most usually in graphic or prose form. These require the musician to elaborate upon a suggested schema to invent musical material. These structures (in my experience) distract musicians from the sonic material and the personal engagement with other musicians. I have come to consider these open form compositions as negatively enclosing improvisations.

5 | Wright, Seymour (2011): CD notes, in: Allum, Jennifer; Prévost, Eddie: Penumbrae, Matchless Recordings MRCD79.

„Ambige Interpretationen musikalischer Zeichen sind vielleicht die wirksamsten Quellen musikalischer Innovation und musikalischen Wandels: Das heißt, wenn einen die sozialen Umstände dazu ermuntern, Musik auf eine eigenwillige statt einer kulturell akzeptierten Weise zu hören, ist die Wahrscheinlichkeit höher, dass man Musik komponiert, die in eine neue Richtung ausholt." (Blacking 1995: 229)

Die *zweite Natur* ist die kulturelle Evolution des Homo sapiens.[6] Sie bewegt uns vom Instinktiven zur Teilhabe an einer kollektiven Form von Bewusstsein. Musik wird zu einem Reservoir sozialer Ausdrucksweisen. Mehr noch: Sie wird zu einem Fortsatz unseres kollektiven Gefühls von Menschlichkeit – dabei härtet sie sich zuweilen zur Chiffre –, anstatt Vehikel für die Ausbildung eines Seinsgefühls zu bleiben.

Wie erlangen und erhalten wir uns eine aufgeschlossene Reaktionsfähigkeit in Bezug auf unsere Umwelt und die daraus resultierende Kultur? Gibt es in uns einen Ort, wo wir uns Alternativen zu dem Konsens ausmalen können, auf den man sich konservativ geeinigt hat? Materielle und ökonomische Bedingungen lenken Entwicklung. Wenn sie günstig sind, kann sich das menschliche Bewusstsein (kollektiv und individuell) mit Wahlmöglichkeiten befassen. Musik ist einer dieser Bereiche, in denen gewählt werden kann. Doch, wie Seymour Wright bemerkt, »ist ein großer Teil des Treibens der Entwicklungen versteckt, aufbereitet oder unsichtbar.«[7]

Ich bin sicher, dass Musiktheorie und Musikethnologie sich rasch vorwärts bewegen werden und sich ihrer selbst bewusster werden. Das hoffe ich. Bisher fehlt es noch an jeglicher tiefgehenden, strukturellen Analyse. Und die Verbindung mit wichtigen menschlichen Werten ist verloren gegangen. Der Schwerpunkt, so scheint mir, wurde auf Konstruktion und Komparation gelegt. Die Untersuchung hat sich in einigen Fällen als potentiell destruktiv erwiesen.

»Die Rolle von Sammlern – mit deren Technologien und Prestige – ist an zahlreichen Stellen enorm; wir haben von asiatischen und afrikanischen Performern gehört, die nicht in Abwesenheit »ihrer« Ethnomusikologen auftreten wollen.« (Nettl 1983/2005: 170)

Worin auch immer die Motivation der Musiker, auf die sich Nettl in dem Zitat bezieht, besteht, ihre musikalische Priorität hat sich von ihrer ursprünglichen kulturellen Basis entfernt. Sie haben sich von der Gemeinschaft, die sie geboren und aufgezogen hat, abgelöst. Der Zusammenschluss dieser Musiker und »ihrer« Ethnomusikologen stellt eine selbstbezogene Symbiose zur Schau. Es

6 | Es gibt einen zum Nachdenken anregenden Bericht von der »Gen-Kultur-Koevolution«, zu finden in: Lumsden, Charles; Wilson, Edward Osborne (1981).

7 | Wright, Seymour (2011): CD-Notes, in: Allum, Jennifer; Prévost, Eddie: Penumbrae, Matchless Recordings MRCD79.

sounds are intended as music. Listening. Tactility is also important. The most subtle of musicians develop the feel, the weight of material, and marvel at the miraculous way sounds emerge from stuff. The deceptive (and perhaps deleterious) mystery of second nature is that our consciousness hardens into formality. Creativity is elusive and at times illusory.

Conservatism in culture is restrictive. Whereas our social institutions are repositories of knowledge and technical information, they are less good at promoting innovation.

John Blacking remarked:

"Ambiguous interpretations of musical signs are probably the most potent sources of musical innovation and change: that is, when one's social circumstances encourages the development of an idiosyncratic, rather than culturally approved way of listening to music, one is more likely to compose music that strikes out in a new direction." (Blacking 1995: 229)

Second nature is the cultural evolution of *homo sapiens*.[6] It moves us from the instinctual to a share in a collective form of consciousness. Music becomes a reservoir of social expression. More: it becomes an appendage to our collective sense of humanity – hardening at times into a cypher – rather than remaining a vehicle for developing our sense of being.

How do we acquire and maintain an open response to the environment and our ensuing culture? Is there a point within ourselves where we can picture alternatives to the conservatively agreed consensus? Material and economic conditions direct development. When they are favorable, human consciousness (collective and individual) can address choice. Music is one such arena for selection. Yet, as Seymour Wright notes, so much of "[...] the on-goings of [musical] development are hidden, edited or simply unseen [...]."[7]

I am sure the theory of music and ethnomusicology is moving apace and becoming more self-aware. I hope so. Hitherto, there has been an absence of any deep structural analysis. And a loss of connection with important human values. Emphasis, it seems to me, has centered upon construction and comparison. Examination has, in some cases, been destructive.

"The role of collectors, with their technology and prestige, has in various places been enormous; we have heard of Asian and African performers who won't perform without the presence of 'their' ethnomusicologists." (Nettl 1983/2005: 170)

6 | There is a thought-provoking account of "gene-culture coevolution" to be found in Lumsden, Charles; Wilson, Edward Osborne (1981).

7 | Wright, Seymour (2011): CD notes, in: Allum, Jennifer; Prévost, Eddie: Penumbrae, Matchless Recordings MRCD79.

gibt keinen Hinweis auf ein daraus folgendes kulturelles und kreatives Moment.[8] Ein Großteil von Musik innerhalb der westlichen politischen Ökonomie wird durch Sitten des Marktes eingeschränkt. Welche wahrgenommenen kulturellen Werte auch immer im klassischen Repertoire verankert sind, es liegt am bequemsten innerhalb des Geldzusammenhangs – Kommissionen, Konzerte, Aufnahmen. Auch der Gebrauch von Musik als Ausdruck von Religion ist geschwunden. Neue Stimmen für den »Pop«-Markt müssen so klingen wie andere, »etablierte« Stimmen, um Verkäufe zu sichern. Darin besteht für die meisten die »konservative« musikalische Realität.

Vielleicht gibt es inzwischen kein anderes Spielfeld für musikalisches, künstlerisches Leben und kulturelle Zugehörigkeit. Das zeugt von einer sehr engen Auffassung von Zweck: ein ästhetischer Hohlraum und ein ethisches Vakuum. Die englische Philosophin Iris Murdoch empfahl, dass wir der Religion die Idee von Spiritualität entreißen. (Murdoch 1992: ohne Seitenangabe). Von wo aus kann dann ein erneuertes Gefühl von Staunen entstehen? Es gibt, natürlich, keine andere Quelle als unsere Beziehung mit der Materialität der Welt. Eine bewusste Symbiose. In Anbetracht unserer ko-evolutionären Prozesse hat die Menschheit durch Technologie natürlich andere Perspektiven entwickelt. Die aktuelle Phase von Computer-Entwicklung und elektronischen Klanghilfen ermöglicht uns neue Wege für Empirismus. Wir haben die faszinierende Aussicht auf einen Techno-Schamanismus.

Um einmal das Offensichtliche festzuhalten: Wir müssen zu unseren menschlichen Sensibilitäten zurückkehren. Zu lange Zeit haben wir einem angehäuften kulturellen Konsens das Diktat über unsere Handlungen und Reaktionen gestattet. Natürlich bewundern wir, geschichtlich betrachtet, Vorbilder. Viele dieser Vorbilder sind trotz ihrer technischen Errungenschaften im Hinblick auf ihre Kreativität unbeweglich geworden und in irrelevanten oder vielleicht überholten Konventionen festgefahren. Dieses Zeitalter verlangt jedoch nach einem neuen Gefühl von Sinnhaftigkeit. Die größtenteils unberücksichtigten äußerlichen Konsequenzen menschlicher Aktivität haben die Bio-Sphäre stark strapaziert.[9] Wann sollte sonst eine kulturelle Agenda angesprochen werden, um den Fortbestand des menschlichen Abenteuers zu ermöglichen? Die Art, wie wir uns auf die materielle Beschaffenheit unserer Welt beziehen (ihre spürbaren und materiellen Bestandteile) und wie wir mit unseren Mitmenschen arbeiten, könnte uns Bedenkzeit, Ziele und die fortwährende Existenz als Spezies stiften.

---

8 | Oder zynischer: »gegenseitiger Parasitismus« wäre eine angemessenere Metapher.

9 | In einer sozioökonomischen Rechnung werden den schädlichsten Auswirkungen der Industrialisierung beispielsweise nicht die wahren Kosten zugeschrieben. Luft, Wasser und Land stehen einfach zur Verfügung. Es existiert noch keine universelle Vorstellung von Bewirtschaftung.

Whatever the motivation of the musicians to which Nettl refers, their musical priority has shifted from its original cultural base. They have been detached from their birth or nurturing community. The association of these musicians, and "their" ethnomusicologists displays a selfish symbiosis. There is no evidence of any ensuing cultural creative moment.[8] Most music within the Western political economy is constrained by marketplace *mores*. Whatever perceived cultural values are embedded within the classical repertoire it sits most comfortably within the cash nexus – commissions, concerts, recordings. Even its use as an expression of religion has faded. New voices for the "pop" market are required to sound like other "established" voices to secure sales. This is the "conservative" musical reality for most.

Maybe musical, artistic life and cultural affiliations now have no other arena. This speaks of a very narrow sense of purpose: an aesthetic lacuna and an ethical vacuum. The English philosopher Iris Murdoch recommended we wrest the idea of spirituality away from religion (Murdoch 1992: no page reference). So, from where can a renewed sense of wonder arise? There is, of course, no other source but our relationship with the materiality of the world. A conscious symbiosis. Given our co-evolutionary processes, humanity has, of course, created other vistas through technology. The current phase of computer development and electronic aids to sound offer us new avenues for empiricism. We have the intriguing prospect of a techno-shamanism.

To state the obvious: we need to return to our human sensibilities. For too long, we have allowed an accreted cultural consensus to dictate our actions and responses. Of course, historically we admire exemplars. Many such models, despite their technical achievements, have become creatively immobile and cemented into irrelevant or perhaps outworn conventions. However, the age requires a new sense of purpose. The largely unconsidered external consequences of human activity have taken a huge toll on the bio-sphere.[9] When better to address a cultural agenda to allow the human adventure to continue? It is how we relate to the material fabric of our world (its sentient and material parts) and how we work with fellow human beings that may give us respite, purpose and continued existence as a species.

Tinkling with sounds is no better than playing the fiddle while Rome burns. Meanwhile, the planet is heating and the weather often inclement and increasingly capricious. How can art help solve human-induced problems? Philip Guston's retreat from abstraction is perhaps a good first object lesson for us all.

---

8 | More cynically, "mutual parasitism" might be an apt metaphor.

9 | For example, in a social economic accounting no real cost is attributed to the most deleterious effects of industrialization upon our environment. The air, sea and land are simply there for the taking. A universal sense of husbandry does not yet exist.

Klänge zu klimpern ist nicht besser, als zu fiedeln, während Rom brennt. Währenddessen erwärmt sich der Planet, und das Wetter ist oft rau und zunehmend launenhaft. Wie kann Kunst helfen, solche von Menschen gemachten Probleme zu lösen? Philip Gustons Rückkehr aus der Abstraktion bietet vielleicht guten Anschauungsunterricht für uns alle.

»Als die 1960er daherkamen, fühlte ich mich gespalten, schizophren. Der Krieg, was mit Amerika vor sich ging, die Brutalität der Welt. Was für eine Art Mann bin ich, dass ich zu Hause sitze, Zeitschriften lese und mich in frustrierter Rage über alles verrenne – und dann gehe ich in mein Studio, um ein Rot zu einem Blau zu korrigieren. Ich dachte, es müsste eine Möglichkeit geben, etwas dagegen zu tun. Ich wusste, dass vor mir ein Weg lag. Ein sehr roher und undefinierter Weg. Ich wollte mich wieder vollständig fühlen, wie damals als Kind [...]. Ich wollte Einheit zwischen dem, was ich dachte und was ich fühlte.« (Philip Guston quoted by Robert Storr 1986: 53)

Der erste Schritt besteht sicherlich darin, nichts schlimmer zu machen. Als nächstes sollten wir unsere menschliche Verfassung überprüfen. Nicht in flüchtigen Launen von Abstraktion, in denen sich der menschliche Verstand mit seinem Können brüstet. Wir sollten die Praxis des Erkundens zu einer Kunstform oder einer alternativen (oder parallelen) Route in Richtung menschlichen Verständnisses werden lassen. Erkunden als Leitfaden für das Leben. Erinnern wir uns, der Großteil von Musik – selbst einige informell konstruierte (das heißt improvisierte) Formen – ist in erster Linie eine »[...] Präsentation von verfügbaren Fertigprodukten«.[10] Des Weiteren unterliegen Musiker (selbst improvisierende) viel stärker einer »Ästhetik der Imitation« als den meisten bewusst ist. Und unsere Nachahmung anderer Musiker ist mit dem Maß vergleichbar, in dem Messiaen auf seine fedrigen Freunde angewiesen war. Außerdem ergehen wir uns mit großer Wahrscheinlichkeit in Selbstplagiaten.[11] Nichts davon ist zwingend schlecht. Durch Imitation lernen wir so viel. Aber sie ist nicht an sich kreativ. Es ist unwahrscheinlich, dass aus ihr etwas Neues entsteht. So dient zum Beispiel eine Improvisation, die ihre Klangwelt Anton Webern verdankt, in erster Linie dessen Anerkennung, und sie zelebriert vielleicht seinen konkreten Beitrag. Um davon zu lernen, etwas daraus zu entwickeln, muss ein signifikanter Bestandteil hinzugefügt werden. Welchem Zweck dient man, indem man die informelle Nachbildung eines formalen Musikstücks erzeugt?

Dennoch gibt es Möglichkeiten, kreative Beziehungen zu pflegen, indem wir zu unseren biologischen Imperativen zurückkehren und diese weiterent-

10 | Wright, Seymour (2011): CD-Notes, in: Allum, Jennifer; Prévost, Eddie: Penumbrae, Matchless Recordings MRCD79.

11 | Dieses Thema wird, neben anderen, dazugehörigen Diskussionsfeldern, ausführlicher behandelt in: Prévost (2011)

"So when the 1960s came along I was feeling split, schizophrenic. The war, what was happening to America, the brutality of the world. What kind of man am I, sitting at home, reading magazines, going into a frustrated fury about everything – and then going into my studio to adjust a red to a blue. I thought there must be some way I could do something about it. I knew ahead of me a road was laying. A very crude, inchoate road. I wanted to be complete again, as I was when I was a kid [...]. Wanted to be whole between what I thought and what I felt." (Philip Guston quoted in Storr 1986: 53)

The first step, surely, is not to make things worse. Thereafter, let us review our human condition. Not in flighty fancies of abstraction in which the human mind preens its prowess. Let us make the practice of enquiry into an art form and an alternative (or a parallel) route to human understanding. Investigation as a guide to life. Remember, most music – even some informally constructed (in other words: improvised) forms – are mostly a "[...] presentation of ready-worked-out on-tap outcomes [...]".[10] Further, musicians (even improvisers) are more subject to an "aesthetic of imitation" than most realize. And, we emulate other musicians just as much as Messiaen relied on his feathered-friends. We are also likely to indulge in self-plagiarism.[11] None of this is necessarily bad. Imitation is how we learn so much. But it is not in itself creative. It is unlikely that anything new will emerge. An improvisation, for example, which owes its sound world to Anton Webern serves only to acknowledge and maybe celebrate his particular contribution. To learn from it, to develop from it, something significant must be added. What purpose is served by making an informal analogue of a formal piece of music?

However, there are ways we can pursue creative relationships by returning to, and developing from, our biological imperatives. *Homo sapiens* is contrasted with fellow hominids by the creative confluence of our technical and social intelligence centers. Steven Mithen – a leading figure in the emergence of "cognitive archaeology" – calls this process *cognitive fluidity*.[12] Let us withdraw (stand back, if only temporarily) from our understanding of music as an autonomous artistic phenomenon and focus upon three features of primary significance for us as human beings.

1. *Technical intelligence* A strong feature of this capacity is curiosity. Why are things how they are? What can they do?

10 | Wright, Seymour (2011): CD notes, in: Allum, Jennifer; Prévost, Eddie: Penumbrae, Matchless Recordings MRCD79.

11 | This issue is visited, along other attendant areas of discussion, more fully in: Prévost (2011).

12 | Mithen, Steven (1996): The intermittent quality of *cognitive fluidity* suggests it is an active evolutionary process.

wickeln. Der *Homo sapiens* hebt sich von anderen Hominiden dadurch ab, dass es einen kreativen Zusammenfluss seiner/unserer technischen und sozial intelligenten Zentren gibt. Steven Mithen – eine führende Persönlichkeit in der Entstehung »kognitiver Archäologie« – nennt diesen Prozess *kognitive Fluidität* (*cognitive fluidity*).[12] Nehmen wir einmal Abstand (gehen wir, wenn auch nur vorübergehend, einen Schritt zurück) von unserem Verständnis von Musik als autonomes, künstlerisches Phänomen und konzentrieren uns auf drei Merkmale, die für uns als Menschen von vordergründiger Bedeutung sind:

1. *Technische Intelligenz.* Ein starkes Merkmal dieser Fähigkeit ist Neugierde. Warum sind die Dinge, wie sie sind? Was vermögen sie?
2. *Soziale Intelligenz.* Theory of Mind. Was denken andere Menschen? Wie können sie mir helfen? Einfühlungsvermögen.[13]
3. *Selbstbewusstsein* (als Individuum, als Teil einer Familie, anderer sozialen Gruppierungen oder einer Spezies).

Für Musiker ist es wichtige und erste Priorität, die Welt um uns zu betrachten und ihre akustischen Eigenschaften zu bemerken. Schließlich ist dies initialisierender Bestandteil unserer Menschlichkeit – unserer *ersten Natur.* Nach akustischen Eigenschaften Ausschau halten. An die Körnung, die Textur und das Gefühl der Klänge gelangen. Deren Einfluss auf und Macht über uns als fragende und empathische Wesen spüren, das führt zur *zweiten Natur.* Dies ist der kulturschaffende Prozess, der ständige Aufsicht fordert – Optionen neben den historisch bestimmten bemerken oder finden. Wir benötigen eine kreative und empathische Rückkehr zu einem Moment, bevor kulturelle Formationen begannen, einen vertrauten und danach formellen (»normalen«) Charakter zu haben. Diese Fähigkeit, die *zweite Natur* zu reflektieren, ist möglicherweise unsere *dritte Natur.* Sie führt uns vielleicht zu Tätigkeiten, die über die »[...] Präsentation von verfügbaren Fertigprodukten hinausgehen«. Wir können uns in eine aktive, künstlerische Position bewegen. In Richtung *Exploratoria.*

Die Idee von einer Kunst des Erkundens und der Kooperation geht gegen den Strom und stellt den Invidiualismus in Frage, der von unserer gegenwärtigen kulturellen Hegemonie so gerühmt wird: Der Künstler als einsamer Held.[14] Dieses Bild ist viel mehr als nur eine Metapher für eine bewusste Reaktion auf

12 | Mithen, Steven (1996): Der periodische Charakter der kognitiven Fluidität legt nahe, dass es sich dabei um einen evolutionären Prozess handelt.

13 | Wir sollten nicht davon ausgehen, dass Einfühlungsvermögen automatisch zu Altruismus führt. Zu wissen, wie andere Menschen denken, ist ein starkes Werkzeug, um deren Handlungen zu beeinflussen oder zu kontrollieren – zum Guten oder Bösen.

14 | Oder auch der Künstler als modellhafter Entrepreneur. Diese Art des Individualismus trägt auch dazu bei, dass wir atomisiert werden; dazu, Unterschiede auszubeuten

2. *Social intelligence* Theory of mind. What are other people thinking? How can they help me? Empathy.[13]
3. *Self-awareness* (as an individual, as part of a family, of other social groupings and as a species).

As musicians, examining the world around us and noting its sonic properties is an essential first priority. This, after all, is an initializing part of our humanity – *first nature.* Looking for sonic properties. Getting to the grain, texture and feel of sounds. Sensing their effects and power upon us, as enquiring and empathic beings, leads to *second nature.* This is the enculturing process which requires constant monitoring – to note or find options other than the historically determined. We need a creative and empathic return to a moment before cultural formations began to have a familiar and thereafter a formal ("normal") character. This ability to reflect upon *second nature* is, possibly, our *third nature.* Potentially, it moves us into an activity beyond the "presentation of ready-worked-out on-tap outcomes" (Seymour 2011). We can move into an active artistic situation. Towards *Exploratoria.*

The idea of making an art of investigation and cooperation goes against the grain and counters the individualism so vaunted by our present cultural hegemony: artist as a lonely hero.[14] It is, also, far more than a metaphor for a conscious response to our total environment. It is not simply an analogue to green principles (although it might help to develop such a philosophy). There is a more fundamental and personal reason for developing skills of dialog and heurism. It is a playful construct from where the improviser, the informal musician, can locate an infinite source of new material. It is an idea of how we can take ourselves beyond the confines, the dictates, the numbing paralysis of conservatism – towards new vistas and soundscapes. This is *cognitive fluidity* – the seat of creativity? – an albeit intermittent characteristic we have inherited from the struggles of our prehistoric ancestors.

There is curious reluctance within our culture to attribute creativity to any particular human characteristic. The serendipitous is treated as mysterious and shrouded in a sacred silence. It is as if talking about it scares creativity away: speaking about it rationally prevents its occurrence. Yet few now would accept inspiration as something visited upon us by the divine (sacred breath). Where do new ideas come from? I tend to think the more we search the more likely it is we will find. The nature of the research and our relation-

13 | We should not assume that empathy necessarily leads to altruism. Knowing how other people think is a strong tool for influencing or controlling their actions, for good or ill.

14 | Or, artist as some kind of model entrepreneur. This kind of individualism also acts to atomize us. To exploit differences and nurture short-term advantages for those with the guile and (in my opinion) warped empathy.

unser gesamtes Umfeld. Es ist nicht einfach eine Analogie zu grünen Prinzipien (obwohl es dazu beitragen könnte, solch eine Philosophie auszubilden). Es gibt einen grundlegenderen und persönlichen Grund für die Ausbildung von Fähigkeiten des Dialogs und der Heuristik. Es ist ein spielerisches Konstrukt, von dem ausgehend der Improvisierende, der informelle Musiker, eine unendliche Quelle neuen Materials finden kann. Es ist eine Idee davon, wie wir uns selbst über die Grenzen hinwegsetzen, über das Diktat, die betäubende Lähmung durch den Konservatismus – in Richtung neuer Perspektiven und Klanglandschaften. Das ist *kognitive Fluidität* – der Sitz der Kreativität? –, ein, wenn auch periodisches, Charakteristikum, das wir durch die Anstrengungen unserer prähistorischen Vorfahren geerbt haben.

Es gibt ein seltsames Widerstreben in unserer Kultur, Kreativität auf irgendeine bestimmte menschliche Charakteristik zurückzuführen. Die Glückliche wird als mysteriös angesehen und in sakrales Schweigen gehüllt. Es ist, als ob das Sprechen über die Kreativität sie verscheuchen würde: Das vernünftige Sprechen darüber verhindert ihr Auftreten. Dennoch würden heutzutage nur wenige die Vorstellung akzeptieren, dass Inspiration uns durch das Göttliche (Hauch Gottes) übertragen wird. Woher kommen neue Ideen? Ich denke, dass die Wahrscheinlichkeit dafür, etwas zu finden, davon abhängt, wie viel wir suchen. Vielleicht steckt die Lösung im Wesen der Forschung selbst und in unserer Beziehung zu den Materialien, die wir betrachten; obwohl nichts sicher ist.[15]

Künstlerische Modelle, Imitation und eine sorgfältige Fähigkeit, Ideen und Strukturen zu entwickeln, sind nützliche Werkzeuge in der menschlichen Gemeinschaft. Wir ignorieren sie zu unserem Nachteil. Die gedankenlos Hinnahme dieser Eigenschaften zeugt vom Verfall kultureller Partizipation. Unser erster biologischer Imperativ besteht darin, dass wir uns, jeder für sich selbst, einen Platz in dieser Welt einrichten. Unsere kulturellen (und daher kollektiven) Reaktionen tragen hoffentlich zur Bahnung zukünftiger menschlicher Entwicklung bei – wie klein dieser Beitrag auch sein mag. Wir alle profitieren stark von der Arbeit und dem Einfallsreichtum anderer. Wir stehen immens nd unermesslich in der Schuld unserer künstlerischen, intellektuellen und physischen Vorfahren. Aber jeder Mensch (durch eine wundersame Laune unserer komplexen, genetischen Veranlagung) sieht die Welt ein wenig anders. Jede unserer Geschichten trägt zu einem größeren Narrativ bei.

und kurzzeitige Vorteile für diejenigen zu fördern, die die Arglist dafür haben und (meiner Meinung nach) ein verzerrtes Einfühlungsvermögen.

15 | Ich muss an die Geschichte der amerikanischen Golfer-Legende Ben Hogan denken. Er wurde beschuldigt, ein Spieler zu sein, der Glück hat. Er reagierte darauf, indem er sagte, je mehr er trainierte, desto mehr Glück hätte er.

ship to the materials looked into perhaps holds the key; although nothing is certain.[15]

Artistic models, imitation and a careful ability to develop ideas and structures are all useful tools in human society. We ignore them to our disadvantage. However, to accept them without thought is a dereliction of cultural participation. Our initial biological imperative is for each to make a place for ourselves in this world. Our cultural (and therefore collective) responses will hopefully contribute to the trajectory of future human development – no matter how small each contribution may be. We all benefit hugely from the work and the imagination of others. Our debt to our artistic, intellectual and physical forebears is immense and immeasurable. But each human being (by the miraculous quirk of our complex genetic make-up) sees the world slightly differently. Each of our stories adds to the greater narrative.

In 1967 composer turned improviser Cornelius Cardew, concerned with the nature of the collective musical initiative that was (and still is) *AMM*, wrote: "We [*AMM*] are *searching* for sounds and for the responses that attach to them, rather than thinking them up, preparing them and producing them."[16]

Within this deceptively simple sentence, Cardew articulated the essential features of a unified practice of collective enquiry. I have spent most of my musical life doing this, trying to understand its implications and bring the idea – and its practical and philosophical considerations – to the notice of whoever will listen. Two words govern the axiom. "We" is the socializing denominator and "searching" describes the proactivity. There can be no more fundamental description of what makes human culture. Contrast this proposition with what is generally on offer in current Western cultural life. The socializing "we" is subverted by authority. "We" are generally commanded, educated or manipulated into accepting particular social norms. There is always pressure to conform rather than seek potential. Likewise, "searching" is placed in the hands of experts. In music, the composer is the approved innovator and a market ethos generally confirms and supports both intellectual property rights and ideological precedence.

In a strange way, I see the collective "searching for sounds and the responses that attach to them" as a way of practicing to be a human being. It is not guaranteed to solve problems or create lasting or great art (Prévost 2006). However, if only as an antidote to the excesses of our present cultural industry with its buried (and often toxic) imperatives, I commend it to you all.

15 | I am reminded of American golfing legend Ben Hogan. He was accused of being a "lucky" player. He acknowledged this, remarking the more he practiced he luckier he became.

16 | „Towards an Ethic of Improvisation" (1967), in: Prévost (2006).

1967 schrieb Cornelius Cardew, einst Komponist, dann Improvisator, in Beschäftigung mit dem Wesen der kollektiven musikalischen Initiative, die – damals wie heute – AMM ist: »Wir [AAM] *suchen* nach Klängen und den Reaktionen, die sich daran knüpfen, anstatt sie uns auszudenken, vorzubereiten und zu erzeugen.«[16]

Innerhalb dieses täuschend simplen Satzes formuliert Cardew die wesentlichen Merkmale einer vereinheitlichten Praxis kollektiver Forschung. Ich habe den größten Teil meines musikalischen Lebens damit verbracht, eben das zu tun, die Implikationen dessen zu verstehen und die Idee – und ihre praktischen und philosophischen Betrachtungen – all jenen nahezubringen, die dafür ein offenes Ohr haben. Zwei Wörter leiten das Axiom. »Wir« ist der sozialisierende Nennwert und »suchen« beschreibt die Proaktivität. Es kann keine grundlegendere Beschreibung davon geben, was menschliche Kultur ausmacht. Wird dieser Vorschlag dem gegenübergestellt, was das aktuelle, westliche kulturelle Leben zu bieten hat, dann wird das sozialisierende »Wir« von Autorität untergraben. »Wir« werden für gewöhnlich dazu aufgefordert oder manipuliert, uns wird gelehrt, dass wir bestimmte soziale Grundsätze akzeptieren. Es wird immer eher Druck ausgeübt, um konform zu gehen, anstatt um nach Potential zu suchen. Außerdem wird das »Suchen« in die Hände einiger Experten gelegt. In der Musik ist der Komponist der anerkannte Innovator und ein Markt-Ethos bestätigt und unterstützt sowohl intellektuelle Besitzrechte als auch ideologische Vorläufer.

Auf eine merkwürdige Weise erscheint mir das kollektive »Suchen nach Klängen und den Reaktionen, die sich daran knüpfen« als ein mögliches Einüben von Menschsein. Es bietet nicht die Garantie, Probleme zu lösen oder überdauernde oder großartige Kunst zu schaffen. Dennoch, wenn auch nur als Gegenmittel gegen die Exzesse unserer gegenwärtigen kulturellen Industrie mit ihren verborgenen (und oft toxischen) Imperativen, empfehle ich es Ihnen und euch allen.

Übersetzung aus dem Englischen: Solveig Raschpichler, Berlin

16 | »Towards an Ethic of Improvisation« (1967), in: Prévost (2006).

Literatur/References

Blacking, John (1995): Music, Culture & Experience, selected papers, Chicago: University of Chicago Press.
Lumsden, Charles; Wilson, Edward Osborne (1981): Genes, Mind and Culture: The Coevolutionary Process, Harvard: Harvard University Press.
Mithen, Steven (1996): The Prehistory of the Mind: The Cognitive Origins of Art, Religion and Science, London: Thames and Hudson.
Murdoch, Iris (1992): Metaphysics as a Guide to Morals, London: Penguin Books.
Needham, Joseph (1997): "Sound Acoustics", in: Science & Civilisation in China, Volume IV: 1, Cambridge: Cambridge University Press.
Nettl, Bruno (1983/2005): The Study of Ethnomusicology, Illinois: University of Illinois Press, (new edition 2005).
Prévost, Edwin (Hrsg./Ed.) (2006): Cornelius Cardew: A Reader, Essex, UK: Copula.
Prévost, Edwin (2011): The First Concert – An Adaptive Appraisal of a Meta-Music, Essex, UK: Copula.
Storr, Robert (1986): Guston, New York: Abbevile Press.

Intermezzo 8

HBW: Es ist wichtig, nicht zu vergessen, dass wir eigentlich permanent die Rechnung ohne die Köche machen, wenn wir über andere urteilen, obwohl wir gar nicht wissen können, was sie tun. Wir können vermuten, was sie tun, wir können das klangliche Ergebnis beschreiben, das ist da. Aber wir wissen von keinem einzigen der Musikerinnen und Musiker, die gespielt haben, was sie wirklich gemacht haben. Das können wir nur erfahren, wenn die Forschung partizipativ auch mit denen arbeitet, die spielen, und nicht über sie. Sonst geraten wir in eine Distanz, die zwar manchmal gut zu sein scheint, aber ich glaube, dass die Beweglichkeit, innen drin zu sein in der Erzeugung der Klänge, wichtig ist und auch wieder ganz weit weg gehen zu können und die größtmögliche Distanz einnehmen zu können und die größtmögliche Intensität in Form von Empathie. Darin steckt der große Vorteil auch dieser Versammlung, dass wir sowohl über Improvisieren Denkende als auch Improvisierende sein können. Da mischt sich das idealer als in vielen anderen wissenschaftlichen Veranstaltungen.

WS: Mir kommt es schizophren vor, wenn wir versuchen, beides möglichst weit voneinander getrennt perspektivisch aufeinander gerichtet in einer Person zu sein. Deswegen würde ich sagen, ich betreibe Forschung wirklich als Researcher im Sinne eines, der darüber steht oder eine Abstraktion bedient. Aber ich suche nicht, sondern ich finde, indem ich die Dinge zulasse, anstatt sie zu forcieren und dadurch zu verfälschten Ergebnissen komme, weil ich eigentlich immer aus einer Außenposition etwas von innen zu beschreiben versuche.

Intermezzo 8

HBW: It's important not to forget that, when judging someone, we permanently tend to leave them out of our consideration although we can't really know at all what they are doing. We can surmise what they are doing, we can describe the resulting sounds, that's there, but we don't know from any single musician, who was playing, what they were really doing. And we can only find that out if research is participatory and works with, rather than about those playing – otherwise we will generate too much distance; that might seem a good thing sometimes, but I believe that the flexibility of being right inside sound creation is just as important as also being able to get really far away from it; creating the biggest distance possible as well as the greatest intensity possible in the form of empathy. Therein lies the big advantage of this gathering of musicians, in my opinion, that we can be those who think about improvisation and also improvisers ourselves, it's a much better mix, I think, than at many other scientific events.

WS: It seems schizophrenic to me trying as one person to embody both perspectives which are as far away as they can possibly be. For this reason I would say I conduct research – as a real researcher, in the sense of being apart from the thing or by means of abstraction, but I don't search – instead I find – and I do this by allowing things to be, rather than forcing them and then coming to incorrect results because of always trying to describe something internally from an external position.

RC: Mit meinen Studenten mache ich es so, dass wir zunächst spielen und danach eine Diskussion haben, eine Konversation über Improvisation. Eine Menge an Themen entstehen aus der Debatte und diese werden dann zum Gegenstand systematischer Forschung. Ich denke also nicht, dass es ein Problem ist, innen drin zu sein. Eigentlich denke ich, dass es für den Forscher, der über Improvisation spricht, gerade gut ist, wenn er auch selbst Improvisator ist.

Diskussionsbeiträge von Helmut Bieler-Wendt (HBW), Wolfgang Schliemann (WS) und Rogério Costa (RC), Mai 2014

RC: With my students, we always play and after we've played we have a discussion, a conversation about improvisation. Lots of topics arise from the debate and discussion and become issues for systematic research. So I think there is no problem of being inside ... actually I think it's good for the researcher when he speaks about improvisation that he is also an improviser himself.

Helmut Bieler-Wendt (HBW), Wolfgang Schliemann (WS) and Rogério Costa (RC)
in a public discussion, May 2014

Translation into English: Louise & Phil Loxton, GB-Wales

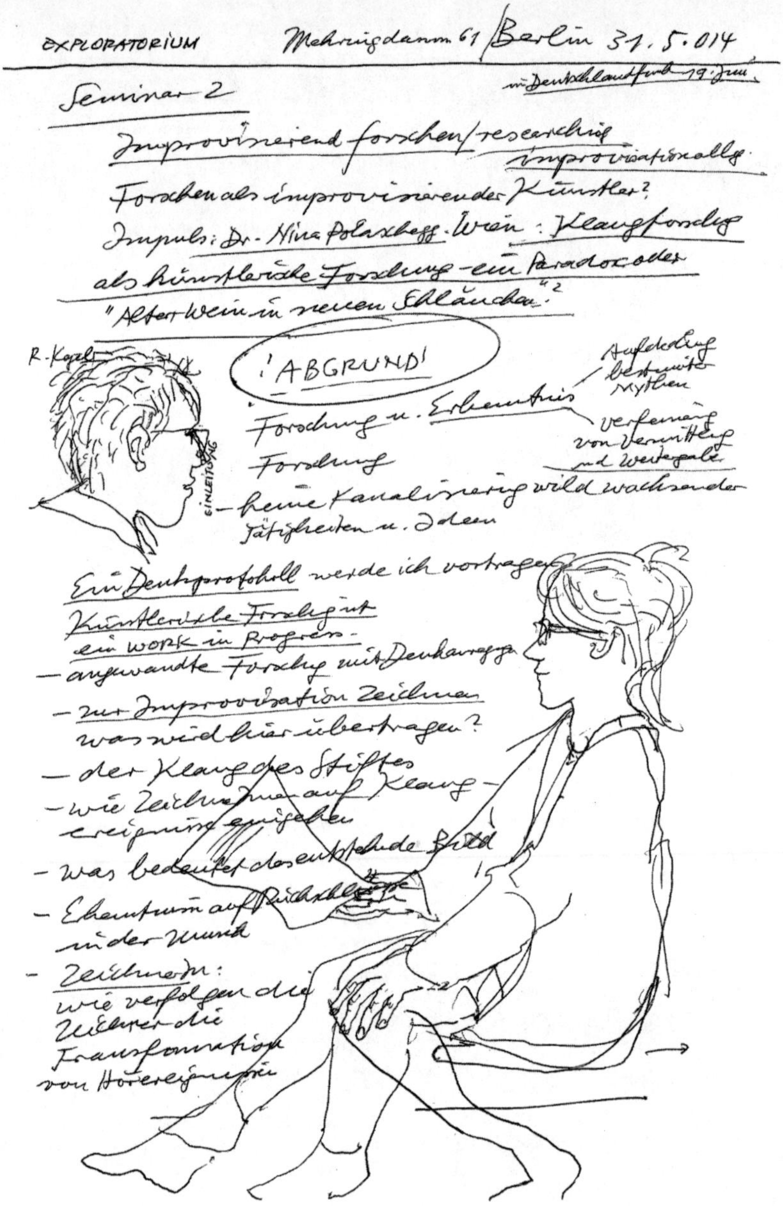
EXPLORATORIUM Mehringdamm 61 Berlin 31.5.014
in Deutschlandfunk 19. Juni
Seminar 2
Improvisierend forschen / researching improvisationally
Forschen als improvisierender Künstler?
Impuls: Dr. Nina Polaschegg, Wien: Klangforschung als künstlerische Forschung – ein Paradox oder „Alter Wein in neuen Schläuchen“?
R. Kapel
EINLEITUNG
ABGRUND
Forschung u. Erkenntnis
Forschung
Aufdeckung bestimmter Mythen
Verfeinerung von Vermittlung und Weitergabe
– keine Kanalisierung wild wachsender Tätigkeiten u. Ideen
Ein Denkprotokoll werde ich vortragen
Künstlerische Forschung ist ein WORK in Progress
– angewandte Forschung mit Denkanregungen
– zur Improvisation Zeichnen
was wird hier übertragen?
– der Klang des Stiftes
– wie Zeichnungen auf Klangereignisse eingehen
– was bedeutet das entstehende Bild
– Erkenntnis auf Rückschlüsse in der Kunst
– Zeichnerin:
wie verfolgen die Zeichner die Transformation von Hörereignissen

Klangforschung als künstlerische Forschung: ein Paradox oder »Alter Wein in neuen Schläuchen«? | Sound Studies as arts-based Research: A Paradox or "old wine in new bottles"?

Nina Polaschegg

Vorbemerkung

Der folgende Text ist als Impulsreferat entstanden, nicht als wissenschaftliche Abhandlung. Ziel war es, diverse Grundfragen, die beim Nachdenken über die an mich gerichteten Fragen auftraten, zu stellen, um eine anschließende Diskussion präziser führen zu können. Anstatt davon auszugehen, dass x oder y an sich schon künstlerische Forschung seien, fragte ich, ob dies überhaupt der Fall sei und wenn nicht, warum nicht. Die Adressaten und Teilnehmenden des Symposiums waren, bis auf weitere Referenten, keine Fachwissenschaftler. Entsprechend ging es nicht darum, herrschende Fachdiskurse zu referieren und zu diskutieren. Vielmehr war es mein Ziel, die Zuhörenden an einzelnen Gedankengängen teilhaben zu lassen, die gedanklichen Schritte hin zur Thesenbildung und zu vorläufigen Urteilen möglichst einfach nachvollziehbar zu machen. Die Funktion des Textes als Impuls zur anschließenden Debatte bringt zudem mit sich, dass einige Thesen dabei bewusst provokativ gestellt sind. Ziel war es ebenso, das Nachdenken über eine möglicherweise neue Disziplin – die künstlerische Forschung – zu präzisieren, nicht aber abschließende Antworten zu formulieren. Im Folgenden werde ich mich auf einige Fragen bzw. Thesen beziehen, die mir als Themen für mein Impulsreferat gestellt wurden.

Ausgangspunkt meiner Gedanken

In der Literatur verschiedener geisteswissenschaftlicher Disziplinen finden sich zum Teil vergleichbare, zum Teil divergierende Ansätze. Eine umfassende, präzise bzw. eindeutige Begriffsdefinition künstlerischer Forschung scheint zum momentanen Zeitpunkt noch nicht ausgearbeitet zu sein. Vielmehr präsentiert sich das Denken über »künstlerische Forschung« als ein Thinktank, ein Experimentieren mit neuen Begriffen und damit verbundenen Interpretationsmöglichkeiten künstlerischen Handelns und des Schreibens darüber. Künstlerische Forschung ist ein »work in progress«, eine Suche nach Erkenntnis anderer Ausprägung und Form, eventuell auch anderen Inhalts als diejenige traditioneller wissenschaftlicher Forschung. Als kleinsten gemeinsamen Nenner lässt sich künstlerische Forschung auch als einen dritten Weg der Erkenntnissuche neben reinem Kunstschaffen auf der einen Seite und wissenschaftlicher Forschung auf der anderen Seite beschreiben. Klare Forderungen, wie zum Beispiel der Anspruch auf eine intersubjektive Nachvollziehbarkeit und die Entwicklung neuer Methoden, neuer Epistemologien und neuer Forschungsansätze unter anderem mit ästhetischen Mitteln als explizites Ziel, werden beispielsweise vom FWF, dem Wissenschaftsfond Österreichs als klare Ziele von geförderten Projekten definiert. Doch solch klare und damit auch vergleichbare Konzepte scheinen (meines Wissens) nicht die gesamte Debatte zu prägen.

Author's note

The following text started life as a brief talk, not a scholarly essay. Its aim was to explore a range of basic issues that occurred to me when reflecting on questions I was asked so as to facilitate a productive ensuing discussion. Instead of assuming that x or y in themselves represent arts-based research, I asked whether this was the case at all and if not, why not. Apart from the other speakers, the audience at the conference were not specialists. It was therefore not an appropriate setting in which to give a lecture on current scholarly discourse, but rather it was an opportunity to share aspects of my thinking with the listeners and lay out the mental steps involved in the crystallization of a hypothesis and ad hoc judgments as transparently as possible. A further corollary of the text's function as a stimulus for the ensuing discussion is that a number of statements were formulated in a deliberately provocative way. The aim was to channel reflection on what is potentially a new discipline – arts-based research – yet not provide conclusive answers. In the following text I will refer to a number of issues and ideas that were given to me as topics for my talk.

Points of departure

The literature published in the many different humanities subjects sometimes adopts comparable approaches and sometimes divergent ones. An all-embracing, precise, and clear definition of arts-based research does not appear to have been fully elaborated at the present time. Instead, scholarly thought on the topic is a kind of think-tank, an experiment in new concepts and the associated interpretative possibilities of artistic production and the writing devoted to it. Arts-based research is a "work in progress", the pursuit of knowledge of expression, form, and potentially content, which is different to that in traditional scholarship. Reduced to its lowest common denominator, arts-based research may also be described as a third way situated between artistic works on the one side and scholarly research on the other. A clear agenda, for example the need for intersubjective understanding and the development of new methods, new epistemologies, and new approaches to research, for example using aesthetic resources, as the explicit objective, has been defined by institutions such as the Austrian Science Fund (FWF) as central to projects that it sponsors. But these clear, and thus also comparable, concepts do not (in my opinion) appear to characterize the entire discussion.

Following on from the Berlin conference, the question arises of whether aspects of the discussion do indeed productively link the concept of "arts-based research" to a new research approach, or whether it is simply a new term that is being used – which could be discussed as justified for various reasons, for example its general recognition in the scholastic community of the 21st century.

Gerade im Anschluss an das Berliner Symposium stellt sich die Frage, ob Teile der Diskussion tatsächlich zielführend den Begriff der »künstlerischen Forschung« mit einem neuen Forschungsansatz verbinden oder ob hier zum Teil nicht vor allem ein neuer Begriff verwendet wird – was aus diversen Gründen, etwa der gesellschaftlichen Akzeptanz in der Wissenschaftsgesellschaft des 21. Jahrhunderts, zu diskutieren wäre. Oder auch, um einzelne Schritte im Kunstschaffen bewusster zu reflektieren oder ins öffentliche Bewusstsein zu bringen. Provokant gefragt: Verbirgt sich hinter dem Begriff (oder hinter mancher Anwendung des Begriffs) »künstlerische Forschung« doch »Alter Wein in neuen Schläuchen«?

Mir wurde vorgeschlagen, als Ausgangspunkt für meinen Impulsvortrag unter dem Stichwort »klangforschende Improvisationsmusiker« improvisierende Musiker vorzustellen, die ihre künstlerischen Forschungen – damit gemeint waren ihre Klangforschungen – in schriftlicher Form, das heißt in Textform festhalten. Als ein weiteres zu untersuchendes Beispiel für künstlerische Forschung und für improvisierendes Forschen könnte das improvisierende Zeichnen zu musikalischer (Live-)Improvisation herangezogen werden, so ein an mich herangetragener weiterer Vorschlag, den ich aufgegriffen habe. Die Annahme, diese beiden künstlerischen Prozesse als künstlerische Forschung zu bezeichnen, ist Ausgangspunkt meiner folgenden Erörterungen.

Warum findet sich zum Thema Klangforschung wesentlich mehr Literatur von Interpreten als von Improvisierenden? Was wäre daran künstlerische Forschung, wenn Improvisierende Texte verfassen, wie es auch Musikwissenschaftler tun? Handelt es sich bei künstlerischer Forschung von Improvisierenden nicht vielmehr um angewandte Forschung? Ist Zeichnen zu improvisierter Musik ein Beispiel für künstlerische Forschung? Zu diesen und weiteren Fragen soll mein Vortrag in gegebener Kürze Diskussions- und Denkanregungen geben.

1. Zeichnen zu improvisierter Musik: ein Beispiel für künstlerische Forschung – improvisierend forschen?

Ist es ein Beispiel für künstlerische Forschung, wenn zur (Live-)Improvisation gezeichnet und dies dann ausgewertet wird? Der erste Schritt scheint einfach und plausibel. Das Zeichnen zur Improvisation kann man als Übertragung einer Kunst in eine andere, von Klang in Bild beschreiben. Doch was bedeutet dies genau? Was wird hier wie übertragen? Ein Beispiel aus eigener Erfahrung: Es ist viele Jahre her, als ich an einem Workshop für Improvisation teilgenommen habe. Eine Mitmusikerin, eine Designstudentin, wollte damals genau diesen Versuch unternehmen, nämlich zu Improvisation zeichnen. Das sollte mit verbundenen Augen geschehen, um sich ganz auf die Musik konzentrieren zu

Or rather, to shore up knowledge of, or to raise public awareness of the steps involved in making art. Put bluntly: might the term “arts-based research” or its use not simply be “old wine in new bottles”?

As the point of departure for my talk on improvising musicians engaged in sound studies, it was suggested to me that I present examples of artists who codify their arts-based research – in other words, their sound studies – in textual form. As a further example of artistic and improvisational research to be examined, I drew on one other idea that was brought to my attention, that of improvisational drawing accompanying live musical improvisation. The hypothesis that both of these artistic processes might be designated arts-based research is the starting point for the discussion below.

Why is the literature on sound studies dominated by performers and not improvisers? What aspect of it would be arts-based research if improvisers were to write essays in the way that musicologists do? Is arts-based research conducted by improvisers in fact just applied research? Is drawing to improvised music an example of arts-based research? My essay will provide ideas for discussion and reflection on these and other questions.

1. Drawing to improvised music: an example of arts-based research – improvisational research?

Is drawing to (live) improvisation and its subsequent analysis an example of arts-based research? The first step appears simple and plausible enough; drawing to improvisation may be described as the rendering of one art form, the aural, in another, the visual. But what exactly does this mean? What is re-rendered, and how? To give a first-hand example, I took part in an improvisation workshop many years ago at which a fellow musician, a design student, wanted to do just this, in other words, draw to improvisation. It would be done blindfolded to allow us to focus fully on the music and not be influenced by what was taking shape on the paper. She had brought along drawing paper and charcoal pencils, and using these we started to experiment. With just one exception, the results were all surprisingly similar; most of the paper was filled with wild figures. Only one person had used relatively little space, a narrowly-defined ambit, and had evidently applied greater pressure or stronger colors at some points on the paper. I was this nonconformist. The different approaches taken were soon explained. While some had applied a “substantive and emotional interpretation of the music”, my drawing was guided purely by the sound of the pencil on the paper; I acted as a musician who had swapped her double bass for the diverse sounds and timbres of a charcoal pencil striking paper. The statement that drawing to improvised music involves the rendering of one art form in another is thus anything but unambiguous.

können und sich nicht von dem entstehenden Visuellen am Papier leiten zu lassen. Sie hatte Zeichenpapier und Kohlestifte mitgebracht und wir fingen an zu experimentieren. Die Ergebnisse fielen erstaunlich ähnlich aus – mit einer Ausnahme. Weitausschweifende, zeichnerische Gesten füllten die meisten Blätter. Nur eine Person hatte relativ wenig Platz benötigt, zeichnete kleinräumig, hatte an manchen Stellen offensichtlich mit höherem Druck oder stärkerem Farbauftrag gearbeitet. Der Sonderling war ich. Die unterschiedlichen Herangehensweisen waren bald geklärt. Während die anderen mehr oder weniger an einer »inhaltlichen-emotionalen Text-, sprich Musikausdeutung« gearbeitet hatten, zeichnete ich rein nach dem Klang des Stiftes am Papier, sprich, ich handelte als Musikerin, die ihren Kontrabass gegen die vielfältigen Geräuschmöglichkeiten und Klangfarben eines Kohlestiftes am Papier getauscht hatte. Die Aussage, beim Zeichnen nach improvisierter Musik werde von einer Kunst in die andere übertragen, ist also alles andere als eindeutig.

Der zweite Schritt nach dem Zeichnen wäre nun die Auswertung, also die Verbalisierung dessen, was in diesem Beispiel als künstlerische Forschung bezeichnet wird. Wie wir gesehen haben, muss dabei zunächst die Frage geklärt werden, aus welcher Perspektive Zeichner an die Übertragung von Klang in Zeichnung herangehen, aus der des Musikers oder der des Bildenden Künstlers. Doch wie werten wir das entstandene Bild aus? Welche Erkenntnisse können wir aus der Zeichnung ziehen, welche Rückschlüsse auf die Musik? Zur Erinnerung: Wenn wir unter »wir« die Außenstehenden, also die Beobachter von Musiker und Zeichner verstehen würden, dann befänden wir uns außerhalb der künstlerischen Forschung und bewegten uns im traditionellen Feld der Kunst-, beziehungsweise Musikwissenschaft. Das über improvisierte Musik forschende »wir« ist also die Zeichnende als Forschende.

Wie verfolgen also unsere beiden zeichnenden Forscher die Musik? Wie transformieren sie diese quasi »aufs Papier«? Geht es ihnen überhaupt um eine Übertragung – sei es auf formal-struktureller, (klang-)farblicher oder Texturen und Dichtegrade verfolgender Ebene oder aus der Perspektive gestaltpsychologischer Ansätze et cetera? All diese Fragen müssen nachvollziehbar beantwortet werden. Wenn sie sich gar dazu entschließen, wie auch immer geartete emotionale Elemente in der Musik zu übertragen, so sind diese noch schwieriger intersubjektivierbar, da es sich hier um einen sehr stark mit den Hörerfahrungen und dem Wissen um musikalische Tradition und Ausdeutung gekoppelten Aspekt handelt. Womit sich eine weitere Frage stellt, nämlich diejenige, wie viel implizites oder auch explizites Wissen um die jeweils andere Kunstform notwendig ist, um überhaupt mit gegenseitigem Respekt interdisziplinär im künstlerischen Raum agieren zu können – oder eben mithilfe der einen Kunstgattung eine andere erforschen zu können.

Was aber, wenn die Improvisation den beiden zeichnenden Künstlern lediglich als Sprungbrett dient, als loser oder subjektiver Inspirationsfaktor zu

After drawing comes the analysis, in other words, the verbalization of what in this example is termed arts-based research. As we saw, the first issue to be resolved is the role adopted by the person holding the pencil when rendering sound as drawing, that of the musician or that of the visual artist. But how can we analyze the resulting picture? What insights can we gain from the drawing and what does this allow us to say about the music? It is worth noting that if we were to understand the "us" as outside observers of musicians and visual artists, we would not be acting in the spirit of arts-based research, but rather in the traditional realm of fine art or musicology. "We" who conduct research into improvised music are thus the visual artists actively engaged in research.

How then, do our two illustrator researchers follow the music? How do they express it, as it were, "on paper"? Are they concerned with achieving a rendering – be it on the formal/structural, timbral, textural and density level or from the angle of Gestalt psychology? All these questions demand transparent answers. Any particular emotional elements found in the music that they decide to render are even less intersubjectifiable, due to their very strong associations with auditory experience and knowledge of the musical tradition and its interpretation. This raises a further question, namely the issue of how much implicit or even explicit knowledge of the "other" art form is necessary to ensure mutual respect on interdisciplinary activity in the artistic arena – or to be in a position to explore an art form using the means of a different genre.

What, though, if the paper-based improvisation performed by the two artists is merely a point of departure, a loose or subjective source of inspiration for their own art? What would be new about this approach that was previously known simply as "art"?

Up to this point, we have assumed that the drawings created in these sessions are works of art. But is arts-based research a matter of taking one work (musical improvisation in this case) to create another (a drawing)? According to the FWF, the creation of a further work of art is not a condition of arts-based research but does, however, represent a gain in knowledge, albeit one that is regarded as a "third way" between artistic and scholarly knowledge. In other words, neither the simple creation of art, nor pure scholarly research into art (for example the production of figurative graphic scores or sketches representing notation of improvised music), can be considered arts-based research. Conversely, acquiring insights has, in itself, always been the objective of art.

Initial conclusions:

- Arts-based research is a way of acquiring insights.
- Arts-based research must, however, go beyond the simple creation of art, but need not result in a new work of art.

ihrem eigenen Kunstwerk? Was wäre an einem solchen Vorgehen neu, nannte man so etwas bislang nicht schlicht »Kunstschaffen«?

Bislang wurde davon ausgegangen, dass die entstehenden Zeichnungen Kunstwerke sind. Doch geht es denn in künstlerischer Forschung darum, aus einem Kunstwerk (hier der musikalischen Improvisation) ein weiteres Kunstwerk (hier eine Zeichnung) zu schaffen? Laut FWF wäre die Entstehung eines weiteren Kunstwerkes keine Bedingung für künstlerische Forschung, wohl aber ein Erkenntnisgewinn, allerdings ein solcher, der als dritter Weg neben künstlerischer und wissenschaftlicher Erkenntnis gehandelt würde. Reines Kunstschaffen kann also genauso wenig künstlerische Forschung bedeuten wie reine wissenschaftliche Forschung über Kunst (wie zum Beispiel das Anfertigen von graphischen Verlaufspartituren oder graphischen Skizzen zur Notation improvisierter Musik). Umgekehrt ist ein Erkenntnisgewinn an sich allerdings seit jeher auch Ziel der Kunst.

Erste Schlussfolgerung:

- Künstlerische Forschung ist Erkenntnisgewinn.
- Künstlerische Forschung muss über reines Kunstschaffen hinausweisen, sie muss jedoch kein neues Kunstwerk schaffen.
- Künstlerische Forschung muss nachvollziehbar sein, sie muss Methoden, mithin eigene intersubjektiv nachvollziehbare Forschungskriterien entwickeln und offen legen.
- Künstlerische Forschung muss vergleichbar sein.[1]

2. »Klangforschung« als künstlerische Forschung?

Der Begriff der »Klangforschung« ist im 20. und 21. Jahrhundert eng gekoppelt an die Erforschung diverser Geräusche jenseits des traditionellen Instrumentalklangs. Klangforschung zu betreiben, das gehört unter Improvisierenden schon zum selbstverständlichen Handwerk. Es wird allerdings (immer noch) quasi als ein Gütesiegel gehandelt. Und zwar nicht nur für die improvisierte Musik der 1970er und 1980er Jahre oder der zweiten radikalen Phase der Klangforschung Ende der 1990er, Anfang der 2000er Jahre während des sogenannten Reduktionismus[2]. Und ungeachtet dessen, was sie heute noch

---

1 | Vgl. *URL: http://www.fwf.ac.at/fileadmin/files/Dokumente/FWF-Programme/PEEK/ar_PEEK_dokument.pdf*, abgerufen am 19.03.2015.

2 | Kennzeichen waren unter anderem eine minuziöse Feinarbeit in der Geräuschdifferenzierung – ein »unter dem Mikroskop Betrachten einzelner Geräusche oder Klangpartikel«, eine Fokussierung auf Nuancen und Details statt aufs große Ganze und auf hohe

- Arts-based research must be transparent; it must develop and demonstrate methods and consequently personal, intersubjective and verifiable research criteria.
- Arts-based research must be capable of comparison.[1]

2. "Sound studies" as arts-based research?

In the 20th and 21st centuries, the term "sound studies" has been, and still is, closely linked with research into noises beyond the scope of traditional instrumental sound. Sound studies may be part of the improvising musician's natural toolkit, but are (still), to a certain extent, treated as a seal of quality – not only the improvised music of the 1970s and 80s or the second radical "reductionist"[2] phase of sound studies at the end of the 1990s and early 2000s, irrespective of what the term may mean today. Can sound studies be seen as a quality criterion at all? In the search for "novelty" is what is often called sound studies today not rather a refinement of sensitivity to sound, which is characteristic of any good performers? Furthermore, is it not something that has already been practiced for centuries, and not just in instrument making?

But let us stay with the phenomenon of noise and sound studies that, especially in their early days during the radical emancipation of noise in the 20th century, revolutionized musical thinking – among both improvisers and composers (as well as in historically informed performance practice and thus interpretation). The search for and development of new, previously unknown material as the basis of musical composition, here, opened the door to innovative methods in many different areas of music-making (and consequently also in other performance practices, in rock, jazz, folk music, et cetera).

The sound studies process

Improvisers, performing musicians, and composers all conduct sound studies. Only in the rarest cases are sound studies carried out in improvisation; they usually involve direct experimentation, mostly at home in a quiet room while "practicing" or trying things out. However, as always, there are exceptions to this rule:

---

1 | See *URL: http://www.fwf.ac.at/fileadmin/files/Dokumente/FWF-ProgrammePEEK/ar_PEEK_dokument.pdf*, accessed on 19 March 2015.

2 | Characterized, for example, by minutely detailed differentiation of noises – an "analysis of individual noises or sound particles under the microscope", a focus on nuances and details instead of the whole, and on high levels of energy. The term "reduction" is a makeshift device, like "real-time music", and primarily refers to reduction in comparison to a formerly prevailing density.

bedeuten kann. Kann Klangforschung an sich heute überhaupt noch als Qualitätsmerkmal angesehen werden? Im Sinne der Suche nach »Neuheit«? Ist das, was so oft als Klangforschung betrieben wird, heute nicht eher eine Verfeinerung der Klangsensibilität wie sie auch guten Interpreten eigen ist? Und wie sie letztlich seit Jahrhunderten nicht nur im Instrumentenbau betrieben wird?

Doch bleiben wir beim Phänomen der Geräusch-Klangforschung, die gerade in ihren Anfangszeiten im Zuge der radikalen Geräuschemanzipation im 20. Jahrhundert das musikalische Denken revolutioniert hatte – und dies sowohl in Kreisen der Improvisation wie der Komposition (und im Übrigen auch in der historisch informierten Aufführungspraxis, mithin der Interpretation). Die Suche nach und Entwicklung von neuem, bislang unbekanntem Material als Grundlage zur musikalischen Gestaltung öffnete Tore zum Weiter- und Neudenken musikalischen Gestaltens in verschiedensten Formen des Musikmachens (und in Folge natürlich auch in weiteren Spielformen der Musik, im Rock, Jazz, der Folkmusic et cetera).

Zum Prozess der Klangforschung

Klangforschung betreiben sowohl Improvisierende als auch Interpretierende und Komponierende. Klangforschung geschieht im seltensten Falle improvisierend. Sondern meist gezielt experimentierend, meist zu Hause im stillen Kämmerlein beim Üben oder Ausprobieren. Ausnahmen bestätigen, wie immer, die Regel:

- Wenige Fälle des improvisierenden Klangforschens wären, wenn man beim Improvisieren einen Klang entdeckt oder zum Beispiel feststellt, dass man etwas anderes intendiert hatte, an dem Entdeckten aber nun weiter arbeiten wolle. Und das geschieht dann wiederum zu Hause. Der Ursprung war hier ein scheinbarer »Fehler«.
- Klangforschung über das Improvisieren selbst kann auch dann entstehen, wenn während der Improvisation ein rein an der Handlung ausgerichteter Verlauf verfolgt wird und dann scheinbar zufällig bislang unbekannte Klänge entstehen.[3]

Energie. Der Begriff »Reduktion« bleibt dabei ein Hilfsbegriff wie der der »Echtzeitmusik« und bezieht sich vor allem auf die Reduktion im Vergleich zur vorab herrschenden Dichte.

3 | Wie fein man das Raster »unbekannt« ausrichtet, wäre ebenso zu befragen wie die vehement vertretene These des Unvorhersehbaren in improvisierter Musik. Wie unvorhergesehen ist sie wirklich? Wie fein muss man zoomen, um das Unvorhersehbare im Detail zu finden? Oft genauso fein wie in der Interpretation, die ebenfalls Grade des Unvorhersehbaren in der Live-Aufführung bereithält. Oder aus Hörerperspektive beim erstmaligen Hören einer Komposition.

EXPLORATORIUM
Berlin 31.5.014
SOAP2
TEXT
Reinhard Gagel und Matthias Schwabe dirigierten die SOAP NR.2

Klangforschung kann also nicht per se gleichgesetzt werden mit improvisierender Forschung, wie auch immer man diese definieren mag.

Ist Klangforschung künstlerische Forschung?

Handelt es sich beim relativ neuen Begriff der künstlerischen Forschung doch nur um »Alten Wein in neuen Schläuchen«? Sei es, um das eigene Tun als Künstler in Zeiten gesellschaftlich-kulturellen Wandels auf eine höhere Ebene zu hieven, sei es, um das eigene Image im Vergleich zur traditionellen Wissenschaft zu heben, um für die Kunstproduktion neue Chancen der Förderung zu eruieren? Oder ist Klangforschung an sich schon künstlerische Forschung? Oder aber wird Klangforschung dann zur künstlerischen Forschung, wenn die Klangforschenden selbst die Ergebnisse ihrer Klangforschung dokumentieren, etwa die Klänge beschreiben oder deren Herstellung nachvollziehbar und reproduzierbar machen?

Wer schreibt über Klangforschung?

Überlegen wir, wer denn der vielen klangforschenden Improvisierenden tatsächlich auch verbalisiert, verschriftlicht. In summa sind es nicht viele, Eddie Prévost zum Beispiel oder aber der enge Zirkel der Echtzeitmusikszene um Burkhard Beins, Andrea Neumann und andere. Sind ihre Texte künstlerische Forschung? Oder künstlerischer Forschung entsprungen? Das würde ja unter Umständen bedeuten, dass traditionelle (Musik-)Wissenschaftler solche Texte niemals hätten verfassen können, da sie ja wissenschaftlich zu forschen gelernt haben. Worin sich Texte von Wissenschaftlern und Musikern unterscheiden, ließe sich diskutieren. Ob sich dabei aber tatsächlich zwei fundierte, jeweils nachvollziehbare Schreibkulturen, Argumentationslinien und Denkmethoden voneinander unterscheiden ließen, wäre zu prüfen.

Was wäre also das besonders Künstlerische an von Improvisierenden verfassten Texten? Was würde diese unterscheiden von Texten, die von Wissenschaftlern über die Klangforschungen improvisierender Musiker verfasst werden? Was wären intersubjektiv nachvollziehbare Merkmale dieser Texte, was Denk- und Forschungsmethoden, die sich gerade in den Texten selbst zeigen? Worin würden sich beispielsweise zwei Texte zum Thema »Improvisation üben – nach Klängen forschen« unterscheiden, der eine verfasst vom Improvisator selbst, der andere von einer Musikwissenschaftlerin, die den Musiker zuvor interviewt und beobachtet hat? Zur Erinnerung: Eine Methodik und eine intersubjektive Nachvollziehbarkeit, mithin auch Eindeutigkeit von Begriffen, müssten (laut FWF) auch den Texten der künstlerisch Forschenden eigen sein. Solche Methoden und Schreibweisen zu untersuchen und zu prüfen wäre not-

- Isolated cases of improvisational sound studies could involve situations in which a sound is discovered or noticed during improvisation that is different to that which was intended, but is used as a source of further inspiration. This takes place at home and arises from a putative "mistake".
- Sound studies in improvisation can also occur if, during improvisation, the player follows the course of the music that, apparently by chance, produces previously unheard sounds.[3]

Sound studies cannot therefore be equated with improvisational research *per se*, no matter how the latter is defined.

Are sound studies arts-based research?

Is the relatively new concept of arts-based research simply "Old wine in new bottles"? Is it an attempt to raise one's own work as an artist to a higher level in times of societal and cultural change, or to differentiate oneself from traditional scholarship and acquire new sources of funding for art? Or are sound studies in themselves already arts-based research? Put another way, do sound studies become arts-based research if we record their results, for example, by describing the sounds or showing how to reconstruct them?

Who writes on sound studies?

Let us consider which of the many improvisers engaged in sound studies actually verbalize or fix in writing, their findings. In the final analysis, there are only a few, for example, Eddie Prévost or those involved in the real-time music scene with Burkhard Beins, Andrea Neumann, and others. Do their texts represent or originate from arts-based research? This, however, might imply that traditional musicologists who learned to conduct research in scholarly terms could never have written such texts. The differences between texts written by scholars and musicians is an area ripe for discussion, but whether two separate, substantiated, transparent writing cultures, lines of reasoning, and analytical methods could be discerned would require detailed investigation.

What then would constitute the specifically artistic content in texts written by improvisers? What would differentiate them from texts on sound stu-

3 | How the term "unheard" is understood would be worthy of investigation, similar to the vehemently justified theory of the unpredictable in improvised music. How unpredictable is it in truth? How far must we zoom in to find the unpredictable? Frequently just as far as in interpretation, which also contains degrees of unpredictability in live performance. Or from the listener's point of view when hearing a composition for the first time.

wendig, um eine Annahme »ihr Tun verbalisierende Improvisierende sind künstlerisch Forschende« verifizieren zu können.

Über Klangforschung schreiben – welche Möglichkeiten gibt es überhaupt und sind es letztlich nicht öfter Interpreten, die dies tun?

Beispiel 1: Dokumentation von Spieltechniken und Sounds

Auffallend ist, dass sich vermutlich mehr Interpreten finden, die ihre Ergebnisse der Klangforschung verbalisieren beziehungsweise minuziös und ausführlich dokumentieren: Marcus Weiss untersuchte Saxophonklänge, Robin Hayward (aus der Perspektive des Improvisators und des Komponisten) Obertöne der Tuba. Irvine Arditti katalogisierte Spieltechniken der Violine, Bertram Turetzky kategorisierte und dokumentierte Spieltechniken und Klangfarben am Kontrabass, Peter Veale nahm selbige Mühen für die Oboe auf sich. Allen Arbeiten gemeinsam ist eine methodisch klare und intersubjektiv nachvollziehbare Dokumentation. Der Grund ist einfach erklärt, der Nutzen offensichtlich. Interpreten geben hier nicht nur ihre Erfahrungen an eine nächste Generation weiter, die sich weite Strecken der Klangforschung und Suche dann ersparen und die Zeit gleich in deren Umsetzung investieren kann. Des Weiteren bilden diese Konvolute bestes Rüstzeug und Hintergrundinformation für Komponierende. Solche Arbeiten sind sinnvoll, gerade weil hier mehrere Individuen an einem Werk arbeiten: Komponist und Interpret. Improvisierende arbeiten alleine an ihrem Klang, auch wenn alle möglichen Hilfsmittel genutzt werden, so scheint doch (immer noch) die eigene Suche, das Individualistische im Zentrum zu stehen. X oder y habe »eine ganz eigene Klangsprache entwickelt«, dieser Satz findet sich oft als Kommentar und damit verbunden als Qualitätsmerkmal. Wie ganz eigen diese Klangsprache heute noch sein kann, bleibe hier einmal unbeantwortet.

Beispiel 2: Improvisierende, die über ihre Arbeit und über improvisierte Musik allgemeiner reflektieren und diese Reflexionen zu Papier bringen

Worin unterscheiden sich solche Texte von denjenigen Gedanken, die Wissenschaftler verfassen? Um nachvollziehbare Methodik und Argumentationsstruktur versus »künstlerische Freiheit im Schreiben« kann es ja nicht gehen, vor allem wenn man an die Forderung des FWF denkt, dass auch künstlerische Forschung methodisch vorzugehen habe (auch wenn neue Methoden zu entwickeln wären) und vergleichbar sein solle.

Reicht allein die Perspektive aus, aus der heraus die Forschung betrieben wird? Also eine Innenperspektive der Improvisierenden im Gegensatz zur Außen- mithin Beobachterperspektive, die Wissenschaftler einnehmen? Aber ist denn die Improvisierendenperspektive ausschließlich eine Innensicht oder wechseln die Künstler beim Schreiben nicht vielmehr die Seite, indem sie zu Beobachtern werden, wenn auch zu Beobachtern ihrer selbst? Was wäre mit

dies carried out by improvisers composed by scholars? What would be the intersubjectively transparent qualities of these texts, or the analytical and research methods evident from the words themselves? What would be the difference between two texts on the topic of "practicing improvisation – studying sounds", one written by the improviser themselves, the other by a musicologist who had interviewed and observed the musician? It is worth remembering that methodology and intersubjective understanding, including the unambiguity of terminology, should also be inherent in arts-based research texts (according to the FWF). It would be necessary to investigate and review such methods and styles in order to verify the assumption that "improvisers who verbalize their activities are arts-based researchers".

Writing on sound studies – what are the options, and is it not usually the domain of performers?

Example 1: Records of performance techniques and sounds

It is striking that there appear to be more performers who verbalize or record the results of their sound studies in minute detail: Marcus Weiss explored saxophone sounds, Robin Hayward (from the perspective of improviser and composer) looked at tuba overtones. Irvine Arditti cataloged violin performance techniques, Bertram Turetzky categorized and documented performance techniques and timbre on the double bass, Peter Veale did the same on the oboe. Common to all these efforts is a methodically distinct and intersubjectively transparent documentation. The reasoning is clear, the benefits obvious. Performers are not only passing on their experience to future generations, who are thus saved the effort of repeating these sound studies and can instead invest their time in reproducing them. These documents also represent ideal tools and background information for composers. This work is meaningful and important because results are obtained from the interplay of several individuals: the composer and the performer. Improvisers work on their sound alone, and even when all potential resources have been exploited, it is the personal discovery, the individualistic that (still) appears to take center stage. A sentence such as "x or y has developed a kind of trademark sound" is often heard and accepted as a criterion of quality. It remains to be seen, however, if there is any trademark sound that can still be considered unique today.

Example 2: Improvisers who reflect on their work and improvised music more generally and commit these thoughts to paper

What differentiates such texts from the ideas that scholars express in writing? The difference cannot be one of a transparent methodology and line of reasoning versus "artistic freedom in writing", especially if we consider the FWF requirement that arts-based research also proceed on a methodical basis (even if this demands the development of new methodologies) and be capable of com-

Wissenschaftlern, die die Innenperspektive der aktiven Improvisatorin durchaus aus eigener Erfahrung kennen und sich in ihren Reflexionen auch auf diese Erfahrungen beziehen? So einfach lassen sich wissenschaftliche Forschung und Beobachtung aus Künstlerperspektive also nicht trennen. Die reine Tatsache an sich, dass Künstler ihre Arbeit verbal beschreiben oder über sie reflektieren, ist zunächst eine Beobachtung – manchmal wissenschaftlich, manchmal subjektiv essayistisch. Pauschal als künstlerische Forschung, verstanden als einen dritten Weg, lassen sich Texte von Musikschaffenden nicht bezeichnen.

Versuchen wir einen Perspektivenwechsel, weg von der Verbalisierung, also der traditionellen Ausformung und Äußerung von Forschungsergebnissen durch die Wissenschaft, hin zur Kunst selbst und fragen, ob sich künstlerische Forschung eventuell durch ihre Anwendungsbezogenheit auszeichnet.

3. Ist künstlerische Forschung Grundlagenforschung und angewandte Forschung zugleich?

Forschung ist stets mit Erkenntnisgewinn verbunden. Der Unterschied von künstlerischer zu wissenschaftlicher Forschung kann sich aber nicht darin erschöpfen, dass in einem Falle praktizierende oder ausgebildete Künstler, im anderen Falle qua Studienabschluss dazu auserkorene Wissenschaftler am Werke sind – wie an zwei Beispielen zur Verbalisierbarkeit nur andeutungsweise gezeigt wurde. Eine weitere Möglichkeit, künstlerische und wissenschaftliche Forschung zu unterscheiden, wäre, zu überlegen, auf welcher Art und Weise Schlüsse gezogen werden und wie und ob Begründungen für die Schreibenden relevant sind oder warum nicht. Hier besteht allerdings die Gefahr, dass unter der künstlerischen Forschung all das subsumiert werden kann, was von Kunstschaffenden ausgeht und sich nicht den tradierten wissenschaftlichen Kriterien unterordnet, im Extremfall diese unterläuft. Dann aber würden Tür und Tor geöffnet zur Beliebigkeit. Es müssen also andere Kriterien entwickelt werden, um einen Erkenntnisgewinn nachvollziehen zu können. Wir befinden uns in einer Welt der Verbalisierung, der Falsifizierung und der kommunikativen Aushandlung. Kommunikation muss daher intersubjektiv über Aushandeln ermöglicht werden, da wir sonst schlicht handlungsunfähig sind. Und genau diese intersubjektive Nachvollziehbarkeit wird auch von Fördergebern wie dem FWF gefordert.

Blickwechsel: Kann es künstlerische Forschung geben, die nicht an Verbalisierbarkeit gebunden ist?

Zurück zu »klangforschenden Improvisationsmusikern«. Warum betreiben sie Klangforschung? Um aus deren Ergebnissen Kunst zu schaffen. Die Klangforschung ist also ergebnisorientiert. Ergebnisorientiert heißt aber nicht, dass ich

parison. Is the context in which research is conducted sufficient on its own, in other words, the improviser's insider perspective as opposed to the outsider or observer stance adopted by scholars? But then is the improviser's mindset exclusively that of the insider or do artists in fact switch sides when writing and become observers, even in the sense of self-reflection? What about scholars who have personal experience of improvising musicians' insider perspective and reference these experiences in their own writing? Thus it is not a simple matter of separating scholarly research and analysis from the artist's perspective. The mere fact that artists describe or reflect on their work in verbal terms is initially an observation – sometimes scholarly in nature, sometimes as a subjective essay. Texts composed by musicians cannot be described generally as arts-based research in the sense of the "third way".

Let us now put issues of verbalization, in other words the traditional expression of research results in academia, to one side and look at art itself and ask if arts-based research is distinguished by its practical application.

3. Is arts-based research both basic and applied research?

Research is always associated with the acquisition of new findings. The difference between arts-based and scholarly research, however, cannot be reduced to distinguishing between practicing or trained artists and scholars predestined for academia on the basis of their degrees – as was suggested in the two verbalization examples above. Another way to delineate arts-based and scholarly research might be to consider the way in which conclusions are drawn and how and whether particular arguments are relevant to the authors. There is a risk here, however, of arts-based research subsuming anything created by musicians that does not fall within traditional scholarly criteria or, in extreme cases, even subverts them. This would open the flood gates to arbitrariness. We thus need to develop new criteria that can make new insights transparent. We live in a world of verbalization, falsification, and communicative negotiation. Communication must therefore be intersubjectively possible through negotiation to prevent us from inaction. And it is precisely this intersubjective understanding that is demanded by funding bodies such as the FWF.

Change in perspective: Is arts-based research which is not tied to verbalization possible?

Let us return to the "improvising musicians engaged in sound studies". Why do they do it? To create art from the results. Sound studies are thus a results-driven activity; this does not mean, however, that I, as a musician, purposefully

als Musikerin gezielt auf etwas hin arbeite. Das heißt, das Ergebnis muss nicht schon in »Hörweite« des ersten Klanges sein, es muss nicht geplant sein. Schon die Klangforschung selbst könnte das Ergebnis sein, aber auch die Verwendung neu gefundener Sounds im Improvisationskontext. Oder aber die Einbettung verschiedenster Geräuschfarben in unterschiedliche Form- und Strukturprozesse et cetera. Das heißt, die Anwendung der Klangforschung kann verschiedenste und auch stilistisch unterschiedlichste Ausformungen haben. Aus den Ergebnissen der Klangforschung entsteht – im Idealfall – neue Kunst.

Einige Beispiele neuen Kunstschaffens aus der Improvisationsgeschichte auf Basis von Klangforschung:

- Ablehnung traditioneller Gestaltungsmittel (Free Jazz, Geräuschimprovisation der 1970er, New Phonic Art)
- Vinko Globokars *Laboratorium* zur Entwicklung neuer Spieltechniken
- *AMM* – Texturales, laminares Spiel, Geräuschtexturen
- Derek Baileys oder Keith Rowes »Neuerfindungen« der Gitarre
- Reduktion: Mikroskopierung von einzelnen Klängen und »Nebengeräuschen«
- Bricolage/selbstgebaute Instrumente/Kleinelektronik
- bewusste Re-Integration von einst Verdrängtem

Und ist nicht genau das, was wir hier als künstlerische Forschung versuchen zu beschreiben, nämlich künstlerische Forschung als anwendungsorientierte Forschung, exakt das, was Kunst seit der Moderne und in Ansätzen schon viel früher charakterisiert? Unter anderem charakterisiert? Nämlich künstlerischen Erkenntnisgewinn sowie die Erneuerung, die Neuentdeckung, die Neukontextualisierung? Also das Erforschen neuer künstlerischer Äußerungen im Material, in Form, in der Struktur, im Prozess oder in der Generierung neuer Spielidiome. Benötigen wir hierzu einen neuen Begriff? Müssen wir hier wirklich das Wort »Kunst« durch »künstlerische Forschung« ersetzen, um das Selbstbewusstsein der Kunst im Kontext von Marke und Verwertbarkeit zu heben? Wenn es das wäre, dann würde ich dafür plädieren: Nein! Die Kunst an sich hat ihren Wert – sie muss sich kein Mäntelchen umhängen, keines, das aus der Wissenschaft abgeleitet wirkt. Sorgen wir lieber für gegenseitiges Interesse von Kunst und Wissenschaft – und fördern gegenseitige Zusammenarbeit und Inspiration, Emergenz nicht ausgeschlossen!

Nachwort

Ich wurde gebeten, ob ich noch etwas über spezielle Konzerte der Berliner Echtzeitszene hinzufügen könnte, in denen eine oder mehrere Improvisieren-

work to achieve something – the result need not be within "earshot" of the first sound, it need not be planned. Sound studies themselves could also be the result, as could the use of sounds newly discovered in the context of improvisation, or the embedding of diverse timbres in different formal and structural process. In other words, the application of sound studies can assume a wide range of forms and styles. In an ideal situation, the results of sound studies produce new art.

A few examples of new art from the history of improvisation based on sound studies:

- The rejection of traditional artistic means (free jazz, sound improvisation of the 1970s, new phonic art)
- Vinko Globokar's *Laboratorium* to develop new performance techniques
- *AMM* – textural aspects, laminar layers, sound textures
- Derek Bailey's or Keith Rowe's "rediscovery" of the guitar
- Reduction: microscoping of individual sounds and "ambient noise"
- Bricolage / home-made instruments / small electronics
- Conscious reintegration of the formerly suppressed

And is it not the case that the object we are attempting to describe as arts-based research, namely a form of applied research, is precisely that which has been at the center of art since the modern age and, in part, much earlier times – artistic insight and renewal, rediscovery, recontextualization? In other words: the exploration of novel artistic expression in material, form, structure, process or in the emergence of new performance idioms. Do we need a new term to describe this? Must we really replace "art" with "arts-based research" to raise art's self-assurance in the context of "brand" and use value? My response to this would be a resounding no! Art has intrinsic value – it need not take on a false guise, and certainly not one that appears to be derived from scholarship. Let us rather encourage mutual interest in art and scholarship – and promote mutual collaboration and inspiration, without excluding the possibility of emergent processes.

Afterword

I was asked if I had anything to add in relation to concerts given in Berlin's real-time music scene, where one or more improvisers "translate" the music made by their colleagues to their own instruments.

The Berlin-based guitarist Annette Krebs performed music by EFZEG during the "sound of the second hand clapping" event at Berlin's Labor Sonor festival in 2013. She describes her approach using terms such as analysis, copy-

de die Musik von KollegInnen nachgespielt und auf ihre Instrumente transferiert haben.

Die Berliner Gitarristin Annette Krebs interpretierte in der im Jahre 2013 im Berliner Labor Sonor stattfindenden Reihe »The sound of the second hand clapping« die Musik von EFZEG. Sie beschreibt ihr Vorgehen mit den Worten analysieren, abschreiben, reflektieren und daran anschließend ein interpretatives Konzept entwickeln[4].

Die ersten Schritte waren also dieselben, die auch ein Musikwissenschaftler unternommen hätte – eine musikalische Analyse der Musik. Während der Musikwissenschaftler seine Analyse dann in Worte gefasst hätte, sucht der Musiker nach einer Übertragung der Ergebnisse seiner Analyse, nämlich dessen, was er als »Seele« oder auch Kern der Musik beschreibt, auf sein Instrumentarium. Der Musikwissenschaftler fertigt eine Übertragung in Worte an, der Musiker eine in andere Musik, in Kunst. Ob er zuvor in seiner Analyse eventuell dieselben Begriffe verwendet hat wie sein Wissenschaftskollege, bleibt der Öffentlichkeit verschlossen.

Doch welchen Grund gäbe es, diesen Vorgang alleine schon als künstlerische Forschung zu begreifen? Der Vorgang unterscheidet sich zudem von traditioneller Interpretation allein durch eine einzige Tatsache: dass statt Noten (und eventuell Literatur zur historisch informierten Aufführungspraxis oder Hilfestellung der Komponistin oder des Komponisten zur Umsetzung des Notentextes in Klang) Aufnahmen zur Analyse zur Verfügung stehen. Die jeweiligen Urheber können ebenso befragt werden. Interpretation in sogenannter freier Improvisation ist kein völlig neues Phänomen. Jede individuelle Ausprägung eines Spielidioms lässt sich als eine Interpretation (mit Variation) dieses Spielidioms beschreiben. Wobei eine solche Interpretation auch sehr frei gestaltet werden kann und sich im Laufe der Zeit neue Spielidiome entwickeln können. Im konkreten Falle wird der Interpretationsgegenstand weiter eingeschränkt, nämlich auf ein ganz individuelles Spielidiom einer Band. Die Idee unterscheidet sich im Wesentlichen nicht von herkömmlicher Interpretation eines Notentextes. Hier wie dort muss man sich entscheiden, wie viele Freiheiten ich mir als Interpret nehmen kann oder will, hier wie dort muss ich zunächst analysieren und verstehen, muss ich mir eine Version der Interpretation und der Übertragung erarbeiten.

Neu wäre alleine eine akribische Dokumentation des künstlerischen Tuns. Nicht aber die Sache an sich, die Übertragung. Für künstlerische Forschung bestünde also als minimale Forderung die Pflicht zur Dokumentation der verschiedenen Handlungsschritte, Begründung inklusive. Reine Notationsskizzen reichen nicht aus, es müssen auch die Gedanken zur Analyse angefügt werden. Wie komme ich von A nach B, wie nehme ich die Musik der Band xy wahr, die

4 | *URL: http://www.annettekrebs.eu/texte/text/Interpr.html*

ing, reflection, and the subsequent development of an interpretative concept.[4] The first steps are thus the same ones a musicologist would have adopted – a musical analysis of the work. While the musicologist would then have expressed their analysis in words, however, the musician seeks to translate the results of her analysis, in other words, what she describes as the "soul" or heart of the music, to her instrument. The musicologist produces a translation in words, the musician in music, in art. Whether she may have at first used the same terminology as her scholarly colleague in her analysis must remain a matter of conjecture.

But what reason might there be to conceive of this process in itself as arts-based research? It is distinguished from traditional interpretation by one single fact: the use, not of notes (and perhaps also literature on historically informed performance practice or the assistance of the composer in translating the score into sound), but of recordings for the purpose of analysis: the authors can thus also be consulted. Performance in free improvisation is not a new phenomenon. Every personal performance idiom can be described as an interpretation (with variation) of that idiom, although it may be very free and give rise to new idioms over time. In the present case, the subject of interpretation is further restricted to the highly individual performance idiom of a band. The idea does not essentially differ from the conventional interpretation of a score: in both cases, I must decide how much freedom I can or will allow myself as the performer and must first analyze and understand the work, must create my own version of interpretation and performance.

What would be new, however, is the meticulous documentation of the artistic activity as it is, or was, performed. For arts-based research, the minimum requirement would be a duty to document the various actions taken, including their reasoning. Pure notation is insufficient; thoughts or reflections on the analysis must also be added. How do I get from A to B, how do I hear the music by band xy that I want to play on my instrument? The crux of the matter involves reflecting on our own artistic endeavours. It remains to be seen if this constitutes an adequate description of arts-based research, as scholars also interview artists on their work, challenge them to reflect on their methods, and then put this into words.

Have artists, then, always been engaged in "arts-based research", but perhaps not always verbalized and written down their findings? If so, it would be only the bottles that are new – while the wine tastes just as good as it always did.

Übersetzung aus dem Deutschen: Oliver Dahin, Berlin

4 | *URL: http://www.annettekrebs.eu/texte/text/Interpr.html*

ich auf mein Instrumentarium übertragen möchte? Es geht um eine bewusste Reflexion des eigenen künstlerischen Tuns. Ob dies eine hinreichende Definition künstlerischer Forschung sein mag, ließe sich diskutieren. Denn auch Wissenschaftler interviewen Künstler zu ihrem eigenen Tun, fordern sie heraus, ihr Vorgehen zu reflektieren und in Worte zu fassen.

Haben Künstler also immer schon »künstlerisch geforscht«? Nur eventuell nicht immer verbalisiert und niedergeschrieben? Dann wären also doch nur die Schläuche neu, wobei der Wein in den alten Schläuchen doch nicht weniger gut geschmeckt hat.

Nocturne · Köln hübsch 8
29.5.014

Intermezzo 9

Ich möchte anregen, zwei Positionen zu überprüfen und sie möglicherweise zu verlassen. Nämlich einerseits, in der Improvisation zu denken, wir müssten nur improvisieren, damit Kunst dabei herauskommt, und zwar die Kunst, die wir kennen. Und zum anderen die Position, zu denken, wir wüssten, wie Wissenschaft geht, und das auf die Improvisation zu übertragen. Vielleicht sollten wir auch mal neue, andere Modelle überprüfen und versuchen, Improvisation und Forschung parallel gehen zu lassen. Wir könnten das unter dem Aspekt von »Inklusion« tun und überlegen, ob es nicht noch ein Drittes gibt, was wir vielleicht noch gar nicht im Blick haben. Wo gerade unsere Gesellschaft in dieser Hinsicht einen neuen Aufbruch wagt und versucht Dinge, die bisher undenkbar schienen, in ihre Systeme aufzunehmen.

Diskussionsbeitrag von Helmut Bieler-Wendt, Mai 2014

Intermezzo 9

I would like to propose examining maybe two standpoints and possibly departing from them. On the one hand, thinking that with improvisation we only need to improvise in order for art to be produced, and that means the kind of art that we are familiar with. And on the other hand, thinking that we know how science works and applying it to improvisation. Why not take a look at some new and different models and try to do improvisation whilst carrying out research parallel to this. We may do this under the aspect of "inclusion" by considering if there is a third approach we haven't even thought of yet. Especially since our society is currently daring to push forward in this respect and trying to include things in its systems which up to now were deemed impossible.

Helmut Bieler-Wendt in a public discussion, May 2014

Translation into English: Louise & Phil Loxton, GB-Wales

Symposion Berlin 30.5.014

- Auswertung einer Forschung über 'freie Improvisation'
- Improvisation ist in der 'Neuen Musik' eine Spezialrichtung
- Exploratorium mit einer 'Ein Mann Forschungsabteilung'

Denken u. Spielen
Spielen u. Musizieren
Denken in Versunkenheit
...

- das allmähliche Gestalten von Ungestaltetem
- Sehnsucht nach Intensität gemeinsamen Tuns
- die Hervorbringung von Forschung ist selbst Forschung

Reinhard Gagel

Improvisation improvisierend erforschen | An Improvisational Approach to Exploring Improvisation

Das künstlerisch-wissenschaftliche Projekt |

The artistic-scientific project

Reinhard Gagel

»Das unterscheidet künstlerische Forschung von wissenschaftlicher Forschung: Ihr Untersuchungs-Gegenstand liegt nicht vor, er wird vielmehr in jedem Augenblick erst erschaffen und auf die Probe gestellt. Sie beruft sich damit auf keine Methodik, die sich zuvor bewährt und legitimiert hat, sondern sie bedeutet zu allererst die Entwicklung eines Verfahrens, das gleichsam im Prozess des Textens laufend im Entstehen begriffen ist.« Dieter Mersch (zitiert nach Mersch/Ott 2007: 100)

Vorüberlegungen

Mit improvisierendem Erforschen der Improvisation meine ich, dass die Vermittlung theoretischer Aspekte der Improvisation in engem Kontakt zum Improvisieren und durch es selbst geschieht. Nachdenken und Praktizieren sollen so eng wie möglich verknüpft werden. Ich möchte der Improvisation als musikalischer Kunst den Aspekt der Reflektion hör- und sichtbar beifügen und nicht in Nachgespräche verbannen. Dadurch wird Erforschen sofort auf den Kontext bezogen, den sie beschreiben und erklären soll. Sie geschieht mit denen, die teilnehmen wollen und ist als allen zugängliches Ereignis beziehungsweise als öffentliche Aufführung gedacht. Dazu werde ich Formate vorstellen, in denen das musikalische und das sprachlich-denkende Improvisieren eine wesentliche Rolle als Performance spielen. Sie sind Möglichkeiten einer lebendigen Vermittlung von theoretischen Aspekten und eines forschenden Lernens, aber auch öffentlich stattfindende, beobachtbare und partizipative Forschung. Ich verstehe mich in diesem Zusammenhang als Lehrender, als Forschender *und* als Künstler: was mir vorschwebt und was ich zu realisieren suche, ist ein Konzept der Verbindung – gar Versöhnung – von Kunst und Forschung.

Was ist Forschung in diesem Zusammenhang?

Diese Gedanken basieren auf der Grundlage einer Einstellung zu Forschung, die den Forschungsbegriff pragmatisch – als auf die Anwendung in der Realität gerichtet – sieht: Ich nutze die Definition des amerikanischen Philosophen und Wissenschaftstheoretikers John Dewey:

»Forschung ist die gesteuerte oder gelenkte Umformung einer unbestimmten Situation in eine Situation, die in ihren konstitutiven Merkmalen und Beziehungen so bestimmt ist, dass die Elemente der ursprünglichen Situation in ein einheitliches Ganzes umgewandelt werden«. (Dewey [deutsch] 2008: 131)

Dieser Forschungsbegriff lässt sich auch auf musikalisches Improvisieren umdeuten: Die Umformung einer unbestimmten Situation (eine unmarkierte Situation) in eine bestimmte Situation (eine markierte Situation), die in ein

"Das unterscheidet künstlerische Forschung von wissenschaftlicher Forschung: Ihr Untersuchungs-Gegenstand liegt nicht vor, er wird vielmehr in jedem Augenblick erst erschaffen und auf die Probe gestellt. Sie beruft sich damit auf keine Methodik, die sich zuvor bewährt und legitimiert hat, sondern sie bedeutet zu allererst die Entwicklung eines Verfahrens, das gleichsam im Prozess des Textens laufend im Entstehen begriffen ist."[1] Dieter Mersch (zitiert nach: Mersch/Ott 2007: 100)

Preliminary thoughts

What I mean by an improvisational approach to exploring improvisation is that the conveying of theoretical aspects of improvisation is closely connected to improvising and is done through improvisation itself. Practice and reflection should be as closely connected as possible. I would like to address the aspect of reflection in a way that is audible and visible to improvisation as a musical art, and not relegate it to follow-up discussions. In this way, exploration is immediately related to the context which it is intended to describe and explain. Exploration happens for all those who are willing to participate and is perceived as an event which is accessible to all or as a public performance. To this end, I will present formats in which musical improvisation and talking about improvisation plays a significant role during performance. These offer possibilities for the live communication of theoretical aspects and research-based learning and also for a research format that takes place in public and is observable and participatory. Within this context, I see myself as a teacher, a researcher *and* an artist: what I have in mind and what I am trying to realize is a concept that connects – even reconciles – art and research.

What is research in this context?

These ideas are based on an approach to research that views the term – and also its application in reality – pragmatically. I use the American philosopher and scientific-theorist John Dewey's definition:

"Inquiry is the controlled or directed transformation of an indeterminate situation into one that is so determinate in its constituent distinctions and relations as to convert the elements of the original situation into a unified whole." (Dewey [english] 1937: 123)

1 | "Artistic research differs from scientific research: the subject of investigation is not given, rather it is created and put to the test in each and every moment. This is the concept on which artistic research is based, rather than on a methodology that has already been tested and legitimized. It means, first and foremost, the development of a procedure which is, as it were, continually realized in the process of creating text." (Translation Louise & Phil Loxton, GB-Wales)

einheitliches Ganzes (eine Struktur) umgewandelt wird. Damit dieses Forschen funktioniert, muss sein Verlauf offen sein: »[Bei der] Methode, die zum Entdecken, zum systematischen Forschen verwendet wird, ... befindet sich das Denken in einer suchenden Haltung, es verfolgt, plant, versucht dies und das« (Dewey [deutsch] 1951: 118f). Eine solche suchende Haltung führt über Erfolg und Scheitern zu einer übertragbaren Einsicht und Nachhaltigkeit dadurch,

> »dass schon im Zweifel, im Erwägen von Möglichkeiten, im Versuchen ein Hinweis auf die Lösung enthalten ist. Nachdem ein Schluss erreicht wurde, wird ein nochmaliges Betrachten der einzelnen Stufen des Prozesses, dessen was nützlich, schädlich, wertlos ist, dazu beitragen, spätere analoge Fälle rascher und erfolgreicher zu behandeln. Auf diese Weise wird nach und nach eine recht klare Methode aufgebaut«. (Dewey [deutsch] 1951: 118f)

Mir geht es jedoch nicht um das Finden einer Lösung. Vielmehr geht es um eine dieser »Sache Improvisation« und den jeweiligen Menschen gemäße Annäherung an Probleme der musikalischen Improvisation. Tatsächlich kann man aus den Sätzen von Dewey einen Prozess des Lernens aus dem Forschen herauslesen, der in vielem dem Improvisieren – im allgemeinen, aber hier besonders dem musikalischen – ähnlich ist: Spielen mit dem Risiko des Scheiterns, aus Fehlern Hinweise auf neue Wege herausfinden, durch Reflektion auf den Prozess rückbesinnen, Erfahrungen für neue Prozesse sammeln, gar eine (eigene) Methode des Improvisierens entwickeln. Damit ist Forschen sehr breit definiert und das ist für das hier behandelte Thema nützlich: Forschen ist improvisatorisch, ist gleichzeitig Suchen, Finden und Lernen: »forschendes Lernen« beziehungsweise »Lernen durch Forschen«. Es ist aber auch forschendes Lehren: die Anwendung, die ich als ein die Improvisation Lehrender hier vorschlage, soll auch Wissen und Erkenntnisse weitergeben. Sie ist ein ästhetisches Format, eine Performance, die Fragen der Improvisation (auch der Forschung) aus dem Experimentieren und Reflektieren und seiner öffentlichen Präsentation zu beantworten sucht.

Was ist Performance in diesem Zusammenhang?

Ich möchte, was geschieht – musikalisch und textlich – öffentlich machen. Dies nicht in den üblichen Lern- und Lehr- oder Vortragsformaten: nicht durch einen Vortrag, nicht durch ein Seminar, nicht durch Schulformate. Ich möchte Theorie und Forschung aufführen, durch eine performative Spannung verbinden und ich möchte andere daran teilhaben lassen. Aktiv und passiv. Wer sich beteiligt, wird Teil einer *Aufführung*. Diese baut auf Bühnenpräsenz, die eine immanente Spannung aufbaut und sie über eine gewisse Zeit nicht mehr auflöst. Alle sind durch die gleiche Konzentration auf den Verlauf und die Gestaltung der Qualität jeder sprachlichen oder musikalischen Äußerung miteinander verbun-

This understanding of research can be reinterpreted for musical improvisation: the transformation of a non-specific situation (an unassigned/unmarked situation) to a specific situation (an assigned situation) which is converted into a unified whole (a structure).

In order for this research to work, its process must be open. "In the genuine operation of inference, the mind is in the attitude of search, of hunting, of projection, of trying this or that." (Dewey [english] 1910: 118f) This kind of stance goes beyond success and failure to transferrable understanding and sustainability.

"The dilemma is at least suggestive, for it points to the true alternative: the use in inquiry of doubt, of tentative suggestion, of experimentation. After we have reached the conclusion, a reconsideration of the steps of the process to see what is helpful, what is harmful, what is merely useless, will assist in dealing more promptly and efficaciously with analogous problems in the future. In this way, more or less explicit method is gradually built up." (Dewey [english] 1910: 112f)

My concern here is not in finding a solution. I am more interested in this "thing", improvisation, and bringing people closer to the problems of musical improvisation. One can indeed read Dewey's sentences and find a process of learning from research that is in many respects similar to improvisation in general, but in particular to musical improvisation: playing with the risk of failure, finding potential new directions in mistakes, returning to the process through reflection, collecting experiences for new processes, even developing (one's own) method of improvising. These points mean that research can be very broadly defined, which is useful for the topic being addressed here. Researching is improvisatory – simultaneously searching, finding, and learning – it is "investigative learning" or, in other words, "learning through researching". However, is also investigative teaching. The approach that I, as an improvisation teacher, suggest is to pass on knowledge and insight. This takes an aesthetic format; a performance that attempts to answer questions of improvisation through experimentation, reflection and public presentation.

What is performance in this context?

Whatever happens – musically or with text – I would like to do publicly, not in the usual learning or teaching presentation formats, such as lectures, seminars or school formats. I would like to perform theory and research together, to connect them with performative tension, and I would like others to be able to participate both actively and passively. Those who participate become part of a *performance*. This relies on a stage presence that builds up an immanent tension and maintains it for a certain period of time. Everyone is connected to each

den. Dies geschieht durch die Art und Weise, wie eine Aufführung strukturiert ist, welche Rollen den Teilnehmenden zufallen oder welche sie wählen: Sind sie Musiker und improvisieren sie? Sind sie Zuschauer und geben Statements ab? Sind sie Experten und haben Gelegenheit, Wissen weiterzugeben? Sind sie bereit, interessiert, gar darauf aus, gemeinsam in unbekannten Konstellationen zu improvisieren? Dies geschieht dann in einer Art und Weise, die auch auf anderes übertragbar ist: deutlich, moduliert, den Qualitäten des Klangs nachgehend, aufeinander bezogen. Meine Funktion ist die des Anleiters; ich halte die Dynamik aufrecht, ich gebe das Zeichen: Nun beginnt die Performance, nun wird alles zu Kunst, zum Forschen in Kunst und durch Kunst. Den Teilnehmenden muss bewusst sein, dass von nun an alles zu der Performance dazu gehört. Es wird etwas vor sich gehen, dass durch die Intensität, das gemeinsame Interesse, durch die Versenkung in die Musik und den Verlauf quasi *rituell* wird.

Zielformulierung

Die Investigation, die ich in Gang setzen möchte, soll Menschen an einem gemeinsamen Denk- und Gestaltungsprozess innerhalb einer Performance beteiligen. Sie können sich in ihrer Individualität und als Experten ihrer selbst und ihres Handelns einbringen. Erkenntnisse, die aus verschiedenen Wissenschaftszweigen – Neurologie, Psychologie, Philosophie und Musikwissenschaft – gewonnen wurden, werden dazu in Beziehung gesetzt. Praktisches Improvisieren – als Erproben, als offene Bühne – soll mit Nachdenken, Sprechen und Diskutieren immanent und als ein Prozess verbunden werden. Die auf diese Weise entstehende Veranstaltung dient den Teilnehmenden als Vertiefung ihrer Einsichten in die Theorie und Praxis der Improvisation. Sie ist dadurch eng verbunden mit ihrer Spiel-Praxis.

Das künstlerisch-wissenschaftliche Projekt

Diese Erforschung wird nun im Einzelnen ausdifferenziert. Ich nenne das vorgestellte Format das *künstlerisch-wissenschaftliche Projekt*. Es ist

- thematisch eingegrenzt, stellt eine Frage oder einen Forschungsanlass in den Raum (zum Beispiel »woher können wir das?«).
- multiperspektivisch: die Teilnehmer arbeiten mit allen zugänglichen Ressourcen wie eigener Spiel-Erfahrung, eigenem Nachdenken, Angelesenem, Texten, wissenschaftlicher Forschung, Medien.
- ereignishaft und situativ: es wird das verhandelt, erforscht, erarbeitet, was mit den jetzt vorhandenen Mitteln zu Denk- und Gestaltungsprozessen führt.

other through their concentration on the process and the shaping of the quality of each verbal or musical expression. How this occurs is based on the manner in which a performance is structured, which roles the participants are given or which they choose to take: are they musicians who improvise? Are they observers who contribute statements? Are they experts that have the opportunity to share information? Are they prepared, interested, or even willing to improvise collectively in unknown constellations? All this happens in a way that can be transferred to other situations: clear, modulated, following the qualities of the sound, coordinated. My function is that of a guide. I keep the dynamic going, I give the signal: now the performance begins; now everything becomes art, to be investigated in and through art. The participants are aware that "from now on" everything is part of the performance. Something is going to happen that will become a kind of ritual through its intensity, mutual interest and the immersion in the music and the process.

Aims

The investigation that I would like to initiate should include people in a collective thought and formative process within a performance. They can participate as individuals and as experts on themselves and their own acting. Insights gained from diverse scientific disciplines – neurology, psychology, philosophy and musicology – will be applied to this. Practical improvisation – exploration, open stage – should be connected to reflecting, speaking and discussing as part of a process. The events that develop in this way serve to further the participants' understanding of improvisation in theory and in practice, and are as such closely related to their performance practice.

The artistic-scientific project

This investigation will now be differentiated in more detail. I call the formats presented here the *artistic-scientific project*. The project:

- is confined to specific topics and poses questions or grounds for research (for example, "How can we do it?", "Where does our ability to do it come from?")
- has multiple perspectives: the participants work with all of the resources they have access to, such as their own playing experience, reflection, what they have read, texts, scientific research, media.
- is event-based and situational: we negotiate, investigate and develop that which leads to thought processes and formative processes using the means currently available to us.

- performativ: Über die Dauer des Projektes (zwischen ein bis zwei Stunden) werden Diskurse und Lectures abgehalten und kurze oder längere Stücke instrumental beziehungsweise stimmlich improvisiert.

Der Künstler und Kunstpädagoge Gert Selle prägte für die Kunstpädagogik in den frühen 90er Jahren den Begriff des Projektes:

»Es sind Vorhaben – Projekte –, die eine Wahrnehmung (auch Selbstwahrnehmung) vertiefen und in die Formrepräsentanz von Kunst überführen, das heißt in einen verdichteten Zustand von Erfahrung, dessen Wahrnehmung wiederum unsere Erfahrungsfähigkeit beflügelt.« (Selle 1992: 16)

Die Teilnehmenden werden in gewissem Maße zu Künstlern, deren Kunstäußerung wiederum zum Verstehen führt: »Auf den Spuren solcher Prozesse der ästhetischen Objektivation gewinnen wir als Teilhabende nicht nur ein Verständnis vor allem gegenwärtiger Kunst, sondern auch ein Verständnis unserer Selbst«. (Ebd.)

Diese Beschreibung übertrage ich nun auf die Improvisation und möchte im folgenden Abschnitt zunächst die praktischen Formate meiner Arbeit in Berlin vorstellen. Diese werden bisher als einmalige, eine begrenzte Zeit dauernde Performances mit einer thematischen Fragestellung angeboten.[1]

Formate

Vorbild: Vortrag als Performance: Kunst durch Kunst verstehen

Cages Vortrag *Silence* aus dem Jahr 1952 soll hier unter dem einen Aspekt betrachtet werden, dass Cage Erkenntnisse seiner Philosophie als Kunst (als Performance) vorträgt. Die Lesung wird durch das gedruckte Schriftbild geleitet, das durch Lücken zwischen den Wörtern (als Pausen) und fixierte Abschnitte einen relativen zeitlichen Rahmen vorgibt und so zu unterschiedlichen Sprechtempi und Phasen der Stille führt. Cage äußerte sich dazu: »Ich halte diese Vorträge nicht, um die Leute zu überraschen, sondern aus poetischer Notwendigkeit«. (Cage 1995: 169).

---

1 | Langfristig könnte ein solches Projekt mehrmals mit derselben Fragestellung wiederholt werden. Allerdings werden die Konstellationen jedes Mal anders sein: die Teilnehmenden wechseln, die Besetzungen, die persönlichen Ansichten, die Dauer, der Umfang von Redebeiträgen und fixen Teilen.

- performative: for the duration of the project (between one to two hours), discussions and lectures are held and pieces of differing lengths are improvised.

The artist and art pedagogue Gert Selle influenced the meaning of the term *project* in reference to art teaching in the early 1990s:

"Es sind Vorhaben - Projekte -, die eine Wahrnehmung (auch Selbstwahrnehmung) vertiefen und in die Formrepräsentanz von Kunst überführen, das heißt in einen verdichteten Zustand von Erfahrung, dessen Wahrnehmung wiederum unsere Erfahrungsfähigkeit beflügelt."[2] (Selle 1992: 16)

The participants become, to a certain extent, artists whose artistic expression then leads to understanding: "Auf den Spuren solcher Prozesse der ästhetischen Objektivation gewinnen wir als Teilhabende nicht nur ein Verständnis vor allem gegenwärtiger Kunst, sondern auch ein Verständnis unserer Selbst."[3] (Ibid.)

I will transfer this description to improvisation and, in the following section; I would like to present the practical formats of my work in Berlin. So far, these have been one-off performances of limited duration, offering a thematic line of questioning.[4]

Formats

Model: Lecture as performance: understanding art through art

In his 1952 lecture *Silence,* Cage presents his philosophical insights as art (performance). It is this aspect that we focus on here. The reading is guided using different typefaces, spaces between the words (used as pauses), and fixed sec-

2 | "Projects are initiatives that deepen perception (also self-perception). In terms of art, they are transferred into and represented by forms. This means, they are transferred into a concentrated state of experience, the perception of which in turn inspires and stimulates our ability to experience even more." (Translation Louise & Phil Loxton, GB-Wales)

3 | "On the trail of such processes of aesthetic objectivation, we as participants not only gain an understanding of contemporary art, but also an understanding of ourselves." (Translation Louise & Phil Loxton, GB-Wales)

4 | In the long term, a project like this could be repeated several times with the same line of questioning. Although the constellations would be different every time: the participants change, the instruments, the personal perspectives, the duration, the amount of speeches and fixed sections.

Lecture Performance

Silence ist die Urmutter des Vortrags als Kunst, der Lecture Performance. Diese hat in den letzten Jahren eine gewisse Karriere gemacht: Künstlerische Forschung formuliert sich oft als Lecture Performance[2]. Meine eigenen Arbeiten folgen der Faszination einer Performance, in der Musik und Text eng verbunden sind; ein Konzert, in dem die Musizierenden auch (über sich) oder ihr Thema sprechen, Textfetzen und Erkenntnisse vermitteln, und ihre Musik davon beeinflusst ist oder einen Gegenpart liefert. Ein eigenes Format dazu als Beispiel: *theory on stage* – Bibliothekseröffnung im *exploratorium berlin* 2014. Ich habe mit meinem *Whathappensnext-Ensemble Berlin*[3] dafür eine Performance entwickelt, deren Ablaufplan nun folgt[4].

theory on stage
Eine interaktive Performance
Whathappensnext-Ensemble Berlin
(im folgenden *WHN* abgekürzt, Anm. d. Red.)
Am 4. März 2014 im *exploratorium berlin*

Stühle im Viereck um den Teppich im Saal.
Auf dem Teppich Instrumente von *WHN Berlin*

Spielleiter begrüßt: Wir werden nun eine Performance mit den Elementen einer Bibliothek machen, um musikalisch zu verstehen, welche Relevanz die Theorie für die Praxis hat.

Vorspiel: Element Papier
Auf allen Sitzen liegt Papier. Ein Blatt nehmen, es spüren, streicheln, rascheln und so weiter. Der Nullpunkt des Elementes – der Übergang aus der Stille zum Klang...

Dann WHN Ritornell 1: die **Kategorien der Bibliothek** (Musikpädagogik, Theorie der Improvisation und so weiter): kurze Stücke in kleinem engem Kreis.
Pause

2 | Vgl. ausführlich dazu: Peters, Sibylle (2011).

3 | Das *Whathappensnext-Ensemble Berlin* (WHN) ist ein Ensemble, das ich 2013 ins Leben gerufen habe und das seitdem kontinuierlich probt und konzertiert, vor allem mit experimentellen Formaten.

4 | Das Videodokument dieser Lecture Performance kann in der Bibliothek des *exploratorium berlin* eingesehen werden.

tions with relative time frames, which lead to different speech tempos and periods of silence. In Cage's words: "I don't give these lectures to surprise people, but out of a need for poetry." (Cage 1973: x)

Lecture performance

Silence is the mother of lecture as art, the lecture performance. This has really come into its own in recent years: artistic research is often formulated as lecture performance.[5] My own works stem from a fascination with performance in which both music and text are closely connected; a concert in which the performers speak about themselves or their subject, communicate fragments of text and insights and influence their music with these, or in which their music itself becomes a counterpart. Here one of my own formats serves as an example: *theory on stage* – the opening of the *exploratorium berlin* library in 2014. I developed a performance with my *Whathappensnext-Ensemble* Berlin,[6] the plan of which can be seen below.[7]

theory on stage
An interactive performance
Whathappensnext-Ensemble Berlin (Abbr. WHN)
March 4th 2014, *exploratorium berlin*

Chairs set out in a square around the carpet in the hall
WHN instruments placed on the carpet

Performance leader says: We will now conduct a performance with the elements of the library using music to understand what relevance theory has to practice

Prelude: paper
There is paper on all the seats. Take a sheet, feel it, stroke it, rustle it, et cetera. The zero point of the element – the transition from silence to sound...

Then WHN Ritornello 1: The **Categories of the Library** (music pedagogy, theory of improvisation, et cetera): Short pieces in a small tight circle. Break.

---

5 | For further reading see: Peters (2011).

6 | *The Whathappensnext-Ensemble Berlin* is an ensemble that I founded in 2013. It performs and rehearses regularly, in particular with experimental formats.

7 | A video documentation of this lecture performance can be found in the library of the *exploratorium berlin*.

Spielleiter liest:
»›Improvisatoren sind denkende und wissende Leute. Improvisierte Musik tritt schon lange nicht mehr so vereinzelt auf in der Musikliteratur. Sie wird heute in Zeitschriften, nicht zuletzt in ihren eigenen, in gutverbreiteten Publikationen und in PhD- und Doktorarbeiten studiert und vermittelt. Nicht zu sprechen von der Fülle von CDs und Netzpublikationen von Aufnahmen der Musik selbst. Seit wir das Internet bekamen, wurde alles noch durchsichtiger und integrierter.‹ Sandte uns unser dänischer Freund Carl.«

Währenddessen haben sich alle *WHN* in ein Buch vertieft.
Ritornell: auf Zeichen: Jedes Mitglied von *WHN* liest aus einem Buch zufällige Textpassagen. Eine/r liest vor, die anderen reagieren musikalisch sparsam oder auch nicht und so weiter .

Musikalische Debatte
Geladene Gäste spielen mit:
2 *WHN* + 2 Gäste.
Eventuell wiederholen...

WHN Ritornell 2: **Texte** sprechen und **laut performen**.
Vorgeschlagene Version: mit viel Pausen, zuhören, es entstehen seltsame Kombinationen von Worten verschiedener Texte. Diese Kombinationen können andere wiederholen.

Freeplay: Ad Libitum: verschiedene Worte aus gefundenen Büchern **pointieren**. Zwischen den Zitaten kommentierende Soli/Duos und so weiter. Diese Texte werden nach und nach durch Grafikblätter ersetzt.

WHN Ritornell 3: **Grafik Blätter (grafische Notationen)**. Als Ausgangspunkt: Jeder wählt ein Blatt, anschauen, dann weglegen, aus der Erinnerung (oder Imagination) spielen, eventuell entwickeln. Ad Libitum: Die Blätter beim nächsten Stück wechseln, weitergeben oder sich ein Blatt aussuchen von einem anderen.

Finale
Der Spielleiter spricht:
»Unser dänischer Freund Carl schreibt: ›Worüber sind wir Improvisatoren besonders wissend? Wohl über den Prozess und darüber, was es bedeutet, in der Musik gegenwärtig zu sein. Um Prozesse gut in Gang zu halten, braucht man aber auch Bastionen. Das *exploratorium* ist so eine Bastion, und tritt jetzt ein in den sehr exklusiven Kreis internationaler Spezialbibliotheken für

Performance leader reads:
"This was sent to us by our Danish friend Carl. 'Improvisers are thinking and knowing people. A long time ago improvised music only appeared sporadically in musical literature. Today it appears and is studied in journals - not least its own - in well-circulated publications and PhDs. Not to mention the vast number of CDs and internet publications of recordings of this kind of music itself. Since we have had the internet, everything has become more transparent and integrated.'"

During the reading all *WHN* have buried themselves in books.
Ritornello: on cue: Every member of *WHN* reads random text passages out of a book. One reads aloud, the others react (to differing degrees) musically, for example, sparsely, not at all, and so on.

Musical Debate
Invited guests play along:
2 *WHN* + 2 guests
possibly repeat...

WHN Ritornello 2: speak and **perform texts aloud**.
Suggested version: with many pauses, a lot of listening, strange combinations of words from different texts result. These combinations can be repeated.

Free play: Ad libitum: **Emphasize** different words from the books. Solos/duos/et cetera are performed as a commentary between the quotations. These texts are gradually replaced by pages of graphics.

WHN Ritornello 3: **Pages of graphics (graphic notations)**. Point of departure: everyone chooses a page, looks at it, then puts it down, plays it from memory (or imagination) and possibly develops it further. Ad libitum: Change pages for the next piece, pass on or choose a page from someone else.

Finale
The performance leader speaks:
"Our Danish friend Carl writes: 'What do we improvisers know a lot about in particular? We know about the process and about what it means to be in the present moment in music. In order to keep processes going well, bastions are needed. The exploratorium berlin is such a bastion and now joins the very exclusive circle of special international libraries for improvised and contemporary music. This opens up a whole new area for information and exchange. Congratulations!'"

improvisierte und neue Musik. Damit erschließt es einen ganz neuen Bereich von Information und Austausch. Prost, und herzliche Glückwünsche dazu!«

Es ist nicht immer explizit als ad libitum ausgeschrieben, aber man kann ersehen, dass in dem Ablaufplan eine Vielzahl von »offenen Stellen« sind, in die Situatives, Improvisiertes, Spontanes einfließen kann. Die Musik des Ensembles, die erklingt, ist nicht vorher festgelegt und nicht geprobt. Wir improvisieren aus dem Moment. Zu diesem Ablaufplan ergaben sich – und das war auch gewollt – während der Performance Varianten im Detail, dennoch bildete der Plan ein Gerüst. Und das Publikum hatte auch Gelegenheit, sich einzubringen: In diesem Fall haben am Ende fast alle aus dem Publikum die Rollen gewechselt: aus Hörern wurden Rezitatoren, Tänzer, Musiker...

Im Januar 2012 präsentierten wir in einem Abschluss-Symposium Resultate, Erfahrungen und Ausblicke des Forschungsprojektes *Quo vadis Teufelsgeiger?*[5] an der Universität für Musik und Darstellende Kunst, Wien. Dies geschah ebenfalls in einer Lecture Performance, in der wir präsentierten, referierten und das Publikum einluden, auf der Bühne zu improvisieren. Die Bühne war mit Forschungspapieren übersät, das Publikum erhielt Nummern, die wir aufriefen, damit die zugehörigen Personen auf die Bühne kommen. Das Forschungsteam war Hauptakteur auf der Bühne: Wir wechselten die Kleidung, je nach dem, was wir gerade verkörperten, wir improvisierten auf Klavier, Synthesizer und Fagott, wir hielten kurze Vorträge und befragten uns gegenseitig. Ein Experte, der das Forschungsprojekt von außen begleitet hatte, hielt einen kurzen Vortrag. Video- und Audioausschnitte unserer Forschungsarbeit wurden gezeigt.

Im Folgenden ist das Gerüst zu sehen, das in seinen Details in der Situation emergierte, das heißt, in Details und in seinem Verlauf variierte beziehungsweise die Richtung wechselte. Die Lecture Performance wurde per Video dokumentiert, und der Film ist zugänglich[6].

Quo Vadis Teufelsgeiger – Abschluss-Präsentation
Wien Januar 2012
(Autoren und Performer: Magda Bork, Reinhard Gagel, Maria Gstättner)
ABLAUF (so oder ähnlich)

THEMA: Probespiel

Maria spielt, nach ihrem Gefühl, wenn sie nicht mehr mag (noch schärfer: wenn Magda oder Reinhard sagen: »Danke, das genügt«), kommt sie hervor

5 | *URL: http://www.quovadisteufelsgeiger.at.* Auf dieser Website ist auch in Ausschnitten die im Folgenden skizzierte Lecture Performance zu sehen.

6 | *URL: https://www.youtube.com/watch?v-Bf2jZcgzdL4&feature-plcp*

Ad libitum is not always explicitly written out, but one can see that in the structural plan there are a number of "open sections", into which the situative, the improvised and the spontaneous can flow. The music which the ensemble generates is not established in advance, nor is it rehearsed. We improvise in the moment. In addition to this structural plan – and this was also intentional – there were variations in the details. Nevertheless, the plan still provided a framework and the audience also had a chance to participate: in this case, almost everyone in the audience changed their role: listeners became speakers, dancers, musicians et cetera.

We presented the results, experiences and perspectives from the research project *Quo vadis Teufelsgeiger?*[8] in a closing symposium at the University of Music and Performing Arts, Vienna in 2012. This also took the form of a lecture performance, in which we presented, lectured and invited the audience to improvise on stage. The stage was covered with research papers and the audience was given numbers that we called out so that the person with that number would come onto the stage. The research team were the main characters on stage: we changed our clothes, depending on what we were embodying at that moment, we improvised on piano, synthesizer and bassoon, we held short lectures and asked each other questions. An external expert who had accompanied the research project gave a short lecture, and video and audio clips from our research were played/shown.

Below is the framework; it shows the details which emerged out of the situation. The details and the direction varied as the situation unfolded. The lecture performance was documented on video and the film is available. [9]

Quo Vadis Teufelsgeiger?
Where to, Devil's Fiddler? – Final Presentation,
Vienna, January 2012
(Authors and performers: Magda Bork, Reinhard Gagel, Maria Gstättner)
PROCESS (like this or similar)

SUBJECT: Audition

Maria plays how she feels. When she doesn't want to play anymore, or when Magda or Reinhard say "Thank you, that's enough", she appears from behind a screen.
Magda reads one to three quotes from musicians about auditions
Reinhard improvises, maybe Maria joins in with him.

---

8 | Excerpts from the performance of the lecture performance sketched out below can be found here: *URL: http://www.quovadisteufelsgeiger.at.*

9 | *URL: https://www.youtube.com/watch?v-Bf2jZcgzdL4&feature-plcp*

Magda liest 1-3 Zitate von den Musikern über Probespiel
Reinhard improvisiert, vielleicht Maria dazu.

THEMA: Forschungsgegenstand

Magda trägt vor, worum es ging (PowerPoint)
»Wie kommt es zur Freien Improvisation in der Klassik«

THEMA: Praxis zeigen

Reinhard zeigt seine Arbeit – kommentiert Audiobeispiele live,
Musikalische Interaktion Beispiel »FREE 22"«
liest dazwischen einen Theorie-Text »Verstehen«
gemeinsam mit Magda zeigen wir »Nur ein Ton« : Zitat und Musik
Maria liest vor »über das Wünschen« und zeigt auch ein Musikbeispiel dazu.
Magda benennt die Phänomene, die wir im Labor beobachtet haben:
»Was kann Improvisation?« gegenübergestellt zu **»Was brauchen klassische Interpreten?«**

THEMA: Konsequenzen

1. Einspielung: Statements von Teilnehmern des Projekt-Ensembles (Hochschullehrer): »Das Akzeptieren von Jetzt, nicht immer weiter weiterdenken«, dann leise Musik und
2. kurze Lesung dreier Statements von Teilnehmenden

THEMA: Ins Gespräch kommen/Eigensprache/Idiolektik

Magda befragt Reinhard und Maria am Stehtisch: »Was ist Euch jetzt wichtig?« Reinhard könnte über Polystilistik et cetera reden beziehungsweise Maria ihr Konzept von »Was wünscht Du Dir jetzt?« erläutern und damit auch den Übergang zu einer eventuellen Publikumsbeteiligung machen – eine Nummer mit den Nummern? Haikus... Blitzlicht aufschreiben, während wir spielen oder auch nicht.
Eventuell hier die DenkraumSpuren spielen?
Eventuell: Texte lesen lassen. Oder Schlagworte aus dem Denkraum.
Leise aus dem Off: Musik aus der Werkstatt von Reinhard (»Saties little noises«)

THEMA: Artistic research

Jens Badura trägt vor: »Aussetzungen ins Mögliche«
Im Hintergrund laufen Workshop-Fotos und/oder -Video
Magda liest ihren Text »künstlerisch forschen« als Brücke zur Improvisation von Reinhard und Maria

SUBJECT: Subject of Research

Magda lectures on what it was about (using PowerPoint)

"How does free improvisation come about in classical music?"

SUBJECT: Demonstrating Practice

Reinhard shows his work – comments on sound examples,

Musical interaction example "FREE 22''"

In between he reads the theoretical text "Understanding in improvised music"

We show "Just a Tone" together with Magda: quote and music

Maria reads "About Wishing" aloud and presents a musical example.

Magda identifies the phenomena that we observed in the laboratory:

"**What can improvisation do?**" as opposed to "**What do classical musicians need?**"

SUBJECT: Consequences

1. Recording: statements from participants of the project ensemble (university teachers): "Accepting the Now, not always thinking ahead," then quiet music and
2. reading of three short statements by participants

SUBJECT: Starting a conversation/personal language/idiolect

Magda asks Reinhard and Maria at the table: "What is important to you now?" Reinhard could talk about polystylism, et cetera or Maria could explain her concept of "What do you wish for yourself now?" and, in this way, possibly make a transition to audience participation – an activity with the numbers? Haiku ... write down quickly while we are playing or not playing. Possibly: Have texts or key words from Thinking Space read quietly from off-stage: Music from Reinhard's workshop (audiofile "Satie's little noises")

SUBJECT: Artistic research

Jens Badura presents: "Abandoning yourself to the possible"

Workshop photos and/or video in the background

Magda reads her text "Artistic Research" as a bridge to an improvisation by Reinhard and Maria

SUBJECT: Declarations Quo vadis Teufelsgeiger (QvT)?
Where to, Devil's Fiddler?

Magda reads five to seven pamphlet texts aloud: "We have realized that..."

THEMA: Bekenntnisse QvT (Quo vadis Teufelsgeiger?)
Magda liest fünf bis sieben Pamphlettexte vor: »Wir haben erkannt, dass ...«
Maria zieht etwas aus, Reinhard etwas an, Magda nimmt die Perücke
Wir spielen das **Ende** (von der Performance, vom Projekt, von der Weisheit...)
Finale: situativ ohne Vorbereitung

Meine Vorstellung einer Lecture Performance ist, dass das Konzept und der tatsächliche Ablauf oft abweichen und es auch sollen. Es geht mir um die Schaffung einer *improvisierten* Lecture Performance[7]. Etwas innerhalb der Performance geschieht und das fließt wieder zurück in die Lecture Performance selbst. Es entsteht zum Beispiel ein Musikstück, eine Diskussion, die Auswirkungen haben auf den nächsten Schritt. Das meint die Erwartung von Rückkopplungsschleifen, Emergenz und Autopoiesis: sind bestimmte Themen sehr im Vordergrund, werden Richtungen gewählt aufgrund der Beteiligung und des fokussierten Interesses der Anwesenden. Welche Ideen bringen die Anwesenden ein? Zum Beispiel haben wir an einer Stelle der oben konzipierten Wiener Performance zwei durch Nummern bestimmte Personen zum Improvisieren auf die Bühne gebeten. Wir konnten nicht wissen, wer da kommen würde: Es waren in diesem Falle zwei erfahrene Improvisatoren, die den Gedanken der freien Improvisation aus dem Moment wirkungsvoll darstellen konnten. Was wäre gewesen, wenn es Unerfahrene, gar Ängstliche gewesen wären? Dann hätte ich mit ihnen exemplarisch arbeiten können, was eine ganz andere Richtung eingeschlagen und Folgen für den weiteren Verlauf gehabt hätte. Am Ende – »als Finale situativ ohne bestimmte Vorbereitung« im Ablaufplan – habe ich dann ein Audiofile mit einem verblüffenden Stück improvisierter Kammermusik abgespielt, was mir aus dem Verlauf der Performance als Ende schlüssig erschien und ein tatsächlich sehr emotionsgeladenes Finale erzeugte.

Das Berliner Labor

Unter Labor verstehe ich ein Format, in dem die Lecture Performance noch einmal intensiviert wird.[8] Die Teilnehmenden sollen sich weitaus stärker als in einer Lecture Performance selbst beteiligen. Deshalb mischen sich hier länge-

7 | Das unterscheidet sich von den Lecture Performances, die zum Beispiel Sibylle Peters (2011) beschreibt: Sie waren meist fest geplant und auch so durchgeführt.

8 | Es findet regelmäßig viermal jährlich statt und wird über das Programmheft des *exploratorium berlin* als öffentliche Veranstaltung der Abteilung Theorie und Forschung angekündigt.

Maria takes something off, Reinhard puts something on, Magda takes the wig
We play the **End** (of the performance, of the project, of the wisdom...)
Finale: situative without preparation

My idea of a lecture performance is one in which the conception and actual unfolding often differ, and they should. I am interested in creating an *improvised* lecture performance.[10] Something happens during the performance and this flows back into the lecture performance itself. For example, a piece of music, or the outcome of a discussion, has an effect on the next step. This leads to the expectation of feedback loops, emergence and autopoiesis: certain subjects are in the foreground, directions are chosen based on the level of participation and what those present want to focus on. What ideas do those present contribute? For example, at one point during the Vienna performance mentioned above, we called two people to the stage, using a numbers system, in order to improvise. We did not know who would come: in this case they were two experienced improvisers who could really convey ideas of free improvisation in the moment. What would have happened if they had been inexperienced or even afraid? Then I could have worked with them in a more structured and supportive way, which would have changed the direction, which in turn would have had consequences for the further development of the performance. At the end – referred to in the structural plan as "Finale, situative without preparation" – I played a recording of a surprising piece of improvised chamber music, which, given the course of the performance, seemed to me to make more sense as an ending and actually created a very emotional finale.

The Berlin laboratory

I understand the term laboratory as a format in which the lecture performance is further intensified.[11] The participants should be involved to a much greater extent than in a lecture performance. That is why, during a laboratory, longer phases of musical improvisation are mixed with extended discussions. Each laboratory deals with a subject: this should be presented or explored with the aid of improvisation, performance, presence, and with the participation of those present.[12]

---

10 | This differs from the lecture performances described by Sibylle Peters (2011) for example: these were, in general, more planned out and executed accordingly.

11 | It takes place quarterly and is listed in the *exploratorium berlin's* program as a public event hosted by the Department of Theory and Research.

12 | So far there have been three laboratories and two more are planned for Winter 2015/2016.

re Phasen musikalischen Improvisierens mit ausgedehnten Gesprächsrunden. Jedes Labor steht unter einem Thema: Dieses soll dann gemeinsam mithilfe der Improvisation, der Performance, der Präsenz und unter Beteiligung der Anwesenden präsentiert beziehungsweise erforscht werden[9].

Als Beispiel wähle ich das zweite Labor[10]: Dieses konzipierte ich als *Wissensoper.* Das Thema lautete: *Improvisieren. Woher können wir das?* Der Text besteht aus Ergebnissen anderer als musikalischer Forschungsgebiete, trägt Statements der Neurophysiologie, der Psychologie und der Kulturwissenschaft zusammen. Im Laufe des Labors sollen sie durch gemeinsames Improvisieren auf ihre Praxisrelevanz erprobt und mit eigenen Erfahrungen zusammengebracht werden. Der Text sollte im Musik-Text beziehungsweise Musik-Gesang-Verhältnis einer improvisierten Oper aufgeführt werden[11]. Der von mir vorgesehene Ablauf war in diesem Fall ein Opernlibretto. In ihm waren die musikalischen Beteiligungsmöglichkeiten vorgeschlagen: Teilnehmende können Opernrollen übernehmen, singen oder sprechen, Instrumentalisten Begleitungen untermalen, Intermezzi spielen. Auch Diskussionen waren als »Gesprächsinseln« Teil des Librettos. Dabei ist Improvisieren auch deshalb Forschen, weil jede improvisierte musikalische Äußerung eine Art Selbstversuch ist: Was passiert in der Situation? Was passiert mir in der Situation? Was hat das mit mir zu tun? Woher kann ich das, wo hole ich das her? Jede darüber auch geäußerte Selbstkundgabe ist zudem eine weitere Information für den Verlauf und ergibt Daten für weitere Erkenntnisse zum jeweiligen Thema.

Ein Ausschnitt dieses Konzeptes (nur Teil 1) soll hier gezeigt werden:

Woher können wir das?
Eine investigative Performance, erfunden, getextet und angeleitet von Reinhard Gagel

Ablauf
Im Raum ist ein abgetrennter Raum (abkleben). Das kann ein Viereck in der Mitte sein oder aber eine Bühne vor einer Wand. Die Instrumentenwagen sind sichtbar. Dieser Raum ist ausgeleuchtet.
Alle Teilnehmer nehmen, soweit es geht, auf der Bühne Platz. Sie entscheiden sich, ob sie singen, sprechen oder mit Instrumenten musizieren wollen. Sie

9 | Bisher fanden drei Labore statt, für den Winter 2015/2016 sind zwei weitere geplant.

10 | Es fand am 12.5.2015 von 20 – 22 h im *exploratorium berlin* statt.

11 | Diese Idee folgt der Tradition meiner *Offhandopera*. Sie ist ein Musik-Text-Format, an dem (professionelle und nichtprofessionelle) Musiker und Sänger adhoc teilnehmen und aus dem Stegreif ein Libretto vertonen.

The second laboratory serves here as an example.[13] I created this as a *knowledge opera*. The subject was "Improvising. Where does our ability to do it come from?" The text consists of findings from other areas of musical research and is comprised of statements from neurophysiology, psychology and cultural studies. Over the course of the laboratory, these should be examined through collective improvisation in terms of their relevance to practice and combined with personal experience. The text should take the form of an improvised opera and have the corresponding music to text or music to singing ratio.[14] I intended the events to unfold as would an opera libretto. This suggested the following possibilities for musical participation: participants could take on opera roles, sing or speak, perform instrumental accompaniment or play intermezzos. Discussions also formed part of the libretto, as so-called "conversation islands." As such, improvising is also research, because every improvised expression is also a kind of self-experiment: what happens in the situation? What happens to me in the situation? What does this have to do with me? Where does this come from? Where does my ability to do this come from? Every expressed statement of self also provides further information for the process and generates data for further insights into the respective subject.

An excerpt from this concept is shown here (only part one):

Where does our ability to do this come from?
An investigative performance, devised, written and directed by Reinhard Gagel

Sequence
There is a separate area in the room (marked out). This can be a square in the middle or a stage in front of a wall. The instrument wagons are visible. This room is illuminated. All participants take their places on stage, as far as this is possible. They decide if they want to sing, speak or make music with instruments. They take instruments from the instrument wagons or unpack the instruments they have brought themselves.
Greeting. Explanation of form.

Part 1 Epiphany

A sound field improvisation. Instruments and singers. No motifs, only sounds. No development, dynamic remains as pp, various instruments, singers with vowels and consonants.

13 | It took place on May 12th 2015, 8:00 – 10:00 pm at the exploratorium berlin.
14 | This idea is in the tradition of my *Off-hand opera*. This is a music/text format in which (professional and amateur) musicians and singers participate in an ad hoc way and create an impromptu libretto.

holen sich Instrumente vom Instrumentenwagen oder packen ihre mitgebrachten Instrumente aus.
Begrüßung. Form erklären.

Teil 1 Epiphanie

Eine Klangflächenimprovisation. Instrumente und Sängerinnen. Keine Motivik, nur Sounds. Keine Entwicklung, Lautstärke bleibt pp. Beliebige Instrumente, Sängerinnen mit Vokalen und Konsonanten.

Dahinein: *Sprecher A* (eventuell mehrmals wiederholen):

Wie kommen wir von Ton zu Ton?
Was geschieht in mir beim Erfinden?

Die Klangflächenimprovisation wird fortgesetzt bis zu einem klaren Ende (in pp als fade out).

Stille

Sprecher A: In der ästhetischen Theorie verwendet Gumbrecht für den Moment Epiphanie = »Die Erscheinung des Herrn«, es ist ein Bild für das Plötzliche, Überraschende, Unvorhersehbare, das jede Improvisation auszeichnet.

Stille

Sprecher B: Epiphanie ist ein flüchtiges Phänomen.

Stille

Das Ensemble erfindet Klänge mit der Vorstellung von »flüchtig«.
Währenddessen stehen sechs Sängerinnen auf. Sie sprechen oder singen die folgenden Sätze.
Es wird im Moment entschieden, ob die Texte einfach in die Musik gesprochen werden oder ob eine Arienform entsteht: sechs kurze Arien mit Begleitung durch einzelne Instrumente.

a. Wir wissen nie, wann eine Epiphanie vorkommt…
b. Wenn sie eintritt, wissen wir nicht, welche Form sie annimmt und wie intensiv sie wird…

Speaker A joins in (possibly repeated several times):

How do we get from tone to tone?
What happens inside me when I create?

The sound field improvisation continues until a clear end is reached (pp as a fade out).

Silence

Speaker A: In aesthetic theory Gumbrecht uses "the appearance of the Lord" to indicate the moment of epiphany. It is an image of the spontaneous, surprising, unpredictable that characterizes every improvisation.

Silence

Speaker B: Epiphany is a fleeting phenomenon.

Silence

The ensemble develops sounds, imagining "fleeting."
While this is happening, six singers stand up. They speak or sing the following sentences.
They decide in the moment if the texts are simply spoken to the music, or if an aria form develops: six short arias with accompaniment of instruments.

a. We never know when an epiphany will happen...
b. When it happens, we don't know what form it will take and how intense it will be...
c. As the event happens, it simultaneously undoes itself...
d. One forgets what has happened immediately when one experiences intense moments ...
e. Epiphany is when one "feels that it is coming towards you"...
f. Epiphany appears in the timeframe of the moment...[15]

Conversation Island 1 on epiphany.
How do we connect the terms to our personal experience?

Rules of the conversation islands:
Remain in the tension of the performance.

15 | Ulrich Gumbrecht formulated these criteria: 2004: 133ff.

c. Das Ereignis macht sich selbst ungeschehen, während es in Erscheinung tritt...
d. Man vergisst sofort, während man intensive Momente erlebt, was war...
e. Epiphanie ist, wenn man »das Gefühl hat, es komme auf einen zu«...
f. Epiphanie taucht in der Zeitform des Augenblicks auf...[12]

Gesprächsinsel 1 über Epiphanie.
Wie bringen wir die Begriffe mit unserer eigenen Erfahrung in Verbindung?

Regeln der Gesprächsinseln:
In der Spannung der Aufführung bleiben.
Kurze Statements formulieren (Vorbild eine kurze Melodie).
Pausen lassen.
Reihenfolge rituell: im Kreis. Oder auf Zeichen des Anleiters.
Möglich auch: in einen weiteren markierten räumlichen Bereich gehen (speakers corner).

Der tatsächliche Verlauf des Labors wich von dem gezeigten Gerüst jedoch ab. Es ging von einer bestimmten Anzahl von Teilnehmenden aus: An dem Abend kamen jedoch viel weniger als erwartet – und darüber hinaus keine Sänger –, sodass manche geplanten Rollenverteilungen, auch ein eventuelles Vertonen von Texten nicht funktioniert hätte. Ich habe also den Plan ganz schnell umgedacht. Viele Texte habe ich in Form einer Lecture selbst gesprochen. Die Gesprächsinseln und das gemeinsame Improvisieren konnten auf diese Weise einen breiteren Raum einnehmen, als in dem »Libretto« vorgesehen war.

Allgemeine Charakteristika der Erforschungsprozesse in Projekten

Improvisation erforschen

Ein Projekt – als Lecture Performance, als Labor – bietet die Gelegenheit und den Raum, Probleme und Themen der Improvisation unter einer bestimmten Fragestellung mittels Improvisation zu präsentieren und zu erforschen. Was dann wirklich geschieht, was konkret geäußert wird und wie die musikalischen Prozesse verlaufen, lässt sich nur zum Teil vorplanen. Sie ergeben sich aus dem jeweiligen situativen Zusammenhang (wer und wie viele kommen,

12 | Diese Kriterien hat Hans Ulrich Gumbrecht formuliert: 2004: 133ff.

Formulate short statements (The model is a short melody).
Let pauses happen.
Ritual sequence: in a circle or on cue from the leader.
Also possible: go to another marked-off space (speakers' corner).

The actual course of the laboratory deviated from the framework shown here, which assumed a certain number of participants: that evening there were far fewer participants than expected – and additionally there were no singers – so some of the planned distributions of roles or even a possible singing of the text would not have worked. Therefore, I quickly revised the plan. I spoke many of the texts myself in the form of a lecture. As such, the conversation islands and collective improvising had greater room than was originally conceived in the "libretto".

General Characteristics of the Exploratory Processes in Projects

Researching Improvisation

A project – as a laboratory, as a lecture performance – offers the opportunity and the space to present and explore problems and subjects of improvisation relating to a certain line of questioning using improvisation itself. What really happens, what is concretely expressed, and how musical processes unfold can only be partially planned in advance. These result from the respective situative context (who and how many come, what questions they have, what information and opinions they contribute). A project makes controversial discussions and individual debates possible, but in no way results in a finalized outcome, as a lecture might, for example. This fits with the character of improvisational processes, which have their own forms in each individual situation and are perceivable as event-rich activities with a fleeting sound structure.

Researching by Improvisation

The respective project is an occasion, an exploratory stage and an experimental field in which perceptions and experiences, special opinions and estimations are developed. However, the collective musical improvisation practice is the focal point upon which everything else is based. It forms the stage on which theoretical concepts are proven to be true or not, or gain or lose evidence.

The way the project progresses is also improvised: in spite of some advanced planning (materials, approximate course, sequence of subjects), there are unpredictable reflex outcomes, particular qualities of the music that could possibly

welche Fragestellungen haben sie, welche Informationen und Meinungen bringen sie ein). Ein Projekt ermöglicht kontroverse Diskussionen und sehr individuelle Erörterungen, ergibt aber auf keinen Fall ein abgeschlossenes Resultat, wie es zum Beispiel ein Vortrag bieten würde. Das passt zum Charakter von improvisatorischen Prozessen, die ja in jedem Einzelfall ihre eigene Gestalt haben und als ein flüchtiges Klanggebilde, als eine ereignishafte Handlung wahrnehmbar sind.

Durch Improvisieren erforschen

Das jeweilige Projekt ist Anlass, Forschungsbühne, Experimentierfeld, auf dem durch Wahrnehmungen und Erfahrungen spezielle Meinungen und Einschätzungen zum Thema entwickelt werden. Aber: Die gemeinsame musikalische improvisatorische Praxis ist der Kern, um den sich alles andere ansiedelt. Sie bildet die Bühne, auf der sich theoretische Thesen bewahrheiten, Evidenz bekommen, oder eben nicht.

Auch in seinem Ablauf ist das Projekt improvisiert: Trotz einer gewissen Vorplanung (Materialien, ungefähre Abläufe, Reihenfolge der Themen) gibt es unvorhersehbare Reflexionsergebnisse, besondere Qualitäten der Musik, die eventuell dazu zwingen, in neue Richtungen jenseits des Konzeptes zu denken und Reihenfolgen und Abläufe zu ändern.

Beteiligung

Die gezeigten Lecture Performances und das Labor haben ein unterschiedliches Verhältnis zur Öffentlichkeit. Sowohl die Bibliothekseröffnung als auch die Quo Vadis Performance sind von einem erfahrenen Team konzipiert und aufgeführt worden. Zuschauer und Zuhörer hingegen kamen unplanbar. Sind es viele oder wenige? Sind sie bereit, sich zu beteiligen? Das Labor wird von mir in der Art einer Offenen Bühne[13] konzipiert: Ich heiße alle willkommen und lade sie ein, sich zu beteiligen, also sowohl mit zu diskutieren als auch mit zu improvisieren. Wer kommt mit welchen Interessen? Welche Fähigkeiten können sie einbringen? Der Verlauf hängt sehr viel mehr von Zufälligkeiten ab (siehe oben das Beispiel mit den unerwartet wenigen Teilnehmenden), beteiligt aber umfassender und identifiziert mehr, weil ja der Verlauf nur von den Anwesenden bestimmt wird.

13 | *Offene Bühnen* sind Formate am *exploratorium berlin*, wo Musiker adhoc mit anderen zusammen spielen können. Sie finden mehrmals monatlich in unterschiedlichen Spezialausrichtungen statt (als *Offene Bühne*, als *Offene Bühne Musik & Poesie*, als *Offene Bühne Musik & Bewegung*, als *Offhandopera*).

force a reevaluation in terms of new directions. These depart from the concept and can change sequences and processes.

Participation

The lecture performances and laboratory described here have differing relationships to the public. Both the library opening and the *Quo Vadis* performance were conceived and performed by an experienced team. The audience and listeners were, by contrast, unpredictable: are there too many or too few of them? Are they prepared to participate? I conceived the laboratory as a kind of open stage.[16] I welcome all who come and invite them to participate, both to improvise and to discuss. Who comes and what interests do they have? What abilities can they contribute? The process is far more dependent on coincidences (see the example above with fewer participants than expected) and is more inclusive and reveals more because the process is determined solely by the participants.

Musicians as experts of themselves – experts on improvisation

The participants come with different mindsets. They have their own knowledge, experience, philosophies and opinions about improvisation. These should flow into the project. Since improvising is a very personal creative ability, understanding and exploring such individual information takes on great significance. In a sense, the participants are everyday experts on improvisation.

Exploring as performance. Open stage+

Over the course of an artistic-scientific project, the participants should be given the possibility to find paths between playing and thinking by improvising both musically and with texts. Aesthetic perception and artistic process become a central point of reflection. We therefore perceive the improvising musician as a reflecting artist in a particular way: their criteria for an artistic performance are transferred to a field of thought and discovery which is not primarily musical. A relationship between music and word occurs, in which art and reflection approach each other and interfuse in performative thought and thinking performance. Improvising takes place in an immersed mode of enhanced perception (hearing-listening) and of mutual attentiveness.

---

16 | *Open stages* are formats at the *exploratorium berlin* where musicians can play in an ad hoc way with others. They take place several times a month with different focus areas (such as *open stage, open stage music and poetry, open stage music and movement* and *Off-hand opera*).

Musiker als Experten ihrer selbst – Experten der Improvisation

Die Teilnehmenden kommen mit unterschiedlichen Voraussetzungen. Sie haben eigene Kenntnisse, Erfahrungen, Philosophien und Meinungen über Improvisation. Diese sollen in das Projekt einfließen. Da Improvisieren eine sehr persönliche Gestaltungsfähigkeit ist, kommt für das Verstehen und Forschen solchen individuellen »Daten« eine große Bedeutung zu. Die Teilnehmenden sind gewissermaßen Alltagsexperten der Improvisation.

Forschen als Performance. Offene Bühne+

Im Verlauf eines künstlerisch-wissenschaftlichen Projektes soll ermöglicht werden, dass die Teilnehmenden aktiv Wege zwischen Denken und Spielen finden, indem sie musikalisch und textlich improvisieren. Ästhetische Wahrnehmung und künstlerische Gestaltung werden zu einem wesentlichen Punkt der Reflexion. Damit nehmen wir auch den improvisierenden Musiker als reflektierenden Künstler auf eine besondere Weise wahr: Seine Kriterien für eine künstlerische Performance werden übertragen auf ein zunächst einmal nicht-musikalisches Denk- und Erkenntnisfeld. Es entsteht ein Musik-Wort-verhältnis, in dem Kunst und Reflektion einander näher kommen und durchdringen: im performenden Denken und im denkenden Performen. Das Improvisieren findet im Modus der Versenkung, der gesteigerten Wahrnehmung und der gegenseitigen Achtsamkeit statt.

Diskussionen als Teil der Performance, Gesprächsinseln

Diskussionen spielen eine wichtige Rolle. Sie schaffen die konkrete Auseinandersetzung zwischen den Teilnehmenden und erzeugen neue Informationen zum Gegenstand (individuelle Meinungen, Gelesenes, eigene Philosophien). Diskussionen zwischen Künstlern (als spezialisierte Experten), Hörern (als Hörexperten), Spielern (als Spielexperten) im Interesse des gemeinsamen Projektes und auf Augenhöhe zu ermöglichen, ist wesentliches Ziel eines Projektes. Sie sind zum Teil ritualisiert (im Libretto war vorgesehen, dass eine Reihenfolge und ein Sprechgestus eingehalten werden sollte) oder weitaus öfter offene Gespräche, die ich als Moderator anleite.

Moderation und Anleitung

Zu dem jeweiligen Projekt wird eingeladen mit einer Fragestellung und einem bestimmten Materialfundus und Setting (Beispiel: das oben behandelte Labor »Woher können wir das«?). Je nach Format habe ich unterschiedliche Rollen. Generell vertrete ich die Position dessen, der Informationen von außen ein-

Discussions as part of the performance, conversation islands

Discussions play an important role. They create concrete confrontation between participants and bring new information to the subject (individual opinions, things that have been read, personal philosophies). One primary goal of a project is to facilitate discussions between artists (as specialized experts), listeners (as listening experts), and players (as experts in playing) in the interest of a mutual project and on an equal footing. These are partially ritualized (they follow a sequence and maintain the speech gestures which have been laid out in the libretto) or more often, they are simply open discussions that I facilitate.

Facilitating and guiding

An invitation to the respective project sets out the line of questioning, the specific material pool and the setting (for example the above laboratory "Where does our ability to do this come from?") take on various roles depending on the format. In general, I adopt the position of the person who contributes information from the outside, who facilitates the discussion, delivers short lectures on the subject, poses questions, introduces provocative texts, and contributes practice and performance suggestions that arise out of the line of questioning. This role also includes the function of maintaining the musical and performative tension of the performance project.

Texts

The project is based on a text or collection of texts that I (or other participants) gather regarding a specific subject, and which I then transform into an open text. For example, when collecting texts, I also think about possible performative aspects: spoken/sung by many or few, with instruments or a cappella (see *The Opera of Knowledge* or *Theory on Stage*). I think in terms of processes and segments that are with or without music, I organize solos and small ensembles. By doing so, I enable participation (by providing roles, accompaniment, impulses, variety) and I encourage closeness (by focusing sound qualities, inspiring motifs and so on).

Documentation and sustainability

Each project has its own value in terms of experience, concentration, its presence in the moment – meaning what happens – and what draws one in. However, it also has a process; a form is created, then, within this, come insights, statements, musical structures and performative elements that distinguish the

bringt, moderiert, kurze Lectures zu dem Thema, Fragen, provozierende Texte und aus der Fragestellung abgeleitete Übungs- und Spielvorschläge einbringt. Die Rolle beinhaltet auch die Funktion, die musikalische und performative Spannung eines Performanceprojektes aufrecht zu erhalten.

Texte

Das Projekt baut auf einem Text – beziehungsweise einem Vortragskonvolut – auf, den oder das ich (oder andere Teilnehmende) zu einem bestimmten Thema sammle und welchen/welches ich dann in einen offenen Text umwandle. Zum Beispiel denke ich beim Zusammenstellen von Texten auch eventuelle performative Seiten mit: als von vielen oder wenigen gesungen/gesprochen, mit Instrumenten oder a capella (siehe Beispiele *Wissensoper* beziehungsweise *theory on stage*). Ich denke in Abläufen und Teilen, die mit und ohne Musik sind, ich organisiere Soli und kleine Ensemblepartien. Damit sorge ich auf der einen Seite für Beteiligung (ich biete Rollen, Begleitung, Impulse, Abwechslung) und auf der anderen Seite für Nähe (ich musikalisiere, ich animiere zu Motiven, Klängen und so weiter).

Dokumentation und Nachhaltigkeit

Jedes Projekt hat einen Selbstwert des Erlebens, der Konzentration, der Präsenz dessen, was gerade geschieht und was einen hineinzieht. Außerdem hat es einen Verlauf und eine ästhetische Form geschaffen, dann ist es zu Einsichten, Statements, musikalischen Strukturen, performativen Elementen gekommen. Das Projekt zeichnet sich durch die Prozesshaftigkeit ebenso aus wie durch das konkrete praktische Resultat, das es erbringt. Das kann zum Beispiel ein Videomitschnitt sein, der den Gesamtverlauf als künstlerisches Ereignis dokumentiert und zum erneuten Betrachten einlädt.

Erlebnis statt Didaktik

Letztlich soll es auch um das Erlebnis von Kunst gehen, es handelt sich also nicht um eine neue Vermittlungs-Didaktik, denn diese »...weiß nicht, will es nicht wissen, wie die geheimnisvolle Erschütterung durch sensible Wahrnehmung zuwege kommt, die das Ereignis Kunst verheißt« (Selle 1992: 22). Das Projekt kann in der gezeigten Anlage und improvisierten Durchführung diese Erschütterung, die Präsenz, die Versenkung, die Sensibilität der Wahrnehmung mit dem Denken, Sprechen und Formulieren zusammenbringen.

particular project. The project is characterized by the process, as well as by the concrete practical result that it produces. This could be a video for example, which documents the entire process of the artistic event and that invites renewed observation.

Experience instead of didactics

Ultimately, it should also be about experiencing art. It is not about new didactics, as these : "...weiß nicht, will es nicht wissen, wie die geheimnisvolle Erschütterung durch sensible Wahrnehmung zuwege kommt, die das Ereignis Kunst verheißt"[17] (Selle 1992: 22). The project in the form in which it is described here, and its improvised realization, can bring together this shock, the presence, the immersion, the sensibility of perception with thinking, speaking and formulating.

Conclusion

With this concept and the resulting project forms, I am looking for a way which is not about making music or reading books, nor a theory or a sound, but a way where a third thing results; where the participants find themselves in the "Hochspannung einer Kunstwerkerwartung"[18] (Selle 1992: 17), and, in addition, are incited by the performative dynamic that creates a dense presence. What results is sense. Sense not only meaning *sens(e)-ible*, that from which one can grow intellectually, but also *sens(e)-sual* in the moment, when, as the philosopher Georg Picht put it, "die Sinne denken"[19] (Picht 1986: 336). With this I formulate a definition of research where the discoveries lie in the experience of the meaningfulness of a moment of reconciliation between art and theory, no matter how fleeting this moment may be. The person leaving a laboratory was not offered a piece, or a lecture, or a reading – no, they were part of a coming together, in the middle of which is: "...ein einander Näherkommen mit dem Zweck des Hereinholens gemeinsamer Möglichkeiten"[20] (Flusser 1995: 213). Identifying possibilities through this coming together, and through this rese-

---

17 | "... do not know, do not want to know, how the mysterious shock is brought about by sensitive perception – this is the phenomenon that art promises" (Translation: Louise & Phil Loxton, GB-Wales).

18 | "high voltage of the expectation of art" (Translation Louise & Phil Loxton, GB-Wales).

19 | "the senses think" (Translation Louise & Phil Loxton, GB-Wales).

20 | "...a coming closer to each other with the intention of bringing about mutual possibilities" (Translation Louise & Phil Loxton, GB-Wales).

Fazit

Mit diesem Konzept und den sich daraus ergebenden Projektformen suche ich einen Weg, auf dem nicht entweder Bücher gelesen und diskutiert oder Musik gemacht wird, in der nicht eine Theorie oder ein Klang, sondern ein Drittes entsteht; in dem sich die Teilnehmenden in der »Hochspannung einer Kunstwerkerwartung« (Selle 1992: 17) befinden, durch performative Dynamik animiert, die eine dichte Präsenz erzeugen. Was dabei entsteht, ist Sinn. Dabei ist Sinn nicht nur als *Sinn-volles*, das einen intellektuell weitergebracht hat, zu sehen, sondern ebenfalls als das *Sinn-liche* im Moment, dann, wenn »die Sinne denken«, wie der Philosoph Georg Picht es formuliert hat (Picht 1986: 336). Damit formuliere ich einen Forschungsbegriff, dessen Erkenntnis im Erleben der Sinnhaftigkeit eines zwar flüchtigen, aber zwischen Kunst und Theorie ausgesöhnten Momentes liegt. Wer aus einem Labor hinaustritt, hat kein Werk, keinen Vortrag, keine Vorlesung geboten bekommen, nein, er war Teil einer Annäherung und mittendrin: »...ein einander Näherkommen mit dem Zweck des Hereinholens gemeinsamer Möglichkeiten« (Flusser 1995: 213). Möglichkeiten zu eruieren im gemeinsamen Näherkommen, im Forschen Vieler[14], weist einen möglichen Weg der Forschung. Improvisation ist dort der Gegenstand der Erforschung und die Methode selbst.

Ausblick

Das künstlerisch-wissenschaftliche Projekt lässt sich noch weiterdenken. Die bisher realisierten nur kurzen Projektdauern könnten verlängert werden, was eine längere Beschäftigung mit Themen ermöglichen würde. Die Intervalle, in denen zum Beispiel das Labor bisher stattfindet, könnten verkürzt, Themen über mehrere Monate weiter verfolgt werden. Die Labore könnten an anderen Orten und zu anderen Gelegenheiten gezeigt werden: statt im *exploratorium berlin* auch in Universitäten[15], in Schulen, in anderen Improvisationseinrichtungen und Konzertorten. Dabei würden auch andere Zielgruppen erreicht. Zudem wäre denkbar, dass sich ein Team bildet, das die gezeigte Wissensoper

14 | Sibylle Peters (2013) hat unter diesem Titel ein Buch veröffentlicht, in dem kollektive Forschungen beschrieben und reflektiert werden.

15 | In meiner Lehrtätigkeit an der Universität für Musik und darstellende Kunst Wien habe ich mit meinen Studenten ein Format realisiert, in dem ein ständiger Wechsel von improvisatorischer Praxis, Vorträgen und gemeinsamer Diskussion zum Thema *Improvisieren lernen und lehren* stattfindet. Dies findet als improvisiertes Labor statt: Es gibt einen ungefähren Ablaufplan, der sich aber flexibel je nach in der Veranstaltung aufgeworfenen Fragestellungen auch ändern kann.

arch, which is being done by many people,[21] presents a possible way forward for future research. Improvisation is the subject of research here as well as the method itself.

Outlook

The artistic-scientific project could be developed further. The short time-spans of the projects carried out to date could be extended, enabling a longer engagement with the subjects. The intervals at which the laboratory takes place could, for example, be shortened and subjects pursued over the course of several months. The laboratories could be shown at other locations and in other contexts: instead of just at the *exploratorium berlin*, also at universities,[22] schools, and other improvisation spaces and concert venues. Other target groups could be reached this way. It is also conceivable that a team could be put together that performs *The Opera of Knowledge* again and again, and includes others in the performance and the discussion. Such long-term developments and diverse constellations allow for the collection of a multitude of individual statements which could then be used as data. These statements, for example, the question "Where does our ability to do this come from?" could be relevant to research and could then be analyzed. Furthermore, projects create a unity of subject and methods, they include others, and create, both in terms of political culture and scientific theory, a practice which runs counter to current trends in cultural and pedagogical practice, both of which currently exist in their own separate areas. So it is possible to think beyond what has been touched upon here: the project as an interface between the artistic event, and the place of research and reflection. To me this seems to hold great promise.

Translation into English: Louise & Phil Loxton, GB-Wales

21 | Ed. Sibylle Peters (2013) published a book with this title, in which collective research is described and reflected upon.

22 | As a teacher at the University of Music and Performing Arts, Vienna, I put together a format with my students in which a constant shift takes places between improvisational practice, lectures, and collective discussion on the subject of teaching and learning improvising. This occurs as an improvised laboratory: There is an approximate formal plan that can be adjusted depending on what questions come up during the event.

immer neu aufführt und andere an der Aufführung und Diskussion beteiligt. Mit solchen langfristigen Verläufen und verschiedenartigen Konstellationen lässt sich eine Vielzahl von individuellen Äußerungen als Daten sammeln, die – zum Beispiel für die gezeigte Frage »woher können wir das« – auch forschungsrelevant werden könnten. Dieses könnte dann in Dokumentationen ausgewertet werden. Projekte ermöglichen zudem eine Einheit von Gegenstand und Methode, beteiligen andere, und bilden sowohl kulturpolitisch als auch wissenschaftstheoretisch eine quer verlaufende Praxis zu kulturell und pädagogisch Gängigem, das vor allem aus der Trennung in separate Bereiche besteht. Es lässt sich also weiterdenken, was hier angerissen wurde: Das Projekt als Verbindung von Kunstereignis, Recherche- und Reflexionsort scheint mir sehr vielversprechend.

LITERATUR/REFERENCES

Cage, John (1973): Silence. Middletown: Wesley University Books. (Deutsch: (1995): Silence. Frankfurt am Main: Edition Suhrkamp).

Dewey, John (1910): How we think. Boston D.C.: Heath & Co. (Deutsch: (1951): Wie wir denken. Zürich: Morgarten Verlag).

Dewey, John (1937): Logic: The Theory of Inquiry. New York: Holt, Rinehart and Winston. (Deutsch: (2008): Logik. Die Theorie der Forschung. Frankfurt am Main: Suhrkamp Verlag).

Flusser, Vilém, (1995): Gesten. Versuch einer Phänomenologie. Frankfurt am Main: Fischer Verlag.

Gumbrecht, Hans Ulrich (2004): Diesseits der Hermeneutik. Frankfurt am Main: Edition Suhrkamp.

Mersch, Dieter; Ott, Michaela (2007): Kunst und Wissenschaft. München: Fink Verlag.

Peters, Sibylle (2011): Der Vortrag als Performance. Bielefeld: transcript Verlag.

Peters, Sibylle (Hrsg./Ed.) (2013): Das Forschen Vieler. Bielefeld: transcript Verlag.

Picht, Georg (1986): Kunst und Mythos. Stuttgart: Klett Cotta.

Selle, Gert (1992): Das ästhetische Projekt: Plädoyer für eine kunstnahe Praxis in der Weiterbildung und Schule. Unna: LDK Verlag.

Intermezzo 10

MS: Welche Rolle spielt die Suche nach Neuem in der improvisierten Musik?

BP: Ich habe den Eindruck, dass der ehrlich performende Musiker, wenn er für Leute spielt, über eine Menge angesammeltes Material verfügt, das er kennt und umsetzen kann. Aber wenn er ehrlich ist, dann liegt sein Interesse nicht dort, denn diese Sachen sind nicht mehr spannend. Stattdessen sind für den Musiker die Teile der Performance spannend, die noch unbekannt »da draußen« sind, die vage sind und die er nicht genau festmachen kann. Diese Dinge existieren trotzdem, man kann sie irgendwie hören. Man hat sie im Kopf, im Ohr, im inneren Gehör, im Körper, aber umsetzen kann man sie nicht. Ausschau nach neuen Klängen zu halten, bedeutet deswegen für mich, dass sie schon da sind, und es ist meine Hauptaufgabe, an sie zu gelangen, sie zu ordnen und tiefer in ihr Wesen einzusteigen.

EP: Ich schlage vor, dass wir damit noch einen Schritt weiter gehen. Wir sollten uns nicht zu sehr auf die Klänge konzentrieren oder auch darauf, was für einen Eindruck sie wohl auf das Publikum machen. Klänge werden zum Produkt – man könnte auch sagen »zum Ausdruck« – der Suche. Die Suche schließt dabei jedoch jede Vorstellung davon aus, was »ein guter« Klang sein könnte. Darüber hinaus hat die Person, die auf der authentischen musikalischen Suche ist, keine Vorahnung davon, was der Klang sein oder werden soll. Beim Suchen und Finden geht es genau darum, dass man keine Vorstellung davon hat, »was es da draußen so gibt«, und das Vergnügen liegt natürlich genau darin, diese neue Sache zu finden. Ironischerweise bedarf dieser Vorschlag sehr strenger Disziplin, ist aber auch ein möglicher Weg in Richtung Erhabenheit.

INTERMEZZO 10

MS: How important is the search for the unknown in improvised music?

BP: I feel that the honest performing musician, when playing for people, has all this accumulated material that he knows and he can play. But if he is honest, he is not interested in playing what he knows because it's not exciting anymore. What is exciting in a performance for the player is the stuff that is unknown out there, that is vague, of which you don't know exactly what it is. But it's there. You can hear it, kind of. It's in your mind. It's in your ear, it's in your inner hearing, it's in your body, but you can't quite pin it down. And so looking for new sounds means to me that they are already there, and it's a major part of my job to be able to get to them and put them in order and to get deeper into what they really are.

EP: I am suggesting we take things a stage further. Let us not be too focused on the sounds or how we perceive they might affect an audience. Sounds become the product – "the expression" if you wish – of the search. However, the search precludes any sense of what "a good" sound might be. Further, the authentic musical searcher does not have a presentiment of what the sound ought to be or might become. The point about searching and finding is that you have no idea "what is out there", and the joy is, of course, finding this new thing. Ironically, this proposal demands very severe discipline, but it is also a possible route to sublimity.

BP: How do you search?

BP: Wie suchst du denn?

EP: Vielleicht benötigen wir reduktives Werkzeug, um die Vorgehensweise zu erfassen. Meiner Meinung nach gelten die folgenden analytischen Zwillings-Imperative:

1. Suchen ohne die Erwartung, etwas zu finden. Das schließt die Bereitschaft ein, über normale Musikgeschichte oder -bräuche hinauszuschauen. Die Suchenden sollten in jeder Art Material nach Klängen suchen und dabei über die Technologie herkömmlicher Musikinstrumente hinausgehen. Diese Vorgehensweise erfordert es, die Materialien ständig auf ihr Potential für die Klangproduktion hin zu untersuchen, das sich auf einem Makrolevel wie auch auf einer mikroskopischen Ebene befinden könnte. Sehen wir uns einige Beispiele an:

   a) durch Atem eine Trommel bearbeiten;
   b) ständig nach Ergebnisvariationen suchen, die entstehen, indem Bogendruck und Streichwinkel verändert werden. Eine wunderbare Beschreibung der Möglichkeiten, die dieser Herangehensweise innewohnen, findet sich in Schilderungen von antiker chinesischer Musikproduktion auf einem Instrument, das »The extinct great Lute« (Die verschwundene große Laute) genannt wird. Es handelt sich um einen horizontalen Psalter mit 25 Seidensaiten. Dazu nur ein Beispiel: das als Yin bezeichnete Vibrato.

Ein Finger der linken Hand bewegt sich schnell über dem gekennzeichneten Punkt auf und ab. »Eine kalte Zikade beklagt den ankommenden Herbst«. Das klagende, schwingende Summen der Zikaden soll dabei imitiert werden. Von diesem Yin gibt es mehr als zehn Spielarten. Es gibt das Chhang-Yin, ein langgezogenes Vibrato, das an den »Schrei einer den Regen ankündigenden Taube« erinnern

EP: Maybe we have to use reductive tools to grasp the practice. To my mind, the following twin-analytical imperatives are in place:

1. Searching without an expectation of finding anything. This means being prepared to look beyond the normal history or customs of music. The searcher should look for sounds in any material and go beyond the technology of conventional musical instruments. This practice demands constant observation of the materials for their sound-making potential. This could be at a macro- or microscopic level. Take a few examples:

    a) applying breath to a drum.
    b) constantly looking for variations of results to be gained by adjusting bow pressure and angle of trajectory. A beautiful description of the possibilities inherent in this approach can be found in accounts of ancient Chinese music-making on what is described as "The extinct great lute" – a horizontal psaltery with twenty-five silk strings, [and reviewing] one example only, the vibrato termed yin.

A finger of the left hand moves quickly up and down over the spot indicated. "A cold cicada bemoans the coming of autumn." The plaintive, rocking drone of the cicadas should be imitated. Of this yin there exist more than ten varieties. There is the chhang-yin, a drawn-out vibrato, which should recall "the cry of a dove announcing rain"; the hsi-yin, a thin vibrato, which should make one think of "confidential whispering"; the yu-yin or swinging vibrato, which should evoke the image of "fallen blossoms floating down with the stream", et cetera. Remarkable is the ting-yin, where the vacillating movement of the finger should be so subtle as to be hardly noticeable. Some handbooks say that one should not move the finger at

soll; das Hsi-Yin, ein dünnes Vibrato, das an »vertrauliches Geflüster« denken lassen soll; das Yu-Yin, oder auch schwingendes Vibrato, das das Bild von »mit dem Strom abwärts fließenden, gefallenen Blüten« hervorrufen soll, et cetera. Bemerkenswert ist auch das Ting-Yin, wobei die schwingende Bewegung des Fingers so subtil sein soll, dass sie kaum wahrnehmbar ist. In einigen Handbüchern steht, dass man den Finger überhaupt nicht bewegen soll, sondern dass das Timbre stattdessen durch das Pulsieren des Blutes in der Fingerspitze beeinflusst werden soll, indem die Saite ein wenig vollständiger und stärker als sonst auf das Griffbrett gedrückt wird.[1]

Wenn wir erst über diese gründliche Suche nach Varianz im Vibrato gelesen haben, haben sich die Ergebnisse natürlich bereits in kulturellen Bildern verfestigt. Dennoch eröffnet sich darin eine Vorstellung davon, was möglich sein könnte. Und meine eigene Erfahrung legt nahe, dass es immer neue (wenn auch mikroskopische) Dinge gibt, die gefunden werden können. Die Suche wird zu Kunst, nicht die daraus resultierenden Klänge.

2. Der zweite dieser Zwillings-Imperative könnte (wenn auch unter Vorbehalt) in dem Begriff »Empathie« verankert werden. Denn während all dies, oben aufgezählte, Suchen vonstatten geht, versucht der Beteiligte außerdem auf das zuzugreifen, was darum herum vorgeht. In unserem Fall sind das besonders die anderen beteiligten Musiker. Von dem Eindruck kollektiver Teilnahme abgesehen – dem gemeinsamen Musizieren – bieten unsere Mitmusizierenden uns auch eine großartige Quelle von möglicherweise inspirierendem Tonmaterial, technischen und emotionalen Informationen.

---

1 | Needham, Joseph (1977): »Sound Acoustic«, Science & Civilisation in China, Vol. IV:1, Cambrigde: Cambridge University Press, S. 132.

all, but let the timbre be influenced by the pulsation of the blood in the fingertip, pressing the string down on the board a little more fully and heavily than usual.[1] Of course, by the time we come to read about this exhaustive search for variety in vibrato, the results have hardened into cultural images. However, it reveals a sense of what may be possible. And, my own experience suggests that no matter how long you have been working in this way, there are always new (even if microscopic) things to be found. It is the search that becomes the art not the resultant sounds.

2. The second of the twin imperatives could be enshrined (if conditionally) in the term "empathy". For while all the searching recounted above is going on, the participator is also trying to attend to what is going on around. Especially, in our case, the other participating musicians. However, apart from a sense of collective participation – making music together – our fellow musicians also offer us a great source of potentially inspiring audio, technical and emotional information.

These two analytical propositions are especially creative when entwined. Each has an impact upon the other. The difficulty in this practice is giving the two elements equal and simultaneous attention. I notice, success in acquiring this dual facility is an intermittent human condition.

Matthias Schwabe (MS), Barre Phillips (BP) and Edwin Prévost (EP)
in a public talk, May 2014

---

1 | Needham, Joseph (1977): "Sound Acoustic", Science & Civilisation in China, Vol. IV:1, Cambrigde: Cambridge University Press, p. 132.

Diese beiden analytischen Vorschläge sind besonders in Kombination kreativ. Jeder hat Einfluss auf den anderen. Die Schwierigkeit dieser Vorgehensweise besteht darin, den beiden Elementen gleichwertige und gleichzeitige Aufmerksamkeit zu widmen. Diese doppelte Fähigkeit erfolgreich zu erlangen, ist nach meiner Erfahrung nur mit Unterbrechungen möglich.

Matthias Schwabe (MS), Barre Phillips (BP) und Edwin Prévost (EP)
im Podiumsgespräch, Mai 2014

Übersetzung aus dem Englischen: Solveig Raschpichler, Berlin

EXPLORATORIUM Berlin 1.6.2014

OFFENE BÜHNE

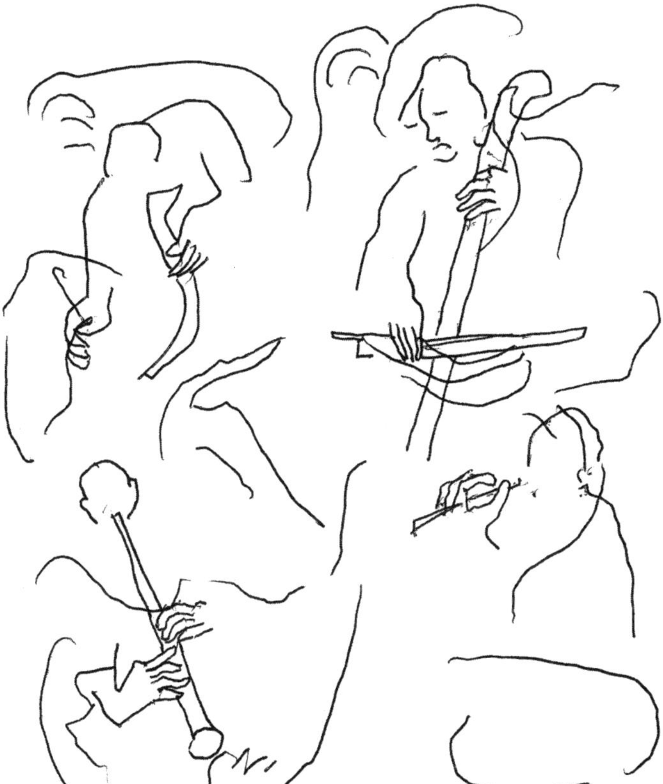

EXPLORATORIUM Berlin 29-5 014

~~Begrüßung~~ Eröffnung Matthias Schwabe

Wir haben tolle Leute eingeladen!

Spiel als Abenteuer

Diverses als Anleitung zum Symposion

Exploring Improvisation – Exploring Music | Exploring Improvisation – Exploring Music

Künstlerische Erkundungen im improvisatorischen Alltag |
Artistic investigation as part of the everday life of improvisation

---

Matthias Schwabe

Explorieren, das bedeutet erforschen, untersuchen, erkunden, ergründen, ermitteln, ausloten. Jenseits seiner Verwendung im wissenschaftlichen Kontext beschreibt dieser Begriff auch eine Haltung, die das alltägliche Tun charakterisieren kann: genau wahrnehmen, sich nicht auf Gewohntes verlassen, den Dingen immer wieder neu auf den Grund gehen, bereit sein, neue Wege einzuschlagen und sich dem Ungewissen auszusetzen, offen sein für neue Erkenntnisse.

Genau darum geht es in diesem Text: um das Explorieren im musikalischen »improvisatorischen Alltag«, ein Erkunden, das einerseits dem Improvisieren von Natur aus eigen ist und das wir andererseits zur Positionsbestimmung und zur immer wieder erneuten Hinterfragung unseres Tuns benötigen.

In der improvisatorischen Praxis sind wir kontinuierlich mit Fragestellungen konfrontiert, die unser forschendes Interesse einfordern. Dafür bedarf es geeigneter explorativer Strategien und Settings. Diese Fragestellungen, Strategien und Settings des improvisatorischen Alltags möchte ich beispielhaft an meiner Arbeit im *exploratorium berlin* beschreiben. Als Zentrum für improvisierte Musik und kreative Musikpädagogik hat es sich das Explorieren nicht nur zum Programm gemacht, sondern auch einen Namen gewählt, der diesem Thema eine besonders wichtige Rolle zuweist. Die Auseinandersetzung mit Improvisation erfolgt hier auf breiter Ebene. Entsprechend findet sich Exploration

- als künstlerischer Ansatz, der die gesamte Tätigkeit durchzieht
- als pädagogischer Ansatz
- in der Auseinandersetzung mit (externer) Theorie und Forschung
- im Entwickeln spezieller explorativer Veranstaltungsformate

1. Exploration als künstlerischer Ansatz: Settings und Fragestellungen

a) Improvisation als künstlerischer »Versuchsaufbau«

Exploration und Improvisation sind eng miteinander verknüpft. Beim Improvisieren geht es stets um das spontane Ausloten der Möglichkeiten und um das (Er-)Finden von Unvorhergesehenem (lat.: improvisus), ganz gleich, ob innerhalb festgelegter überlieferter Regeln, beispielsweise im Umgang mit einem Fugenthema oder einem indischen Raga, oder in einem ganz freien Kontext.

Im *exploratorium* nimmt die sogenannte »Freie Improvisation« eine zentrale Rolle ein, frei im Sinne eines Sich-frei-Machens von traditionellen Regelwerken. Das hat künstlerische und pädagogische Gründe. Zu den pädagogischen

Exploring means researching, examining, investigating, feeling, touching, determining, fathoming. Aside from its use in the scholarly context, this term also describes an attitude that can characterize a way of acting in everyday life: to perceive something in precise detail, not to rely on what we are accustomed to, to revisit things in a new way again and again at their very root, to be prepared to go in new directions, to be open to the unknown and to new perceptions. This is the theme of this text: to explore "the everyday life of improvisation in music", to conduct an investigation that on the one hand is inherent to the nature of improvisation and which on the other requires us to define our position and to repeatedly question our behavior anew.

In improvisatory practice we are continuously confronted with lines of questioning that demand we take an exploratory interest in them. This requires appropriate explorative strategies and settings. I would like to describe these lines of questioning, strategies, and the settings of the everyday life of improvisation using my work at the *exploratorium berlin* as an example. As a center for improvised music and creative music education, it has not only made exploring its main focus, but has also chosen a name that emphasizes the fact that this subject plays a particularly significant role. The engagement with improvisation takes place on a broader scale here. To this end, we find exploration

- as an artistic approach, which pervades all activity
- as a pedagogical approach
- in the engagement with (external) theory and research
- in the development of special explorative presentation formats

1. Exploration as an Artistic Approach: Settings and Lines of Questioning

a) Improvisation as an artistic "experimental construction"

Exploration and improvisation are closely connected. Improvisation is about a constant feeling and working out of possibilities and discovering (creating) the unanticipated (lat: improvisus), regardless of whether it is within the framework of fixed rules of tradition – for example, the treatment of a fugal subject or an Indian raga – or in a completely free context.

At the *exploratorium*, so-called "free improvisation" plays a central role; free in the sense of freeing one's self from traditional sets of rules. This is based on artistic and pedagogical reasons. I will elaborate further on the pedagogical reasons later. Regarding the artistic perspective, free improvisation is, for us, a special approach in the further development of contemporary music, as well as other art forms.

Gründen später. In künstlerischer Hinsicht ist Freie Improvisation für uns ein besonderer Ansatz zur Weiterentwicklung aktueller beziehungsweise zeitgenössischer Musik wie auch anderer Künste.

Auf der Suche nach einer aktuellen beziehungsweise sich immer wieder selbst aktualisierenden Musiksprache arbeitet die Freie Improvisation mit einer Art alternativem »Forschungs-Setting«, das auf ganz spezielle »kreative Triebfedern« setzt, nämlich

- kollektive Kreativität und deren synergetisches Potential (im Falle der Ensemble-Improvisation)
- die intensive Wahrnehmung einer Gesamtsituation
- die daraus resultierende Logik des Augenblicks
- das intuitive Potential der Akteure
- motorische und taktile Impulse im experimentellen Umgang mit den Klangerzeugern
- Flow-Phänomene[1]

Dies ist vergleichbar mit Strömungen in der Bildenden Kunst des 20. Jahrhunderts, die beispielsweise auf Spontaneität oder das Primat des Unbewussten setzten und so zu ganz eigenen Ergebnissen kamen. Inwieweit die genannten Faktoren andere »Forschungs-Ergebnisse« generieren als kompositorische Ansätze, welcher Art die Unterschiede sind, ob komponierte und improvisierte Resultate auch ununterscheidbar sein können und wenn ja, unter welchen Bedingungen, wäre ein lohnendes Thema musikwissenschaftlicher Forschung.

b) Themen künstlerischer Erkundung

Abgesehen von dieser ganz grundsätzlichen Interpretation von Improvisation als »Forschungs-Setting« haben sich in der Arbeit des *exploratorium* bestimmte Themen und Fragestellungen heraus kristallisiert, die teils die alltägliche Arbeit prägen, teils in besonderen Projekten vertieft und erkundet wurden:

- Die »Erkundung des Augenblicks«
- Raum als künstlerische Inspirationsquelle
- »Klangforschung«: Instrumente und Materialien als künstlerische Dialogpartner

1 | Mit Flow wird ein von Mihály Csíkszentmihályi beschriebener Zustand bezeichnet, in welchem ein Mensch vollständig in seinem Tun aufgeht (Csíkszentmihályi 2000). In improvisierter Musik gibt es ein besonderes Flow-Phänomen, das mit »es spielt« bezeichnet wird. Dabei scheint kein eigener Impuls nötig zu sein und die Musik sich wie von alleine zu entwickeln.

In the search for a current, or constantly self-renewing musical language, free improvisation works with a kind of alternative "research setting" based on very special "creative driving forces", namely

- collective creativity and its synergetic potential (in the case of ensemble improvisation)
- the intense perception of a whole situation
- the resulting logic of the moment
- the intuitive potential of the actors
- motoric and tactile impulses during the experimental engagement with the sound-producing elements
- flow phenomena[1]

This is comparable to trends in the visual arts of the 20th century which, for example, relied on spontaneity or the primacy of the subconscious and in doing so, came up with their own very individual results. To what extent the above-mentioned factors generate different "study results" compared to compositional approaches, what kinds of differences are generated, whether composed and improvised results can be indistinguishable from one another, and if so, under what conditions, would all be worthy subjects for musicological research.

b) Themes for artistic exploration

Regardless of this fundamental interpretation of improvisation as a "research setting," certain themes and lines of questioning have emerged from the work of the *exploratorium*. Some of which influence everyday work, whereas others are more intensively explored in specific projects:

- The "exploration of the moment"
- The physical setting itself as a source of artistic inspiration
- "Sound research": Instruments and materials as partners in artistic dialog
- Sound material, structure and form
- Interdisciplinary nature
- The interlacing of art and pedagogy

1 | Flow refers to a condition described by Mihály Csjkszentmihályi, in which a person completely merges with their actions (Csíkszentmihályi 2000). There is a particular flow phenomenon in improvised music described as "playing by itself", in which individual impulse does not seem to be necessary and the music unfolds as if by itself.

- Klangmaterial, Struktur und Form
- Interdisziplinarität
- Die Verschränkung von Kunst und Pädagogik

– Die »Erkundung des Augenblicks«

Was braucht es, um im Moment adäquat zu agieren? Welche Wahrnehmungs-Kanäle muss ich öffnen, um dem Augenblick gerecht werden zu können?
Was heißt überhaupt »Augenblick«? Ist das nur der Bruchteil einer Sekunde? Oder heißt es, Vergangenes und potentiell Zukünftiges wie in einem einzigen Bild zugleich im (Augen-)Blick zu haben?
Wie kann ich mich in einen Zustand versetzen, in dem ich zu einer solchen Wahrnehmung in der Lage bin?
Wie kann ich beurteilen, welche Aktion für einen solchermaßen wahrgenommenen Augenblick angemessen ist?
Auf welcher Ebene fällt die Entscheidung?
Was bedeutet »angemessen«? Was ist der Maßstab?

Die »Erkundung des Augenblicks« ist in zweierlei Hinsicht *das* zentrale Thema improvisatorischen Arbeitens. Ganz konkret ist sie gleichbedeutend mit der Tätigkeit des Improvisierens, sofern ich das Improvisieren wirklich ernst nehme, wirklich *im Moment* agiere. Dann ist jede Improvisation ein Akt der Erkundung des Augenblicks.

Zugleich haben wir es mit einer Fragestellung grundsätzlicher Art zu tun, die auch der kontinuierlichen Reflexion bedarf. Dabei ist in diesem Fall der Weg das Ziel, nämlich das Aufrechterhalten des Fragens, die ständige Beobachtung: Explorieren als Grundhaltung.

– Raum als künstlerische Inspirationsquelle

Raum, seine Akustik, seine architektonischen und vielleicht auch historischen Eigenheiten sind ein wichtiger Bestandteil der improvisatorischen Exploration im Allgemeinen und der Erkundung des Augenblicks im Besonderen. Das Thema rückt vor allem dann in den Fokus der Aufmerksamkeit, wenn gezielt ungewöhnliche Räume aufgesucht werden, die das improvisatorische Agieren in besonderer Weise beeinflussen.
Wie interagiere ich musikalisch mit der individuellen Nachhallzeit des Raumes, wie mit Besonderheiten bei bestimmten Frequenzen oder bestimmten Lautstärke-Graden?
Welche besonderen Gestaltungsmöglichkeiten ergeben sich durch spezielle räumliche Positionierungen oder Wege der Musiker?
Welche eigenen Klänge besitzt der Raum?
Welche Assoziationen bietet der Raum durch sein Aussehen oder seine Geschichte (Abbruchhaus, ehemalige elektrische Schaltzentrale, Kirche, verlasse-

– The "exploration of the moment"

What does it take to act appropriately in the moment? Which channels of perception do I need to open in order to be able to cope with the demands of the moment?
What does "moment" even mean? Is it only a fraction of a second? Or does it mean having past and potential future in sight at the same time?
How can I put myself in a position so that I am capable of such perception?
How can I judge which action is appropriate for the perceived moment?
On what level does this decision take place?
What does appropriate mean? How is it measured?

The "exploration of the moment" is *the* central theme of improvisational work in two different respects. It is tantamount to the act of improvising, providing I really take improvising seriously and really act *in the moment*. When this aspect is fulfilled, every improvisation is an act of "exploration of the moment."

At the same time, we are dealing with a fundamental line of questioning, which also continuously requires reflection. As such, in this case the path is the goal. Namely, maintaining the questioning, the constant observation: exploring as a fundamental attitude.

– The physical setting itself as a source of artistic inspiration

The physical setting, its acoustics, its architectural, and maybe also its historical qualities, are an important aspect of improvisational exploration in general and the exploration of the moment in particular. The issue becomes the focus of attention when specific physical settings are chosen that affect improvisational action in a particular way.
How do I interact musically with the individual resonance of the physical setting, with the special qualities of specific frequencies or specific amplitudes?
What creative possibilities result from special positioning or how the musicians move around the physical setting?
What sounds does the physical setting itself provide?
What associations does the physical setting evoke with its appearance or its history (condemned building, former electricity power plant, church, abandoned factory) and what meaningful referential or inspirational possibilities result?[2]

– "Sound research": instruments and materials as partners in artistic dialog

The approach to the instrument or any (more or less) sonorous material is fundamentally different for many improvisers compared to that of conventional musical practice. While classical musicians aspire to "master" their instrument,

2 | This subject is addressed from various perspectives in another publication (ringgespräch über gruppenimprovisation 2012).

ne Fabrikhalle) und welche sinnvollen Bezugs- und Inspirationsmöglichkeiten ergeben sich daraus?[2]

– »Klangforschung«: Instrumente und Materialien als künstlerische Dialogpartner

Der Umgang mit dem Instrument beziehungsweise mit jedwedem mehr oder weniger klangvollen Material ist für viele Improvisationsmusiker von grundsätzlich anderer Art als in der konventionellen Musikausübung. Während klassische Interpreten anstreben ihr Instrument zu »beherrschen«, die absolute Kontrolle darüber zu haben, bietet sich in der Improvisation ein explorativer Ansatz an, der darin besteht, sich in eine Art »Dialog« mit dem Instrument (beziehungsweise Material) zu begeben, das Instrument/Material immer wieder zu »befragen«: Wer bist du? Was kannst du? Wie klingst du? Wozu regst du mich an? Wie können wir miteinander interagieren? Wie können wir auf ganz andere Weise interagieren, uns quasi neu begegnen? So entsteht nicht nur im Probenkontext, sondern auch während einer Performance immer wieder klanglich Neues und Unerwartetes.

– Klangmaterial, Struktur und Form

Die Erforschung von Klangmaterial sowie dessen Strukturierung und Form steht im Mittelpunkt jeder Art von Musik, die den Anspruch hat, zeitgenössisch zu sein. Ich möchte mich in diesem Zusammenhang auf einige exemplarische Aspekte beschränken, die aufzeigen, wie die Besonderheiten des improvisatorischen Settings diesem Experimentieren eine ganz eigene Richtung geben können.

- In der Improvisation sind Klangfindung, Zusammenklang, Struktur und Form nicht nur musikalisch begründet, sondern resultieren zugleich aus dem Verhalten der Einzelnen und der Interaktion zwischen den Spielern. Daher entstehen Ideen zur Gestaltung des Materials auch aus dem Erproben von Verhaltensweisen, inneren Haltungen und Interaktions-Modi. Beispiele dafür sind das Ausloten von Nähe und Distanz (durch verschiedene Grade von Klangverschmelzung und Kontrastierung), Absichtslosigkeit beziehungsweise Beiläufigkeit von Aktionen, Spiel mit verschiedenen Energie-Levels, als Ensemble agieren wie ein einziger Organismus, »jede/r für sich und alle gemeinsam«, Experimente mit der Interaktions-Geschwindigkeit und verschiedenes mehr.
- Wer improvisiert, agiert als Instant-Komponist, zugleich aber auch als Instrumentalist. Entsprechend spielt der unmittelbare Umgang mit dem In-

2 | Dieses Thema ist in einer eigenen Publikation von verschiedenen Perspektiven beleuchtet worden (ringgespräch über gruppenimprovisation 2012).

to have absolute control over it, improvisation offers an exploratory approach that consists of entering into a kind of "dialog" with the instrument (or material), to constantly "ask" the instrument/material: Who are you? What can you do? How do you sound? What do you inspire me to do? How can we interact with one another? How can we interact in a completely different way, as if we were meeting for the first time? In this way, sonically new and unexpected things happen time and again, and not just in a rehearsal context but also during performance.

- Sound material, structure and form

Investigating sound material, as well as its structure and form, is central to any kind of music that aspires to be contemporary. I would like to focus on a few examples that show how specific aspects of the improvisational setting can give this experimentation a distinct direction.

- In improvisation, sound discovery, harmony, structure and form do not just come into being through the music, they also result from the behavior of the individuals and the interaction between the players. Thus ideas about the shaping of materials also result from testing out ways of behaving, internal attitudes, and modes of interacting. Examples of this are exploring distances (using varying grades of blending and contrasting sound), unintentionality or randomness of actions, playing around with different energy levels, acting as an ensemble which performs as a single organism, "everyone for themselves and yet all together", experimenting with the speed of interaction, as well as many other things.
- Those who improvise act as instant composers and also as instrumentalists. Accordingly, the direct interaction with the instrument plays an important role in the creative impulse. In traditional forms of improvisation, this has usually expressed itself as a high level of virtuosity. In current free improvisation, the emphasis has shifted towards the search for new and unknown sounds by testing out the sonic possibilities and extreme boundaries of the instrument or voice.
- Some things are easier when improvising, others more difficult. The subtle and differentiated balancing of timbres is easier to realize in the spontaneous improvisational process than the combining of complex pitch relationships, at least when these are spread out among various instruments. Regardless of whether at extremely slow or extremely quick tempos, gradual developmental processes lend themselves better than do repeated references to formal sections and their variations, although the latter is certainly possible. These experiences influence the course of the research: do I want to dedicate myself to the specific potential that improvisation has to offer? Or do I find it intriguing to explore themes which basically require me to

strument eine wichtige Rolle für die kreativen Impulse. Dies hat sich in traditionellen Formen der Improvisation meist durch ein hohes Maß an Virtuosität geäußert. In der aktuellen Freien Improvisation spielt die Suche nach neuen und unbekannten Klängen durch das Austesten der klanglichen Möglichkeiten und äußersten Grenzen des Instrumentes beziehungsweise der Stimme eine wichtige Rolle.

- Es gibt manches, was beim Improvisieren leichter, anderes, was schwieriger ist. Das subtile und differenzierte Ausbalancieren von Klangfarben ist im spontanen improvisatorischen Prozess leichter zu realisieren als das Kombinieren komplexer Tonhöhenverhältnisse, zumindest dann, wenn diese auf verschiedene Instrumente verteilt sind. Graduelle Entwicklungsprozesse, egal ob in extrem langsamem oder rasend schnellem Tempo, sind näherliegend als das wiederholte Aufgreifen von Formteilen und deren Varianten, obwohl letzteres durchaus machbar wäre. Diese Erfahrungen beeinflussen die Richtung der Erforschung: Will ich mich dem widmen, was die Improvisation an besonderen Potentialen zu bieten hat? Oder reizt mich die Erkundung dessen, was ich den improvisatorischen Möglichkeiten geradezu abtrotzen muss? Zugleich stellt sich die Frage nach dem Umgang mit den »traditionellen Werten«. Soll die Tonhöhe weiterhin der primäre Gestaltungsparameter von Musik bleiben? Gibt es zwingende Gründe für die in Rezensionen und Analysen nach wie vor verbreitete Auffassung, die Wiederholung oder Variation von Formteilen sei ein Merkmal qualitativ hochwertiger Musik, eine ABA-Form sei »wertvoller« als beispielsweise eine ABCDEF-Form?

– Interdisziplinarität

Es gibt keinen Klang, der ohne Bewegung zustande kommt. Andersherum erzeugt, wer sich bewegt, mit hoher Wahrscheinlichkeit auch Klang. Darüber hinaus sind Musizierende und sich Bewegende immer auch als Bild wahrnehmbar, insbesondere, wenn sie im Ensemble agieren. Die Verbindungen zwischen den Künsten sind so eng, dass ein Ausloten ihrer möglichen Beziehungen sich geradezu aufdrängt. Solche Erkundungen können sich sowohl auf die Gleichzeitigkeit mehrerer Künste in der Tätigkeit einzelner oder mehrerer Performer beziehen als auch auf das Zusammenspiel von Akteuren verschiedener Kunstformen. Das wirft spannende Fragestellungen auf. Wie kann ich so agieren, dass Klang, Bewegung und Bild zu einer überzeugenden Einheit werden? Welche künstlerischen Möglichkeiten bietet dieses Ineinandergreifen der Künste? Wie kann gleichberechtigte Interaktion zwischen Vertretern unterschiedlicher Kunstgattungen entstehen? Wie ein spannungsvolles Mit-, Neben- oder gar Gegeneinander? Wie können Künstler der verschiedenen Genres ihre Rollen sinnvoll aufteilen, angleichen oder gar vertauschen?[3]

3 | Siehe auch Schwabe 1994.

challenge improvisational possibilities? At the same time, there is also the question of how to approach "traditional values." Should pitches continue to be the primary shaping parameter of music? Are there necessary reasons for the idea, still common in reviews and analyses of music, that repetition or variation of formal sections is a sign of qualitatively valuable music, for example an ABA form is "more valuable" than an ABCDEF form?

- Interdisciplinary nature

There is no sound that is produced without movement; to put it another way: when one moves, one is most likely to produce sound in the process. Furthermore, those who make music and move are also always perceivable as an image, particularly when they are performing in an ensemble. The arts are so closely connected that an exploration of their possible relationships is an obvious step. Such investigations can refer to the simultaneity of multiple arts in the actions of individual or multiple performers, or to collaboration between actors from different art forms. This raises interesting questions: how can I act so that sound, movement and image become a convincing whole? What artistic possibilities does this interconnection of arts offer? How can equal interaction between representatives of different art forms occur? Like dynamic tension with one another, in juxtaposition, or even against one another? How can artists from different genres divide, share or even trade their roles in a way that makes sense?[3] Improvisation offers a chance to pursue these questions as a practical experiment. The impact of this subject became apparent at the *exploratorium* where several special kinds of events on the subject were created, most of which referred back to impetus given by visitors and users and which illuminated the interdisciplinary nature of improvisation from various perspectives.[4]

- Interlacing art and education

One research subject specific to the work of the *exploratorium berlin* is the intertwining of artistic and pedagogical work. Decades of experience in the film genre have shown that when amateur actors are allowed to improvise, they can activate surprising artistic potential. Similarly, we have discovered in our work in the areas of dance and music that so-called amateurs who have relevant

3 | See also Schwabe 1994.

4 | Specifically *Offene Bühne Musik & Bewegung* (open stage for music and movement), a "research laboratory voice, sound and movement" entitled *Grenzgänge*, and the course offerings *K plus B*" - experiments with the simultaneousness of sound and movement" - and *Performance* "on the fringe of performing and visual arts, music and movement". *Offhandopera* and *Offene Bühne Poesie & Musik* (open stage for poetry and music) address the connections between text and improvised music. Temporary events and performances also include visual and/or theatrical elements.

Die Improvisation bietet die Chance, diesen Fragen im praktischen Experiment nachzugehen. Die Brisanz des Themas wurde im *exploratorium* deutlich, wo mehrere spezielle Veranstaltungsformate dazu geschaffen wurden, die großenteils auf Impulse von Besuchern und Nutzern zurückgehen und Interdisziplinarität aus verschiedenen Perspektiven ausleuchten.[4]

– Die Verschränkung von Kunst und Pädagogik

Ein für die Arbeit des *exploratorium berlin* spezifisches Erkundungsthema widmet sich dem Ineinander-Übergehen von künstlerischer und pädagogischer Arbeit. Im Genre Film gibt es schon seit Jahrzehnten die Erfahrung, dass schauspielerische Laien, lässt man sie improvisieren, verblüffende künstlerische Potentiale aktivieren können. Ganz ähnlich haben wir in unserer musikalischen und tänzerischen Arbeit festgestellt, dass sogenannte Laien mit entsprechender Workshop-Erfahrung in einem gut gewählten experimentellen Setting mit hoher künstlerischer Kompetenz agieren können, ohne als »Amateure« identifizierbar zu sein. Das ist möglich, weil intensives experimentelles Spielen häufig eine hohe Performance-Qualität aufweist und Laien oft bessere »Spieler« – im ursprünglichen Wortsinn – sind als beispielsweise viele ausgebildete Instrumentalisten. Entsprechend arbeiten wir an Performance-Formaten, die experimentelle Kompetenzen in den Mittelpunkt stellen und keine künstlerisch-professionelle Ausbildung erfordern.[5]

c) Künstlerisch-experimentelle Erkundungsprojekte zu besonderen Themen

Zahlreiche weitere Themen verdienen unsere Aufmerksamkeit, weil sie unsere künstlerischen Möglichkeiten erweitern können. Hierfür gilt es, geeignete Settings zur Erkundung zu entwickeln. Dazu zwei Beispiele.

---

4 | Konkret sind das die *Offene Bühne Musik & Bewegung*, ein »Forschungslabor Stimme, Klang und Bewegung« mit dem Titel *Grenzgänge* sowie die Kursangebote *K plus B*, »Experimente mit Gleichzeitigkeit von Klang und Bewegung« sowie *Performance* »im Grenzbereich von Darstellender und Bildender Kunst, Musik und Bewegung«. Der Verbindung von Text und improvisierter Musik widmen sich die *Offhandopera* und die *Offene Bühne Poesie & Musik*; temporäre Angebote und Performances beziehen bildnerische beziehungsweise theatralische Aspekte mit ein.

5 | Beispielhafte Projekte dieser Art waren *Odysseus 2008*, verschiedene Beiträge zum *FeldForschungsFestival_Kultur 2010* und zur *Langen Nacht der Museen* im Januar 2011 sowie die *Under Ground Symphony 2011*. Näheres dazu habe ich in zwei Artikeln ausführlich beschrieben (Schwabe 2011 und Schwabe 2012b).

workshop experience can perform with a high level of artistic competence in well-chosen experimental settings, so much so that they cannot be identified as "amateurs." This is possible because intensive experimental playing often exhibits a high level of quality and amateurs are often better "players" – in the original sense of the word – than, for example, many trained instrumentalists. Therefore we work on performance formats that focus on experimental competence and that do not require professional artistic education.[5]

c) Artistically experimental research projects on particular subjects

Many other subjects deserve our attention because they are capable of expanding our artistic potential. For this, appropriate settings for research must be developed. Here are two examples.

The subject of the project with the title *Listen to my car,*[6] was about improvising in places in the inner city of Berlin that are influenced by the variety of traffic sounds. Specifically, these were street intersections and a train underpass; in each case these places were investigated at different times of day. The challenge was to react to sounds, which to a certain extent were predictable, but which did not themselves interact. What results is an asymmetrical communication that is irritating for the players at first, but then ultimately generates new creative strategies. My personal experience was that I could act appropriately when I operated as a non-communicative element in accordance with my own rules in the different places and whole-heartedly committed myself to the poetry of the coincidental juxtaposition. This experience was of fundamental significance to me because it could feedback as an improvisational "repertoire" and expansion of horizons.

One exemplary project was the performance *43200 Seconds,* which took place in May 2015. It was a twelve-hour interdisciplinary improvisational performance, with a total of 26 performers from music, dance and the visual arts. The concept was understood mainly as a self-experiment with time: how do my playing, my perception, my creativity, my behavior during interaction, my concentration and my perception of the passing of time change over such a long period? Do my sources of creativity, from which I play, change?[7]

---

5 | For example *Odysseus 2008*, various contributions to *FeldForschungsFestival_Kultur 2010* and *Lange Nacht der Museen January 2011*, and *Under Ground Symphony 2011* represent projects of this kind. I have been writing about those projects in two articles (Schwabe 2011 and Schwabe 2012b).

6 | One of seven projects with which the *exploratorium* participated in the *1st FeldForschungsFestival_Kultur 2010.*

7 | More information about this project can be found online at: *http://exploratorium-berlin.de/43200-sekunden-dokumentation/.*

In einem Projekt mit dem programmatischen Namen *Listen to my car*[6] ging es um das Experiment, an Berliner Innenstadt-Orten zu improvisieren, die durch vielfältige Verkehrsgeräusche geprägt sind. Im konkreten Fall handelte es sich um Straßenkreuzungen und eine Bahn-Unterführung, jeweils zu unterschiedlichen Tageszeiten. Die Herausforderung bestand darin, auf Klänge zu reagieren, die zwar bis zu einem gewissen Grad vorhersehbar sind, aber selbst nicht interagieren. Dadurch entsteht eine asymmetrische Kommunikation, die für die Spieler zunächst irritierend ist, aber letztlich neue kreative Strategien generiert. So war meine persönliche Erfahrung, dass ich dann angemessen agieren konnte, wenn ich mich selbst als nicht-kommunikatives, sondern nach eigenen Gesetzen handelndes Element dieser Situation verhalte und auf die Poesie des zufälligen Nebeneinanders setze. Diese Erfahrung war für mich von grundsätzlicher Bedeutung, weil sie sich als improvisatorische »Repertoire-« und Horizont-Erweiterung auch auf andere Situationen rückkoppeln lässt.

Ein Projekt mit exemplarischem Charakter war die Performance *43200 Sekunden*, die im Mai 2015 stattfand: eine zwölfstündige interdisziplinäre Improvisations-Performance mit insgesamt 26 Akteuren aus den Bereichen Musik, Tanz und Bildende Kunst. Das Konzept war vor allem als Selbstversuch mit der Zeit zu verstehen: Wie verändern sich mein Spiel, meine Wahrnehmung, meine Kreativität, mein Interaktionsverhalten, meine Konzentration und mein Zeitgefühl in einem solch langen Zeitraum? Ändern sich die Quellen, aus denen sich mein Spiel speist?[7]

Dieses Experiment war insofern beispielhaft, als es alle der oben genannten Erkundungsthemen enthielt.

- Die *Erkundung des Augenblicks* fand wie unter einem Mikroskop statt, weil der lange Aktions-Zeitraum quasi den Augenblick dehnte und somit einen außergewöhnlichen Fokus darauf ermöglichte.
- Als *Raum* stand eine Kirche[8] zur Verfügung, die durch ihre Akustik, ihre baulichen Besonderheiten und ihre Atmosphäre zur Auseinandersetzung und Erkundung einlud und eine reichhaltige Inspirationsquelle für viele der Aktionen war.
- Daneben standen diverse *Materialien* bereit, die zu klanglichen und visuellen Explorationen einluden: Holzstangen, Metallschalen, 800 Tischtennisbälle, Orgelpfeifen, rot bemalte Leinwand-Elemente und verschiedenes mehr.

---

6 | Eines von sieben Teilprojekten, mit denen das *exploratorium berlin* sich am *1. FeldForschungsFestival_Kultur 2010* beteiligte.

7 | Nähere Informationen zu diesem Projekt sind im Internet zu finden unter: *http://exploratorium-berlin.de/43200-sekunden-dokumentation/*.

8 | St. Johannes-Evangelist in Berlin Mitte.

This experiment was exemplary in as far as it contained all of the above-mentioned research subjects.

- The *exploration of the moment* happened under a microscope because the extended time span stretched the moment, thereby making it possible to place an extraordinary focus on it.
- There was access to a church as *the physical setting*,[8] which was a rich source of inspiration for many of the actions on account of its acoustics, the particularities of its construction and its atmosphere.
- There were diverse *materials* available that invited acoustic and visual explorations: wooden poles, metal bowls, 800 ping pong balls, organ pipes, canvas materials painted red and many more.
- The approach to musical *form* was a completely new experience on account of the unusually long duration of the piece and the resulting change in the perception of the passing of time. The idea of silence/stillness gained an especially significant meaning in the selection of sound and movement material; as such this was primarily used as a form-defining element: silence/stillness as a way to settle or calm down a formal section, as well as to bring activity to a complete standstill.
- Eleven musicians, twelve dancers and three visual artists worked simultaneously. Far from "interpreting" each other, the *different arts* and artists were, to a great extent, mutual sources of inspiration for each other. The setting offered the possibility of continuously exploring various forms of collaboration and non-collaboration, with each other as well as in juxtaposition. Ultimately, the key common element was the mutually-maintained presence of the participants in the moment.
- The performance was realized by an ensemble that was put together specifically for this project. It was a colorful mix of *professional and non-professional performers,* the majority of whom were non-professionals. Considering this, it was remarkable how naturally the artistic process unfolded during the performance. In this respect, the variety of inspirational sources was very helpful: the physical setting, the various art forms and various materials. Moreover, the extended time span was not only a challenge but also a relief, as it allowed one to really delve deeply into the artistic process. In terms of the task of finding an appropriate setting for professionals and non-professionals to explore artistic juxtaposition, the experiment was a success, and not in spite of, but because of, the diversity of the artistic dimensions. The intensive preparation (see below: "Exploration as a pedagogical approach") was another important factor which contributed to the success of the setting. This took place both short term – in the form of a preparatory

8 | St. Johannes-Evangelist in Berlin Mitte.

- Der Umgang mit musikalischer *Form* war durch die ungewöhnlich lange Stückdauer und das dadurch veränderte Zeitgefühl eine ganz neue Erfahrung. Bei der Wahl des *Klang- und Bewegungsmaterials* kam dem Thema Stille eine besonders große Bedeutung zu, wobei auch dies primär zu Formgebung eingesetzt wurde: Stille als Zur-Ruhe-Kommen eines Form-Abschnitts sowie als vollständiger Stillstand des Geschehens.
- Elf Musiker, zwölf Tänzer und drei Bildende Künstler arbeiteten simultan. Weit entfernt davon, sich gegenseitig »auszudeuten«, waren die *verschiedenen Künste* und Künstler einander in hohem Maße gegenseitige Inspirationsquelle. Das Setting bot die Möglichkeit, in einem kontinuierlichen Mit- und Nebeneinander unterschiedliche Formen des Zusammenspiels und Nicht-Zusammenspiels zu erkunden, wobei letztlich die gemeinsam aufrecht erhaltene Präsenz das entscheidend Verbindende war.
- Die Aufführung wurde von einem nur für dieses Projekt zusammengestellten Ensemble realisiert, das aus einer bunten Mischung von *professionellen und nicht-professionellen Akteuren* bestand, wobei die nicht-professionellen in der Mehrheit waren. In Anbetracht dessen verblüffte die Selbstverständlichkeit, mit der in der Performance der künstlerische Prozess vor sich ging. Dabei half die Vielfältigkeit der Inspirationsquellen: des Raumes, der verschiedenen Künste, der verschiedenen Materialien. Dazu kam, dass die Dehnung der Zeit nicht nur Herausforderung, sondern auch Erleichterung war, da sie ein besonders intensives Eintauchen in den künstlerischen Prozess erlaubte. Unter dem speziellen Aspekt, ein geeignetes Setting für ein künstlerisches Nebeneinander von Professionellen und Nicht-Professionellen zu erkunden, war der Versuchsaufbau also nicht trotz, sondern wegen der Vielfalt der künstlerischen Dimensionen erfolgreich. Ein weiterer wichtiger Gelingensfaktor dieses Settings war die intensive fachliche Vorbereitung (siehe auch weiter unten: »Exploration als pädagogischer Ansatz«), die sowohl kurzfristig – durch einen vorbereitenden Workshop – als auch langfristig stattfand, durch die Begrenzung der Akteure auf Personen, die sich in den künstlerisch-pädagogischen Strukturen des *exploratorium* schon seit längerer Zeit intensiv mit Freier Improvisation auseinandersetzen.

Die beschriebenen Projekte stehen für eine Art künstlerisch-praktischer Forschung, in der ein besonderes Setting zu Erkundungen und Erfahrungen im praktischen künstlerischen Tun führt und im besten Fall in eine Erweiterung der individuellen Handlungsmöglichkeiten und des ästhetischen Horizontes mündet. Dazu gehört immer auch ein anschließendes Reflektieren, um das Erlebte zu vertiefen und zu verankern. Dies ist umso fruchtbarer, wenn es im Kontext einer Gruppe geschieht, wo Erfahrungen miteinander geteilt, verglichen und abgewogen werden können.

workshop – and long term by limiting participation to people who have engaged with free improvisation over a longer period of time in the artistic-pedagogical structures of the *exploratorium.*

The projects described represent a kind of artistic-practical research, in which exploration of a particular setting and practical experience in artistic action ideally result in an expansion of the individual possibilities and the aesthetic horizons. Subsequent reflection is always a part of this, in order to deepen and ground the experience. This is even more fruitful when it takes place in a group context where experiences can be shared, compared and evaluated.

2. Strategies of artistic exploration

There are observable processes and mechanisms that can be monitored in the artistic exploration that was discussed. I would like to illustrate these here using the following model.

This model, which I describe as the *vortex of artistic exploration*, consists of three levels: the **activity level** is the outer ring, shown in medium grey. This compares with the **resource level**, which is in the center circle in light-grey. The interactions between these two levels are shown on the **process level** in the form of dark gray arrows (see page 375).

Three elements of activity are connected to each other on the **activity level** in a circular and/or spiral form: the conception of performance rules or settings, practical artistic exploration and observation, reflection and realization.

This set of three is also common in empirical sciences. There is, however, a fundamental difference compared to empirical science. Artistic research is less concerned with the pursuit of objective truths that can be generalized as natural law, and more with subjective experiences and realizations which influence the artistic action of the performer, broaden their artistic horizons and, in the best case, lead to artistic innovation. The focus is not external observation but internal (and inward).

A particular quality of these three elements is that they connect experimental practice and theory. This takes place in the form of a spiral. The spiral-shaped process begins when new discoveries emerge from these three steps (conception – exploration – observation/reflection) and these lead to more new concepts, explorations and observations/reflections.

The level of **resources** complements the activity level. The resource level contains our wealth of knowledge, ability and experience; a "treasure trove" – in the fairytale sense – of incomparable value, which comprises our consciousness, as well as our unconsciousness, and which also influences our attitudes, actions and patterns of reaction. The totality of things that we call upon when

2. Strategien künstlerischer Erkundung

In den beschriebenen künstlerischen Erkundungen lassen sich wiederkehrende Abläufe und »Wirk-Mechanismen« beobachten, die ich in nachfolgendem Modell veranschaulichen möchte.

Dieses Modell, das ich als *Spiralwirbel künstlerischer Erkundung* bezeichne, beinhaltet drei Ebenen: Die **Aktivitätsebene** ist im äußeren Ring mit mittelgrauen Textfeldern dargestellt. Dem gegenüber steht die Ebene der **Ressourcen**, die im hellgrauen Mittelkreis zu finden ist. Die Wechselwirkungen zwischen diesen beiden Ebenen sind auf der **Prozess-Ebene** in Form dunkelgrauer Pfeile verbildlicht.

Abbildung 1: Der Spiralwirbel künstlerischer Erkundung. ©Matthias Schwabe 2015

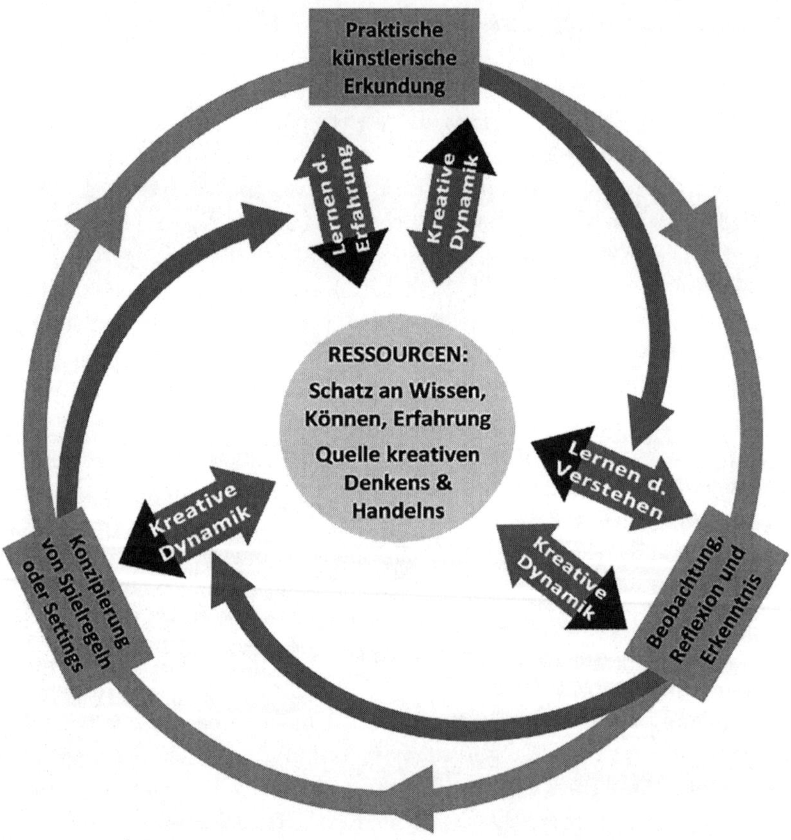

Auf der **Aktivitätsebene** werden drei Handlungsschritte kreis- beziehungsweise spiralförmig miteinander verbunden: die Konzipierung von Spielregeln oder

Figure 1: The Vortex of Artistic Exploration. ©Matthias Schwabe 2015

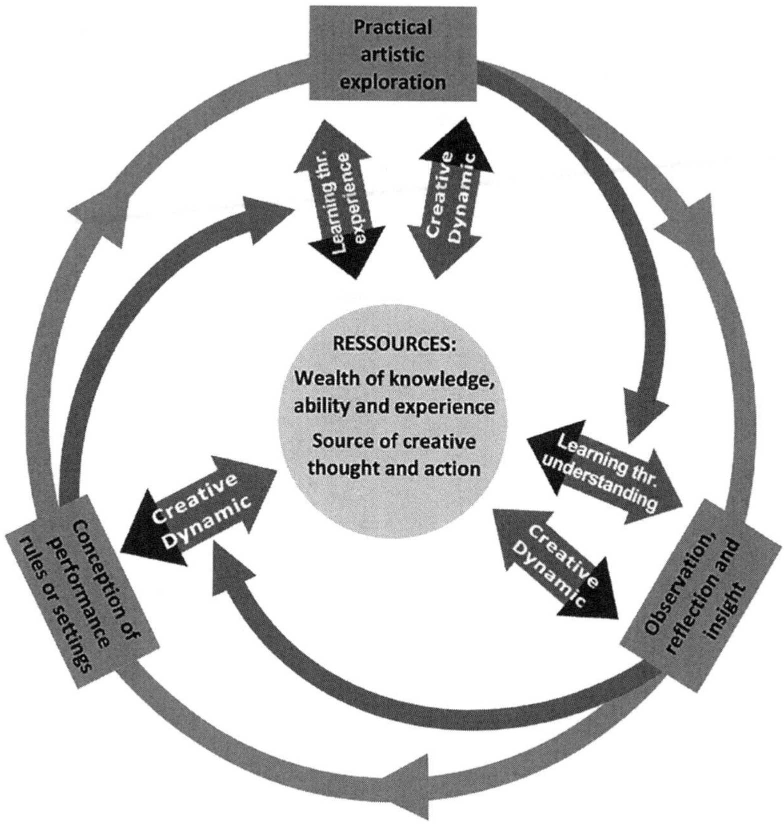

we think and act, are what I term resources. In the context of this model, it is not necessary to examine the exact composition and mode of operation of this level; as, given the multitude and complexity of the many existing explanatory models, to do so would also exceed the scope of this article. I would like to content myself with the conclusion that, on the one hand, our resources are the basis for our thoughts and actions, and on the other, that these are enriched by our thoughts and actions. Our resources are *also* – and this is crucial for artistic work – the source of our *creative* thought and action if new ideas and possibilities for action are to emerge out of new internal connections.

The **process level**, which describes the interactions between the activities and the resources, is critical to all this. Here, a constant feedback takes place between the respective activity and the resources. We act or think based on our resources. New experiences or thoughts that occur on the activity level enrich these resources and make such actions or thoughts possible on a new level, which in turn contributes to a further enrichment of our resources and so on.

Settings, die praktische künstlerische Erkundung sowie Beobachtung, Reflexion und Erkenntnis.

Dieser Dreischritt ist auch in den empirischen Wissenschaften gang und gäbe. Allerdings besteht ein grundlegender Unterschied zur naturwissenschaftlichen Forschung darin, dass es bei künstlerischen Erkundungen weniger um das Erzielen objektiver Wahrheiten geht, die sich als Naturgesetze verallgemeinern lassen, als vielmehr um subjektive Erfahrungen und Erkenntnisse, die das künstlerische Handeln der Ausführenden beeinflussen, deren ästhetischen Horizont erweitern und im besten Fall zu künstlerischen Innovationen führen. Im Mittelpunkt steht also nicht der Blick von außen, sondern von (und nach) innen.

Eine besondere Qualität dieses Dreischritts besteht darin, dass er experimentelle Praxis und Theorie miteinander verknüpft. Dies geschieht in Form einer Spirale. Wenn aus dem ursprünglichen Dreischritt Konzipierung – Erkundung – Beobachtung/Reflexion neue Erkenntnisse resultieren, die zu wiederum neuen Konzepten, Erkundungen und Beobachtungen/Reflexionen führen, wird damit ein spiralförmiger Prozess in Gang gesetzt.

Komplementär zur Aktivitätsebene ist die Ebene der **Ressourcen**. Sie beinhalten unseren Schatz an Wissen, Können und Erfahrung, einen im märchenhaften Wortsinn wirklichen »Schatz« von unvergleichbarem Wert, der unser Bewusstes ebenso wie unser Unbewusstes umfasst und auch unsere Einstellungen, Haltungen und Reaktionsmuster prägt. Als Ressourcen bezeichne ich also die Gesamtheit dessen, worauf wir zurückgreifen, wenn wir denken und handeln. Im Kontext dieses Modells ist es nicht nötig, die genaue Zusammensetzung und Funktionsweise dieser Ebene zu beleuchten. Aufgrund der Vielzahl und Komplexität der verschiedenen existierenden Erklärungsmodelle würde dies auch den Rahmen des Artikels sprengen. Ich möchte mich mit der Feststellung begnügen, dass unsere Ressourcen einerseits die Grundlage unseres Denkens und Handelns bilden und andererseits durch unser Denken und Handeln bereichert werden. Unsere Ressourcen sind *auch* – und das ist entscheidend für die künstlerische Arbeit – die Quelle unseres *kreativen* Denkens und Handelns, wenn aus neuen internen Verknüpfungen neue Ideen und Handlungsmöglichkeiten hervorgehen.

Entscheidend dafür ist die **Prozessebene**, die die Wechselwirkungen zwischen den Aktivitäten und den Ressourcen beschreibt. Hier findet eine ständige Rückkopplung zwischen der jeweiligen Aktivität und den Ressourcen statt. Wir handeln oder denken auf Grundlage unserer Ressourcen, neuer Erfahrungen oder Gedanken, die auf der Aktivitätsebene auftreten, bereichern diese Ressourcen und ermöglichen so ein Handeln oder Denken auf neuem Level, was zu einer weiteren Bereicherung unserer Ressourcen beiträgt und so fort.

Die Bereicherung der Ressourcen, die dabei stattfindet, ist als *Lernvorgang* aufzufassen. In der Phase der praktischen Erkundung handelt es sich dabei um *Lernen durch Erfahrung*, in der Phase der Reflexion um *Lernen durch Verstehen*.

The enrichment of the resources that takes place can be understood as a *learning process*. During the practical investigation phase, there is *learning through experience*, during the reflection phase there is *learning by understanding*.

As I currently see it, the stage of concept development is not about learning. Here, the second important aspect of the interactions, that which I call *creative dynamic*, becomes significant. When new experiences and ideas do not fit into our existing structure of knowledge, ability and experience, meaning that the structure must therefore be modified, new connections can (but do not have to) develop and, as such, generate *creativity*. This process is also influenced by frequent interactive feedback when new impulses lead to modifications that generate new activities, which in turn create new connections and so on. This kind of creative dynamic is possible at every stage of activity.

The previous stage of each activity plays an important role as a catalyst for both the learning processes and the creative dynamic. The setting is crucially responsible for the extent to which creative dynamic and learning processes are initiated (or prevented) during the practical investigation. A particularly successful – or indeed unsuccessful – exploratory phase is in turn the best possible precondition for subsequent reflection and any (new) insights that may ensue. Ultimately, productive reflection is a useful point of departure for the conception of a new exploratory phase.

The dynamic that results from the activities in their interaction with the resources not only resembles a spiral in visual representation, but can also evoke a vortex in practice, when the spiral begins to move in the manner described. This is because settings, practical explorations and insights continuously lead to new explorations, reflections and settings.

In order to understand the model, it is important to observe that the processes described can unfold at completely different time dimensions. Where there is very fast rotation, particularly in the practical exploration phase, an action can be observed and reflected on virtually simultaneously to its execution. This leads to its categorization as successful or unsuccessful and, consequently, to the decision as to whether or not the strategy should be maintained or changed. On a different time scale, for example in a rehearsal context, post-performance observation and reflection of one improvisation setting can result in a modified setting for the next improvisation. A far greater time scale is imaginable where an artistic project is "understood" after many years, leading to new ideas for projects.

Admittedly, the model should not be seen as an absolutely necessary process, but rather as an example of an approach in which theory and practice can both be fully appreciated. Conversely, the value of reflection is highly debatable. The *New Phonic Art Ensemble* for example, one of the most renowned free improvisation ensembles of the 1960s, made it a policy not to talk about their pieces because they were concerned that (self) critical examination would hinder spontaneous decision-making and, by doing so, impede artistic freedom.

Im Stadium der Konzept-Entwicklung geht es nach meiner aktuellen Auffassung nicht um Lernen. Hier kommt vielmehr der zweite wichtige Aspekt der Wechselwirkungen zum Tragen, den ich als *kreative Dynamik* bezeichne. Wenn neue Erfahrungen und Ideen nicht in unser bestehendes Gefüge aus Wissen, Können und Erfahrung einzuordnen sind und infolgedessen das Gefüge modifiziert werden muss, können (nicht müssen) neue Verknüpfungen entstehen und damit *Kreativität* generieren. Auch dieser Prozess ist durch vielfache wechselseitige Rückkopplung geprägt, wenn neue Impulse zu Modifikationen führen, die neue Aktivitäten generieren, die wiederum neue Verknüpfungen verursachen und so fort. Solche kreative Dynamik ist in jedem Aktivitäts-Stadium möglich.

Sowohl für die Lernvorgänge als auch für die kreative Dynamik spielt der jeweils vorhergehende Aktivitätsschritt eine wichtige Rolle als Impulsgeber. So ist das Setting entscheidend dafür verantwortlich, in welchem Maße während der praktischen Erkundung kreative Dynamik und Lernprozesse in Gang gesetzt (oder im Gegenteil verhindert) werden. Eine besonders gelungene – und übrigens auch eine besonders misslungene – Erkundungsphase wiederum ist die bestmögliche Voraussetzung für eine anschließende Reflexion und daraus resultierende (neue) Erkenntnisse. Eine ergiebige Reflexion schließlich ist ein hilfreicher Ausgangspunkt für die Konzipierung einer neuen Erkundungsphase.

Die Dynamik, die durch die Folge der Aktivitäten in ihrer Wechselwirkung mit den Ressourcen entsteht, hat nicht nur in der bildlichen Darstellung den Charakter eines Wirbels, sondern kann auch in der Praxis einen wirbelförmigen Sog erzeugen, wenn in bereits beschriebener Weise die Spirale in Bewegung kommt, weil Settings, praktische Erkundungen und Erkenntnisse zu immer wieder neuen Erkundungen, Reflexionen und Settings führen.

Wichtig zum Verständnis des Modells ist die Beobachtung, dass die beschriebenen Abläufe sich in zeitlich ganz unterschiedlichen Dimensionen abspielen können.

So gibt es insbesondere in der Phase der praktischen Erkundung einen sehr schnellen Kreislauf, in welchem eine Aktion quasi zeitgleich mit der Ausführung beobachtet und reflektiert wird, was dazu führt, dass sie als erfolgreich oder auch nicht erfolgreich eingestuft und entsprechend die aktuelle Strategie beibehalten oder geändert wird. In einer anderen zeitlichen Dimension kann – beispielsweise in einem Probenkontext – aus dem Setting für eine Improvisation nach Durchführung, Beobachtung und Reflexion ein modifiziertes Setting für die nächste Improvisation erfolgen. Aber auch ein zeitlich sehr viel größerer Maßstab ist denkbar, wenn ein künstlerisches Projekt erst im Abstand von vielen Jahren »verstanden« wird und zu neuen Projektideen führt.

Das Modell ist wohlgemerkt nicht als zwingend notwendiges Verfahren zu verstehen, sondern als Muster eines Vorgehens, in dem Theorie und Praxis

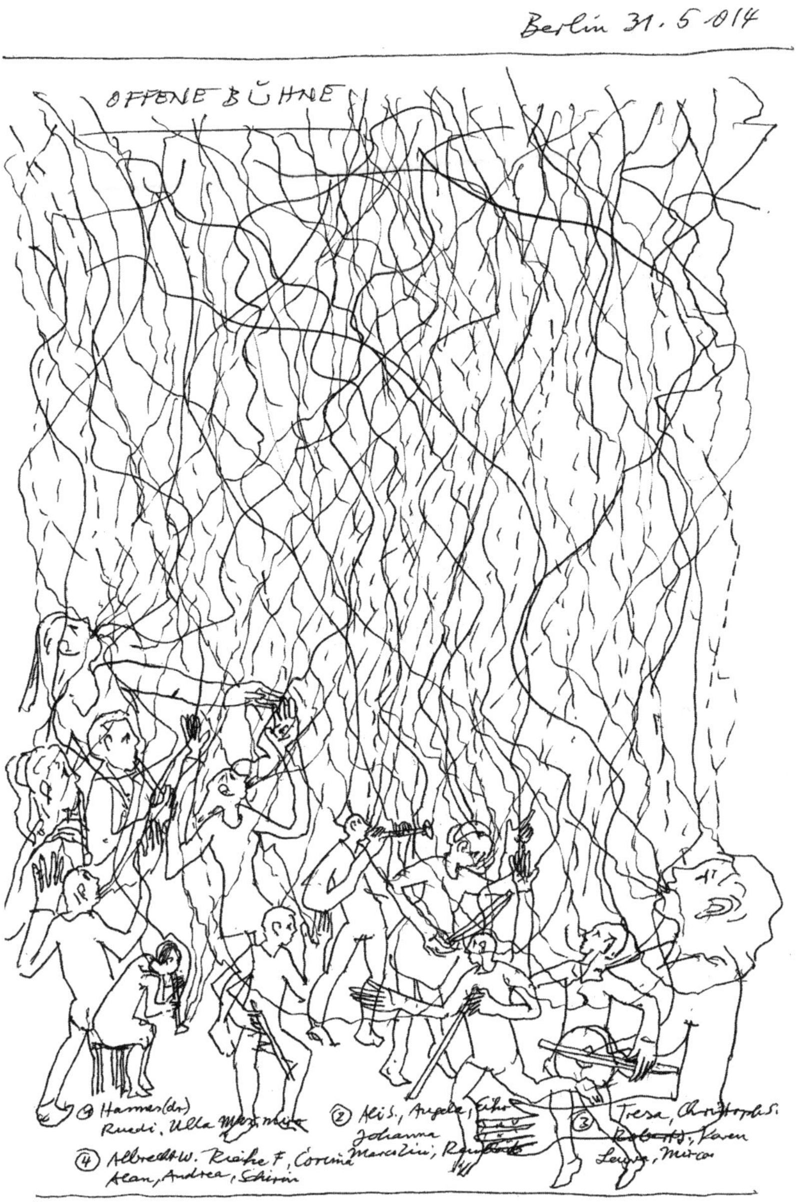
Berlin 31. 5 014
OFFENE BÜHNE

gleichermaßen zur Geltung kommen. Der Stellenwert der Reflexion ist dabei durchaus umstritten. So hatte es sich das *New Phonic Art Ensemble,* eines der renommiertesten Freie Improvisation-Ensembles der 1960er Jahre, zum Prinzip gemacht, nicht über seine Stücke zu sprechen, weil durch (selbst-)kritisches Beleuchten eine Einschränkung der spontanen Entscheidung und somit der künstlerischen Freiheit befürchtet wurde.

3. Improvisieren(d) lernen – Exploration als pädagogischer Ansatz

Improvisieren(d) lernen unterscheidet sich insofern ganz grundsätzlich von vielen anderen Arten des Lernens, als der Lerngegenstand – die Improvisation – ergebnisoffen ist. Es gibt keinen verbindlichen Wissenskanon und kein verbindliches Handwerk, der beziehungsweise das die Fähigkeit gewährleisten könnte, in selbstbestimmter Weise *Eigenes* zu schaffen, also kreativ zu sein. Einer Belehrung im traditionellen Sinn fehlt somit die Grundlage.

Der Schlüssel zum Lernen ist deshalb auch hier die Suchbewegung, die sowohl Weg als auch Ziel des Lernprozesses ist. Suchbewegung als Ziel, das heißt, dass es um die Befähigung geht, eigene Musik neu zu (er)finden, anstatt Eingeübtes zu reproduzieren. Suchbewegung als Weg bedeutet, sich durch praktisches Erkunden mit der »Sprache Musik« vertraut zu machen.

Deshalb ist es sinnvoll, in der pädagogischen Arbeit der künstlerischen Erkundung einen zentralen Stellenwert zuzuweisen. Das Modell des Spiralwirbels zeigt, wie damit sowohl Lernvorgänge als auch Kreativität initiiert werden können.

Die Besonderheit des pädagogischen Ansatzes besteht darin, dass eine improvisationserfahrene Person die »Reiseleitung« übernimmt, geeignete Settings anbietet, die Erkundungen (mitspielend oder nur hörend) begleitet, die anschließende Reflexionsphase durch gezielte Fragen fokussiert und weitere geeignete Spielregeln beziehungsweise Settings vorschlägt oder die kollektive Erarbeitung von Settings moderiert.

Für eine solche Vorgehensweise ist es wichtig, dass die Exploration bei ganz elementaren musikalischen Erlebnissen ansetzen kann. In der Freien Improvisation ist das möglich, weil ihr Material der Klang an sich ist. Es gibt somit keine verbindlichen Systeme für die Gestaltung von Tonhöhen (wie Skalen oder Harmonik) und Zeitabläufen (Metrum, Rhythmen, Formschemata), die man zuerst erlernen müsste, um damit spielen zu können. Deshalb sind von Seiten der Spieler keinerlei Vorkenntnisse oder Fertigkeiten wie Rhythmusfestigkeit oder Intonations-Sicherheit erforderlich. Und weil für diese Musik jede Art von Klang oder Geräusch zu Musik werden kann, bedarf es auch keiner elaborierten Instrumentaltechnik.

3. Learning improvising/improvising learning – exploration as a pedagogical approach

Learning improvising is fundamentally different from many other kinds of learning. This is because the subject – improvisation – is open with regard to the outcome. There is no obligatory canon of knowledge or technique that can guarantee the ability to create *something by yourself* in a self-determined way, in other words, to be creative. The basis for instruction in the traditional sense is therefore absent.

Thus, here, the key to learning is also searching which is both the way and the goal of the learning process. Searching as a goal means that it is about the ability to find (invent) one's own music anew, instead of just reproducing what one has practiced. Searching as a way means to acquaint oneself with the "language of music" through practical exploration.

Therefore, it makes sense to give artistic exploration a central role in pedagogical work. The vortex model shows how both learning processes and creativity can be initiated by doing so.

What is noteworthy about this pedagogical approach is that a person with experience of improvisation takes on the role of a "travel guide", who offers appropriate settings, guides explorations (playing or just listening), steers the subsequent reflection phase with pointed questions, and suggests other suitable rules for playing or settings, or who manages the collective development of the settings.

With such an approach it is important that the exploration can start with the most elementary of musical experiences. This is possible in free improvisation because the material is the sound itself. There is, therefore, no obligatory system for organizing pitches (like scales or harmony) or time (meter, rhythms, formal schemes) that one must first learn in order to play around with them. That is why the performer does not need to have any prior knowledge or skills such as rhythmic stability or clean intonation. In addition, for this music, every kind of sound or noise can become music. What is more, no elaborate instrumental technique is needed either.

The performers can then dedicate themselves completely to the exploration. The "sound itself" can be re-experienced as a phenomenon that deserves our full attention. Finding and creating sounds, whether with instruments or materials, can itself be a very sensual exploratory exercise. This raises central questions about music-making: how can these sounds work together? How can we piece them together as a convincing process over (in) time? These questions can be pursued as a continuous process of research and learning that make it possible to experience musical creation, as well as social interaction "from the inside out".[9]

---

9 | I have described the method I practice myself in detail in numerous publications, for example in Schwabe 1992, Kieseritzky; Schwabe 2001, Schwabe 2012a.

So können sich die Spieler ganz der Erkundung widmen. Der »Klang an sich« kann als Phänomen, das unsere gesamte Höraufmerksamkeit verdient, neu erlebt werden. Schon das Finden und Erfinden von Klängen ist eine sehr lustvolle Erkundungsaufgabe, egal ob auf Instrumenten oder Materialien. Daraus ergeben sich die zentralen Fragestellungen musikalischer Gestaltung: Wie können diese Klänge zusammenwirken? Und wie können wir sie zu einem überzeugenden Ablauf in der Zeit zusammenfügen? Diese Fragen lassen sich in einem kontinuierlichen Forschungs- und Lernprozess verfolgen, der musikalische Gestaltung und parallel dazu soziale Interaktion immer weiter differenziert und »von innen heraus« erfahrbar macht.[9]

Es gibt zahlreiche methodische Details, wie unterschiedliche »pädagogische Reiseleiter« einen solchen Erkundungsprozess gestalten können, welche Art von Settings sie wählen, ob sie die Settings selbst vorgeben oder sie gemeinsam mit der Gruppe entwickeln, in welchem Maße Lernvorgänge und/oder kreative Impulse initiiert werden und verschiedenes mehr.

In diesem Kontext sei darauf hingewiesen, dass es keine Situation ohne Setting gibt. Auch »keine Vorgabe« ist ein Setting, wobei natürlich dann besonders die Zusammensetzung der Gruppe eine Rolle spielt (große oder kleine Gruppe, vertraute oder unbekannte Mitspieler), deren Vorkenntnisse und der situative Kontext.

Eine besondere Herausforderung der pädagogischen Arbeit ist die Beobachtungs- und Reflexionsphase. Selbst-Beobachtung während des Spiels ist sehr anspruchsvoll, lohnt aber geübt zu werden. Hilfreich ist, wenn ein Teil der Spieler als Zuhörer agiert oder die Improvisationen aufgenommen und gemeinsam angehört werden. Für die Reflexion gilt es, durch gezielte Fragen den Diskussionsprozess zu moderieren und zugleich geeignete Begrifflichkeiten und Kriterien zu erarbeiten, die für improvisatorische Prozesse relevant sind.

Im *exploratorium* haben wir noch eine zusätzliche pädagogische Erkundungs-Ebene zu bieten: Hier ist ein breit aufgestelltes Kollegium tätig, das nicht nur verschiedene fachliche Schwerpunkte vertritt, sondern auch verschiedene methodische Ansätze und damit unterschiedliche Settings. In einem explorativen Kontext ist diese Vielfalt für alle Beteiligten eine Bereicherung, weil sich die verschiedenen »Forschungsideen« gegenseitig ergänzen.

Je mehr wir die pädagogische Arbeit als künstlerischen Erkundungsprozess gestalten, desto mehr verschwimmen die Grenzen zwischen Kunst und Pädagogik. Wenn Unterrichtende und Unterrichtete sich gemeinsam auf die Suche begeben, gemeinsam kreative Höhen und Tiefen durchlaufen und ge-

---

9 | Details zu der von mir selbst praktizierten Methodik habe ich in zahlreichen Publikationen beschrieben, beispielsweise in Schwabe 1992, Kieseritzky; Schwabe 2001, Schwabe 2012a.

There are many factors which different "pedagogical travel guides" can draw upon to put together such an exploratory process: what kind of settings they choose, whether they choose the settings themselves or develop them together with the group, to what extent learning processes and/or creative impulses are initiated, and many others.

In this context, it should be pointed out that there is no situation without a setting. Even "no stipulation" is a setting, in which the constellation of the group is of particular importance (large group or small group, familiar or unknown players), as are their prior knowledge and the situational context.

A particular challenge of pedagogical work is the observation and reflection phase. Self-observation while performing is very demanding but worth practicing. It is useful to have some of the players act as listeners, or record the improvisation and then listen to it together. Developing appropriate terminology and criteria that are suitable for improvisational processes, asking pertinent questions and managing discussion processes are all relevant to the reflection.

At the *exploratorium* we have another pedagogical exploratory level to offer: there is a wide diversity of teaching staff here, not only in terms of their areas of expertise, but also their methodological approaches; these, in effect, create variety in the settings as well. In terms of the explorative context, this diversity is enriching for everyone involved because the different "research ideas" complement one another.

The more we develop the pedagogical work as an artistic, exploratory process, the more blurred the lines between art and pedagogy become. When those who teach and those who are being taught set off on their journey together, learn together and go through artistic ups and downs together, then Joseph Beuys' often quoted motto "everyone is an artist" is experienced in reality.

4. Engaging with External Theory and Research

Reflecting on our artistic experience is a multidimensional and therefore demanding activity. What is more, we are initially limited, in terms of exchanging ideas, to those people in our immediate vicinity. For these two reasons, it can make sense to gain insights from other people who

- are involved with the same subjects in other locations
- have engaged with our subjects in a particular way, for example in distinctly academic settings
- are experts in a more or less related field (for example body therapy, psychology, therapy, pedagogy, philosophy, aesthetics, neuroscience), and as such, shed a special light on our activities

meinsam lernen, wird Joseph Beuys' vielzitiertes Credo »Jeder Mensch ist ein Künstler« in der Praxis erlebbar.

4. Die Auseinandersetzung mit externer Theorie und Forschung

Das Reflektieren unserer künstlerischen Erfahrung ist eine vieldimensionale und daher ausgesprochen anspruchsvolle Tätigkeit. Dazu kommt, dass wir beim Austausch über unsere Ideen zunächst auf die Personen aus unserem unmittelbaren Umfeld eingegrenzt sind. Aus beiden Gründen kann es sinnvoll sein, sich darüber hinaus mit den Erkenntnissen anderer Personen auseinanderzusetzen,

- die sich denselben Themen an anderen Orten widmen,
- die sich mit unseren Themen auf besondere Weise auseinandersetzen, beispielsweise in ausdrücklich wissenschaftlich angelegten Settings,
- die als Experten einer mehr oder weniger verwandten oder entfernten Thematik (beispielsweise Körperarbeit, Psychologie, Therapie, Pädagogik, Philosophie, Ästhetik, Hirnforschung) einen besonderen Blick auf unsere Tätigkeit werfen,
- die als ebensolche Experten zwar keinen Blick auf unsere Tätigkeiten werfen, deren Erkenntnisse aber dennoch für uns wertvoll sein können.

Im *exploratorium* gibt es dafür seit 2012 den Bereich *Theorie & Forschung*, der das Reflektieren über Improvisation in vielfacher Weise fördert und realisiert. Hier werden externe Referenten eingeladen, Symposien veranstaltet und eigene Publikationen herausgegeben. Herzstück ist eine kleine Fachbibliothek mit den wichtigsten Schriften über frei improvisierte Musik sowie zahlreiche angrenzende Themen. Reinhard Gagel, der die Abteilung leitet, hat ein ganz eigenes Profil dafür entwickelt, wie dieses externe Wissen nicht nur einfach präsentiert und zur Verfügung gestellt, sondern in besonderen Veranstaltungsformaten mit improvisatorischer Praxis rückgekoppelt wird.

Seine Arbeitsweise und Projekte hat er an anderer Stelle in diesem Buch ausführlich vorgestellt (siehe S. 312ff).

Sein zentrales Anliegen ist es dabei, die Reflexion mit der künstlerischen Erkundung unmittelbar zu verbinden, sozusagen eins werden zu lassen. Innovativ ist außerdem die Idee, theoretische Texte zum Bestandteil von Settings zu machen. Auf diese Weise kann Theorie sowohl in der Praxis erfahrbar gemacht, als auch zugleich auf ihre Realitätstauglichkeit hin überprüft werden. Die praktische Erkundung bietet eine Basis für vertieftes Verständnis und – gegebenenfalls auch kritische – Hinterfragung.

- do not deal with our activities, but whose insights as experts might still be valuable to us.

The *Theory & Research* department has existed at the *exploratorium* since 2012. It supports and realizes reflection on improvisation in a number of ways. It invites external lecturers, organizes symposiums and publishes our works. A small library dedicated to the subject is at the center of this, containing the most important writings on free improvisation as well as on numerous related subjects. Reinhard Gagel, who leads this department, has developed a unique profile that not only presents and makes external knowledge available, but which also provides feedback on improvisational practice via special event formats. His approach and projects are comprehensively detailed in this book (see p. 312ff).

His main priority is to connect artistic exploration directly with reflection, so in effect they become one. The idea of making theoretical texts an integral part of settings is also innovative. In this way, it is possible to experience theory in practice and, at the same time, to test its validity. Practical exploration offers a basis for deeper understanding and – possibly also critical – questioning.

5. Explorative event formats for improvisational practice

Settings for improvisational investigation can also become event formats in their own right. The context of an event space such as the *exploratorium* lends itself to developing new formats and exploring beyond the common categories of artistic presentations and pedagogical offerings. Some of these forms of presentation have already been addressed. Now I would like to present a "classic" example, the so-called *open stage*. This event lies somewhere between a concert and a workshop and offers people who already have experience of improvising the possibility to explore the "critical situation", namely the situation of improvising on stage. However, this takes place in a playful setting because the active participants – usually between 20 and 30 people – do not perform in existing rehearsed formations, but are repeatedly divided up into new ad hoc ensembles, sometimes by drawing lots, sometimes on the basis of who wants to play with whom. The playful nature of the event offers stimulation and protection at the same time. Stimulation comes from the repeated change of partners, whereas protection results from the fact that an "unsuccessful" piece does not really question the competence of the individual performers, given the fact that the ensembles are thrown together spontaneously. The term "unsuccessful" does indeed make sense here, because even if the criteria are debatable, both performers and listeners make subjective value judgments.

5. Explorative Veranstaltungsformate für die improvisatorische Praxis

Settings für improvisatorische Erkundungen können auch zu eigenständigen Veranstaltungsformen werden. Im Kontext eines Veranstaltungsortes wie dem *exploratorium* bietet es sich an, besondere Formate zu entwickeln und zu erkunden, jenseits der üblichen Kategorien von künstlerischen Präsentationen einerseits und pädagogischen Angeboten andererseits.

Auf einigen solcher Veranstaltungstypen wurde bereits hingewiesen. Ich möchte nachfolgend exemplarisch einen »Klassiker« vorstellen, die sogenannte *Offene Bühne*. Diese Veranstaltung ist zwischen Konzert und Workshop angesiedelt und bietet Personen mit improvisatorischer Vorerfahrung die Möglichkeit, den »Ernstfall«, nämlich die improvisatorische Bühnensituation, zu erkunden. Allerdings geschieht dies in einem sehr spielerischen Setting, weil die aktiv Teilnehmenden – in der Regel 20 bis 30 Personen – nicht in bestehenden und aufeinander eingespielten Formationen auftreten, sondern zu immer wieder neuen Adhoc-Ensembles zusammengestellt werden, teils im Losverfahren, teils mit Wunschpartnern. Dieser spielerische Charakter bietet Anregung und Schutz zugleich. Anregung durch die immer wieder neuen Partner, Schutz insofern, als ein »misslungenes« Stück in Anbetracht der spontan zusammengestellten Besetzung die eigene Kompetenz nicht wirklich in Frage stellt. Der Begriff »misslungen« macht dabei übrigens durchaus Sinn, denn wenngleich die Kriterien dafür streitbar sind, fällen doch sowohl Spieler als auch Zuhörer subjektive Werturteile.

Verbale Reflexionen finden während der Veranstaltung nicht statt. Da aber pro Abend circa 20 Stücke (die auf fünf bis sieben Minuten Dauer angelegt sein sollen) gespielt werden und die Spieler jeweils nur an drei bis vier davon aktiv beteiligt sind, sind sie über einen langen Zeitraum hinweg, nämlich bei allen anderen 16 – 17 Stücken, »nur« Zuhörer. Hier geschieht – bewusst oder unbewusst – ein kontinuierliches Reflektieren darüber, welche Stücke sie überzeugt haben, welche nicht und warum das so war. Sie entwickeln Kriterien, erproben deren Anwendung bei verschiedenen Stücken und können sich, wenn sie möchten, nach der Veranstaltung mit anderen darüber austauschen.[10]

Zweifellos hat die *Offene Bühne* einen wichtigen Stellenwert als sozialer Treffpunkt und »Partner-Börse« für improvisatorische Unternehmungen. Die wichtigsten Gründe dafür, warum sich dieses Setting auch nach derzeit mehr als elf Jahren immer noch sehr großer Beliebtheit erfreut und zu den am meisten frequentierten Veranstaltungen gehört, sind jedoch – das belegen zahlreiche Gespräche – zum einen die Möglichkeit, die Bühnensituation mit verschiedenen

---

10 | Eine ausführliche Beschreibung der Erfahrungen mit der *Offenen Bühne* und ähnlichen Veranstaltungen ist zu finden in improfil 2015.

Verbal reflection does not take place during the event. However, since approximately 20 pieces are performed in an evening (each lasting between five and seven minutes), and the participants only actively take part in three or four of these, they are listeners for a longer period of time, namely for the other 16 or 17 pieces. During all this, continuous reflection takes place – consciously or unconsciously – regarding which pieces the participants found convincing, which ones they did not, and why this was the case. They develop criteria, test their applicability during different pieces and, should they so wish, they can share their feedback with others after the event.[10]

Without a doubt, the open stage is of great value as a social meeting place and "partner exchange" for improvisational activities. The most important reasons why this setting is so popular and why it is one of the most well-attended events – and many conversations bear this out – are the possibilities of exploring the stage situation with various players, the many different artistic encounters and the exchange (practical and, when desired, theoretical) that comes with them. All of these are important "drivers" for creative production and the broadening of the horizons of the artistic experience.

Event formats such as these encourage exploration and investigation by the musicians. At the same time, they are the subjects of our research as event organizers who are searching for appropriate settings and ways to improve them.

Concluding remarks

This paper has dealt with "research" in the sense of artistic investigation and exploration without any claims to scholarly objectivity. Instead, the focus has been on personal subjective artistic insight and the broadening of horizons, which can, in the best case, lead to the further development of contemporary artistic practice. The questions that arise may only seem to be relevant to improvisation, whereas in fact, they lend themselves to an enrichment of our musical or cultural life as a whole: *exploring improvisation* also means *exploring music.*

This applies to artistic work in which freely improvised music can be an unusual impulse for contemporary creation. This can be applied to pedagogical work where employing artistic exploration as a way of learning and teaching is an unconventional approach, which unfolds the learners' potential to a greater extent and takes them seriously, ultimately enabling them to gain a musical understanding "from the inside out". This also applies to reflection on music, which can be intensified in a special way when it is tested on one's own impro-

10 | A detailed description of experiences with the *Open Stage* and similar events can be found in improfil 2015.

Spielpartnern zu erkunden sowie zum anderen die vielen verschiedenen künstlerischen Begegnungen und der damit einhergehende (praktische und bei Bedarf theoretische) Austausch. All dies sind wichtige »Treibmittel« für kreatives Schaffen und die Erweiterung des künstlerischen Erfahrungshorizontes.

Veranstaltungsformate wie dieses sind einerseits dem Erproben und Erforschen von Seiten der Spieler gewidmet. Zugleich sind sie aber auch Objekte unseres Erforschens als Veranstalter, auf der Suche nach geeigneten Settings und deren Verbesserung.

Schlussbemerkung

In diesem Beitrag ging es um »Forschen« im Sinne eines künstlerischen Erkundens beziehungsweise Explorierens, jenseits wissenschaftlicher Ansprüche an Objektivierbarkeit, stattdessen fokussiert auf die eigene subjektive künstlerische Erkenntnis und Horizonterweiterung, die im besten Fall zu einer Teilhabe an der Weiterentwicklung zeitgenössischen Kunstschaffens führen kann.

Die Fragen, die dabei auftreten, sind nur scheinbar improvisationsspezifisch. Tatsächlich sind sie dazu geeignet, unser musikalisches beziehungsweise kulturelles Leben insgesamt zu bereichern: *exploring improvisation*, das heißt eben auch *exploring music*. Dies gilt für die künstlerische Arbeit, wo frei improvisierte Musik ungewöhnliche Impulse für zeitgenössisches Schaffen geben kann. Dies gilt für die pädagogische Arbeit, wo künstlerisches Erkunden als Weg des Lehrens und Lernens einen ungewöhnlichen Ansatz darstellt, der die Potenziale der Lernenden in besonderem Maße herausfordert und ernst nimmt und ihnen ein musikalisches Verständnis »von innen heraus« ermöglicht. Dies gilt auch für das Reflektieren über Musik, das, wenn es in der eigenen improvisatorischen Praxis auf die Probe gestellt wird, in besonderer Weise vertieft werden kann. Und es gilt schließlich für die Möglichkeit, in ungewöhnlichen improvisatorischen Formaten musikalischen Zusammenspiels neue anregende musikalische Erfahrungen zu sammeln.

Bei all dem nimmt das Explorieren einen zentralen Stellenwert ein. Und genau diese Eigenschaft von Improvisation, dass Musik nicht ausgeführt, sondern primär erkundet wird, ist aus meiner Sicht einer der wichtigsten Impulse, den die improvisatorische Praxis zu unserem kulturellen Leben beisteuern kann: Exploration als künstlerische Grundhaltung.

visational practice. Finally, it also applies to the possibility of collecting new and inspiring musical experiences in unusual improvisatory formats for the purpose of collective music-making.

Exploration plays a central role in all of these. It is precisely this quality of improvisation – that music is primarily explored rather than performed – that, from my perspective, makes it one of the most important impulses that improvisational practice can contribute to our cultural life: exploration as a fundamental artistic approach.

Translation into English:: Louise & Phil Loxton, GB-Wales

Literatur/References

Csíkszentmihályi, Mihály (2000): Das Flow-Erlebnis. Jenseits von Angst und Langeweile im Tun aufgehen. 8., unv. Auflage, Stuttgart: Klett (English (1975): Beyond Boredom and Anxiety. The Experience of Play in Work and Games, San Francisco: Jossey-Bass Publishers).

improfil Nr. 78 (2015): Offene Bühne – Improvisation adhoc, April.

Kieseritzky, Herwig von; Schwabe, Matthias (2001): »Gruppenimprovisation als musikalische Basisarbeit«, in: Kraemer, Rudolf-Dieter; Rüdiger, Wolfgang: Ensemblespiel in Schule und Musikschule. Ein Handbuch für die Unterrichtspraxis, Augsburg: Wissner Verlag, 155-174.

ringgespräch über gruppenimprovisation LXXV (2012): Raum, April.

Schwabe, Matthias (1992): Musik spielend erfinden, Kassel: Bärenreiter.

Schwabe, Matthias (1994): »Musik – Bewegung – Improvisation«, in: ringgespräch über gruppenimprovisation LIX, August 1994, 16-18. Auch nachzulesen im Internet unter *URL: http://www.matthiasschwabe.com/musik-bewegung-improvisation/ (August 2015).*

Schwabe, Matthias (2011): »Experimentelle Improvisation im öffentlichen Raum«, in: ringgespräch über gruppenimprovisation LXXIV, April 2011, 79-81.

Schwabe, Matthias (2012a): »Improvisation als Basiskompetenz im Musikunterricht«, in: Pabst-Krueger, Michael; Terhag, Jürgen (Hg./Eds.): Musikunterricht heute 9. Musizieren mit Schulklassen. Praxis – Konzepte – Perspektiven, Handorf: Lugert Verlag, 106-113.

Schwabe, Matthias (2012b): »Wie Raum inspiriert – Underground Symphony 2011«, in: ringgespräch über gruppenimprovisation LXXV, April 2012b, 29-31.

Performance 29-5-014 · 15^{30}
FK

Autoren | Authors

Dr. Alan Bern (USA/Deutschland) ist Komponist, Improvisator, Pianist, Akkordeonist, Musikdirektor, Philosoph und Pädagoge. Er ist der Gründer und Vorsitzende von *othermusic e.V.*, einem Verein, der sich der Umsetzung interkultureller und interdisziplinär kulturell/bildender Projekte widmet, und er ist Leiter von *Yiddish Summer Weimar* und *Winter Edition*. Er studierte bei einer bemerkenswerten Reihe von Musikern und Denkern, darunter John Cage, Karl Berger, dem *Art Ensemble of Chicago*, Anthony Braxton, Frederic Rzewski, Leonard Shure, Daniel Dennett, Joel Hoffman und weiteren.

Er hat den Ruth Lifetime Achievement Award für seine innovative Arbeit als Musiker und Pädagoge erhalten. Seine CDs verschiedener Genres sind auf EMI, Winter & Winter, Jazz Werkstatt, Wergo, Rounder, Pinorekk und anderen Labels erhältlich. Er komponiert außerdem Musik für Theater und Zeitgenössischen Tanz, und seine Kompositionen wurden in den USA, Europa und Israel ausgezeichnet.

Bern hat einen Magistertitel in Philosophie und einen Doktortitel in Klassischer Komposition. Geboren in Bloomington, Indiana, lebte er viele Jahre in Boston und Brooklyn und seit 1987 in Berlin.

Mirio Cosottini hat 1992 seinen Abschluss an der *Akadamie für Musik* in Florenz gemacht. 1999 erhielt er einen Abschluss in Philosophie an der *Universität von Florenz*. Er ist eines der Gründungsmitglieder von Timet, einer zehnjährigen Kollaboration, die zu seinem Beitrag als Performer und Komponist führte. In der Folge hat er sich ausführlicher der Komposition, Musikalischen Analyse und Improvisation gewidmet. Er hat viele Artikel zum Thema Improvisation aus einer philosophischen, didaktischen und musikologischen Perspektive veröffentlicht. 2005 hat er *GRIM (Music Improvisation Research Group)* mit Alessio Pisani gegründet. Von 2005 bis 2010 hat er Improvisation am *Konservatorium von Padua* in Italien unterrichtet. Er promoviert momentan an der *Universität von Triest* mit einem Forschungsprojekt zur musikalischen Ästhetik.

Prof. Rogério Costa ist außerordentlicher Professor, Komponist, Saxophonist und Forscher, er gehört dem *Musikinstitut der Universität von São Paulo* (Brasilien) an. Als Komponist hat Costa Werke für verschiedene Besetzungen geschrieben wie Oktette, Quartette, Trios, Duos und Soli. Maßgebliche Künstler in Brasilien und Europa wie *Abstrai* aus Rio de Janeiro, *Camerata Aberta* aus São Paulo und das *Pierrot Lunaire Ensemble* aus Wien haben seine Kompositionen gespielt. Als Forscher entwickelt Professor Costa ein Forschungsprojekt zur Improvisation und ihren Verbindungen zu anderen Forschungsgebieten. Seine umfangreichen Arbeiten zum Thema Improvisation sind in Fachzeitschriften, Tagungsbeiträgen und Büchern veröffentlicht worden. Drei der wichtigsten aktuellen Projekte, die er betreut, sind die Gruppen für freie Improvisation *Entremeios, Musicaficta* und *Orquestra*

Dr. Alan Bern (USA/Germany) is a composer, improviser, pianist, accordionist, music director, philosopher and educator. He is the founder and chairman of *othermusic e.V.*, an association dedicated to creating intercultural and interdisciplinary cultural/educational projects based in Weimar, and the director of *Yiddish Summer Weimar and Winter Edition*. He has studied with a remarkable range of musicians and thinkers, including John Cage, Karl Berger, the *Art Ensemble of Chicago*, Anthony Braxton, Frederic Rzewski, Leonard Shure, Daniel Dennett, Joel Hoffman and others.

He has received a Ruth Lifetime Achievement award for his innovative work as a musician and educator. His CDs in several genres are available on EMI, Winter & Winter, Jazz Werkstatt, Wergo, Rounder, Pinorekk and other labels. He also composes music for theater and contemporary dance and his compositions have won awards in the USA, Europe and Israel.

Bern has a Master's degree in Philosophy and a Doctorate in Music Composition. A native of Bloomington, Indiana, he lived for many years in Boston and Brooklyn and has been based in Berlin since 1987.

Mirio Cosottini graduated from the *Florence Academy of Music* in 1992. In 1999, he obtained a degree in Philosophy from the *University of Florence*. He is one of the founding members of *Timet*, a 10-year collaboration that led to his contribution as a performer and composer. Subsequently he has delved further into composition, musical analysis and improvisation. He has published many articles on Improvisation from a philosophical, didactical and musicological point of view. In 2005 Cosottini founded the *GRIM (Musical Improvisation Research Group)* with Alessio Pisani. From 2005 to 2010 he taught improvisation at the *Conservatory of Padova* in Italy. He is currently doing a Ph.D at the *University of Trieste* with a research project in the Aesthetics of Music.

Prof. Rogério Costa is an associate professor, composer, saxophonist and researcher affiliated to the *Music Department at the University of São Paulo/Brazil*. As a composer, Costa has written compositions for various formations including octets, quartets, trios, duos and soloists. Leading artists in Brazil and Europe, such as *Abstrai* of Rio de Janeiro, *Camerata Aberta* of São Paulo and the *Pierrot Lunaire Ensemble* of Vienna, have played his compositions. As a researcher, Professor Costa is developing a research project on improvisation and its connections with other areas of study. He has written extensively on the theme of improvisation, with publications in journals, conference papers and books. Three of the most important current projects under his supervision are the free improvisation groups *Entremeios, Musicaficta* and *Orquestra Errante*. *http://www.rogeriocosta.mus.br/; https://usp-br.academia.edu/Rog%C3%A9rio Costa; http://www3.eca.usp.br/?q=node/236*

Errante. http://www.rogeriocosta.mus.br/; https://usp-br.academia.edu/Rog%C3%A9rioCosta; http://www3.eca.usp.br/?q=node/236

Corinna Eikmeier studierte Violoncello, zeitgenössische Musik und Improvisation. Sie interessierte sich schon während des Studiums für Zusammenhänge zwischen Ausdruck und Bewegung und machte parallel zu ihrem Musikstudium die Feldenkrais-Ausbildung in Wien (1992 – 1995).

Sie ist an zahlreichen interdisziplinären Projekten beteiligt, ist Lehrbeauftragte an der *Hochschule für Musik, Theater und Medien Hannover* für Feldenkrais und Improvisation, und freiberufliche Cellolehrerin.

Von 2007 bis 2009 führte sie ein Projekt zum Thema Feldenkrais und Improvisation durch. Die Projektdokumentation ist 2010 unter dem Titel *Ungewohnte Positionen* erschienen. Seit 2010 führt sie das Projekt wissenschaftlich weiter und promoviert an der *Universität für Musik und darstellende Kunst Wien* im Fach Musikpädagogik. *www.corinna-eikmeier.de*

Lara Frisch promoviert an der *Bauhaus-Universität Weimar*. Ihr Thema setzt sich mit der Gruppenkommunikation improvisierender Ensembles auseinander. Dabei interessiert sie ganz besonders welche Kommunikationsformen benutzt werden, die die kreative Zusammenarbeit der Ensembles fördern. Nach ihrem Abiturabschluss in Luxemburg, studierte sie in England. Dort hat sie ihren BA in Kultur- und Kunstwissenschaften an der *University of Kent* in Canterbury, und ihren MA in Zeitgenössischer Kunsttheorie am *Goldsmiths College* in London erhalten. Ihre Forschungsinteressen beziehen sich auf Gruppenkommunikation und -dynamik, Systemdenken (Niklas Luhmann, Donella Meadows), kreative Zusammenarbeit und Dialog (nach David Bohm). Sie ist zudem eine zertifizierte Dialogprozessbegleiterin des Instituts *Dialog Transnational* in Berlin.

Reinhard Gagel, Improvisationsmusiker (Klavier, Moog Synthesizer), Ensembleleiter, Improvisationsforscher. Duo und Ensembleprojekte mit namhaften Musikern der Improvisation. Rundfunk- und CD-Produktionen mit eigenen Ensembles. Am *exploratorium berlin* zuständig für Theorie und Forschung. Schwerpunkt seiner praktischen und theoretischen Arbeit: musikalische Improvisation als partizipative Kunst-Praxis, Lecture Performances zur Theorie der Improvisation und Konzeption und Realisierung der multistilistischen Musiktheaterform *Offhandopera*. Lehrbeauftragter für die Ensemblefächer Musikalische Kommunikation, Didaktik der Improvisation und Freie Kammermusik an der *Universität für Musik und darstellende Kunst, Wien*. Dissertation über *Improvisation als soziale Kunst* bei Prof. Dr. Peter Röbke, Wien. Vorsitzender des *Ring für Gruppenimprovisation e.V.* und Mit-Herausgeber der Improvisa-

Corinna Eikmeier studied the cello, contemporary music and improvisation. During her studies she became interested in the relationship between expression and movement and as a result of this undertook a parallel study of the Feldenkrais method in Vienna (1992-1995). She is involved in numerous interdisciplinary projects, teaches Feldenkrais and improvisation at the *Hanover University of Music, Drama and Media* and is a freelance cello teacher. From 2007 to 2009 she led a project on Feldenkrais and Improvisation. The project documentation titled "Ungewohnte Positionen" (Unfamiliar Positions) was first published in 2010. Since then she has continued to work on this project in a scientific capacity and is currently doing a doctorate in musical education at the *University of Music and Performing Arts, Vienna. www.corinna-eikmeier.de*

Lara Frisch is a researcher on group communication based in Berlin and is currently completing a Ph.D at the *Bauhaus University Weimar.* Her research explores the group communication processes which facilitate and foster creative collaboration amongst improvising ensembles. After successfully completing her A-Levels (Abitur) in Luxembourg, she graduated from the *University of Kent,* in Canterbury, England, with a BA in culture and cultural sciences and then completed her MA in contemporary art theory at *Goldsmiths College,* University of London. Her research interests are: group communication and dynamics, systems thinking (Niklas Luhmann, Donella Meadows), creative collaboration and dialog (David Bohm). Lara Frisch is also certified as a dialog facilitator by the Berlin *Institute Dialog Transnational.*

Reinhard Gagel is an improvisational musician (piano, Moog synthesizer), ensemble leader and a researcher of improvisation. He is involved in projects for duos and ensembles together with renowned improvisational musicians, as well as radio and CD productions featuring his own ensembles. He is responsible for theory and research at the *exploratorium berlin.* The main focus of his practical and theoretical work is musical improvisation as a participatory art form, lecture performances on the theory of improvisation and design and implementation of the multi-stylistic form of musical theater known as offhand opera. He is a teacher of the ensemble subjects; musical communication, improvisational didactics and free chamber music at the *University of Music and Performing Arts, Vienna.* Reinhard Gagel wrote his thesis on Improvisation as a social art form under the guidance of Professor Dr. Peter Röbke in Vienna. He is chairman of the *Ring für Gruppenimprovisation e.V.* and associate editor of the improvisation journal *improfil.* More information on Reinhard Gagel and his work can be found at: *www.reinhard-gagel.de; www.exploratorium-berlin.de; ww.quovadisteufelsgeiger.ac.at; www.impro-ring.de*

tions-Fachzeitung *Improfil. www.reinhard-gagel.de; www.exploratorium-berlin.de; www.quovadisteufelsgeiger.ac.at; www.impro-ring.de*

Marc Godau, Studium Musik und Germanistik auf Lehramt an der *Universität Potsdam*. Seit 2007 Lehrtätigkeit in einer allgemeinbildenden Schule und der Erwachsenenbildung (darunter Universität Potsdam, *Universität der Künste Berlin (UdK)*, Hoffbauer Stiftung). Mitgründer der Forschungsstelle *Appmusik: Formen musikalischer Praxis mit Apps* an der UdK Berlin. Derzeit wissenschaftlicher Mitarbeiter im Projekt TOUCH:MUSIC, ein BMBF-gefördertes Entwicklungs- und Erprobungsvorhaben zur musikpädagogischen Weiterbildung von Musikerinnen im Einsatz von Smartphones und Tablets in der freien Jugendarbeit und im außerunterrichtlichen Bereich an Schulen. Daneben Tätigkeit als Workshopleiter, Musiker, Arrangeur und Komponist. Forschungsschwerpunkte: informelles Musiklernen, systemisch-konstruktivistische Musikdidaktik. Laufendes Promotionsprojekt zu *Gruppenprozessen beim Musizieren im Musikunterricht*.

Matthias Haenisch, Studium der Musikwissenschaft und Germanistik, sowie Psychologie und Philosophie an der Freien Universität und Technischen Universität Berlin. Magisterabschluss 2008. Seit 2011 Wissenschaftlicher Mitarbeiter am *Bereich Musik und Musikpädagogik* der *Universität Potsdam*. Laufendes Promotionsprojekt mit einer empirischen Studie zur Ästhetik und Aufführungspraxis improvisierter Musik. Langjährige Tätigkeit als freiberuflicher Musiker sowie als Projektmanager in der Berliner Kulturveranstaltungsbranche.

Prof. em. Fridhelm Klein, geboren 1938 in Berlin, von 1969 bis 2004 Professor für Experimentelles Spiel und Medien an der *Akademie der Bildenden Künste*, München. Ausstellungen im In- und Ausland. Gastdozent an verschiedenen Hochschulen, Workshops, Seminare, Vorträge im In- und Ausland. Von 1989 bis 1999 Arbeit an der »Besucherschule« der *ART Frankfurt*. Schwerpunkt der eigenen künstlerischen Arbeit: Umgang mit Natur, Kunst und Kommunikation. Lebt und arbeitet in München und auf Kreta. Betreut die *Hallertauer Akademie* seit 2007.

Urban Mäder, geboren 1955, lebt in Luzern/Schweiz. Lehr- und Forschungstätigkeit an der *Hochschule Luzern – Musik* (Klavier- und Gruppenimprovisation, Music and Art Performance). Rege Tätigkeit als Komponist und Improvisator. Entwickelt auch sogenannte installative Musik im interdisziplinären Kontext. Mitbegründer des *Forum Neue Musik Luzern*. Zahlreiche Kompositionsaufträge, Werkverzeichnis mit über 70 Werken. *www.urbanmaeder.ch*

»Es gibt nur Improvisation – anschieben, aufbrechen, öffnen, verflüchtigen.«

Marc Godau studied to be a teacher of music and German literature at the *University of Potsdam* (1st exam 2009). Since 2007 he has been a teacher of educational programs for adults. He teaches in schools and at colleges of higher education (including *Potsdam University, Berlin University of the Arts (UdK), Hoffbauer Stiftung*). He co-founded the research center *Appmusic: ways to practise music using Apps* at the *Berlin University of the Arts (UdK)*. He is currently working on the scientific project TOUCH:MUSIC – a development and test initiative funded by the BMBF focusing on the musical education and further education of musicians who use smartphones and tablets in their work with youths outside of school and in extra-curricular school activities. In addition, he is a workshop leader, musician, arranger and composer. The main focus of his research is learning music in an informal setting and the systematic and constructive didactics of music. He is currently doing a doctorate on *Group Processes Whilst Making Music in the Music Classroom.*

Matthias Haenisch studied musical sciences and German literature, as well as psychology and philosophy at the Free University and the Berlin Technical University, obtaining a Ph. D in 2008. Since 2011 he has been a Research and Teaching Fellow at the *Potsdam University Institute of Music and Musical Education*. Matthias Haenisch is currently working on his doctoral thesis with an empirical study of the Aesthetics and Performance Practice in improvised music. He has been a freelance musician for many years, as well as a project manager in the cultural events sector in Berlin.

Prof. em. Fridhelm Klein, geboren 1938 in Berlin, von 1969 bis 2004 Professor für Experimentelles Prof. em. Fridhelm Klein, born 1938 in Berlin, was a professor of Experimental Play and Media at the *Academy of Fine Arts*, Munich, from 1969 – 2004. He holds exhibitions in Germany and abroad, is a visiting professor at various universities and gives workshops, seminars and lectures at home and abroad. From 1989 – 1999 he worked at the *Frankfurt ART* "School of Visitors". The focus of his own artistic work has centered on dealing with nature, art and communication. Fridhelm Klein lives and works in Munich and on the island of Crete. He has been head of the *Academy of Hallertau* since 2007.

Urban Mäder, born 1955, lives in Lucerne, Switzerland. He teaches and researches at the *Lucerne University of Applied Sciences and Arts – School of Music* (piano- and group improvisation, Music and Art Performance) and is very active as a composer and improviser. He develops what is termed "installed music" in an interdisciplinary setting and was the co-founder of the *Forum New Music Lucerne* and has published more than 70 titles. For more information visit *www.urbanmaeder.ch.*

"There is only improvisation – initiate, start anew, open, evaporate."

Mathias Maschat, Studium Kulturwissenschaften und ästhetische Praxis mit Hauptfach Musik in Hildesheim; Diplomarbeit (2006): *Frei improvisierte Musik im Spannungsfeld von Selbstorganisation und öffentlicher Förderung. Studie zu Musikerkooperativen und zur kulturpolitischen Verankerung der improvisierten Musik in Deutschland;* 2007/08 Volontariat im Musikreferat des *Niedersächsischen Ministeriums für Wissenschaft und Kultur,* Hannover; 2009 tätig bei *ohrenstrand.net,* dem Berliner Netzwerk für neugieriges Hören (Presse- und Öffentlichkeitsarbeit); 2010–2013 Stipendiat im Strukturierten Promotionsprogramm *Erinnerung – Wahrnehmung – Bedeutung. Musikwissenschaft als Geisteswissenschaft* an der Universität Osnabrück mit dem Promotionsprojekt: *Improvisationsästhetik im Kontext musikalischer Avantgarde;* Mitveranstalter der Reihe *biegungen im ausland,* Berlin; Mitbegründer der *Berlin Improvisation Research Group (BIRG).*

Dr. Nina Polaschegg studierte Musikwissenschaften, Soziologie und Philosophie in Gießen und Hamburg, wo sie auch promovierte. Ihre Forschungsschwerpunkte liegen im Bereich der Musiksoziologie, der zeitgenössischen komponierten, improvisierten und elektronischen Musik sowie im zeitgenössischen Jazz. Sie lebt als Musikwissenschaftlerin, Musikpublizistin und Kontrabassistin in Wien, arbeitet für diverse öffentlich-rechtliche Rundfunkanstalten in Deutschland, Österreich und der Schweiz und schreibt für verschiedene Fachzeitschriften. Lehraufträge an den Musikhochschulen bzw. Universitäten Hamburg und Klagenfurt. Als Kontrabassistin spielte sie historisch informiert mit Barockorchestern und widmet sich vor allem der (freien) Improvisation.

Edwin (Eddie) Prévost, Perkussionist und Schlagzeuger, wurde 1942 in England geboren. 1965 Mitbegründer des wegweisenden Improvisationsensembles *AMM*. Ein Großteil von Prévosts Diskographie (*AMM* und andere) ist auf *www.matchlessrecordings.com* zu finden.

Er hält gelegentlich Vorlesungen und schreibt über Musik. Er hat die folgenden Bücher geschrieben: *No Sound Is Innocent* (Copula, 1995), *Minute Particulars* (Copula, 2004) und *The First Concert: An Adaptive Appraisal of a Meta-Music* (Copula, 2011) geschrieben. Er hat die veröffentlichten Schriften von Cornelius Cardew herausgegeben – *Cornelius Cardew: A Reader* (Copula, 2006) – und John Tilburys Cardew-Biographie *Cornelius Cardew: A Life Unfinished* (Copula, 2008) verlegt. Seit 1999 veranstaltet Prévost einen wöchentlichen Improvisations-Workshop in London. Bisher haben daran mehrere hundert Musizierende von über 20 verschiedenen Nationalitäten teilgenommen.

Matthias Schwabe, geboren 1958 in Karlsruhe. Studierte Komposition und Musiktheorie in Karlsruhe und Hamburg. Ausbildung, später Mitarbeit bei Lilli Friedemann in Musikalischer Gruppenimprovisation.

Mathias Maschat studied cultural sciences and aesthetic practice with a major in music in Hildesheim. His list of accomplishments reads as follows: Dissertation (2006) on *Freely improvised music in the conflicting fields of self-organisation and public funding. A study on musicians' cooperatives and on the politico-cultural integration of improvised music in Germany*; 2007/08 traineeship in *the music department at the ministry for science and culture* in Hanover, Lower Saxony; press and public relations work for *ohrenstrand.net*, the Berlin-based network for interested listening; 2010-2013 scholarship holder on the Structured Doctorate Program *Memory – Perception – Significance. Musical Science as a Science of the Arts* at the University of Osnabrück. His doctorate project is on *Improvisational Aesthetics in the Context of Musical Avantgarde*; co-organizer of *biegungen im ausland*, Berlin; co-founder of the *Berlin Improvisation Research Group (BIRG)*.

Dr. Nina Polaschegg studied musical sciences, sociology and philosophy in Gießen and Hamburg where she also attained her doctorate. Her research focuses mainly on the fields of music sociology, as well as contemporary composed, improvised and electronic music and contemporary jazz. She works as a music scientist, music publisher and double-bassist in Vienna, also working for various radio stations in Germany, Austria and Switzerland. In addition, Nina Polaschegg writes for different trade journals and teaches at various Conservatories and at the Universities of Hamburg and Klagenfurt. As a double-bassist she has played with baroque orchestras and is dedicated, above all, to the pursuit of (free) improvisation.

Edwin (Eddie) Prévost, percussionist and drummer, born in England in 1942. Co-founder in 1965 of seminal improvising ensemble *AMM*. Most of Prévost's discography (*AMM* and other) can be found on *www.matchlessrecordings.com*.

He occasionally lectures and writes about music. His books are *No Sound is Innocent* (Copula 1995), *Minute Particulars* (Copula 2004) and *The First Concert – an adaptive appraisal of a meta-music* (Copula 2011). He edited the published writings of Cornelius Cardew: *Cornelius Cardew:* A *Reader* (Copula 2006). And, subsequently published John Tilbury's biography of Cardew: *Cornelius Cardew a life unfinished* (Copula 2008). In 1999, he first convened a weekly improvisation workshop in London. So far, this has been attended by many hundreds of musicians representing over twenty different nationalities.

Matthias Schwabe was born in Karlsruhe in 1958. He studied composition and theory of music in Karlsruhe and Hamburg. He was trained, and later worked with Lilli Friedemann in the field of musical group improvisation.

He has been working in Berlin as a freelance composer, improviser, music pedagogue and author on music pedagogy since 1984. Matthias Schwabe is a founder member of the improvisation ensemble *Ex Tempore*.

Seit 1984 freiberuflich tätig in Berlin als Komponist, Improvisator, Musikpädagoge und Musikpädagogik-Autor. Gründungsmitglied des Improvisationsensembles *Ex Tempore.*

Fortbildungstätigkeit im Bereich kreativer Musikpädagogik im In- und Ausland. Lehraufträge am *Sozialpädagogischen Institut Berlin* (Erzieher-Ausbildung) und an der *Universität der Künste Berlin.*

Zahlreiche Veröffentlichungen zu den Themen Improvisation, Kreativität im Instrumentalunterricht sowie in Elementarer Musikpädagogik. Gründer und Leiter des *exploratorium berlin.*

Weitere Informationen unter *www.matthiasschwabe.com.*

In den Intermezzi kommen außerdem zu Wort:
Helmut Bieler-Wendt (Musiker, Improvisator, Komponist; Bildungsreferent am LWL-Bildungszentrum *Jugendhof Vlotho*; Vorstandsmitglied des *INMM* Darmstadt)
Christoph Irmer (Geiger, Improvisationsmusiker und Pädagoge)
Barre Phillips (Kontrabassist, Improvisationsmusiker und Komponist)
Stefan Roszak (experimenteller Musikpädagoge, Klangkünstler und Instrumentenbauer)
Wolfgang Schliemann (Perkussionist, Improvisator, Musikwissenschaftler, Pädagoge)

He has expanded his training in the area of creative music pedagogy both at home and abroad. He teaches as well at the *Social-Pedagogical Institute* in Berlin (teacher-trainer) and the *Berlin University of the Arts (UdK)*. Matthias Schwabe has published countless works on the themes of improvisation, creativity in instrument lessons and rudimentary music education, and is in addition the founder and head of the *exploratorium berlin*.

For more information, visit *www.matthiasschwabe.com*.

In addition, the "Intermezzi" contain statements of
Helmut Bieler-Wendt (musician, improviser, composer; education consultant at *Jugendhof Vlotho*; board member of *INMM* Darmstadt)
Christoph Irmer (violinist, improvising musician and pedagogue)
Barre Phillips (double-bass player, composer and improvising musician)
Stefan Roszak (experimental music teacher, sound artist and instrument maker)
Wolfgang Schliemann (percussionist, improviser, musicologist, pedagogue)

FRIDHELM KLEIN

EXPLORING IMPROVISATION

10 Jahre exploratorium Berlin
29.5. – 1.6.2014

Festival Freie Improvisation in Theorie und Praxis

In begleitenden Zeichnungsnotizen von Fridhelm Klein

Festival-Programm | Festival-Program

Exploring Improvisation | Exploring Improvisation

10 Jahre *exploratorium berlin* Festival Freie Improvisation in Theorie und Praxis | 10 years of *exploratorium berlin* Festival Free Improvised Music in Theory and Practice

---

29.05.2014

15.30 h	Eröffnung/Opening **Performance:** *Sarotti Instant & TanzArtLabor*
16.15 – 18 h	*Why do we improvise?* **Podiums-Gespräch** mit/**Talk** with Barre Phillips & Eddie Prévost
20 h	**Konzert/concert:** *Ensemble hübsch acht* Carl Ludwig Hübsch (tub, comp), Isabelle Duthoit (cl), Joris Rühl (cl), Philipp Gropper (sax), Wolter Wierbos (trb), Joker Nies (electr), Philip Zoubek (p), Christian Lillinger (dr)

30.05.2014

10 – 12.30 h	**Symposium** Improvisation erforschen – improvisierend forschen | Researching Improvisation – Researching by Improvisation Urban Mäder, Matthias Haenisch & Marc Godau, Corinna Eikmeier, Rogério Costa
12.30 – 13 h	**Offene Bühne/Open Stage**
14.30 – 16.30 h	**Workshops** mit/with Barre Phillips & Ariel Shibolet
14.30 – 16.30 h	**Seminar A** Improvisierend forschen | Researching by Improvisation Impulse: Prof. Fridhelm Klein
17 – 18 h	**Tutti Improvisation SOUP 1**
20 h	**Konzert/concert:** *Neumann – Phillips – Prévost – Shibolet* Andrea Neumann (inside-p, electr), Barre Phillips (bass), Eddie Prévost (perc), Ariel Shibolet (sax)

31.05.2014

10 – 12.30 h	**Symposium** Improvisation erforschen – improvisierend forschen | Researching Improvisation – Researching by Improvisation Alan Bern, Mirio Cosottini, Lara Frisch, Mathias Maschat
12.30 – 13 h	**Offene Bühne/Open Stage**
14.30 – 16.30 h	**Workshops** mit/with Barre Phillips & Ariel Shibolet
14.30 – 16.30 h	**Seminar B** Improvisierend forschen/Researching by Improvisation Impulse: Dr. Nina Polaschegg
17 – 18 h	**Tutti Improvisation SOUP 2**
19.30 h	**Konzert/concert:** *Fritz Hauser & Jean Laurent Sasportes* Fritz Hauser (dr, perc), Jean Laurent Sasportes (dance)
21 h	**Buffet & Fest** 10 Jahre exploratorium berlin **Celebration** 10 years of exploratorium berlin

01.06.2014

11 h Saal 1	**Offene Bühne/Open Stage**
11.30 – 13.30 h	*»Improvisation ist mehr!« | "Improvisation is more!"* 50 Jahre Improvisation in der künstlerischen, pädagogischen und therapeutischen Arbeit – 50 Jahre »Ring für Gruppenimprovisation« | 50 years of improvisation in arts, education and therapy – 50 years of "Ring für Gruppenimprovisation" (Association for improvised music) **Roundtable** mit/with: Prof. Peter Jarchow, Prof. Gerd Lisken, Ulrike Matthes, Dr. Nina Polaschegg, Willem Schulz, Wolfgang Schliemann, Prof. Dr. Eckhard Weymann. Moderation: Matthias Schwabe, Dr. Reinhard Gagel

14.30 h	**Vor-Konzert/pre-concert:** Ensembles des/of exploratorium berlin: *Wednesday-Night-Ensemble* Ensemble *Vocalia Improva* *Whathappensnext Ensemble Berlin*
16 h	**Konzert/concert:** *Ensemble Explorativ* Anna Barth (dance), Reinhard Gagel (p, moog), Thomas Gerwin (electr, perc), Agnes Heginger (voc), Klaus Holsten (fl), Wolfgang Schliemann (dr), Matthias Schwabe (fl, vla), Ute Wassermann (voc)

Musik und Klangkultur

Martha Brech, Ralph Paland (Hg./eds.)
Kompositionen für hörbaren Raum/ Compositions for Audible Space
Die frühe elektroakustische Musik und ihre Kontexte/The Early Electroacoustic Music and its Contexts

2015, 354 Seiten, kart., zahlr. Abb., 34,99 €,
ISBN 978-3-8376-3076-3

Camille Hongler, Christoph Haffter, Silvan Moosmüller (Hg.)
Geräusch – das Andere der Musik
Untersuchungen an den Grenzen des Musikalischen

2014, 198 Seiten, kart., 24,99 €,
ISBN 978-3-8376-2868-5

Jörn Peter Hiekel, Wolfgang Lessing (Hg.)
Verkörperungen der Musik
Interdisziplinäre Betrachtungen

2014, 234 Seiten, kart., zahlr. Abb., 29,99 €,
ISBN 978-3-8376-2753-4

Leseproben, weitere Informationen und Bestellmöglichkeiten finden Sie unter www.transcript-verlag.de

Musik und Klangkultur

Frédéric Döhl
Mashup in der Musik
Fremdreferenzielles Komponieren, Sound Sampling und Urheberrecht
Juni 2016, 416 Seiten, kart., 39,99 €,
ISBN 978-3-8376-3542-3

Lena Nieper, Julian Schmitz (Hg.)
Musik als Medium der Erinnerung
Gedächtnis – Geschichte – Gegenwart
Mai 2016, 268 Seiten, kart., 34,99 €,
ISBN 978-3-8376-3279-8

Marion Saxer (Hg.)
Spiel (mit) der Maschine
Musikalische Medienpraxis in der Frühzeit von Phonographie, Selbstspielklavier, Film und Radio
April 2016, 418 Seiten, kart., zahlr. Abb., 39,99 €,
ISBN 978-3-8376-3036-7

Marie-Anne Kohl
Vokale Performancekunst als feministische Praxis
Meredith Monk und das künstlerische Kräftefeld in Downtown New York, 1964-1979
2015, 430 Seiten, kart., zahlr. Abb., 39,99 €,
ISBN 978-3-8376-3223-1

Martha Brech
Der hörbare Raum
Entdeckung, Erforschung und musikalische Gestaltung mit analoger Technologie
2015, 304 Seiten, kart., zahlr. Abb., 34,99 €,
ISBN 978-3-8376-3096-1

Omar Ruiz Vega
Musik – Kolonialismus – Identität
José Figueroa Sanabia und die puerto-ricanische Gesellschaft 1925-1952
2015, 336 Seiten, kart., zahlr. Abb., 44,99 €,
ISBN 978-3-8376-2900-2

Daniel Siebert
Musik im Zeitalter der Globalisierung
Prozesse – Perspektiven – Stile
2014, 228 Seiten, kart., 32,99 €,
ISBN 978-3-8376-2905-7

Teresa Leonhardmair
Bewegung in der Musik
Eine transdisziplinäre Perspektive auf ein musikimmanentes Phänomen
2014, 326 Seiten, kart., 37,99 €,
ISBN 978-3-8376-2833-3

Christina Richter-Ibáñez
Mauricio Kagels Buenos Aires (1946-1957)
Kulturpolitik – Künstlernetzwerk – Kompositionen
2014, 342 Seiten, kart., zahlr. Abb., 39,99 €,
ISBN 978-3-8376-2662-9

Christian Utz
Komponieren im Kontext der Globalisierung
Perspektiven für eine Musikgeschichte des 20. und 21. Jahrhunderts
2014, 438 Seiten, kart., zahlr. Abb., 39,99 €,
ISBN 978-3-8376-2403-8

Steffen Scholl
Musik – Raum – Technik
Zur Entwicklung und Anwendung der graphischen Programmierumgebung »Max«
2014, 236 Seiten, kart., zahlr. Abb., 31,99 €,
ISBN 978-3-8376-2527-1

Leseproben, weitere Informationen und Bestellmöglichkeiten finden Sie unter www.transcript-verlag.de